Why Veterans Run

JEREMY M. TEIGEN

Why Veterans Run

Military Service in American Presidential Elections, 1789–2016

TEMPLE UNIVERSITY PRESS
Philadelphia • Rome • Tokyo

TEMPLE UNIVERSITY PRESS
Philadelphia, Pennsylvania 19122
www.temple.edu/tempress

Copyright © 2018 by Temple University—Of The Commonwealth System
 of Higher Education
All rights reserved
Published 2018

Library of Congress Cataloging-in-Publication Data

Names: Teigen, Jeremy M., 1971– author.
Title: Why veterans run : military service in American presidential
 elections, 1789–2016 / Jeremy M. Teigen.
Description: Philadelphia : Temple University Press, [2018] | Includes
 bibliographical references and index.
Identifiers: LCCN 2017022786| ISBN 9781439914359 (cloth : alk. paper) |
 ISBN 9781439914366 (paper : alk. paper) | ISBN 9781439914373
 (e-book)
Subjects: LCSH: Presidents—United States—Election—History. |
 Presidential candidates—United States—History. | Presidents—United
 States—Biography. | Veterans—Political activity—United States—
 History.
Classification: LCC JK524 .T36 2018 | DDC 324.9730086/97—dc23
 LC record available at https://lccn.loc.gov/2017022786

9 8 7 6 5 4 3 2 1

For two U.S. Navy veterans:

my father, Michael Teigen, who served

on the U.S.S. *Daniel Webster* in the Vietnam War,

and my maternal grandfather, Gene Smith, who served

on the U.S.S. *Jason* in World War II

Contents

	Acknowledgments	ix
1	Veterans Running for President	1
2	Explaining Why Veterans Run	9
3	Early Republic: George Washington through James Monroe	49
4	Antebellum Generals: Andrew Jackson through the Civil War	61
5	Civil War Generals and the Bloody Shirt: George McClellan through William McKinley	98
6	Early Twentieth Century: Theodore Roosevelt through Adlai Stevenson	127
7	The "Greatest Generation": Dwight Eisenhower through Bob Dole	141
8	Mixed Legacy of Vietnam: Bill Clinton through Donald Trump	204
	Conclusion: Contemplating a Future with Fewer Veterans in Politics	238
	Appendix	249
	References	257
	Index	277

Acknowledgments

When a project runs long, it accumulates a commensurately extensive list of individuals who deserve appreciation for their help along the way. I finished this book when I was a full professor, but the moment that created a spark for what would shape a book idea happened twenty-five years ago. I was a young man in the air force, filling out an absentee ballot in the 1992 presidential election. Many of my fellow airmen had felt incensed and almost hostile about the fact that Bill Clinton had avoided the draft during the Vietnam War. They expected presidents to be "real veterans"—a political criterion that I inadvertently stored for later empirical exploration as a scholar. The amount of time between then and now translates to a lot of good people helping along the way.

When I showed up at the University of Wisconsin to start studying on the G.I. Bill, Robert Booth Fowler, Charles Jones, Anne Khademian, and Ken Mayer were all great mentors and were very much the reason I decided to chart a course toward a doctorate and try this college professor thing out. The Wisconsin Veterans Museum not only employed me while I was an undergrad in Madison; it also provided a great environment to talk about veterans' issues. Mark Van Ells and the late Richard Zeitlin and Charlie Howe at the museum both helped with my first writing about veterans.

I got tremendous help from my mentors at the University of Texas when I worked toward the dissertation that began to explore military veterans in the electorate as well as why American political parties nominated so many military veterans to run for office. Zoltan Barany, Bruce Buchanan, Walter Dean Burnham, Wendy Hunter, Tse-Min Lin, Bob Luskin, Phil Paolino, Brian Roberts, John Sides, Bat Sparrow, and especially David Leal and Daron Shaw showed me how to do a lot more than "spin the ANES tapes one more time." Thanks also go to Nancy Moses and Gary Freeman for repeatedly finding me space and opportunity to work. My fellow Americanist and political behavior graduate students in Austin also provided a loving peanut gallery and a core faction of Burdine Hall friends—I believe that we all helped each other improve our social science. Neal Allen, Brian Arbour, Mijeong Baek, Brian Brox, Joe Giammo, Danny Hayes, So Young Lee, Seth McKee, Jaesung Ryu, Mike Unger, and Don Zinman all read proto-drafts of a lot of the ideas in this book's pages or their antecedents. I especially thank Rich Holtzman among that crew for a kind act.

Some colleagues at Ramapo College have been very supportive. Robert Becklan, Paul Elovitz, Michael Fluhr, Bernard Roy, Stacie Taranto, and Mike Unger read different chapters and helped me improve them. A handful of undergraduates at Ramapo College deserve recognition for help with data collection and other important assists: Alex Cordaro, Justine D'Elia Kueper, David Ermann, Anthony LaRosa, Kamila Marek, Tom McGeady, Zach Stavros, Annika Wouters Hill, and especially Erik Topp.

Experts who have been a terrific boon include some kind souls who have reacted to iterations of later stages of the book project: Shawn Ambrose, Allison Dagnes, Peter Feaver, Keith Gaddie, Andrew Polsky, Pat Shields, and most especially Kent Jennings, who could not have been a more kind and helpful sounding board and mentor. I am also glad for Seth Lynn and his work at VeteransCampaign.org and for connecting with me.

Many whose paths I crossed doing archival work deserve appreciation as well. I am grateful to Meredith Sleichter and the Eisenhower Foundation at the Dwight Eisenhower Presidential Library for financial support, as well as to Chris Abraham and Mary Burtzloff for archival help there. Many others helped me in different ways at other archives: Nan Card at the Rutherford B. Hayes Presidential Center, Stacey Chandler at the John F. Kennedy Presidential Library, Barbara Cline at the Lyndon B. Johnson Presidential Library, Sarah D'Antonio Gard and Kristine Schenk at the Robert and Elizabeth Dole Archive, MaryAnn McSweeney at the Jimmy Carter Presidential Library, Thaddeus Romansky at the George H. W. Bush Presidential Library, Ann Sindelar at the Western Reserve Historical Society, and James Zobel at the archives of the Douglas MacArthur Memorial. At Ramapo College, librarians Katie Cohen, Christina Conner, and Sam Wittenberg deserve thanks for various data and citation help.

I also thank Aaron Javsicas at Temple University Press for scores of things but particularly for cautioning me against my first book title idea, *Tippecanoe and Hanoi Hiltons Too*. And I owe a lot to my copyeditor for her fantastic work. Both Temple University Press and I are especially grateful to Jason Dempsey and Joe Barbato for saving us from publishing a book with an epic stock photography fail on the cover.

On the home front, Amelia Teigen helped with perfect positivity, while Doug Busam helped me finish the book by literally saving the roof above my head. Last, this book represents probative evidence that I married up. The novelist Bruce Holsinger did a book-text search across time for front matter phrases in which male authors thanked their wives for typing up manuscripts and found countless examples of throwaway gratitude; some writers did not even include their wife's name. I seek to assure readers that I did not marry my wife, Professor Julie George, for her typing skills, but I do thank her for all the writing help on this book: all the last-minute reads, the margin comments, and help with framing. Shortcomings within these pages belong to me alone, of course, but this book, and a good bit elsewhere, is better because of her help.

Why Veterans Run

1

Veterans Running for President

Being in on this here D Day is goin' to be worth 250,000 votes back home.
—Strom Thurmond, quoted in Hadley, *The Invisible Primary*

The Normandy invasion into Hitler's stranglehold of Europe started on the early morning of June 6, 1944, and the certainty of the Allies' success in establishing a beachhead to defeat Germany became apparent only in the days that followed. Those brutal hours involved hundreds of thousands of combatants. Survivors would commemorate the bloody experience afterward—manifesting dramatic effects not only on the outcome of the war but on their individual lives and fortunes after returning home. Waves of men parachuted, flew, or came aboard landing boats to face an entrenched enemy. Strom Thurmond, an American soldier from South Carolina, rode into battle in a particularly risky fashion. He was a lieutenant colonel serving in a civil-affairs unit that contended with ordinary legal matters, so he convinced a combat unit in the 82nd Airborne to allow him to ride shotgun. He volunteered to leave his army desk job in Great Britain to fly in a glider to Normandy to secure area behind the German beach defenses. He was older, a forty-one-year-old among younger soldiers, and he elected to ride in the back of an engineless plane, a disposable airborne combat ferry. They landed harder than intended in an apple orchard near St. Mère-Eglise, and his newly adopted squad was instantly under enemy fire. After engaging in firefights and contending with casualties, he ended up in a foxhole with Captain Stuyvesant Wainwright II, who would later be elected to Congress. Thurmond yelled to Wainwright the words quoted in the epigraph to this chapter, asserting that serving in such a titanic battle would win him "250,000 votes" after the war.¹

A large photo of Thurmond in uniform receiving the Bronze Star ran on the front page of a major South Carolina newspaper in 1944 after the successful invasion, and it was "the best free advertising a gubernatorial hopeful could imagine."² Soon after his return stateside, he went back to South Carolina and won the Democratic Party primary to become governor in 1946, a position that served as a launching platform toward national fame and higher office. Thurmond's electoral math about the quarter-million-vote yield of military service was naturally hyperbole, but the sentiment behind it, that past military service for the nation enhanced a candidate's ability to attract votes, relies on a logic that extends back to the beginning of the republic and forward to today's elections.

A generation later, another man confronted large questions about his potential wartime service. In 1969, American involvement in Vietnam continued along with the draft that compelled men into the war. Bill Clinton was a Rhodes Scholar who would later become Arkansas attorney general, governor, and U.S. president. In 1969, he was twenty-three years old and against American involvement in the war. He sought to avoid the draft and the war he felt was wrong. However, rather than become a conscientious objector, abscond to Canada, or choose other means to avoid the draft illegally, he expressed interest in the University of Arkansas Reserve Officer Training Corps (ROTC), which would defer his immediate draft eligibility, stating he would attend law school there. He ultimately attended Yale after spending time at Oxford University, however, and had written a letter to an ROTC recruiting officer apologizing for misrepresenting the depth of his antiwar feelings. He viewed the ROTC option as a means to avoid the draft, and the letter spelled out that his interest in the program was not genuine. He expressed great admiration for those who defied the law and the draft, but he felt he could not take this route for a critical reason: "I decided to accept the draft in spite of my beliefs for one reason: *to maintain my political viability* within the system."³ In essence, the young Clinton foresaw a political career for himself and believed avoiding military service would portend negative political consequences for his prospects in public life. Looming large for the future politician were concerns that breaking the draft laws would exclude him from public service later, but implied in his letter is also recognition that military

---

1. Quoted in Hadley 1976, 3.
2. Bass and Thompson 2005, 72.
3. Ifill 1992, A1 (emphasis added).

service was an expected path toward a life in politics for men of his generation. To embody the logically opposite role of military hero, "draft dodger," would proscribe political options, so he sought a middle course, a legitimate means to avoid war service.

The implied logic behind both Thurmond's optimistic appraisal of the votes that his medals would attract and Bill Clinton's apprehensions assumes that military service helps candidates attract votes while lacking it harms a candidate's chances. This perception has been an article of faith since the electoral coronation of George Washington in 1789. Washington successfully commanded a patchwork of militias and regulars to win independence from British rule and was a national hero because of his service. This experience was part of what made him the sole candidate for the new executive position. Subsequent candidates for high political office have shared the belief that military service is a boon for gaining popular support and votes.

Perhaps the most compelling fact driving the perception that military service helps win votes is the large number of veterans who have held public office. More than two-thirds of the roughly forty elected presidents have been military veterans. At one point in the 1970s, approximately three-quarters of the members of Congress had served in the armed forces in their early adulthood. Large numbers of elected leaders in governors' mansions, state legislatures, and local political offices also share a common military experience. The perceived appeal of military service has occasionally been so strong that political candidates have overstated their service records. In recent years, observers have caught candidates in congressional and other elections describing their military service in terms that strayed beyond their actual experience. The very fact that candidates risk getting caught in an exaggeration or fabrication of military service underlines the perception that wearing the uniform helps win office.

Yet sufficient counterexamples undermine the idea that military veterans enjoy an advantage when seeking high political office. William Henry Harrison's two candidacies raise doubts. If his military heroism on the frontier became such an important factor in 1840, why did his service fail to become a campaign asset in his first attempt to defeat Martin Van Buren in 1836? Military time simply does not guarantee that voters will always be moved toward candidates running on their martial laurels. Another notable illustration of how time in uniform pointed away from electoral victory rather than toward it happened after the Vietnam War. Following Strom Thurmond thirty years later, William Westmoreland ran for governor of South Carolina in 1974. He was *Time* magazine's "Man of the Year" in 1965 and held a far more well-known military record than

Thurmond's, yet he even failed to obtain his party's nomination despite being a retired four-star general, commander of forces in Vietnam, and in the discussion for the Republican presidential nomination in 1968.[4]

This book helps explain why, given the uneven electoral success of military veterans running for president, parties repeatedly nominate them. Military veterans run for the presidency after our wars, and the major parties nominate them frequently: more than half of the major party candidates for president have been in the armed forces. The parties choose veterans as their standard-bearers more often than the simple number of veterans in the population would suggest. Despite important political implications for veterans in office, no one has systematically sought to understand why they appear on our presidential ballots with such high frequency. I examine and describe the factors that shape veteran candidate emergence patterns over time. The kinds of leaders that become the president of the United States of America, or lose an election trying, reflect on what Americans perceive about themselves. To understand why so many veterans run for office reveals attributes of elections; it also illuminates the relationship between the military and civilian spheres and the preferences of the American electorate.

To achieve this analytic goal, this book understands military veteran candidate emergence as a set of outcomes shaped by factors. The number and kinds of veterans who appear in presidential elections depend on a list of influences stemming from wars, military institutions, and politics. While Chapter 2 elaborates the logic and details, the underlying explanatory power of the book examines how military and political factors shape the outcomes, the veteran candidacies. The outcomes are the number of veterans who run for president, the kinds of veterans who run for president, and the level of salience that candidates' military service attains during campaigns. The factors that shape and constrain these outcomes include (1) an unchanging, elemental bond between military veterans and the state; (2) the size and recruitment patterns for prior wars; (3) the partisan entanglements, federalization, and professionalization of military institutions; and (4) developments in civilian politics, specifically the changing mechanism used by political parties to choose their presidential nominees and the growing presidency as an institution. The book examines how these factors shape veteran candidate outcomes by segmenting U.S. military and electoral history into six postwar eras and analyzing them as distinct case studies.

---

4. He later described his electoral efforts candidly, asserting that he was an "inept candidate ... used to a structured organization." Quoted in Pace 2005, B8.

It is important to understand the reasons behind the high number of veterans in American presidential elections. The framers of the U.S. Constitution were gravely concerned about the dangers that standing armies and militarism present to liberty. Two ancient Romans, Coriolanus and Cincinnatus, provide contrasting visions for how former defenders of the state return to civilian politics after the war. Coriolanus, elevated from either myth or reality into literature within Plutarch's chronicles and later in Shakespeare's verse, was a Roman military leader from the fifth century B.C. He successfully fended off an enemy attack and achieved military honors through battle heroism. With that fame and popularity, he ritualistically showed his war wounds to the people to ascend to power. The framers of the U.S. Constitution clearly feared that such demagoguery might allow a latter-day Coriolanus to use elections to seize power with martial glory and debase the Constitution. Alexander Hamilton wrote in "Federalist 9" that the "petty republics of Greece and Italy" were precisely the examples to avoid by building a more "firm union." Their main pathology for Hamilton was the "perpetual vibration between the extremes of tyranny and anarchy," as ephemeral leaders translated personality and military fame to power only to be torn down in their excess.[5] It was not lost on the American framers that military heroes were frequently the vehicles for these cycles of revolution. The framers also inherited their fear of domestic standing armies from the English tradition, whose memory of Oliver Cromwell and the New Model Army coupled standing armies and despotism. Evidence of their concerns peppers the Constitution, the Bill of Rights, and the *Federalist Papers*. The Second and Third Amendments, with various grievances in the Declaration of Independence, are only the most obvious examples. A dozen *Federalist* papers discuss the militia and military, while only one discusses the Electoral College. The concluding *Federalist* paper promotes ratification of the Constitution specifically as a bulwark against various political perils, including "the military despotism of a victorious demagogue."[6] Those who wrote America's charter feared that a potential Coriolanus could prorogue civilian authority.

It was not Coriolanus but another Roman who became the archetype for George Washington and a tradition of soldiers-turned-leaders. Cincinnatus left his plow to take up arms and lead a defense of the homeland from invaders. With the threat abated, to the fields he returned, voluntarily passing power back to the Roman Senate. The allusions between Cincinnatus and George Washington were too ripe to go unpicked. Lord Byron, in his 1814 "Ode to Napoleon Buonaparte," described Washington's

---

5. Hamilton et al. 2009, 42.
6. Hamilton et al. 2009, 445.

return to Mount Vernon after Yorktown, deeming him the "Cincinnatus of the West," and the poet was not the only one to make the comparison. The spirit of Cincinnatus stands compatible and complementary with the notion of a citizen-soldier defense posture, eschewing martial influence on politics. American voters have not feared presidential candidates' military experiences but instead have celebrated them. Candidates' supporters associate martial experiences not with potential despotic tendencies but with patriotic sacrifice.[7]

If the shadow of Coriolanus had endured, it is doubtful that parties would have nominated a dozen generals, doubtful that more than half of presidential candidates had donned a military uniform. Instead, those seeking elected office heralded and highlighted their experience, sometimes even exaggerating their wartime valor. Parties nominate veterans more frequently than the veterans' share in the electorate at large should predict, despite early fears of standing armies. Such a formative environment could have created conditions that precluded military experience among candidates. It did not. In a pattern that corresponds to wars, their legacies, and other forces, American electoral history has undergone different waves of veterans in presidential contests featuring different types of veterans at different times. These surges and ebbs matter for understanding our elections, but whether and how much our election system is biased toward attracting veterans also matters for other important concerns. The potential implications of military veterans in presidential elections extends to how parties enjoy advantages on defense issues, gender politics, distinctive foreign policy views, and even levels of presidential success.

The two major parties in American politics compete on political issues that face the country, but this competition is not symmetrical on every issue. Each party enjoys a perception of credibility on certain issues over the other party, with voters believing that one party is better than the other at handling that issue. Education policy, for example, belongs more to the Democratic Party in the eyes of the electorate, while the Republican Party has owned defense and national security issues since the Vietnam War.[8] If voters see veteran and nonveteran candidates differently, then there are partisan implications to such differences. My past research using experimental settings demonstrated that candidates with military service provide voters with a "veteran" cue, but more important, potential voters

---

7. One exception was initial fears about the Society of the Cincinnati, the hereditary organization of Revolutionary War army officers and their descendants. Jefferson and others felt the group might perpetuate a permanent war caste that would become "undertakers of republicanism." Hünemörder 2006, 191.
8. Holian 2004; Norpoth and Buchanan 1992; Petrocik 1996.

use that cue to conclude that the candidate is better able to handle issues of national defense and security.[9] The same study did not find that party conditioned these citizens' perceptions of a veteran candidate's future ability to cope with security- and defense-related issues. Another study that used experimental conditions found that candidates' military service influenced voters' hypothetical vote-choice decisions—and also found party asymmetry in the results: Democrat candidates gained more advantage than Republican candidates from being a veteran.[10] However, if Republican candidates in general enjoy an advantage in the eyes of voters pertaining to their ability to contend with defense matters, and voters see military veteran candidates with more credibility on defense, there is a potential for a built-in advantage for Republican veterans on defense issues in elections. This concern depends heavily on whether there is a disproportionate number of Republican or Democratic veterans and on whether Republicans continue to enjoy a defense-issue advantage.[11]

There are also important gender implications that stem from an electoral environment conducive to military veterans when considering the rarity of female veterans in general, certainly among the political class. While the central focus of this book targets presidential elections, its implications extend to other races for federal and state public office. Candidates and incumbents with military service appear to enjoy an advantage over nonveterans when engaging their biography to achieve or at least initiate policy outcomes. Military service aids incumbent legislators' efforts to achieve action and gain media attention for their views over those of nonveterans. Given that military service is still experienced overwhelmingly by men, there is a gender asymmetry to how politicians can frame expertise on defense and security issues.[12]

Central to the importance of understanding an election mechanism that nominates an abundance of military veterans, evidence suggests that there are important differences between political leaders with and without experience in the armed forces.[13] Policy makers with military experience hold different views on war and defense than others who did not serve.[14] One study measured the proportion of key policy makers in the federal government over time since 1816 by tracking biographies of

---

9. Teigen 2012.
10. McDermott and Panagopoulos 2015.
11. Others have written that the George W. Bush administration diminished the Republican advantage on defense and security issues by the way it conducted the Iraq War. See Goble and Holm 2009.
12. Swers 2007; Huddy and Terkildsen 1993.
13. Horowitz, Stam, and Ellis 2015.
14. Feaver and Gelpi 2005; Gelpi and Feaver 2002.

members of the U.S. House of Representatives and the president's cabinet, including the president and vice president. Sometimes veterans have held large numbers of House seats and cabinet posts; as high as 72 percent of House members have had military service, and as high as 92 percent of cabinet members. Other eras have seen far fewer, with 13 percent and none, respectively. The highs and lows correspond with American war making. Peter Feaver and Christopher Gelpi's research shows that the share of veterans in positions of power affects the propensity to start conflicts. When there were more veterans in policy-making roles, the United States was less likely to initiate military action. When there were fewer veterans, the United States was more likely to initiate conflict. The pattern was even stronger for veterans' reluctance to initiate militarized disputes when considering "interventionist" types of wars rather than those with national security more at stake. Such research is not the only scholarly investigation into the political and foreign policy implications of the "gap" between civilian and military cultures, but the empirical evidence supplies a germane policy reason to better understand the mechanisms that propel so many veterans toward major-party nominations.

Last, candidates' pre-presidential experiences influence later perceptions about their success as president. In particular, one study that examined presidents from William McKinley to George W. Bush concluded that military experiences helped presidents become more successful once in the White House.[15] By disaggregating different forms of military service, the study showed that serving during times of war as a young man drives a president toward higher performance in public persuasion, while combat experience buoyed how well a president does in crisis leadership. When assessing all ten arenas of presidential success, having served in combat and being on active duty during a time of war shape how well a man will do as president overall. Some may criticize this type of study because presidential success is too abstract to be quantified or ranked meaningfully or that there are insufficient cases for analysis. Even if we take such studies with a healthy grain of salt, it is at a minimum suggestive that military service and presidential quality are linked. When comparing the loosely defined political and policy success of the presidents since McKinley, the men with wartime military service differed from those without it, warranting the interest in the number of veterans who appear in elections.

---

15. The authors defined presidential success by using a survey commissioned by C-SPAN of "scholars and other professional observers of the presidency" who ranked each president on a scale of 1–10 in ten categories of success, such as "public persuasion" and "crisis leadership." Uscinski and Simon 2012, 522.

2

Explaining Why Veterans Run

> If there is anything proved by the campaigns in which soldiers figured, it is the absence of any factors of predictability common to them all.
> —Dorothy Goebel and Julius Goebel Jr., *Generals in the White House*

> The veteran is always a powerful political force, for good or evil. . . . He has fought for the flag and has absorbed some of its *mana*. He is sacred. He is covered with pathos and immune from criticism.
> —Willard Waller, *The Veteran Comes Back*

By examining all major-party presidential candidates from 1789 to 2016 and classifying their service to create a taxonomy of military experiences as they relate to electoral campaigns, this chapter describes in detail the outcomes, the pattern and number of veterans in presidential elections, and the salience of their military service during the campaign. Then it turns to the factors that shape these outcomes by elucidating the bedrock connection between military institutions and the state; the magnitude and duration of prior wars along with how troops were recruited; the varying partisan hue of military institutions, elites, and political forces over time; the changing way parties choose presidential nominees; and the growing power of the U.S. presidency. To analyze how these factors influence the number and types of veterans parties nominate for the presidency, we must examine how both change over time. Hence, the next step entails dividing American electoral history into six eras that delineate common patterns of military veterans' emergence in presidential elections, which also serve as the case-study chapters that follow. This chapter then confronts an intuitive but unsupported rival hypothesis that military candidates attract more votes in general elections and concludes with a description of the case-study chapters.

Veterans in Presidential Elections and the Salience of Their Service in Campaigns

The key political phenomenon this book explains is how and why so many presidential candidates have been military veterans and why that has changed over time. To best understand these outcomes, we must recognize three ways military-service biography has been important: (1) the increasing and decreasing number of military veterans that parties have nominated over time; (2) the different kinds of veterans, from supply clerks to combat heroes to career generals; and (3) the degree to which veteran candidates' military service became salient during their presidential campaigns.

How Many Presidential Candidates Have Served in the Military?

Limiting the count to only candidates who obtained major-party nominations (Federalists, Democratic-Republicans, Democrats, Whigs, and Republicans) reveals that many seeking the White House have had experience in the armed forces, broadly construed.[1] For the purposes of this count, military service includes time in the activated militias, in volunteer units from the states, or in one of the federal military branches in times of war or peace. From 1789 to 2016, more than half of those who vied for the presidency had served in the military earlier in their life. Of the approximately seventy major-party candidates, forty-six have served in a military capacity.

To understand how large that number is, what "more than half" means, it makes sense to imagine how many veterans ought to appear in presidential elections simply by chance. If there were no bias favoring military service among political candidates and military experience were arbitrarily distributed among males, we should expect to see veterans appearing as candidates roughly as often as veterans appear in the male population (considering only males here, given the late entry of women into electoral politics). Considering even the largest estimates of how many served in the armed forces, a far smaller proportion served in American history than the proportion of presidential candidates with military service.

---

1. Counting the number of major-party candidates is not immediately straightforward and is especially complicated between the beginning and the consolidation of the Whig Party in the 1830s. Even after this change, the decision to include Stephen Douglas and John Breckinridge, both nominated by rival halves of the splintered Democratic Party in 1860, requires including three major-party candidates for 1860 alongside Lincoln.

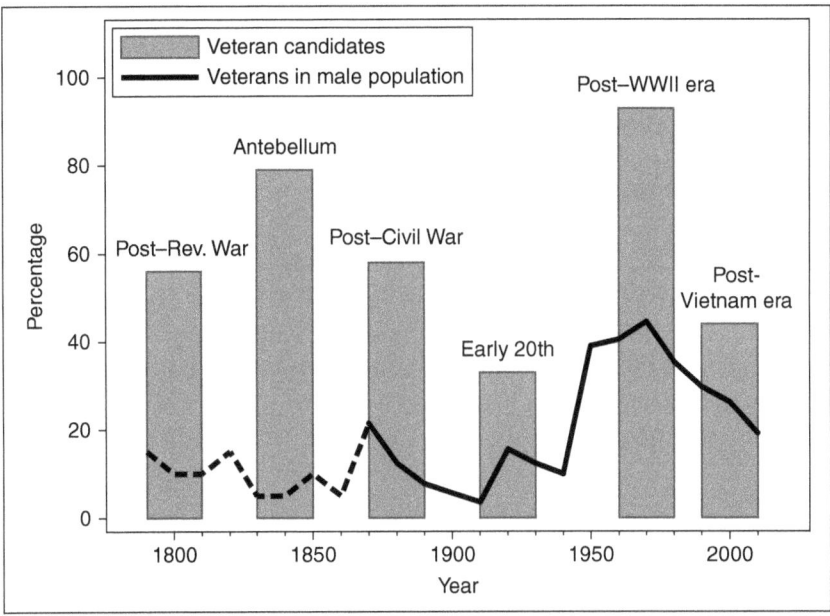

Figure 2.1 Estimated veteran percentage of the adult male population, by decade, and percentage of major-party presidential candidates with military service experience, by cohort (outlined in Table 2.2). Data source: U.S. Census Bureau data, various years; U.S. Department of Veterans Affairs 2017.

In very rough terms, there were some 2 million men in the Union armies out of the approximately 16.2 million men in the United States, using the 1860 census.[2] The 1940 census reported about 66 million men in the United States,[3] and approximately 16 million served during World War II. These numbers are included here not to convey precision but to demonstrate that during the largest U.S. conflicts, roughly 18 percent and 24 percent of the entire male population, respectively, served. Given the rapid demobilization that followed these conflicts and the smaller forces needed for other conflicts and wars in U.S. history, 24 percent is a gross overestimate, and likely a high-water mark, for an all-time approximation of what percentage of American males have served.

The line in Figure 2.1 shows the veteran population as a percentage of the adult male population over time. For the early years, marked by the dashed line, the estimate is little more than a guess, as data for both veterans and the adult male number lack reliability. After the Civil War, the data quality improves, but there are year-to-year inconsistencies; for

---

2. U.S. Census Bureau 1864, xvii.
3. U.S. Census Bureau 1942, 9.

example, the demarcation for adult age varies between sixteen and twenty across the years. Further complicating the consistency is the different ways races are treated across time. While the figures on veterans before the Civil War are rough estimates, it is safe to assume that prior data are never higher than the Civil War numbers, and it is likely they are much smaller. The Department of Veterans Affairs estimates that about 42 million people served in the U.S. military during war, including the Revolutionary War, War of 1812, Indian Wars, Mexican-American War, Civil War, Spanish-American War, World War I, World War II, Korean War, Vietnam War, and Desert Storm.[4] With a back-of-the-envelope estimate of 545 million cumulative Americans, and if males are approximately half of that, then a rough figure for the proportion of all men who served under arms is about 15 percent when considering all eras together.

All of this is to say that 60 percent is much larger than 15 percent: more than half of America's presidential candidates have had military service of some sort, a proportion much higher than one would expect if we somehow randomly selected our candidates from the male population. Figure 2.1 also plots a bar graph of the proportion of party candidates of each era who were military veterans for specific contrast to the percentage of veterans in the male population. Simply, veterans are overrepresented in presidential elections. The American presidential candidate selection mechanism prefers veterans.

Table 2.1 conveys a list of all major-party nominees from 1789 to 2016. The table is organized by candidate, not year, so that individuals are not counted more than once. The reasoning behind this decision relies on the assumption that subsequent runs do not inspire the nomination process to focus on character biography as they presumably do in a candidate's first attempt. Further, it would understate or exaggerate the potential role of military service in presidential elections by overcounting candidates. Assume as an illustration, that Franklin D. Roosevelt's lack of military service reveals something about veterans in elections. Should his four elections count as four nonveterans running in his era or as one? Should Richard Nixon's U.S. Navy service count in 1960, 1968, and 1972 when trying to understand veterans' role in presidential elections? Both candidates should count only once because the fundamental characteristic about them, for the purposes of this analysis, is their unchanging military past. The table shows the candidates' birth year, which elections they contested, and their party; summarizes their service experience; and categorizes how and when they served.

---

4. U.S. Department of Veterans Affairs 2017. One estimate of how many Americans have ever lived, adding births and immigration, is 545 million. See "How Many Americans?" 2010.

TABLE 2.1 MAJOR-PARTY PRESIDENTIAL CANDIDATES' MILITARY SERVICE, 1789–2016

Nominee	Birth year	Presidential elections	Party	Service	Era	Type
George Washington	1732	1789, 1792	None	British officer, commander of Continental Forces during Revolutionary War	REV	Battlefield general
John Adams	1735	1796, 1800	Fed	None	REV	Nonveteran
Thomas Jefferson	1743	1796, 1800, 1804	DR	None	REV	Nonveteran
Charles C. Pinckney	1746	1800, 1804, 1808	Fed	Militia officer during Revolutionary War, POW	REV	Combat veteran
James Madison	1751	1808, 1812	DR	Inactive militia, drilled one march	REV	Common veteran
DeWitt Clinton	1769	1812	Fed	None	REV	Nonveteran
James Monroe	1758	1816, 1820	DR	Officer with Washington, Battle of Trenton	REV	Combat veteran
Rufus King	1755	1816	Fed	Officer during Revolutionary War	REV	Combat veteran
John Quincy Adams	1767	1824, 1828	DR	None	REV	Nonveteran
Andrew Jackson	1767	1824, 1828, 1832	D	General, Indian Wars, hero of Battle of New Orleans	AB	Battlefield general
Henry Clay	1777	1832, 1844	NR, W	None	AB	Nonveteran
William Henry Harrison	1773	1836, 1840	W	General, hero of Battle of Tippecanoe	AB	Battlefield general
Martin Van Buren	1782	1836, 1840	D	None	AB	Nonveteran
James Polk	1795	1844	D	Colonel, local militia during peacetime	AB	Common veteran
Zachary Taylor	1784	1848	W	General, commander during Mexican-American War	AB	Career general
Lewis Cass	1782	1848	D	Militia general, War of 1812, Battle of the Thames	AB	Battlefield general
Winfield Scott	1786	1852	W	General, commander during Mexican-American War	AB	Career general
Franklin Pierce	1804	1852	D	General, officer during Mexican-American War	AB	Battlefield general
John Frémont	1813	1856	R	Officer during Mexican-American War, "Pathfinder"	AB	Combat veteran
James Buchanan	1791	1856	D	Local militia, War of 1812	AB	Common veteran
Abraham Lincoln	1809	1860, 1864	R	Militia officer during Indian Wars	AB	Common veteran
Stephen Douglas	1813	1860	D	None	AB	Nonveteran
John Breckinridge	1821	1860	D	Officer during Mexican-American War, rear guard	AB	Common veteran
George McClellan	1826	1864	D	General, Union commander during Civil War	CW	Career general

(continued)

TABLE 2.1 MAJOR-PARTY PRESIDENTIAL CANDIDATES' MILITARY SERVICE, 1789–2016 (continued)

Nominee	Birth year	Presidential elections	Party	Service	Era	Type
Ulysses Grant	1822	1868, 1872	R	General, Union commander of all forces during Civil War	CW	Career general
Horatio Seymour	1810	1868	D	None	CW	Nonveteran
Horace Greeley	1811	1872	D	None	CW	Nonveteran
Rutherford Hayes	1822	1876	R	General, Union commander during Civil War	CW	Battlefield general
Samuel Tilden	1814	1876	D	None	CW	Nonveteran
James Garfield	1831	1880	R	General, Union commander during Civil War	CW	Battlefield general
Winfield Scott Hancock	1824	1880	D	General, Mexican-American War, Union Commander during Civil War	CW	Career general
James Blaine	1830	1884	R	None	CW	Nonveteran
Grover Cleveland	1837	1884, 1888, 1892	D	None (paid a substitute)	CW	Nonveteran
Benjamin Harrison	1833	1888, 1892	R	General, Union commander during Civil War	CW	Battlefield general
William McKinley	1843	1896, 1900	R	Enlisted and officer with combat experience during Civil War	CW	Combat veteran
William Jennings Bryan	1860	1896, 1900, 1908	D	Joined army between presidential attempts in 1898, fell ill	E20	Common veteran
Theodore Roosevelt	1858	1904	R	Rough Rider officer in Spanish-American War	E20	Combat veteran
Alton Parker	1852	1904	D	None	E20	Nonveteran
William Taft	1857	1908, 1912	R	None	E20	Nonveteran
Woodrow Wilson	1856	1912, 1916	D	None	E20	Nonveteran
Charles Hughes	1862	1916	R	None	E20	Nonveteran
James Cox	1870	1920	D	None	E20	Nonveteran
Warren Harding	1865	1920	R	None	E20	Nonveteran
John Davis	1873	1924	D	None	E20	Nonveteran
Calvin Coolidge	1872	1924	R	None	E20	Nonveteran
Al Smith	1873	1928	D	None	E20	Nonveteran
Herbert Hoover	1874	1928, 1932	R	None	E20	Nonveteran
Franklin Roosevelt	1882	1932, 1936, 1940, 1944	D	None	E20	Nonveteran
Alf Landon	1887	1936	R	Brief commission in army during World War I	E20	Common veteran
Wendell Willkie	1892	1940	R	Army lawyer during World War I	E20	Common veteran

Nominee	Birth year	Presidential elections	Party	Service	Era	Type
Thomas Dewey	1902	1944, 1948	R	None	E20	Nonveteran
Harry Truman	1884	1948	D	Officer, World War I, artillery	E20	Combat veteran
Adlai Stevenson	1900	1952, 1956	D	Navy, following World War I	E20	Common veteran
Dwight Eisenhower	1890	1952, 1956	R	General, World War I, commander of Allied forces, World War II	GG	Career general
Richard Nixon	1913	1960, 1968, 1972	R	Navy, World War II	GG	Common veteran
John Kennedy	1917	1960	D	Navy, World War II, PT-109	GG	Combat veteran
Barry Goldwater	1909	1964	R	Army Air Forces pilot, World War II	GG	Common veteran
Lyndon Johnson	1908	1964	D	Navy liaison, observer	GG	Common veteran
Hubert Humphrey	1911	1968	D	None, denied entry during World War II for medical reasons	GG	Nonveteran
George McGovern	1922	1972	D	Army Air Forces bomber pilot, World War II	GG	Combat veteran
Gerald Ford	1913	1976	R	Navy officer, World War II	GG	Combat veteran
Jimmy Carter	1924	1976, 1980	D	Navy submarine officer	GG	Common veteran
Ronald Reagan	1911	1980, 1984	R	World War II army reserve, public affairs officer	GG	Common veteran
Walter Mondale	1928	1984	D	Army, enlisted	GG	Common veteran
George H. W. Bush	1924	1988, 1992	R	Navy torpedo bomber pilot, World War II	GG	Combat veteran
Michael Dukakis	1933	1988	D	Army, in South Korea after the war	GG	Common veteran
Bob Dole	1923	1996	R	Army officer, World War II, wounded in combat	GG	Combat veteran
Bill Clinton	1946	1992, 1996	D	None	VN	Nonveteran
Al Gore	1948	2000	D	Army enlisted, in Vietnam, journalist unit	VN	Common veteran
George W. Bush	1946	2000, 2004	R	Texas Air National Guard	VN	Common veteran
John Kerry	1943	2004	D	Navy swift-boat captain in Vietnam	VN	Combat veteran
John McCain	1936	2008	R	Navy pilot in Vietnam, POW	VN	Combat veteran
Barack Obama	1961	2008, 2012	D	None	VN	Nonveteran
Mitt Romney	1947	2012	R	None	VN	Nonveteran
Donald Trump	1946	2016	R	None	VN	Nonveteran
Hillary Clinton	1947	2016	D	None	VN	Nonveteran

Note: D = Democratic Party; DR = Democratic-Republican Party; Fed = Federalist Party; NR = National Republican Party; R = Republican Party; W = Whig Party; REV = Revolutionary War era; AB = Antebellum era; CW= Civil War era; E20 = Early twentieth century; GG = Greatest Generation era; VN = Vietnam War era

How Presidential Candidates Served: A Military-Political Taxonomy of Military Service

There is wide variety in how these forty-six veterans served their country in uniform. Up to this point, I have occasionally noted different ways that certain veterans have served, but it is now necessary to formalize different categories. The imagery and personal narratives portraying America's presidents frequently involve military service prior to becoming president. Primary- and secondary-school-level treatments of presidential candidates often recount the martial pasts of the chief executives, such as the story of *PT-109*. Several winning candidates held obvious and oft-repeated military credentials, such as George Washington, William Henry Harrison, Dwight Eisenhower, and Ulysses Grant, but others were not generals, such as James Monroe or John Kennedy. There are also unsuccessful major-party presidential candidates with publicized military service in their past, including Lewis Cass, John Frémont, George McClellan, and Winfield Scott Hancock or, more recently, Bob Dole and John McCain. The centrality of the military service differed among these candidates. With so many memorable examples, one might guess that every presidential election must have featured at least one veteran. While more than half of the aspirants have served prior to their attempt to win the White House, different eras have featured different patterns of veteran candidate emergence: not only have the number of veterans changed, but also the nature of the candidates' service differs over time.

Samuel Huntington was among the first to write specifically about the military biographies of American statesmen and provided a beginning for explaining veterans' repeated entry into politics. He wrote *The Soldier and the State*, the seminal book on the complicated relationship between civilian politicians and the military.[5] In particular, he examined the tensions inherent between two sets of values: those embodied in a system of elected leadership and liberal democracy and the conservative values within the military ranks of those who protect the state. Aside from the antebellum South, the sole tradition in American political development has been classic liberalism. Huntington described how the civilian sphere's ideological dominance has been at odds with those he calls the "conservative realists" within the armed forces responsible for the country's security needs. However, because of this ideological schism between America's civilian and military cultures since the founding, Huntington needed to explain the American tendency to nominate and elect men with military backgrounds. It is difficult to claim that the American polity is ideologically

---
5. Huntington 1957.

incongruent with the military when so many of its leaders have had martial experience, so Huntington needed to differentiate the candidates. To make the case that the dominant liberalism prevailed over the realist military institutions, he needed to delineate the different backgrounds of military experience.

To do so, he compared the electoral wins and losses of those among the professional military class with those of others who served for shorter periods. He saw careerists who made the military their life as fundamentally different from the men who briefly served their nation in war or peace. The few military professionals who have been electorally successful distanced themselves from the uniform. Huntington also defined "military hero" candidates as either amateur servicemen who spent a short amount of time in the ranks or as military professionals who "abandoned [the] military trappings and adopted the guise of liberalism."[6] From his Eisenhower-era vantage point, Huntington counted fifteen military heroes. But if the aversion to militarism was strong, he questions, why then have a third of the thirty-three presidents been generals? His answer lies in looking at the nature of each candidate's service. Only six of the fifteen heroes that he identifies were professional military men; the remaining individuals were military heroes during a time of war, an interlude that interrupted their civilian career. Washington, for example, left his farm to lead a citizen army to secure victory against the British and then eschewed the uniform and returned home to till the ground anew. Similar stories surround Andrew Jackson, William Henry Harrison, and the other heroes, so Huntington uses their numerical advantage in winning elections over the professionals to conclude that American voters prefer the citizen-military hero to the military professional, which supported his logic of American antipathy toward ideological traditions besides classic liberalism.[7]

I have a different purpose than Huntington for highlighting the number and types of military veterans in presidential elections. If, as he suggests, the reason behind the high number of veterans running for the White House is that the American mind eschews military professionals while finding erstwhile military heroes compelling, how do we explain variation over time? America's fixed tradition of liberalism is an insufficient explanation. Huntington sought to contrast ideologies and understand civil-military relations, but if we want to understand why veterans

---

6. Huntington 1957, 158.
7. Morris Janowitz also recognized that the American electorate has been more allergic to professional military men while preferring those who served in the citizen-soldier tradition. See Janowitz 1960.

appear in politics in some periods but not in others, we need to scrutinize the eras and candidates. For example, how do we understand the post–World War II veterans who dominated electoral politics for a generation differently than the large wave that followed the Civil War? The World War II veterans, by and large, served in the entirely federalized twentieth-century military machine as well-trained, professionalized junior officers. It was a citizen army featuring large-scale conscription, concluding with massive demobilization after the war's end. The Boys in Blue, those who served in the northern ranks during the Civil War, were also a large army, somewhere near two million across the span of the war. Some were volunteers and many were conscripted, but most served in state-based units, marching under their state flag along with the Union colors. Their officers were elected more often because of political cunning than drill and weapons knowledge. No one has accused those in the ranks of either side of excessive professionalism; the Prussian military scholar and general Helmuth von Moltke reportedly decided in the 1870s that there was no reason to study the American Civil War because "it had been fought by armed mobs."[8]

The Civil War and World War II, while both massive conflicts that engaged the whole of the nation, differed in important ways related to the armies. Structure, professionalism, officer recruitment, centralized soldier induction, geographic origins, and other matters dramatically differed between the army that won the Civil War and the one that prevailed in World War II. Among the keenest distinctions is the reliance on regionally based units. Huntington and others mark a keen distinction between militia service in the nineteenth century and participation in the postreform professionalized armed forces of the twentieth century. For some, militia participation is not veritable military experience. This divorce is unnecessarily dismissive, precluding comparison of using militia service with service in the more professionalized armed forces for political gain. An easy response to the distinctiveness of the early republic's elections that elevated large numbers of militia veterans to seek the White House might suggest that the militia is different from and incomparable with the professionalized class, only a small number of whom entered politics. I disagree with this separation. While I certainly do not assert that the militia is tantamount to a professionalized military in relation to martial quality, training, or military efficacy, for the purposes of understanding its electoral role, activated militia service was important military service in its era. Toward a better understanding of why military experience peppers our presidential election rosters, this analysis considers activated

---

8. Quoted in Catton 1985, 144.

militia service as a type of military service, worthy of comparison, while noting the inherent differences.

An initial comparison reveals that American voters have clearly preferred citizens with brief military experience to military careerists, especially when one widens the pool to include those office seekers who did not obtain their party nomination, men such as Wesley Clark, Leonard Wood, and Douglas MacArthur. Yet to divide veterans into only two categories is problematic. Contrasting those who had only brief service to careerists, tallying winners and losers after Election Day, is too shallow to understand why the American electorate prefers amateur, citizen-soldiers to military professionals, and it ignores their relationship to candidates without military service. A more specific categorization of military service is therefore necessary to explain the variation in American presidential candidates' military records as they manifest on the campaign trail.

This book divides military service into five categories: nonveteran, common veteran, combat veteran, battlefield general, and career general. This grouping provides an exhaustive typology that comprises presidential candidates' service, and lack thereof, across more than 220 years of elections between 1789 and 2016. To create a taxonomy of an inherently qualitative phenomenon, such as the type of military service a person experienced, involves striking a balance between grouping different examples into the smallest number of categories that encapsulates the broadest range. While the various formal ranks within the military may provide an initially appealing ordered scale, it is unrealistic to think that party elites who make the nomination decisions, primary voters, or general election voters would distinguish civilian candidates simply by their final rank in uniform. Additionally, even the same rank may not mean the same sort of military service. To become a one-star, or brigadier, general in America's twentieth- and twenty-first-century army would take a stellar and speedy military career. General Wesley Clark started at West Point in 1962; graduated at the top of his class; and was awarded his first star, becoming a general, in 1989. Contrast him with General Benjamin Harrison. He was a civilian when the armies first clashed at Bull Run in 1861. He obtained his commission as second lieutenant in 1862. He was almost instantly promoted to colonel, the rank immediately below general, within the same year to command the Indiana 70th Regiment. His experience during the Civil War was deep and bloody as he commanded his men through several battles in the South, but his time in uniform was short. He became a one-star general before the Grand Review in Washington, D.C., and was a civilian before the end of 1865. Should we consider a Clark, an Eisenhower, or a Winfield Scott, each of whom served decades as careerists before attempting to run as a presidential candidate, in the same way we consider a Benjamin Harrison? Harrison's entire military career spanned less than four years, yet the exigencies and norms of the Civil War impelled him up the ranks with dramatic speed. Another distinction should also be preserved in a taxonomy of military service because some men faced combat while others did not. A description of each of the five categories follows.

Nonveterans are men who performed no service in the armed forces. This classification comes irrespective of the reason or justification for the lack of military service. Some men actively avoided military service, others may have simply been ineligible using the laws or regulations of their era, and others in this category simply went through their early adulthood with little interest in the military at a time when their country did not require service. Over the entire span of U.S. history, fewer than half of major-party candidates did not wear a uniform.

The common veteran category comprises individuals who were members of one of the various forms of armed service. This may include enlisted or commissioned service in the regular, federal forces in any branch, the states' National Guards, the federal reserves, or activated militias of the eighteenth and nineteenth centuries. Common veterans may have served in times of peace or war and include volunteers as well as draftees. The duration of the service may be short or long. While enlistments and commitments as officers in today's service generally begin at four years, service in the nineteenth century and earlier might be as short as ninety days. What distinguishes the common veterans from the previous nonveteran category is service. What distinguishes it from the subsequent categories is combat or command experience. For the purposes of understanding the role of military service in elections, it is important to mark a difference between honorable but noncombat service and the more storied experiences from the battlefield.

Combat veterans are those who met the criteria for the common veteran category and additionally were involved in direct combat, whether in the skies, on the ground, or on the seas. Combat veterans underwent risk from enemy fire. Pilots such as McCain and George H. W. Bush are in the combat veteran category because they flew combat missions and were exposed to enemy fire. Experience within ground forces in combat also counts, such as Dole's march against the Germans in the 1945 Italian campaign or Theodore Roosevelt's famous campaign against the Spanish in Cuba. Sailors who were aboard vessels actively engaged against enemy forces also belong in the combat veteran category, such as Kennedy's time as a torpedo-boat skipper in the Pacific.

A category for the nineteenth century comprises the men who obtained general rank on an accelerated schedule during wartime during the preprofessional era of America's armed forces: battlefield general. Benjamin Harrison, the candidate and president who went from civilian to general back to civilian in a short span, typifies this type of service. Unique to wartime and unique to the nineteenth-century preprofessionalized U.S. Army, the speedy promotion to general during the carnage of America's greatest conflict is similar to that in the combat veteran category, but something additionally special is afforded those with the rank of general, hence a separate type of veteran. This group includes men with ephemeral but meteoric military service, such as Harrison, Rutherford B. Hayes, James Garfield, and Franklin Pierce.

Last, there are the career generals who ran for president. These men dedicated the large part of their lives to military service as their career during war and peacetime. Among presidents are Eisenhower and Grant. There were careerists who obtained the nomination but lost on Election Day, such as McClellan, Scott, and Hancock. A unique characteristic of these men is that they can make a lateral entry into presidential politics. George Washington is difficult to classify: he was not a career soldier, but he was able to make a lateral entry into the presidency. They do not need, as most candidates do, to win lower office before consideration for a nomination.

Salience of Military Service in Presidential Campaigns

The different categories of service manifested in different ways in the rhetoric within presidential elections. In some presidential contests, the time in uniform was salient. Consider, for example, Kerry's candidacy in the 2004 election when the Democrats attempted to unseat George W. Bush during a wartime election. Kerry's time in the U.S. Navy on swift boats during the Vietnam War inspired the campaign to substantially highlight his experiences and make his service the de facto theme of the Democratic Convention that year. Other campaigns found more subtle ways of employing their candidate's time as a service member, such as Bob Dole, who mentioned his World War II service but not as prominently or centrally.

Some presidential candidates stepped onto the biggest stage in American politics with an honorable but modest wartime or peacetime service record. The candidates and campaigns made reference to the experience, featured it in introductory advertising in a minor way, and moved on to other issues or candidate attributes. Candidates like Barry Goldwater and

Jimmy Carter, both officers in the 1940s, served honorably but did not make their time in the military central, and neither their opponents nor contemporary issues made the service salient. Candidates in this category proverbially checked a box, fulfilling a perceived prerequirement for higher political office, but did not electioneer loudly about their time in uniform.

Other candidates with vivid military backgrounds made their time in uniform central to their political identity. These candidates ran on their record, using their service to bolster their political credibility. They trumpeted their service through slogans, songs, nicknames, posters, campaign advertisements, and other imagery. William Harrison, Zachary Taylor, Ulysses Grant, Dwight Eisenhower, and John Kennedy typify this type of salience. Their service was more than a perfunctory line on their life résumé; it became woven into their identity, even their moniker, such as Harrison's "Ole Tippecanoe." Volunteers on the campaign trail for John Kennedy wore tie clips in the shape of his naval torpedo boat from World War II. Nineteenth-century campaigns infused songs with martial lyrics while twentieth- and twenty-first-century campaigns splashed the candidates' service on television ads and websites.

For still others, military service was salient but controversial. Their service records in war or peace, or the fact that they had not served, became newsworthy during the campaign. Their service or lack thereof made headlines but not necessarily the kind that campaign managers prefer. For these candidacies, the military experiences or lack of service was either entirely negative or its positivity was contested. John Kerry, a Vietnam combat veteran, made his service central to his campaign. However, an opposition group aired the "Swift Boat" ads, which questioned the veracity of his claims and painted him as an antiwar traitor. Bill Clinton's attempts at avoiding the Vietnam draft was a political headwind both during his 1992 campaign and while he was president. Andrew Jackson's detractors attempted to blunt the large appeal of his New Orleans victory by reminding voters that, as a commander, he had ordered the executions of two British nationals and six American militia members who had deserted the ranks.

Factors That Shape Veteran Emergence

I argue that the historians Dorothy and Julius Goebel did not see the whole picture when they asserted an "absence of any factors" (from their 1945 vantage point) that explain why and when veterans appear in presidential elections.[9] Several factors enable and constrain the number and

---
9. Goebel and Goebel 1945, 267.

types of veterans in presidential elections and the salience of military service during campaigns. First, military service grants a civic legitimacy to veterans because of an unchanging, fundamental, and unique bond between the armed forces and the state, also evident in veterans being treated as first-class citizens and the potential with which "veteran" can be used as a campaign cue. Second, the size, duration, and recruiting methods of prior wars create the veteran population from which political aspirants begin their public careers. Third, the partisan entanglements, federalization, and professionalization of military institutions influence veteran emergence in presidential elections by allowing for or precluding partisan-aligned military elites to run. Fourth, developments in civilian politics regarding party nomination systems and the presidency as an institution are important. The evolving way that political parties choose their presidential nominees has a limited influence, while the growth of the power of the presidency also colors how voters perceive candidates' military service.

Military Institutions and Civic Legitimacy: Veterans' Bond with the State

There are unchanging baseline conditions that allow military experience to confer political legitimacy to veterans. Candidates seeking high political office in the United States attempt to convince voters they are the right man or woman for the job. Candidates with military service can explicitly or implicitly invoke a connection between themselves and a vital institution within the American political sphere. There is something powerful about the bond between the state and its military institutions. This unique relationship engenders appeal for political aspirants seeking the presidency, an appeal more robust than the relationship between the state and other public, civic, or private institutions. This bond has implications for how citizens perceive the potential leaders of their democracy. Candidates have obvious incentives to communicate to voters how "American" they are, and associating themselves with an institution fused tightly to the American state's core helps this goal. To harken back to early-life experiences in the armed forces is to telegraph to voters a bond and association with the most American of American institutions. The military is deeply embedded in holidays and other civic practices at the national, state, and local levels. Memorial Day, Veterans Day, and Fourth of July events generally involve military themes in their traditions. Certainly, the rituals of civic life in America involve its armed forces and have done so since its beginning. John Marshall, the early giant of the Supreme Court, expressed that being in the army enhanced his attachment to country. He was in uniform with Washington during the revolution, having suffered at Valley Forge in the oft-retold circumstances of the winter of 1777–1778. Marshall, who viewed his rival Thomas Jefferson's lack of service as shirking, saw that his own time as a captain in the army had "made a nationalist of him."[10]

This perception that military service contributes to a sense of patriotism did not stop after the founding era. Recent public opinion research depicts that the connection between patriotism and military service is still robust. Contemporary Americans consider military service an extremely patriotic act, second only to the act of voting. A *USA Today*/Gallup survey in 2008 revealed that the number-one and number-two acts that indicated a person as "patriotic" were "voting in elections" (78 percent said it indicated a "great deal" of patriotism) and "serving in the US military" (62 percent of Americans believed it indicated a "great deal" of patriotism).[11]

The armed forces are tied to the state in a way that other institutions cannot surpass. In the case of the United States, the military institutions developed at the same time that the state was created. By definition, America's need for non-British military institutions to confront the Redcoats dates exactly to the Revolutionary era. This shared origin is true in other places, at least in countries where its genesis involves a revolution and armed conflict. The political legitimacy conferred by personal involvement in such an institution reminds voters that a candidate has experience in the part of the U.S. government that enabled the United States to begin and survive. Scholars examining the high frequency of military interventions into politics in the mid-twentieth century, especially in Latin America, found a similar political state-bound legitimacy in those contexts. Besides the fact that the armed forces are indeed armed, offering coercive options that civilians lack, they enjoy another key advantage when usurping civil authorities: they share a common source of legitimacy because the origins of the state and its military are symbolically fused. Samuel Finer, an early scholar on civil-military relations, wrote that coups d'état, or so-called praetorian interventions of military authorities, were in part enabled by the unique relationship between the state and its military. Forged "by a deliberate fiat for the sole purpose of defending [the] state," the military "symbolizes independence, sovereignty."[12] Aside from possessing weapons, the military shares origin stories with the state itself

---

10. Wood 2009, 434.
11. Quoted in Morales 2008.
12. Finer 1962, 29.

and hence embodies the same core legitimacy and association with sovereignty itself, which stems from those revolutionary origins. This logic, perhaps most succinctly captured by Moltke's dictum, "The Army is the most outstanding institution in every country, for it alone makes possible the existence of all civic institutions," helps us understand the military's nonmartial power in politics.[13] What is true about the military in all regime types manifests also in a democratic and electoral setting. The military enjoys a special and early place in the civic narrative of a country. It follows, therefore, that political candidates for high elected office who invoke personal connection to the armed forces are reminding voters of their experience in the institution with the highest possible civic bond to the state's origins and that state itself.

What fortifies the understanding that the military as an institution shares a root-level bond with the state itself is that wars and the armies that wage them create states. The strong bond between a state and its army is intuitive. Charles Tilly's famously titled third chapter in *Coercion, Capital, and European States*, paraphrased, that wars make states and states make wars, powerfully illustrates the link between the state and its martial institutions.[14] The original and basic purpose of a state is to provide security with actual or threatened violence. With the rise of the state as an economic war-making unit and the central locus of power since the seventeenth century, along with the dramatic rise in the costs of war making, armies became part and parcel of states and their origins. But the role of the military in state creation is important toward understanding more than earlier eras and extends beyond European countries. Scholars who focus on the development and rise of the American federal government have examined the transformative role that war plays in politics and state development.[15] Engagement in conflict engendered a rise in state capacity with the armed services frequently being at the nexus of war and state transformation.

The rise of the American state was not linear. There were different periods of American political history that saw fast growth of the apparatus of the state: its revenues, its spending, the number of its workers, and its role in citizens' lives. Consolidating the union, the Civil War in the 1860s also marks a key moment in state growth. While some scholars emphasize that our focus should include the U.S. Army and state building in the Antebellum era,[16] most attention centers on the era following the

---

13. Moltke and Hughes 1993, 22.
14. Tilly 1990.
15. Mayhew 2005.
16. Adler and Polsky 2010; Katznelson 2002; Resch 1999; Jensen 2003.

Civil War and Reconstruction,[17] and for these scholars of American political development, the army was an essential actor in state enlargement. The development and growth of the federal government also occurred later, in the 1940s, in reaction to the epic conflict of World War II. Public policy arenas such as Social Security, labor relations, and public finance changed during the war, engendering a "virtual revolution" in the growth of the federal state driven by the American war effort in World War II.[18] The war created a massive wave of veterans returning stateside after the defeat of the Axis forces, and the federal government initiated policies to assist their social and economic reintegration. The most notable of these programs were mortgage guarantees and the educational assistance programs, commonly known as the G.I. Bill, an expansively used path to college funding still in place today. Veterans who participated in these programs exhibited enhanced levels of civic participation later in life as civilians.[19]

To illustrate further how a country's martial origins influence if and how military service becomes salient for civilian leadership, two democratic contexts in addition to those in the United States frame a contrast. Direct comparisons are impossible because of vast differences in the party and electoral arena because prime ministers and presidents are selected quite differently and the contours of politics generally differ dramatically. Yet, at the risk of stretching a comparison too far, consider the post–World War II electoral history of Japan and Israel in regard to that of the United States. Japan's post–World War II political culture was deeply influenced by the renunciation of military strength. Japan has been concertedly pacifist, and few men who have attained high office have military experience. The path to becoming a prime minister or cabinet minister is very different from America's party nomination and peculiar Electoral College mechanism, but we may consider generally that political conditions in Japan do not favor men with martial pasts.[20] Yet with its many conflicts, security environment, and universal conscription, Israel sits on the opposite side of a spectrum from Japan, with many of its prime ministers having prolific and well-known military experience. Of the individuals who have been prime minister, all the males served in either the militaries of their home countries of their youth, the prestate militias existing before the Israeli Defense Forces (IDF) and statehood, or the IDF itself. It is

---

17. Skowronek 1982; Skocpol 1992; Polsky and Adler 2008.
18. Sparrow 1996, 30.
19. Mettler 2002, 2005.
20. Japan's antimilitarism has taken strong root since the American security umbrella fostered its possibility after World War II. See Berger 1993.

important to remember that this comparison cannot form a perfect analogy with the American case because both Japan and Israel have parliamentary systems and the electorate does not choose the head of government. Despite vastly different means for selecting the chief executive, it is not difficult to infer that systemic forces within each country's contemporary and historical political contexts constrain the pool of men and women who might be in a position to ascend politically. In other words, there must be a reason, or set of reasons, why Israeli politics harbors and places some premium on military service and a related array of reasons why Japanese politics eschews military service.

The connection between the military institutions in the United States and the state was forged in a context of neither imposed pacifism nor hypervigilant defense but somewhere in between. America's armed forces, through their unique and deep association with the state itself, lend their civic legitimacy to their former members. The inherent connection between war and state is an easy one to perceive in the mind of voters. Hence, candidates who showcase their military service during campaigns are invoking their personal connection to the most state-centric institution possible. The armed forces of the United States have a credible claim on the title of "most American" of American political institutions, and one's association with the military symbolically supports the bid to lead those institutions. This fundamental bond between the military, its former members, and the state itself manifests in two ways relevant to understanding veteran candidacies: the tendency to see veterans as first-class citizens and the efficient and easy use of military service as a campaign cue to voters.

We can see clear evidence that experience in the armed forces imbues veterans with a uniquely powerful bond with the state in the way states treat former service members. Veterans of the nation's wars and conflicts, and even those who served during peacetime, enter a heralded status in America's civic space. Americans have collectively decided to recognize that those who have served their country deserve, at a minimum, appreciation. Veterans enjoy a reputation for having shouldered sacrifices large and small. Returning veterans have discovered a government that is sometimes quite grateful for this sacrifice, even if the gratitude began from catalysts elsewhere, either in the electorate or from interest-group pressure. A contemporary military veteran, when considering local, state, and federal governments, can find a substantial array of benefits in the form of cash, considerations, and symbolic recognition.

The eligibility varies, but local, state, and federal governments have each passed various forms of preferential hiring laws that give advantages to veterans seeking government jobs. The Department of Veterans Affairs, formed in the 1930s but with much older origins, is a cabinet-level department charged with managing veterans' benefits. One of the most important and costly forms of tax-supported veterans' benefits is health care for qualified retirees and veterans with service-related injuries. Many states offer specialized automobile license plates for veterans to publicly recognize their service. Since World War II, the celebrated G.I. Bill program and the subsequent programs that have augmented it provide substantial educational benefits for returned veterans going to college. The federal government also guarantees home mortgages for qualified veterans. Veterans experiencing troubles in their life have some tailored preferential treatment, with veterans-only homeless shelters and substance-abuse programs supported by government entities. This list of state-sponsored preferential treatment for veterans, while not exhaustive, is meant to convey generally a policy regime that offers substantial redistribution from the collective funds to a selective group, military veterans. Historically, veterans have been the vanguard of the growth of governmental benefits. Veterans and veterans' benefits factor quite large as evidence for a growing federal government.[21] The evidence suggests therefore, that veterans are a special class of citizen, deserving of preferential treatment. Veterans' benefits are the sole but massive exception to the more usual urge in American politics to make government hiring practices strictly meritocratic.[22]

Part of the rationale behind the inviolable place veterans occupy involves perceptions of their sacrifices.[23] Many candidates for political office have had palpable war wounds, difficult for voters to ignore. The obvious sacrifice made by such a candidate may not have guaranteed electoral victory, but it made military service salient in their nominations. Senator Bob Dole, the Republican nominee for president in 1996, was wounded by enemy fire during World War II, and the injuries prevented the use of his right arm. Senator Max Cleland, a Vietnam War veteran who lost both legs and one arm in 1968, is another example. Another political aspirant, a nineteenth-century veteran-turned-politician, was Lucius Fairchild. He became governor of Wisconsin after serving during the Civil War, when

---

21. Skocpol 1993; Skrentny 1996; Ainsworth 1995. I have glossed over darker times and poorer treatment of veterans in American political history. From the expulsion of the Bonus Marchers to the denial of Agent Orange's effects and other problems, government treatment of veterans has not been invariably positive. See Severo and Milford 1989.
22. Skrentny 1996.
23. Willard Waller's 1944 book on returning World War II vets takes an almost fearful tone: "This pathos is enhanced by the customary period of neglect and mistreatment in the years immediately after a war." Waller 1944, 189.

he lost an arm during the Battle of Gettysburg.[24] Sometimes this political legitimacy is conferred to proxies. Cindy Sheehan rose to prominence in 2005 beyond other antiwar protesters and critics of the Bush administration because of her son's battle death in Iraq.[25]

Another barometer of this civic legitimacy enjoyed by military veterans is how military service has provided a path to political legitimacy for groups seeking political inclusion.[26] African Americans' struggles for civil rights and equitable treatment under the law began after the Civil War, but the culmination of those efforts did not succeed until the civil rights successes in the late 1960s. Before the marches and protests and court cases of the 1950s and 1960s, however, African Americans in uniform found fairer treatment in a desegregated institution well before it occurred in civilian society.[27] Military service also provided agency for blacks seeking to fight civil rights battles after their return to civilian life and Jim Crow.[28] The sacrifices made in wartime are frequently employed by out-groups as rhetorical tools to demonstrate their demands for political legitimacy.[29]

How does this special status correspond to electoral politics? Veterans' benefits do not themselves drive a higher regard for veterans on Election Day or in the mechanisms that select party nominees. Rather, the political atmosphere that engenders state-sanctioned favoritism toward veterans emphasizes the close bond between veterans and the state. The same bond between the state and its military institutions confers a first-class status to those with personal experience in the armed forces. If military veterans have been a favored caste of citizens in the polity, then military service confers a unique civic halo. A similarly close bond that adheres military service to the mechanism by which we select our democracy's leaders should not surprise us.

Another way to understand the context in which the unchanging baseline bond between veteran and the state looks at how voters perceive candidates and campaigns. Military service is a powerful cue for voters to infer characteristics about candidates. Military service resonates with personal traits. Polls reveal that people see time in the armed forces as an expression of patriotism.[30] It is very likely voters place other desirable

---

24. S. Ross 1964.
25. The public and civic veneration of war dead is another example of the special status for those with military experience. See Piehler 1995.
26. Burk 1995.
27. Moskos and Butler 1996.
28. Parker 2009.
29. Krebs 2006.
30. Morales 2008.

traits in the same cognitive space as their perception of veterans, such as selflessness, loyalty, courage, voluntarism, and strength. Because of the way voters view and remember political information about candidates, military experience lends itself as a very effective candidate description. Campaign efforts, at their core, are attempts to convey positive information to potential voters about a candidate or negative information about the alternatives. Because of the expense of creating and conveying electioneering messages, whether they are through the penny press of the nineteenth century, via multimillion-dollar television advertising buys in selected media markets, or in a 140-letter announcement on Twitter, the more data that can be communicated by short messages, the better. The expectation that voters would sift through all available information sources about candidates before coming to a decision is dubious; voters make their call with limited information. Some have termed voters as cognitive misers, choosing to exert only the minimum necessary energy toward acquisition of political information.[31] Rather than civic calculators that store all the political information they receive and then make an evaluation based on that data on Election Day, voters are efficient shortcut takers.[32] Instead of following election news diligently throughout the election season and compiling a list, voters note events that betray substantive facts about the candidates and update their running evaluation of the candidates. Basic biographical information is easy to remember and can communicate a high degree of substantively and politically appealing traits or facts about a candidate.[33] The biographical information that candidates wield is not an arbitrary laundry list or running tally of life experiences but a calculated and succinct ensemble of personal information that comports with generally favorable attributes. For some scholars, personality matters more than issue concerns or partisan-group affiliation: voters evaluate candidates subjectively and assess them in "terms of [their] own embellished perceptions."[34]

More politically relevant characteristics may come to voters' minds when considering military service as well, such as leadership or competence on national defense and security issues. While this does not apply to all cases, military experience may allow some veterans to rise above the partisan politics of their day and be a centrist political candidate. So-called blank-slate presidential candidates, individuals who enter the election year without political baggage, include three types: the centrist, the

---

31. S. Taylor 1981.
32. Popkin 1991.
33. Hayes 2005.
34. Miller, Wattenberg, and Malanchuk 1986, 524.

cross partisan, and the military hero. Individuals running on their military experience are "associated with courage and valor, duty and nonpartisan service to their country."[35]

Military service affords candidates fame and name recognition outside the political framework. Aside from a congressional or gubernatorial path, commanding American troops in a battlefield victory is a path toward national name recognition. Especially among the early presidential candidates, military service was a large part of how the electorate came to know them. For candidates such as Washington, Andrew Jackson, William Harrison, and Zachary Taylor, it is impossible to imagine their political ascent without their time in uniform. Military service not only conferred positive traits, but it was their opportunity to become sufficiently well known in the nation so that party nominating conventions or their antecedents gave blessings to their candidacy. Media coverage of political contests also frequently uses military metaphors and phraseology to describe the contest.[36]

Military experience also humanizes and familiarizes candidates. Candidates from affluent, politically well-connected families often have difficulty making authentic or believable connections to ordinary voters. Many of the men who have been contenders for the presidency have been children of privilege, children of a political dynasty, or both, leaving them open to charges that they fail to understand the concerns facing ordinary, workaday Americans. Because the intentionally homogenizing experience of the armed forces treats all members equally (from the beginning of the twentieth century), military time provides political candidates with evidence they have gone through the same tests and hardships that all service members have. Most voters perceive that special treatment and perpetuation of the normal class system in America has no place in the military, and the pure meritocracy inside the ranks casts positive light on the people who have served.

America's Wars: Troop Strength and Means of Recruitment

No explanation of the number and types of veterans running for the presidency would be reasonable without accounting for the phenomenon that generates large veteran populations: war. The militarized conflicts in which the United States has participated differ dramatically in terms of their magnitude, duration, location, and recruitment of soldiers. The two epic conflicts in American history are the Civil War in the nineteenth

---

35. Crockett 2008, 56.
36. McEuen 1955.

century and World War II in the twentieth century, each creating a massive cohort of veterans that would make up a sizable proportion of the male population for the decades that followed. Exigencies of these two wars required very large conscription-based land armies. The next generation of local, state, and national political elites are simply more likely to have served in the previous war if the previous war enlisted many.

World War II saw approximately sixteen million men in uniform during the 1940s, with the U.S. Army alone peaking at more than eight million. There were approximately twenty-two million men of fighting age in the country, so more than 70 percent of a generation served under arms. The proportion grows when one consider that the population of men of fighting age includes individuals ineligible to serve because of medical or other reasons. George H. W. Bush and John Kennedy were not unique for having World War II experience; rather, they were typical of able-bodied men who were born in the United States between 1910 and 1925. The pool of individuals from which political leaders would arise was replete with those with wartime military experience. The party leaders, ward captains, mayors, assemblymen, congressmen, and senators of that generation were much more likely than men of other generations to be vets—even if there were no relationship between military service and politics. The Civil War also created a generation of men in uniform who fought in war and then went on to shape politics for decades. It was a massive conflict that required the largest armies ever assembled on the continent. Estimates show that roughly half of the white men living in non-southern states served in Union forces from that cohort born between 1815 and 1842.

In contrast with World War II and the Civil War, America's other major conflicts required less manpower to fight and created a smaller pool of military veterans to become the political leaders of their generation. A decade of war in Vietnam put 8.7 million men in service, of whom 3.4 million were deployed to Southeast Asia. About 5.7 million men were in uniform during the Korean War, 1.8 million actually with boots on the Korean peninsula. The rapid mobilization for World War I inducted somewhere near 5 million men for the American Expeditionary Forces' involvement late in that European war. In each conflict, the share of its generation that served was smaller than in World War II and the Civil War. Beyond Vietnam, Korea, and World War I, the other armed conflicts in American history involved proportionally even fewer men of their generation, resulting in extremely small numbers of veterans in the political landscape in the years that followed. Approximately seven hundred thousand were deployed to the Persian Gulf during Operations Desert Shield and Desert Storm in 1990–1991. The Spanish-American War at the turn of the twentieth century involved approximately three hundred thousand. The War of 1812 against Great Britain had fewer than three hundred thousand, and the Mexican War in the 1840s saw fewer than one hundred thousand in uniform. These conflicts, while significant and important in their own ways, did not place as many men in uniform as America's other wars.

It is critical to understand that the number of veterans in the population, while certainly driving the possibilities, does not explain all of the variation in military service records among presidential candidates in American history. The size of the war does not alone explain how many and what kinds of veterans enter presidential politics. This recognition is important for understanding veteran emergence in American presidential elections. To make a more generation-specific articulation of an argument presented earlier in this book, if there were no connection between military service and politics, then the proportion of presidential candidates should resemble the rough proportion of veterans in the male candidate pool. But the number of veterans in presidential politics after World War II exceeds what the raw number of veterans in the population would suggest, even if the World War II veteran pool was larger than other war cohorts. Also, the era prior to the Civil War saw many veteran candidates pursue the White House despite relatively few men with military service overall.

The last important distinction between the eras is how the armies were recruited. The two largest wars, World War II and the Civil War, relied on both volunteers and conscription to fill the ranks. Often, the voluntarism seen was a reaction to likely conscription. Wars in other eras could depend strictly on volunteers—such as the comparatively small wars of the twenty-first century, the Spanish- and Mexican-American Wars, and the Indian Wars. It is obvious that conscription policies shape the size of the forces and, for our purposes, influence the size of the veteran population. These policies also create different kinds of veterans, as the veteran population is roughly a representative cross section of the male population after conscription, while it may not be following all-volunteer periods.

Evolving Military: Federalization, Partisanship, and Professionalization

Without question, the size of the forces under arms in war contributes to the simple availability of veterans who might pursue political paths that lead to a presidential nomination. But another set of elements of the story also explains changing patterns of veterans participating in presidential election politics. They surround how the military institutions have developed across American history. From militia origins with a strong reliance on state government funding and a pure defense posture to a world superpower with the most advanced and professional force on the planet, the U.S. Armed Forces have not stood still. The political identity of the military apparatus is salient to the connection between personal experience with the military and political candidacies.

Not only have the institutions changed, but the way the electorate sees them has also transformed. Public perceptions of America's military institutions have undergone radical change between the founding to the post–Vietnam era, corresponding with the evolution of the armed forces themselves. Early Americans saw a standing army in peacetime as a dangerous antecedent to authoritarian rule, but today's Americans see our standing army as the most trusted part of the federal government, if not all of society. Given the political environment surrounding the foundation of the United States, a subsequent pattern featuring scores of military heroes and other veterans running for office is counterintuitive. Many of the framers who crafted the founding documents of the American republic would likely be quite surprised to know how popular the highly professionalized and federalized U.S. Armed Forces are today and that more than half of the individuals on presidential ballots have been veterans. While the case-study chapters provide more detail about how military institutions have changed with respect to presidential candidates' biographies, the introduction to the broad concept here outlines the fear of standing armies, the way those concerns cultivated a state-based militia system, the slow rise of a regular army, partisanship in the ranks and professionalization, and federalization of the military.

The political history preceding the American Revolution and divorce from the Crown engendered substantial mistrust of standing armies. Dorothy and Julius Goebel refer to it as the "pedigree of prejudice" against the military and militarism.[37] The British Redcoats became the principal instrument with which the most reviled of royal policies pervaded the colonists' lives and survived afterward in political dialogue and action. Whatever political disagreements separated the colonists from the king and parliament, it was the British army regulars alongside the German mercenary-conscript Hessians that became the most prominent expression of British rule before and during the war.[38] Their presence in the colonies was an unsubtle and symbolically important sign that the colonists

---

37. Goebel and Goebel 1945, 3.
38. Ingrao 1982.

were living in a garrison state: the Redcoats "merely intensified the friction that normally exists between garrisons and the civilian population. To the townsfolk the 'Bloody Backs' were visible reminders of 'English Tyranny.'"[39] Samuel Adams made great political hay by using the Redcoats as embodiments of royal rule via his demonization of the British regulars and the Crown, with his broadsheets and speeches on the Boston Massacre being only the most famous.[40]

The disdain for regular armies held by the framers is most richly evident in Thomas Jefferson's catalog of royal transgressions found in the Declaration of Independence. He accuses the British of setting the military "independent of and superior to" the colonial governments.[41] This logic is at least partially sleight of hand borne of the colonial political perspective, for no one believed that King George was under any threat of praetorian urges from his army to usurp royal rule. Yet the advocates for revolution and those who framed the Constitution came to see regular militaries as the embodiment of overbearing executive rule. Among the many complaints found in the Declaration of Independence, the British regulars as well as the "armies of foreign mercenaries" loomed large.[42]

The former colonies waged war on their own territory with a dominant European military power and won independence. The newly independent former colonies faced the need to design a new government to bind themselves together, but preferences about the tightness of those bonds varied. Having served the British during his earlier military career, Washington was the general in command of the various forces that achieved this victory, and Alexander Hamilton served as his adjutant. Their vision for the newly formed confederation's military resembled a European-style, professionalized force.[43] Others also shared this vision, but it ultimately did not triumph, and those who sought a state-based, minimalist defense apparatus prevailed: they saw a standing army in peacetime as steps down a road toward tyranny. Some events in the early period did not help foster an environment conducive to developing a federal force. Beyond the flawed perception of the military efficacy of militia and the troubled financial ability to pay for a professionalized force, the Newburgh Conspiracy played a role in fueling more fear of standing armies.[44] The Articles of Confederation, the first charter binding the former colonies, lasted a

---

39. Schlesinger 1955, 248.
40. The endurance and power of the myths surrounding the British army's culpability in the so-called massacre far exceeded their veracity. See Miller 1960; Maier 1976.
41. U.S. Declaration of Independence, §14.
42. U.S. Declaration of Independence, §27.
43. Weigley 1962.
44. Kohn 1970.

short decade but presaged the skepticism and lack of political will toward creating professionalized military institutions. Those who had fought and won independence among the newly independent states largely eschewed thinking in terms of centralized power when writing the Articles of Confederation. With implications toward what sort of military institutions would subsequently assemble, "Americans lived narrowly," thinking parochially from the perspective of their region and state rather than collectively about defense needs.[45]

The U.S. Constitution included substantial impediments toward developing a professional, federal army. The Constitution is many things: legal framework for a new government, cherished document defining an experiment in democracy, a charter and bulwark protecting liberties, and a symbol for the aspirations of a nation. It is also, however, replete with evidence about the political difficulties facing the men who wrote the document—an incomplete transcript of winners and losers in the many policy and ideological differences that vexed those pushing for and against ratification. The seeds of the country's conflict over slavery are evident, for example, in the spare three-fifths clause. The absence of the word "slavery" is a deafening silence, illustrating the inability to reconcile the matter prior to ratification. On questions about standing armies, militia, the executive's ability to use and misuse the armed forces, and the legislature's role, the Constitution betrays part of the ideological and policy differences between those who feared the army as an instrument of tyranny and those who feared the new republic's inability to defend its shores and borders and maintain order with an anemic, untrained rabble of parochially minded militia. Those who created the documents and constitutional structure of the new nation codified this antagonism toward standing armies in the Declaration of Independence, Constitution, and Bill of Rights. The text of the Second and Third Amendments of the Constitution is only the most palpable reaction to Great Britain's standing army and perceptions about its treatment of colonists. The "well regulated militia" cited in the Second Amendment, as a requirement of a free, secure nation, along with the Third Amendment's prohibition of quartering soldiers in homes without consent, betrays the framers' views of standing armies in the wake of the revolution.[46] The debates around the role of militia occupied much of the framers' attention. Consider that approximately a dozen of the eighty-five *Federalist Papers*, the essays by Alexander Hamilton, James Madison, and John Jay selling ratification of the U.S.

---

45. Jacobs 1947, 13.
46. Zillman 2006.

Constitution, concern some political or military facet of the militia debates, while only one discusses the Electoral College.

The resistance to standing armies, so powerful a sentiment among the men who shaped the Constitution and early republic, was about more than military policy. The Redcoats were the purest embodiment of that against which the former colonists rebelled: those standing armies limited liberty and begat tyranny. While the dynamic changed from the prerevolutionary era to the ratification of the Constitution and beyond, as the shortcomings of a militia-based military establishment became more obvious to more elites, it was an expression of ideological opposition to central authority to oppose a federal army. Lawrence Cress makes a forceful argument about the ideological nature of the various positions held by elites in the early republic over the establishment of military policy.[47] Elbridge Gerry and Alexander Hamilton were on opposite sides of a policy debate, true, but this difference was a manifestation of a larger ideological divide between those seeking stronger state sovereignty and those advocating elevated powers for the fledgling central government. Gerry's vocal and Whiggish protestations against the views of Hamilton and Washington were based on a larger belief system about federalism, state authority, and tyranny as much as or even more so than a question solely of militias and standing armies.

Exigencies due to conflicts with Native Americans and military rivalries between imperial powers on the continent required armed defense. The fighting forces for these needs of the early republic were not innovated in the New World. There is at least a little irony in the origins of colonial unease with standing armies, displeasure of the British Redcoats harnessed by advocates of revolution such as Samuel Adams. The colonists inherited this antimilitarist spirit, like so many other political traditions, from the British.[48] Its manifestation in the new American republic was imported from Anglo-Saxon traditions, and according to one source, the English model was faithfully replicated in the United States.

The militia before and after the Revolution was quite English; "no other American institution bears a closer resemblance to its ancient English ancestor than our militia."[49] We should not confuse a preference for militia and fear of standing armies with pacifism. Richard Kohn reminds us that early republican sentiment against standing armies was not a revelation of pacific spirit. The embrace of volunteer militias celebrates the citizen army contra the "distrust of permanent and professional armies"

---
47. Cress 1982.
48. Ekirch 1956.
49. Ansell 1917, 474.

rooted in the "belief that such institutions are inferior militarily," "wasteful," and dangerous to liberty, which stems from anti-Cromwell English ideology rooted in the seventeenth century.[50]

While the militia was a politically acceptable compromise in the struggle between states' rights advocates and those who sought a stronger central government, the citizen call-up system as a defensive fighting force lacked quality. The de jure classification of militia, compared to the regular federal army, is legally and constitutionally ambiguous. The "militia" as a military term suggests universal or near-universal male citizenry, all able to take up arms to defend the homeland. Washington was repeatedly frustrated by the quality of militia during the Revolutionary War,[51] but the sentiments of those who favored the old system carried the day at the Constitutional Convention. Washington was able to curb one extreme attempt by Elbridge Gerry at codifying a maximum size of standing armies. Gerry proposed a manpower limit of three thousand men-at-arms to constrain the size and hence political danger of a standing army. Washington quelled the motion by whispering a suggestion that Gerry's proposal also stipulate the maximum size of invading armies.[52]

The fears of a centrally organized and commanded military did not recede after ratification of the Constitution. Key debates regarding the power distribution between central and state governments manifested in defense decisions. While political elites in the new nation were divided on the question of standing armies, everyone agreed that some armed force was necessary. The standing armies in which many presidential candidates would later serve were seen by Jefferson's followers as a harbinger of despotism, while the militia, in which other candidates would serve, appeared as a bulwark of liberty. The solution was a militia system with a skeleton of regulars, an arrangement that relied on citizenry to take up arms when necessary. This system was thought to not only protect the country from external aggression but also provide no risk of tyranny. To express both states' rights and fears of standing armies, the early republic placed strong reliance on a state and locally organized militia system. This arrangement would have influences on all the conflicts of the nineteenth century, as political considerations shaped how commanders in chief deployed their armies.

The state-based militia continued as an institution long past its early incarnations both during and before the revolution. Indeed, while the

---
50. Kohn 1979, i.
51. A. Alexander 1946. Washington's complaints are best characterized in his words. See Sparks 1855, 115–116.
52. Herring 1941; L. Smith 1951.

contemporary need for militia in the twenty-fist century is nil, the lore surrounding the Minutemen has endured. A propos the Whiggish mistrust of a standing army discussed earlier, the division of armed entities between the federal government and the peripheral governments in the states was not merely a convenient expression of dual sovereignty; it was an obvious marker denoting the fear of the central government possessing the power to coerce the states.[53] The state-based militias that existed in the decades following the new Constitution's ratification lacked martial skills but served as important civic organizations. The militia as an institution became farcical as a military institution and more a civic habit than defense posture. Reform was difficult because of the militia's dispersed, federalized structure and the political nature of how its leaders were selected.[54] The militia drills and mobilizations were less about training and more a grand civic and social event in the early nineteenth century.[55]

How does understanding the initial fears of standing armies influence the selection mechanisms that parties have used to choose their nominees? The case-study chapters plumb this issue with more thoroughness, but in general terms, the founders' fear of armies and early perceptions of militia victories cemented adoration for citizens who serve their nation in its defense and return home civilians. Despite the poor quality of the Kentucky militia on whom Andrew Jackson had wrongly placed high hopes as reinforcements at New Orleans in 1815, the victory perpetuated a myth of the superiority of militia over European professionals. In reality, artillery carried the day along with luck and British mistakes. The militia "behaved the way American militia units often behaved in the War of 1812: They ran away."[56] Yet mythology overtook reality in the retelling of the battle as the importance of beating the British grew in American consciousness. In creating a narrative in song and story, the citizen-as-temporary-soldier besting the world's preeminent military professionals contributed to a powerful, dominant popularity of militia in the early republic. Jackson himself benefited from this retelling in his own ascent toward the presidency, even though he had complained mightily about the Kentucky reinforcements at the time. This duality of American forces between its professional and federal side and its popular and more civically oriented militia side did not disappear until the twentieth century.

The decline of the militia after the nineteenth century was not the only change with implications for presidential candidacies. While we

---

53. Riker 1957.
54. Cunliffe 1968.
55. Eysturlid 1994; Laver 2002.
56. Anderson 1983, 13.

would chafe at the notion today that our highest-ranking military leaders favor one party or president over another, this apolitical thinking was not fused into the ranks at the beginning. The politicking of men in uniform was common in the Antebellum era. One scholar noted that the high-water mark of partisanship in the military ranks was probably Winfield Scott's presidential candidacy while remaining on active duty in 1852.[57] If the military itself is an incubator of presidential candidates, and the nineteenth century saw several iterations of this sort of candidate, then it is clear how personal military experience translates into political credibility for a presidential run. The higher ranks of the nineteenth-century army were partisan, especially in midcentury. For the upper tiers of the U.S. military establishment, "politics and soldiering were intertwined."[58] The case studies, especially the two that encompass the Antebellum era and the post–Civil War era, spend significant energy on the varying partisan tendencies of elite generals permitted at the time. There is even earlier evidence that partisan differences embodied different military institutions. Among a group of approximately one hundred New York state candidates who stood for election to the constitutional ratifying convention of 1788, about two-thirds had served the revolutionary cause. Among those veterans, about half were Antifederalists and half were Federalists. About 80 percent of the Antifederalists served as militiamen, while about two-thirds of the Federalists served in the Continental Army.[59] The views on the most fundamental political question of the day corresponded with the military experiences of early veterans.

Another aspect of understanding the partisan leanings of the military institutions and how that may shape presidential candidacies must take into account the inherently political missions occupying the army from 1861 to 1876: Civil War and Reconstruction. While foreign policy and external war are political acts, the Civil War and the occupation of the South in its wake were military operations waging domestic political agendas—making the armed forces become a direct actor in a domestic political conflict over the vital issues of the age. Militarily responding to Pearl Harbor entails little or no sense of partisan spirit, while the military response to the attack on Fort Sumter was an internal political struggle between elites and partisans. What had been contested with legislation and politics in 1860 morphed into a conflict of armies and arms. Reconstruction impelled the post–Civil War army into a partisan, domestic enforcement of political reconciliation. One historian makes clear the

---

57. Dempsey 2009.
58. Cunliffe 1968, 305.
59. Burrows 1974.

difficulty: "Upon the defeat of the Confederacy, the desires of various northern groups to elevate ex-slaves and reorder southern society and the southern economy, to enhance the power of a faction of the Republican Party, and to take vengeance on the rebels propelled the army into an extraordinarily difficult task—Reconstruction."[60] Serving one's country in a civil war is different from serving in a war against an external foe. The men who served in the Union army during the Civil War were the party enforcing the administration's political aims in a divisive domestic conflict.

That army underwent change in the following decades. Another key to understanding the twentieth-century case studies relating to the military is increased professionalism. The entirely federalized, standardized military that shares rank and pay structure did not exist prior to the Dick Act, also known as the Militia Act of 1903.[61] Commonalities such as the Uniform Code of Military Justice, standardized uniforms, common basic training, unified command, an overseas-deployable National Guard, and a common education structure within branches are all twentieth-century changes. America's involvement in the twentieth century's world wars and its rise as a world power spurred development of the military institutions. Even though the military rests on long traditions, including trappings such as the contemporary National Guard logo centrally featuring a Minuteman as its symbol, the armed forces of today are unified, federal, apolitical, largely apart from society, and professionalized. Contrast the military innovations of the twentieth century with its antecedents: a largely militia-oriented force with state-based organization, politically sewn into the fabric of civil society within local communities. In short, the electoral appeal of a man who served in a politically and locally oriented preprofessional fighting force differs from the appeal engendered by service in the twentieth century's professional armies.

Political Changes outside War and Military: Evolution of Parties and the Presidency

Major transformations in American politics directly and indirectly shaped the patterns of veteran candidate emergence: the political ascendance of the presidency and alterations to the party nomination process. Both areas of transition produced large implications for politics generally, but these political changes also shaped the patterns of candidate and nominee selection.

---

60. Coffman 1986, 234.
61. Bachman, Blair, and Segal 1977; Adler and Polsky 2010.

The framers, with King George III and other tyrants in mind, sought an executive that would not usurp Congress. Scholarship on the presidency has studied the growth of the executive institution, noting its nonlinear development by focusing on the men who expanded the political reach and grasp of the office. Andrew Jackson and Abraham Lincoln were nineteenth-century presidents who exploited the ambiguity of the constitutional provisions, but their successors allowed the office to contract. Theodore Roosevelt and Woodrow Wilson also expanded energy in the executive, but the dominant presidential government that exists in the United States today emerged during Franklin Roosevelt's administration. The relevance of these changes to the number and types of veterans in presidential contention revolves around citizen perceptions of a president as policy-maker-in-chief as well as the sense of the perpetual need for a commander in chief prepared for war.

The Cold War in the post–World War II era placed the United States in a bipolar world and put the country on a state of alert in the dawn of the nuclear age. This situation put the president more than ever into the role of perpetual commander in chief. This concomitant rise of the presidency spelled out changes in the way voters perceive presidential responsibilities and hence different scrutiny of candidates' backgrounds. In a climate of nuclear readiness and extant adversaries led by the Soviet Union, the electorate made its decisions on whom to elect with an eye more than in the past on their ability to be commander in chief. This is not to say that economic concerns, ideology, or party ceased to drive voters' calculus, but with the centrality of potential military conflicts seemingly continuous, it is natural that voters of the era might be more prone than those in other eras to scrutinize candidates' ability to lead a military. As the importance of the president's role as commander in chief has grown, so too has the potential for voters to use biographical military information to judge candidates.

The key phenomenon of interest in this book is the emergence of veterans as presidential candidates: Why do parties nominate particular candidates? It is important to recognize that the method the parties use to choose their candidate has not remained constant. Another major force that has shaped the veteran emergence patterns evident throughout American history has been changes in the way parties select presidential candidates to run on Election Day. The American electoral environment has been one generally conducive to those with military service, but the process by which candidates obtain their party's presidential nomination has undergone dramatic changes since Washington's time. Shunning political parties as factions prone to political instability, the very early period during the first administration ostensibly lacked a spirit of party conflict. Yet by the time of the third election, a contest between John Adams and Thomas Jefferson, identifiable political camps had been established in Congress, dividing political elites into sides that would become the Federalists and the Democratic-Republicans. The nascent parties faced the dilemma of how to choose their candidate for presidential elections.

The first method was elite driven, the congressional caucus, which was essentially a decision resting in the hands of party members elected to Congress. This mechanism, referred to as "King Caucus" by its critics, lasted for about a generation in the early nineteenth century. It was replaced by the convention method of choosing a candidate. First incorporated by the Anti-Masonic Party in 1832 and then the major parties, nominating conventions placed the nominating decision into the hands of party elites from the various states that convened in late summer. This mechanism opened the door to tracking front-runners as well as "dark-horse" candidates and an open dialogue about the merits of potential choices within the party. Military service was an explicit criteria used by some speakers at these conventions in the nineteenth century, and the case studies elaborate on notable veteran candidacies who benefited from this mechanism of candidate selection.

Starting in the early twentieth century with other progressive reforms to the political system were party primary elections. These contests were open to party faithful where registered partisans could cast ballots within the party to register their candidate preferences. At their onset, party delegates were not bound to honor the results of the primary election when they made their decisions at the national convention. But after the McGovern-Fraser reforms stemming from the implosion of the Democratic Party in 1968, parties enacted a system where the delegates from each state were obligated to vote in accordance with the results of the primary in their state held earlier that year. This internal rule change meant that party members of the electorate held sway, not party elites in smoke-filled rooms, and candidates were given strong incentives to go on the campaign trail and pitch themselves to voters.

Wars and Postwar Eras: Changing Climates after Veterans Return

The patterns of veteran emergence in politics change. There are times replete with veteran candidacies and periods without veterans. At the early twenty-first-century vantage point, Barack Obama, Mitt Romney, Hillary Clinton, and Donald Trump appear unique for lacking service, but this impression comes in contrast to a long-serving World War II generation immediately followed by a handful of Vietnam-era veterans. If there were no relationship between military service and elections, we might see no rhyme or reason for these veterans appearing on the ballot with sporadic nominations here and there. But examination shows that patterns are evident. It seems, from the large changes in the prevalence of veterans in presidential politics, waxing and waning and waxing again, that it is insufficient to simply establish the conditions that make military service prevalent among political aspirants overall.

To make better sense of veteran emergence patterns in presidential politics, this book divides American presidential elections into a periodization scheme that groups candidacies into common patterns of candidates of an era. To explain both the number and types of veterans who have appeared on major-party presidential ballots in the United States, I trace the relevant factors throughout the eras. The case-study chapters examine these elections, candidates, and contexts in detail. Any attempt to delineate history into compartmentalized eras involves necessary compressing and generalizing. The rationale behind the periodization, and therefore the chapter organization, stems from commonalities within patterns among veterans and the contributory factors that map onto America's conflicts and the generations that followed them.

To convey the variation in veteran emergence across time, Table 2.2 depicts the eras for comparison, grouped in a way most meaningful toward understanding the patterns of veterans running in presidential elections. It places each of the six large generations of veterans that follow the conflicts in a row and generalizes the nature of veteran emergence in that era along with the encapsulating dates and candidates. It is clear that different eras hold different levels of demand and supply of veteran candidacies: the parties demand veterans to nominate for elections while wars supply them to different degrees.

The Revolutionary War created the only persona who could have been the first president of the new nation, George Washington. Some of the other eight running for president in this era fought in the war, such as his fellow Delaware River boat mate James Monroe, but Washington stands apart from them. The next era starts with 1824 and closes with Lincoln's candidacies before and during the Civil War in 1860 and 1864. The Antebellum era featured fourteen presidential candidates, eleven with military experience. The veterans of this era served in the War of 1812, the various Indian Wars, and in the Mexican-American War. Collectively, veterans of this era were generals, high-ranking men with well-known party allegiances who achieved fame in combat commanding troops in

TABLE 2.2 ERAS OF VETERAN EMERGENCE

Encapsulating years	Pattern of veteran presidential candidates	Originating wars and conflicts	Size of military and means of recruiting	Military and partisan politics and professionalization	Party nominations and presidency
1789–1820	Washington as prototype	Revolutionary	Medium-size, militia-centered army with few regulars	Regulars as Federalists; militia as states' rights issue; low professionalism	Congressional caucus nominations
1824–1864	Partisan generals with lateral political entry	1812, Indian, Mexican-American	Small volunteer army	Military elites hyperpartisan; low professionalism	Convention nominations
1868–1900	Union generals "waving the bloody flag"	Civil	Large army of volunteers and conscripts with regional units	Regional and partisan conflict over Reconstruction and rise of veterans interest groups	Convention nominations; modern presidency
1904–1948	Veteran hiatus	Spanish-American, World War I	Volunteers only for Spanish-American War; drafted medium-size army for World War I	Veterans interest groups; depoliticization of military	Convention and nonbinding primaries; modern presidency
1952–1990s	Low-ranking World War II officers climb political ladder	World War II, early Cold War	Large conscript and volunteer army	Nonpartisan, professionalizing mass army	Convention and nonbinding and binding primaries; president as commander in chief
1990s–present	Who served and who did not; war with mixed legacy	Vietnam	Medium-size conscript army	End of draft; professionalized army; increased civil-military gap	Binding primaries for nomination; president as commander in chief

small wars. Its exemplar, Andrew Jackson, along with William Harrison, Lewis Cass, and Franklin Pierce, especially embodied this tradition, though Zachary Taylor and Winfield Scott were generals who had spent most of their adult lives in the army as careerists and led prominently during the war with Mexico.

The generation of political candidates following the Civil War, along with the nation they hoped to lead, went through the rending period during and after Reconstruction. This era comprises George McClellan and Ulysses Grant up to and including the last veteran of the Grand Army,

William McKinley in 1896 and 1900. The mainstays of this era were Union generals, the men who commanded soldiers in the Civil War. The new Republican Party and the Democrats fielded twelve candidates, of whom seven were veterans of the Civil War. These veterans included two types, the professionals and the battlefield generals. Ulysses Grant, George McClellan, and Winfield Scott Hancock were West Point graduates and spent many years in service prior to the war. Battlefield generals typified a different sort, those who donned a military uniform only after the Confederacy's opening salvos in 1861. Rutherford Hayes, James Garfield, and Benjamin Harrison were politically connected men of their community who were generally elected to head their regiments and then experienced rapid promotions in a large-scale war.

After the turn of the century and the Spanish-American War, parties rarely nominated men with martial experience. Eighteen men were nominated by their party during this era, and only six had any service at all, and only two with notable service, Theodore Roosevelt and Harry Truman. A form of conscription took place during America's brief involvement in World War I, but the number of men needed for fighting was smaller than the next cohort's global war, World War II.

That epic conflict, involving some sixteen million armed personnel on the American side, or about a fifth of the labor force, generated a massive veteran population after the war. They came from a large-scale conscripted recruitment regime that intended all strata of the population serve, a situation that politically meant that most men running for office of that cohort claimed some sort of war service between Dwight Eisenhower's win in 1952 and Bob Dole's loss in 1996. Only Hubert Humphrey lacked military experience. The number of presidential candidates with military service increased tremendously compared to other cohorts, beyond even what one would expect from the high proportion of veterans in the male population. The most succinct characterization of this group of presidential candidates is brief wartime officers.

Following the World War II generation, the baby boomers entered presidential politics, starting with Bill Clinton, who entered adulthood in the 1960s during the Vietnam War. Al Gore, John Kerry, George W. Bush, and John McCain served in the military, while Bill Clinton, Mitt Romney, Barack Obama, Donald Trump, and Hillary Clinton did not. Bill Clinton beat two World War II veterans in his two elections in 1992 and 1996. Obama, born in 1961, was in his twenties in the 1980s, too young to serve during the Vietnam era. He, along with all the other males who reached their twenties after the end of conscription in 1973, had a choice whether or not to enter the armed forces, and most chose to remain civilians.

Clinton and Trump, on the other hand, were in college when the draft for the Vietnam War was still in effect. Coining a summarizing phrase for this group is impossible, because it includes Vietnam War veterans, heightened political salience of candidates' war records, and an increase in parties nominating nonveterans.

The sheer number of military veterans in an era naturally shapes the number of individuals who might enter the pool of political elites to vie for the White House. The Civil War and World War II involved large proportions of the male population in their time, and correspondingly, the era that followed saw the political entrance of many veterans. But there must be more to the story than the raw number of veterans created by the conflicts. The Mexican-American War and conflicts surrounding the Indian Wars, for example, were comparatively much smaller conflicts, yet we see several notable candidacies in the years that follow. And it is too early to put a firm quantitative figure on it, but the recent wars in Iraq and Afghanistan involved comparatively small numbers of forces with a modestly sized standing army deployed at home and abroad, but men and women returning from these conflicts appear to be entering politics as past veterans have.

Finally, it is important to confront the most intuitive reason why parties nominate veterans. If veterans enjoy a systematic advantage in general elections because voters prefer them ceteris paribus, parties would see incentives in nominating a lot of veterans. To address this question empirically, whether or not veterans hold an advantage over otherwise equivalent nonveterans, I include a quantitative analysis that uses recent presidential and congressional elections to test this hypothesis. The Appendix details the specifics, but analyses there demonstrate no systematic influence on the outcome of general elections stemming from the military biography of the candidates. These nonfindings, using roughly fifty years of presidential elections and almost two thousand pooled congressional elections, do little to support the notion that veterans do well with voters in general elections. While intuitive, a simple advantage at the ballot box cannot explain the large number of veterans nominated by political parties.

Case-Study Analysis: Comparing Eras to Understand Veteran Emergence

This chapter characterizes the influences on veteran emergence for the purposes of explicating an overall account of the changing patterns of veterans in presidential politics, while the case studies hereafter focus narrowly on the eras and candidates. They serve as more than analytic cases in a strict sense of case-by-case methodology. They are also intended to be descriptive. One goal for this treatment of American electoral history is to focus on the presidential candidates themselves, those in contention for the nomination with a military experience angle, as well as notable down-ballot candidates within each period. In large part, the nominees of the major parties remain the key focus of this study. However, notable candidates who enjoyed at least a distant shot at the nomination or made relevant headlines to warrant attention are also included if they were military veterans.

For these candidates, I use secondary and occasionally primary sources to characterize whether or not they had served in some military capacity. If they had served, a summary of that time is detailed. More important, the case studies scrutinize how the service played a role in their later political life. For many candidates, that means examining how military service was featured explicitly in their campaign efforts for their first attempts at public office, such as a congressional race. Using this theoretical framework, each case study analyzes the intersection of military biography and elections through the lens of these dynamics related to the changes that the military institutions themselves portended for candidates, as well as the transformations of civilian politics related to the rise of presidential power and evolution of how parties choose their nominee for president.

3

Early Republic

George Washington through James Monroe

No other man can sufficiently unite public opinion or can give the requisite weight to the office in the commencement of the Government.
—**Alexander Hamilton**, quoted in Washington, *The Papers of George Washington*

The unbroken chain of presidential elections from Washington's first in 1789 to the most recent contest should not imply perfect comparability. The presidential elections of the early republic differed substantially from those that followed. Factions inherited from the founding and earlier coalesced into political parties across the first decade following Washington's second term. The process by which these coalitions chose their candidate was a sporadically evolving work in progress. Even the rules of the general election changed after the ratification of the Twelfth Amendment, the alteration that coupled the presidents and vice presidential candidates. Of the men who rose to become presidential candidates between 1789 and 1820, only one entered politics with military service that shaped his path to the presidency: George Washington.

Before the beginning of regularized competition between Jackson's Democratic Party and the Whigs, and later the Republican Party, the new American republic held nine presidential elections. Before considering the Jacksonian era from John Quincy Adams and Jackson in the 1820s to the Civil War, it is important to understand how the nation's first president portended the military veteran presidential candidates who would follow him.

Military service biography is salient for only one of the candidates. However, the case of George Washington is important for more than his era, because his candidacy and presidency begin a template that others subsequently continue. Four of the nine candidates of this era possessed no military experience. Neither John Adams nor John Quincy Adams served in the armed forces, and Thomas Jefferson and DeWitt Clinton also stayed civilians. The other five served in a variety of ways. Rufus King and James Madison had very brief experiences in the local militia, King briefly seeing combat. The remaining three served as officers. James Monroe and Charles C. Pinckney were battled-tested officers, and George Washington was supreme commander of the war effort.

A pattern that emerged in the next two eras but diminished before the twentieth century is that social and political divisions shaped how military leaders were selected. Who could become a regular army officer was a product of social and political standing. If we see a numerical overrepresentation of Revolutionary War veterans running for president at this time, the bias is a reflection of the initial military recruitment of political elites. Hence, it is not clear that military service, beyond Washington, enabled the candidacies of Pinckney and Monroe. This is truer for Pinckney than Monroe, the latter being quite young when he joined up with Washington at age eighteen. Rather, their military service further codified their prior political elite status in the postwar period. Military service was not a prerequisite for election to public office. On the contrary, Matthew Lyon's fisticuffs in the U.S. House of Representatives, in which he and Roger Griswold tussled on the legislative floor in 1798, ensued after Griswold publicly reminded members about the shame Lyon had endured after being court-martialed for cowardice during the revolution. His punishment forced him to wear a wooden sword, an embarrassment that did not preclude his later election to federal office.[1]

War for Independence: Troop Strength and Means of Recruitment

The Revolutionary War created the Spirit of '76, a sense of citizens taking leave of their routine lives to take up arms against "a despotic foe."[2] America's first war is a unique case—wars of secession are more difficult to analyze and characterize than interstate conflicts. Complicating matters further is that it was not one nation rebelling from the Crown but thirteen colonies in various degrees of synchronization. The conflict between Washington's forces and the British took place in distinct theaters across the whole period of the war. The size of the rebelling army is difficult to estimate, probably the hardest war for which to obtain accurate figures. Reasonable estimates are that slightly more than two hundred thousand

---

1. Wood 2009, 229.
2. Ferling 1984, 258; Royster 1979.

men participated on the American side,³ but the army was never anywhere near that size at any given time. To estimate how many veterans the war created requires placing some faith in uncertain data. Historians surmise that two hundred thousand is on the high side. One estimate avers approximately one hundred thousand "actually bore arms" during the war, "many of them under repeated enlistments."⁴ Most battles were small affairs with only a few thousand involved, excepting the notable battles such as Brandywine and the decisive fight at Yorktown. Figuring the proportion is guesswork, but assuming the white male population of the thirteen colonies was approximately one million, and somewhere between 25 and 50 percent of them were not too young or old, somewhat less than half of those who could serve did so. This is slightly less than the proportion of presidential candidates of the era with wartime experience, but political elites were not chosen randomly. We should not assume that simple numerical likelihood explains the similarity between the ratio of veterans in the population and among the presidential candidates. After all, as a percentage of all males, the share of candidates with military service further outpaces the share of voters who served.

Federalization, Partisanship, and Professionalization of the Military

Weapons and the willingness to use them arrived with the first English settlers. Expectations that all able males could become impromptu soldiers when necessary were unquestioned. The Puritans, the Jamestown settlers, and the other colonists made systems for near-universal militia inclusion. Massachusetts divided its militia into organized regiments as early as 1636. These colonial-era militia organizations drilled only occasionally but more often than the regiments of the nineteenth century. The regiments and other militia organizations were not intended to be deployed as units; rather, they organized for drilling and training purposes to be ready for danger. When conflict with Native Americans required actual combat, volunteers from the local militia would be reorganized into temporary fighting units.⁵

Those serving in the Continental Army would still be citizen-soldiers and return to civilian life after the fight, as their military efficacy was limited. As one expert assessed, "Voluntary militia served on the battlefield only as harassing auxiliaries beside the Continentals, and as a short

---

3. U.S. Department of Veterans Affairs 2017.
4. Peckham 1958, 200.
5. Morton 1958.

term emergency reserve available expeditiously."[6] Outside the home-defense role, generals who attempted to make campaigning and effective fighting forces out of militia were typically disappointed. Washington complained publicly and privately about their ability to deplete his supplies without adding any military effectiveness. A generation later, Andrew Jackson would privately agree, writing that the routine military musters were useless, "much time is lost, much unnecessary expense incurred, and much public property wasted. . . . Little useful knowledge is gained by the musters and drills as now established."[7]

While the militia's military importance is usually discussed as a martial liability in the early republic, some have recognized its more helpful role in early America as a political and party institution. Militia organizations cultivated national and state identity and bonds between citizen and government, bolstered community, and offered opportunities for civilian political elites to reinforce their status. They also played a role in electioneering efforts. Militiamen "supplied the bang and ballyhoo for party banquets and pep rallies," with one unit marching in every village along the Erie Canal to commemorate its completion.[8] Such cases of its social and civic roles eclipsing its military functionality predate the Revolutionary War.[9]

There was an important partisan dimension to military institutions of the era that became a divisive issue between the two parties. The Federalists favored a larger, more standardized, and federally controlled regular army, while Jefferson's followers enshrined militia. The issue was a front in the larger war about the role of the federal government generally, but the debate was more than symbolic. The size and budget of the regulars shrank after the war because of the end of wartime demands but also because of the Federalists' decreasing ability to influence policy outcomes.

Political Changes outside War and Military: Parties and the Presidency Evolve

The first political period in the United States comprised proto-parties that were more like elite-based factions than the broad coalition-building organizations that developed in the Jacksonian era and beyond. The first two elections, in 1789 and 1792, had an outcome foreordained by a preconceived national consensus, choosing the man who had led the country

---

6. Kestnbaum 2000, 18.
7. Stone 1977, 53.
8. Laver 2002, 799; Mahon 1983.
9. Boucher 1973; Carp 1986.

in the revolution, George Washington. The era also saw the culmination of a political rift between the two major factions and the first peaceful transition of power between them in the 1800 election. The aftermath of the second war with Great Britain contributed to the Federalist Party fizzling out, leaving a brief, so-called era of good feelings. While that phrase is an "ironic misnomer," the Republicans reigning as a single party with Monroe running uncontested in 1820 provides an impression of unity.[10] Given that the period comes before the development of major parties as we understand them today, one tendency might be to omit this period because of the indirect comparability with subsequent times. Yet it is impossible to understand Jackson's candidacies without Washington's.

This period of American presidential elections differed substantially from later periods in both the formal rules of the game (for the first four elections before 1804) and in the informal terms of how the proto-parties of the era selected their nominees. The original constitutional provisions for selecting the president gave electors two votes each and forced them to cast at least one vote for a candidate from a different state. This logic stemmed from the Philadelphia convention that presupposed no parties or factions, but the alignment of the Federalists and Republicans became palpable during Washington's second term. The outcome of the 1796 election, with Federalist John Adams winning the presidency while awarding his rival, Republican Thomas Jefferson, the vice presidency, made the need for the Twelfth Amendment obvious.

The other distinction does not concern a constitutional question but marks the development of how the newly emerging political parties selected their nominees to stand for the presidential election. In this early period, parties decided whom to nominate for president within the congressional delegation. Derided later as "King Caucus" by its critics, the congressional caucus was a simple, elite-driven method and helped keep the presidency somewhat beholden to Congress. Members of the party who had been elected or appointed to Congress would simply convene and decide among themselves. It is unlikely that candidates' military biography played a large role in these decisions.

Early Republic Candidates: George Washington through James Monroe

Table 3.1 displays the candidates in chronological order, while the case studies discuss the presidential candidates in descending order of how salient their military service was in elections. Washington's core identity

---

10. Phillips 1971, 363.

TABLE 3.1 ELECTIONS OF THE EARLY REPUBLIC

Election year	Candidate	Party	Veteran type	Detail
1789	*George Washington*		Battlefield general	British officer, commander of Continental Army
1792	*George Washington*		Battlefield general	British officer, commander of Continental Army
1796	*Thomas Jefferson*	DR	Nonveteran	None
	John Adams	Fed	Nonveteran	None
1800	*Thomas Jefferson*	DR	Nonveteran	None
	John Adams	Fed	Nonveteran	None
1804	*Thomas Jefferson*	DR	Nonveteran	None
	Charles C. Pinckney	Fed	Combat veteran	Militia officer, POW
1808	*James Madison*	DR	Common veteran	Inactive militia
	Charles C. Pinckney	Fed	Combat veteran	Militia officer, POW
1812	*James Madison*	DR	Common veteran	Inactive militia
	DeWitt Clinton	Fed	Nonveteran	None
1816	*James Monroe*	DR	Combat veteran	Officer with Washington, Battle of Trenton
	Rufus King	Fed	Combat veteran	Brief combat veteran
1820	*James Monroe*	DR	Combat veteran	Officer with Washington, Battle of Trenton

Note: Winners are italicized. DR = Democratic-Republican Party; Fed = Federalist Party.

as a presidential candidate cannot be untethered from his successful command of the revolutionary army. The wartime service of James Monroe and Charles C. Pinckney was important but not salient for their presidential candidacies. James Madison and Rufus King did technically serve, but their time as officers was brief and did not influence their electoral efforts.

George Washington as Template for Military Hero Candidates

Because of George Washington's unequaled popularity and the breadth and depth of his support, explaining his appeal to the electorate is difficult, leaving a writer to grasp for superlatives. The consensus for him among the delegates at Philadelphia, state leaders, and the general public was certain. Everyone agreed that whatever system was to replace the Articles of Confederation, if it had an executive, George Washington was going to serve in that role. No candidate since has enjoyed such consensus. Hamilton urged his mentor to accept the reality that he was indispensable at the hour when the Constitution's new and untested institution, the presidency, would be filled.[11] The extent of his appeal makes any comparisons to Washington's two elections complicated. When Henry Lee eulogized Washington, his famous phrase, "first in war—first in peace—and first in the hearts of his countrymen," binds Washington's two identities. He was a soldier and civilian leader, the American Cincinnatus, and it is impossible to uncouple them, for one depends on the other.

There was a fear at this time of standing armies and an ideologically based sense that professional men-at-arms were a threat to liberty and the new government. This feeling appears incongruent with the fact that Washington was the most well-known military officer. His service in a Virginia militia unit during the French and Indian War in the 1750s was formative for Washington himself but not the experience in uniform that would give him the popularity necessary to be the only choice for first president. It was instead his formation, organization, and command of the Continental Army that would eventually force the British to surrender in 1781 and bring about the real independence declared in 1776. So, while not precisely a career officer, he was the closest thing to it in the minds of the public.

Sheer military prowess did not solely make Washington into the first president. Beyond the winning and losing of battles and wars, it is difficult to assess the military skills of generals. Washington won the war, of course, but not without losing battles along the way. It is not clear that Washington was the most skilled and qualified man to command the military in the revolution, as arguments can be made for Horatio Gates and Charles Lee. Whether or not this is true is probably immaterial to what made Washington's military experience appealing for his transition from commander to planter to president. The American public and its political elites did not seek or cherish the man because of his martial virtues alone:

> The Americans' restrained conception of their commander's fighting role reflected their ambivalence toward military leadership in general. . . . Lacking tested institutional constraints on the ambitions of strong leaders, and with the ever-present examples of Caesar and Cromwell to justify anxieties about the imposition of dictatorship, Americans at war looked not to their best military man for direction but to the military man in whom they had the most trust.[12]

---

11. Washington 1987, 119.
12. Schwartz 1990, 26.

While the central government's unwillingness and inability to support the army adequately were lamentable, the officers who threatened mutiny to obtain their back pay at war's end created a problem that Washington, perhaps only Washington, had the ability to solve. The role that Washington played in defusing the thinly veiled threats of his officers to march on Congress, the Newburgh Conspiracy, may not contribute to understanding how his military experiences facilitated his political attractiveness, but they demonstrate Washington's preference for the preeminence of civilian government.

Washington broke with long historic precedent at the end of the revolution. Rather than exploit his popularity and the army under his command at the height of his military victory, he retired and went back to his home. For one recent biographer, Washington's departure from the apex of authority in 1783 "remains one of the most remarkable events in the history of war, revolution, and politics."[13] The framers' faith in Washington, based on their observations of his fidelity and retirement, no doubt allowed them to infuse more power in the office of the presidency than otherwise would have been likely. In the end, perhaps Washington's retirement from his inimitable military role as much as the service itself cemented his destiny as first president.

Combat Veterans from the Revolution: Monroe and Pinckney

James Monroe became the final man of the Revolutionary era to ascend to the presidency and the final president to have worn a uniform during the Revolutionary War, earning him the honorific "Last of the Cocked Hats." Historical accounts of the fifth president's time in the revolutionary army detail his involvement, including his injury during the Christmas sneak attack on the Hessians at Trenton.[14] Monroe joined the 3rd Virginia Regiment in 1776 at age eighteen and quickly became a lieutenant in a rifle company. Monroe's outfit marched to New York City in September 1776 to counter the British attack at Harlem Heights. A month later, as a part of the New York and New Jersey movement and retreat in the first year of the war, Monroe's unit saw action at the Battle of White Plains. That battle marked Washington's retreat westward with Monroe's regiment, following the staggering loss of Fort Washington on the northern tip of Manhattan in November.

Monroe's letters in late 1776, that nadir in the revolutionary cause, signaled the desperation facing Washington's forces. The militias shrank

---

13. Larson 2014, 3.
14. Hanser 1976.

as individuals abandoned the cause and leaked away, reducing the army to something smaller than five thousand. Pursued by the British and the Hessians, Monroe and the others under Washington's command marched southwest, crossing rivers and losing men and equipment at every turn. Finally, they made it across the Delaware River into Pennsylvania, having commandeered all the boats from the area. Besides denying the British a means to pursue, this move also gave the impression that Washington planned to winter there and recuperate on the west side of the river, safe from the enemy trailing his forces.

That implied encampment in the cold winter was what Washington exploited when he marshaled his troops and crossed the Delaware again, seeking to surprise the Hessians at Trenton. This "Crossing of the Delaware" and the ensuing battle at Trenton grew into a celebrated turning point for morale and marked the end of the previous months of battle losses and retreats. Monroe, along with Washington and fellow Virginian John Marshall, took part in this battle. Revolutionary forces crossed the river eastward north of Trenton and marched south to surprise the Hessian forces garrisoned there with an early-morning attack. Emanuel Leutze's iconic 1851 painting, *Washington Crossing the Delaware*, fancifully depicts the crossing, featuring Washington standing tall in the Durham boat on the icy waters with Monroe behind him bearing the flag. Once across the water and marching toward Trenton, Washington himself commanded the attack on the morning of December 26, 1776. Monroe was among the first group to cross the river and became the "vanguard of the regiment" in the fast assault.[15]

The Continentals caught the Hessians by surprise, but the mercenaries put up a hasty defense. This attempt to repulse the attack included brass cannons, which pinned down some of the Americans. Lieutenant Monroe, along with his captain, made a fast rush toward the enemy guns and captured them. The next hurdle was east in the small town. His captain fell to Hessian fire, so command transferred to Monroe. A musket ball hit Monroe's shoulder soon thereafter, and his men carried him from the battle to have his wound tended. The bleeding was stopped and Monroe survived, but the ball remained in his shoulder. That battle had not directly led to British surrender and was not decisive in convincing the British to concede American independence. It did provide Washington's army a victory, one that was needed after months of losses. The British had essentially chased Washington's forces from Long Island to Pennsylvania, racking up victories as the revolutionary units retreated and contracted, but the surprise

---

15. Hanser 1976, 150.

attack at Trenton stanched the bleeding in terms of morale. There would be subsequent setbacks before Charles Cornwallis's surrender: Philadelphia, Charleston, Savannah, and others, but Trenton put a high note on what had been a very difficult year for the revolutionary cause.

James Monroe's rank, stature, and experiences during the war appeared to help him establish political credibility. Along with fellow veteran John Marshall, Monroe joined the Virginia House of Delegates in 1782. When they entered the chamber together, they were lauded for their service and chosen for political roles based on their wartime experiences: "Members stood and cheered the two young war heroes, then rewarded their valor by electing them to the . . . executive council," the state's executive arm.[16] This would be the beginning of Monroe's upward political trajectory, later representing Virginia as delegate and senator, and leading it as governor when he was not serving the Jefferson or Madison administration as a minister or secretary. By the time of his nomination for president in 1816, Monroe's political stature was high, and he did not need to rely on his Revolutionary War heroism to obtain nominations or votes. Yet his service in the war as a young man shaped his political outlook and helped his early political career.

The path to a man's highest military rank is occasionally complicated, and perhaps none so much as that of Charles Cotesworth Pinckney, the person the Federalists nominated twice in their waning descent toward nonexistence after John Adams's presidency. Pinckney was an ensign in the Charleston militia before the war, but he became a commander of Continentals in South Carolina when the war began. In 1777 he saw the South as too quiet and departed to serve under Washington to be closer to the action. His regiment arrived in time to fight at the Battles of Brandywine and Germantown. He forged ties with Washington and Hamilton during this period that would become politically important later. British ambitions changed in 1778 as the South became a front in the war, so Pinckney returned to lead his regiment to retake Savannah in 1779. Colonial and French forces failed in their siege and attack, returning to Charleston only to be besieged themselves in 1780. After a month, the colonials capitulated and Pinckney became a prisoner of war. Militiamen were released, but regulars remained imprisoned for another two years, ending Pinckney's military career, though he was rewarded a brevet general star at the end of the war.

The role that Pinckney's military history played in his political life is difficult to describe with authority, but given his frequent appellation of

---

16. Unger 2009, 43.

"general" found in the primary-source material, it seems clear that it must have played at least a small role. While he probably was never sufficiently high in command to bear primary blame for the losses, it is true that the four major battles in which he participated were British victories. One biographer found his military skills lacking: "Pinckney had neither the military talent nor the good fortune which make heroes out of common mortals. In fact if his fellow soldiers were superstitious they might have seen his very presence as an omen of ill luck, for Pinckney was not actively involved in a successful battle during the entire war."[17] What edged Pinckney over King among Federalists may have been his time in uniform: "At a time when the nation was involved in a crisis that could develop into a war, a soldier might have more appeal to the electorate than another member of the Virginia dynasty."[18] However, his service had a potential downside. After initial hesitance to challenge Pinckney's experience, one prominent letter in the *Charleston City Gazette* encapsulated the belief that "no man who loved military honors as Pinckney did and who had held high military office should be transferred to a high civil office."[19]

Low-Salience Military Service and Nonveterans in the Postrevolutionary Era

Rufus King was thirty-three years old and freshly from Harvard when the Revolutionary War intersected with him in August 1778. He joined a militia unit under General John Sullivan on his way to retake Newport, Rhode Island. He became a major and aide to General John Glover. Expected French support did not materialize, so their attack plan turned to defense and King's unit withstood a British attack. King's four-week stint in the war as an officer did little to shape his political career that would eventually see him as the final nominee of the collapsing Federalist Party in 1816. In one biographical sketch of Rufus King on the eve of his nomination to be the Federalist standard-bearer that year, there is no mention of King's military service. Instead, it focuses on his speaking skills as "the most finished orator amongst the moderns" and King's rapport with Alexander Hamilton.[20] He had brief encounters with enemy fire, but King was not "moved by military ambition."[21]

---

17. Zahniser 1967, 69.
18. Zahniser 1967, 252.
19. Zahniser 1967, 223.
20. King and King 1894, 505.
21. Carr et al. 1955, 27.

James Madison technically earned a commission early in the Revolutionary War effort, but he never claimed the title of veteran. The Virginia legislature appointed him colonel of the Orange County militia in October 1775, but Madison's autobiography provides a first-person view that his "feeble health and liability to sudden attacks" precluded "entering the army."[22] His position in the Orange County militia put him in a march as a "revolutionary militiaman" at least once, but it is a mantle he decided not to claim. Table 3.1 lists him as a common veteran, despite Madison's preference, for consistency across time. His legacy as commander in chief is far more well known than his brief march during the revolution, but it is a dubious one, since he was the sole president to flee the capital.

Washington's vice president and America's second president, John Adams, did not take up arms against the British in the revolution. This lack of service was, in his own words, a source of some inadequacy he perceived of himself. For Adams, the revolution was a total war for political existence that elevated the men who ran military risks into civic legitimacy. The war made potential soldiers out of all men. An examination of primary-source letters reveals Adams quite torn on the subject—his lack of service and unwillingness to join the fight vexed him. He later wrote, "I longed more ardently to be a Soldier than I ever did to be a Lawyer."[23] This focus on him is not meant to disparage Adams's dedication—he was serving his country in the legislature—or delve into his mind on the anguish he exhibits in his writings. Rather, it illustrates the sense of obligation that must have been palpable for many during the Revolutionary War period. If Adams felt this way and let this sentiment come through in his letters and other writings, the sense that taking up arms was a civic obligation must have been pervasive.

---

22. Ketcham 1971, 64.
23. Quoted in Ferling 1984, 259.

4

Antebellum Generals

Andrew Jackson through the Civil War

The fact that six of twelve presidents between 1815 and 1860 served as officers demonstrates how political and military elites were often one and the same.
—Jason Dempsey, *Our Army*

I cannot believe that killing 2500 Englishmen at N. Orleans qualifies for the various, difficult and complicated duties of the Chief Magistracy.
—Henry Clay, quoted in Remini, *Henry Clay*

It is impossible to deny the inconceivable influence which military glory exercises upon the spirit of a nation. General Jackson . . . is a man of a violent temper and mediocre talents. . . . But he was raised to the Presidency, and has been maintained in that lofty station, solely by the recollection of a victory which he gained twenty years ago under the walls of New Orleans, a victory which was, however, a very ordinary achievement, and which could only be remembered in a country where battles are rare.
—Alexis de Tocqueville, *Democracy in America*

America underwent massive transformations during the political era from Jackson's presidency to the turmoil of the Civil War. The birth of mass-oriented parties, rising political participation, and dramatically increased speed in communication shaped how parties and candidates persuaded and mobilized potential voters. Political divisions over the tariff, spending on internal improvements, and the expansion of slavery into the new states formed schisms in Washington. The Democratic Party was born as the party of Andrew Jackson but was heir to the Virginia-centered party of Thomas Jefferson, James Madison, and James Monroe. Jefferson's ideological progeny in the Democrats inherited the states' rights, antifederalist banner from the early debates over the size and shape of the central government. Democrats would play the dominant role in a two-party duality over the Whigs, the party born as a reaction to General Andrew Jackson. The Whigs would contest presidential elections with only two successes but remain relevant as an alternative that could occasionally take advantage of regional and national interests to stymie the Democrats until the 1850s.

This era, roughly the period that realignment scholars refer to as the Second Party System, is critical because of the distinctive array of political and military conditions that shape that era's veteran candidacies. Similar to the period after World War II, a high proportion of the Antebellum era's presidential candidates were men with personal military experience. This analysis includes fourteen major-party candidates during this era.[1] This era's presidential candidates were mostly military veterans, with almost 80 percent of them entering national politics after service in the armed forces. Only three of the fourteen men did not serve, which is almost on par with the period between World War II and the 1990s, when thirteen of the fourteen presidential candidates were veterans. What is most notable about the number of veterans in the Antebellum era is the disparity between the number of veterans running for president and the estimated number of veterans in the electorate. In short, the number of veterans running for president was near its highest levels in antebellum politics, while the number of vets in the population was perhaps at its lowest.

War of 1812, Indian Wars, and Mexican-American War: Troop Strength and Means of Recruitment

If the Revolutionary War was the defining military conflict that made the candidacy of George Washington, the War of 1812, the Indian Wars, and the Mexican-American War created conditions for seeing military heroism as a political asset and catapulted a large number of vets to the center of the electoral stage. While the ambiguous term "Indian Wars" can include a wide range of conflicts between the expanding new republic and the various Indian tribes in the nineteenth century, the Indian conflicts around the time of the War of 1812 are relevant as candidate experiences. This includes the Creek War in which Andrew Jackson fought against Creek Indians in the South, the battles with Tecumseh's forces in the Indiana Territory, and the First Seminole War in Florida later that decade. This section details the War of 1812 and the Indian Wars with regard to the size and scope of the conflicts, means of raising troops, and party implications.

---

1. This includes the National Republican, Whig, and Democratic Parties, but I do not consider the Anti-Mason, Free Soil, or Know Nothing nominees.

Parties nominated veterans more than their simple numbers in the population would suggest. The number of Americans who served under arms during the second war with Great Britain is difficult to know with much precision, but estimates suggest that it was probably around 250,000. The Veterans Administration (VA) reports 286,730 total service members during the war, with 2,260 battle deaths and 4,505 "non-mortal woundings."[2] The number of men who actually engaged the British or Indians allied with the British is much lower. The nature of the battles of this war did not resemble the massed formations seen in the Napoleonic Wars or in the U.S. Civil War; they were frontier battles in which thousands rather than tens of thousands of men fought. For example, the Battle of the Thames pitted approximately four thousand men under William Henry Harrison against no more than fifteen hundred British troops. In the Battle of New Orleans about eleven thousand British troops clashed with Andrew Jackson's combined force of about half that number.

To quantify the proportion of veterans in the electorate, we need to assess how many men were eligible to serve. The 1810 federal census reported 571,991 white males between the ages of twenty-six and forty-four and 541,591 white males between the ages of fifteen and twenty-five. If we make a rough guess that about 250,000 men served in either the regulars, volunteers, or activated militia, we can estimate that about 22 percent of "fighting age" men were in uniform.[3] Even if a fifth of this age cohort is a reasonable but high estimate for the percentage of white men who could be counted as veterans of the War of 1812, seeing four men run for president afterward who were on the front lines of those battles (Jackson, Harrison, Cass, and Scott) means that the parties preferred nominating veterans beyond what numbers would indicate.

The second war with Great Britain took place thirty years after gaining independence but with the new nation less prepared for war in terms of manpower than probably any other conflict in which it fought. There was a mix of regulars, volunteers, and militia involved.[4] Emory Upton's authoritative history of the first century of the American military is the most lucid critique of the reliance on activated militia units and the use of short-term volunteer units working under the framework of the regular army. Congress had the opportunity on the eve of the war to raise an army

---

2. U.S. Department of Veterans Affairs 2017.
3. This number is highly unreliable. The figures used to make the estimate are not consensus numbers among sources, and the Census Bureau's numbers in this era do not allow us to see how many men were between fifteen and thirty-five, a probably more realistic upper bound.
4. Russell Weigley says that the authorized strength for the regulars at the war's start was 36,503, and Upton says there were 56,032 employed throughout the war. See Weigley 1967; Upton 1912.

by enlarging the extant regular forces through long-term enlistment yet did not. In Upton's view, this decision prevented an early decisive victory that would have included successful occupation of Canada.[5]

The administration preferred inducting volunteers into the regular army rather than mobilizing existing militia units. This practice may seem at odds with Republican orthodoxy about the fears of standing armies, but the strict constructionists in the Madison administration appear to be more worried about restrictions on militia deployment outside the nation's borders.[6] The military value of the militia volunteers versus that of the regulars might best be summed up by how the British treated them. After the British capture of Fort Detroit in the War of 1812, the British commander released the volunteers to return to their homes but imprisoned the regulars and sent them to Montreal. While not deficient in willingness, the new recruits lacked the military discipline and training to be an effective fighting force because of the constitutional ambiguities about whether the federal government or the states would fund and organize their efforts in war.[7]

The popularity of a war can shape the pattern of veteran emergence into politics, and a war's results shape its popularity. The results of the War of 1812 were more ambiguous than those of America's other conflicts. Historians have debated how to interpret the war's end. For Great Britain, the conflict against Napoleon's armies was the larger concern and the war in North America was only part of its war footing. Americans prefer to see the war as a second war of independence that fully demonstrated its political break with the Crown. The borders between the United States and British territory remained as they were prior to the conflict. The treaty ending the war did not concern itself with the issues that President Madison had used to justify the conflict in his statement to Congress at the onset. The size of the forces engaged in actual combat was small, and claimed victories for either side were more often indecisive than outright triumphs. The Battle of the Thames and the Battle of New Orleans were the only unequivocal victories in the war, and hence, those two battles were hero-making scenes for two presidential candidates down the road. An important political outcome of the war was its role in diminishing the credibility of the quickly waning Federalist Party, which increasingly became a party with strength only in New England, and that region's unwillingness to contribute militia to the cause made the region and the party appear disloyal.

---

5. Upton 1912, 96.
6. Weigley 1967, 118.
7. Skeen 1999.

There are a couple of indirect ways to assess how popular the War of 1812 was with the public. On the one hand, with only two clear victories, the second of which occurred after the end of the war, the war could not have sparked many bursts of patriotism from battlefield outcomes. In what must be considered a low-water mark for the armed forces of the United States, a foreign power successfully invaded the capital and burned down the White House. The war was also quite costly in terms of the growth of the debt. On the other hand, while keeping units on a wartime footing was occasionally a problem, recruiting new volunteers proved easy. Often, more men turned out for enlistment than there were positions to fill, not an indication of an unpopular war.

Further, the war was not long in duration and incurred relatively few battlefield casualties. Using the VA's rough estimate of 2,260 battle deaths across the thirty-two months of the war, there was an average of 71 casualties per month. If one includes those who died from disease and other non-combat-related deaths, then the number increases to 211 deaths per month. The timing of the battles played a role in the war's popularity as well. Even though the Battle of New Orleans took place after the Treaty of Ghent was signed, its tardiness did nothing to diminish the glory Americans felt when the story of the final battle of the war was written as a rout of British regulars by General Jackson and his militia.

The last conflict in which this era's candidates fought was the Mexican-American War. It was another war that offered opportunities to create hero veterans to contest presidential elections. The American war with Mexico was one of the five conflicts in which Congress ever officially declared war with its ordained constitutional powers, but we tend to overlook it because the Civil War happened less than twenty years afterward. The war was short and popular in the United States, as the victory delivered massive territorial gains all the way to the Pacific Ocean. John Tyler, Harrison's vice president who became president after the latter's death only a month into his term, sought annexation of Texas. Obtaining it "headed Tyler's acquisitive agenda."[8] The war is also very important in explaining the role of military service in presidential elections because it certainly enabled the candidacies of Zachary Taylor and Winfield Scott and played an important role in promoting the candidacies of Franklin Pierce and John Frémont.

Compared to larger subsequent wars and the previous War of 1812, the war with Mexico did not put many men in uniform. Taking account of the regulars and the volunteers who mustered in and served during the

---

8. Crapol 2006, 25.

war with Mexico reveals that approximately ninety thousand men served, though this is an estimate because official records were imperfect, again often including redundancies.[9] The various battles of the war were small, taking place across a wide territory in Mexico, and similar to the War of 1812, did not involve large numbers of troops at a time. To frame the size of the fighting forces as a proportion, the 1840 federal census counted 2.1 million white males between the ages of fifteen and twenty-nine. This means that, very roughly, less than 5 percent of those who were eligible were actually in uniform.

The war began when General Zachary Taylor's force of four thousand regulars moved to Texas on the contested border with Mexico, sparking an attack that gave President James K. Polk what he needed to induce a formal declaration of war from Congress in May 1846. After the initial action on the border, it was clear that many more troops would be needed, far more than were serving in the federal army at the time. The need to call on auxiliary troops was therefore high, but the states' militia forces by the 1840s were virtually useless as a fighting force. Further, the militia originally served as a home guard, and eighteenth-century legislation precluded foreign deployment and the militia being used for very long. To get around the legal and practical issues of attempting to summon the states' organized militias to become an invasion force into Mexico, the call for troops was framed not as a summons of the various militias but as an open call for "volunteers," who may or may not have been active in their local militia.

To qualify to be a volunteer required little more than willingness. The mechanism of creating the volunteer units quickly meant that civic leaders who wanted to earn war glory would attempt to create a new unit themselves and hope to win command of it through an election in the ranks. Some men had experience in the militia and had practiced military drills, while others possessed no experience and justified their efforts via less-than-relevant qualifications. One contemporary described the problem during Polk's call for volunteers: "As usual in such elections, the men chosen were selected more for reasons of popularity or political affiliation than for military competency."[10] One extreme example of such a recruiting tactic by a political entrepreneur hoping to earn a captaincy by forming a new unit made his call to arms in low terms. Peter Goff, a new soldier in an Illinois unit, explained to his fellow soldiers that he had been the

---

9. The VA estimates the number at 78,718, while Upton's count is 104,284. Weigley estimates that there were never more than 50,000 in uniform at any given time. See U.S. Department of Veterans Affairs 2017; Upton 1912; Weigley 1967.
10. Viola 1969, 336; see also Buley 1919.

"Butcher of Middletown . . . the man that shot that sneaking, white livered Yankee abolitionist son of bitch. . . . I want to be your Captain, I do. . . . I will serve the yellow-bellied Mexicans the same. . . . I have treated you to fifty dollars [sic] worth of whiskey, I have, and when elected Captain I will spend fifty more!"[11]

The election, which Goff won almost unanimously, took place in a bowling alley and also determined who would be Goff's lieutenants. Goff's abilities to lead men, according to colorful first-person impressions, did not extend beyond his capacity to acquire whiskey. Disgusted, the observer Samuel Chamberlain mustered out of the volunteer unit to join the regular army before he got to the fighting, allowing him to draw comparisons. While it is the impression of a low-ranking enlisted man prone to exaggeration, his view of the differences between the volunteers and the regulars is illustrative: "Our officers were all graduates of West Point, and at the worst were gentlemen of intelligence and education, often harsh and tyrannical, yet they took pride in having their men well clothed, and fed, in making them contented and reconciled to their lot. The volunteer officers on the other hand would tie up a man one day, drink and play cards with him the next, and excuse their favorites from drill and guard duty; in short, most of them were totally incompetent and a disgrace to their profession."[12]

That professionalism that Chamberlain perceived of the regular army officers and their soldiers was relatively new. Not only was the Mexican-American War a victory for the American side, but it was also a vindication of the professionalizing federal army, a process that began after the disasters of the War of 1812.[13] Each of the major battles with Mexican forces across the stages and campaigns demonstrated success: "Whatever its morality or lack thereof, when seen in purely military terms, we must declare the Mexican War a glorious triumph for American arms."[14] The war was America's first fought substantially past its borders. Instead of a desperate defensive struggle for survival for its independence, the war with Mexico was an elective conflict. U.S. forces extended American reach to topple a foreign government by fielding professionals and volunteers under sound commanders, expanding American territory in the process.

Several characteristics of the Mexican War contribute to its relatively high popularity, especially for annexation-minded Southerners. If one measure of the war's approval is the ease of recruiting men to fight, Polk's

---

11. Chamberlain 1987, 31.
12. Chamberlain 1987, 68.
13. Hsieh 2009.
14. Hsieh 2009, 55.

war enjoyed warm support. For example, one order of magnitude larger number of volunteers showed up for Tennessee's call to arms than were needed. Some thirty thousand men from the Volunteer State sought positions in a quota set at only three thousand.[15] Other characteristics of the war also imply its popularity. We do not possess empirical public opinion data, but when one considers the war's short duration, the lack of conscription, the unbroken string of battle victories for the United States, and the zeal for expansionism and manifest destiny, it is easy to see how this war was a popular one with a large capacity for creating heroes with political potential.

One aspect of the Mexican-American War might have diminished its popularity. Casualties as a proportion of the men served were terribly high for the war. Of the 78,718 men mobilized, best estimates indicate 13,283 died on the campaign. That grisly ratio means almost 17 percent of the number of men who served died in the war, a rate much higher than that of the twentieth-century conflicts. Between 2 and 3 percent of the 16 million people serving died in uniform during World War II, and approximately the same casualty rate happened for the 4.7 million serving in World War I. Most of these deaths in the Mexican War, almost 90 percent, resulted from illness and disease rather than from bullets, bayonets, or cannon fire. However, it is unlikely that people back home were disquieted by casualties in Mexico. The scholarly conception of casualty aversion among citizens back home centers on late twentieth-century wars for good reason: they are longer and news about casualties reaches people quickly. While the number of war dead from this war as a proportion is staggering, the conflict's brevity and frequent victories, along with the fact that deaths from disease are probably understood differently than deaths due to direct battle, the war's casualties did not dent its popularity.

Federalization, Partisanship, and Professionalization of the Military

To examine the relationship between the federal and state civilian governments and the military institutions is to watch a moving target. During this period, the ideological attachment to militia as the ultimate fulfillment of defense posture began to recede as its poor military quality became more obvious. This period of civil-military relations in the United States saw a "rationalization" of military policies, a maturation and reconciling of the attachment to localized militia with the growing need for more professionalized forces on the frontier.[16] Jefferson, contrary to his

---
15. McCaffrey 1992, 18.
16. Langston 2003, 8.

treatment of other Federalist preferences, did not "dismantle the army and begin anew" but "institutionalized its functions and moved toward a permanent military establishment."[17]

The allegiance to parties among military generals was high in the period surrounding the Mexican War. Partisan concerns governed the recruiting mechanisms for the volunteers, the maintenance of the regular army, and the most salient issue of open party allegiance by the officer corps, especially those of the highest ranks who held presidential aspirations themselves. Zachary Taylor and Winfield Scott are the best examples of generals with party attachments relevant to their conduct in war as well as for their presidential ambitions.

The U.S. Army was professionalizing in military terms. Its ability to move and fight was improved across the decades in this era, especially when one compares the fighting effectiveness between the War of 1812 and the Mexican-American War. As evidenced by its successes during the latter war, the army's ability to train and lead nascent volunteer units into battle was a new strong suit for the professionalized regulars. However, they were not professional by the standards of civil-military relations in the twentieth and twenty-first centuries. When Samuel Huntington and others wrote the seminal works on civil-military relations in the twentieth century, they thought of military professionalism as concomitant with political neutrality.

Political Changes outside War and Military: Parties and the Presidency Evolve

This post–Federalist Party period in American political history is an era when the Democrats and Whigs institutionalized, began choosing nominees in conventions, and set forth a two-party system that would endure until the Civil War. It was also a period of volatility in presidential duration. Presidents rarely served two terms, as death claimed some in office, while others were turned out by their own party during the next cycle's presidential nomination. The method of obtaining a party presidential nomination was still in flux after the King Caucus congressional system fell out of favor. The disruptive force of Andrew Jackson's popularity in the 1820s was an important influence on what would become the nomination system. His nomination in 1824 took an unusual path that started in his home state of Tennessee's state legislature. That body nominated him for the presidency in 1822, the year following his resignation from the

---

17. Adler and Keller 2014, 168.

military, a move without precedent or promise of success. With only one political banner under which to run in 1824, there was no nomination contest per se; all four candidates were titular Democratic-Republicans. The selection of John Quincy Adams in the House of Representatives, despite Jackson earning more popular and Electoral College votes, galvanized Jackson's supporters, and state legislatures renominated him for the 1828 election only months after Adams's inauguration. The awkwardness of state legislative nominations gave way to the political convention system whereby each state party apparatus would send delegates to a national location to choose a nominee. The way that parties choose their candidates likely influences the types of candidates, though it is difficult to determine how much effect the selection mechanism has on veteran emergence patterns. For Jackson's first nominations, given his broad war-hero popularity coupled with scorn from party elites like Henry Clay, he may have enjoyed a clearer path to a more consolidated party if the conventions had begun prior to the 1830s.

The Antebellum Candidates: Andrew Jackson through Abraham Lincoln

Among the fourteen men who ran for president after nomination by either the Democratic Party or the Whig Party, eleven possessed some military experience. Table 4.1 lists the candidates in chronological order, but the case studies are grouped into substantively meaningful categories to show the different ways military service shaped presidential nominations. Andrew Jackson, William Henry Harrison, Lewis Cass, Franklin Pierce, and John Frémont each had wartime experience, fought a battle or campaign that garnered fame, held public office, and culminated in a presidential nomination. They represent something akin to a Washington model. They were not career military men, but they went to war to lead armies and earned a reputation that helped bolster their political viability. Zachary Taylor and Winfield Scott typify the partisan general. Each was a careerist in the army, led armies in the Mexican War, and was widely understood to align with the Whig Party. They both made a lateral entry into presidential politics without using the Senate or a governor's mansion as a stepping-stone. James Polk, James Buchanan, and Abraham Lincoln were veterans whose military experience varied but was less notable. For these candidates, their military service may or may not have helped establish some prepolitical footing to begin a life in public office, but being a veteran was not central to their electoral identity.

TABLE 4.1 ELECTIONS OF THE ANTEBELLUM ERA

Election Year	Candidate	Party	Veteran type	Detail
1824	John Quincy Adams	DR	Nonveteran	None
	Andrew Jackson	DR	Battlefield general	War of 1812, Battle of New Orleans
1828	John Quincy Adams	NR	Nonveteran	None
	Andrew Jackson	D	Battlefield general	War of 1812, Battle of New Orleans
1832	Henry Clay	NR	Nonveteran	None
	Andrew Jackson	D	Battlefield general	War of 1812, Battle of New Orleans
1836	William Harrison	W	Battlefield general	Battle of Tippecanoe
	Martin Van Buren	D	Nonveteran	None
1840	*William Harrison*	W	Battlefield general	Battle of Tippecanoe
	Martin Van Buren	D	Nonveteran	None
1844	Henry Clay	W	Nonveteran	None
	James Polk	D	Common veteran	Militia colonel
1848	*Zachary Taylor*	W	Career general	Partisan general, Mexican-American War
	Lewis Cass	D	Battlefield general	War of 1812, militia
1852	Winfield Scott	W	Career general	Partisan general, War of 1812 and Mexican-American War
	Franklin Pierce	D	Battlefield general	Mexican-American War
1856	James Frémont	R	Battlefield general	Officer, Mexican-American War, "Pathfinder"
	James Buchanan	D	Common veteran	War of 1812, militia
1860	*Abraham Lincoln*	R	Common veteran	Black Hawk War, militia
	Stephen Douglas	D	Nonveteran	None

Note: Winners are italicized. The elections of 1824, 1836, and 1860 included multiple candidates running under the same party banner, but only those with the highest number of votes are listed. D = Democratic Party; DR = Democratic-Republican Party; NR = National Republican Party; R = Republican Party; W = Whig Party.

Battlefield Generals: Jackson, Harrison, Cass, Pierce, and Frémont

Andrew Jackson was America's second great war hero after George Washington provided the template for obtaining national recognition on the battlefield. Jackson's military career was long and storied, not without controversy, but the moment that catapulted him to national prominence took place on Chalmette Field in 1815 when he beat the British in the Battle of New Orleans. Under Jackson's command, his artillery and volunteer militia used an advantageous position, courage, luck, and British errors to dig in and prevail dramatically against a numerically superior foe. The Redcoats had sought to capture New Orleans but were met with a lopsided defeat, sealing the fame of "Old Hickory" from Tennessee. Jackson earned the appellation in an awkward military campaign in 1813, early in the war against Great Britain. Jackson was initially mobilized into service to bring the Tennessee militia of some two thousand men to New Orleans to buttress the defense of the Gulf Coast. In a turnaround, Jackson was informed he was no longer needed, though he and his volunteers had already made it to Natchez, Mississippi. The return trip was miserable, with many of his men ill, so Jackson gave up his horse and "walked most of the retrograde march" back home.[18] This stoutness earned him the flattering nickname inspired by the hardwood tree.[19]

The nickname came from 1813, but his fame and national reputation date from the Battle of New Orleans in 1815.[20] That the battle victory happened after diplomats agreed to end the war did not diminish the symbolic value of the former colonies beating a world superpower's professional soldiers with armed woodsmen under Jackson's command. The Tennessean used a famous battlefield victory, ripe with symbolic national growth, to further a political career. His time in uniform was a necessary condition toward his presidential aspirations. His appellation in campaign rhetoric and sloganeering was often "General Jackson" or simply "The Hero." His legacy was sufficiently influential on the politics of his era and thereafter that two of the Democratic presidents who followed him, James Polk and Franklin Pierce, earned nicknames that were homages to Jackson: "Young Hickory" and "Young Hickory of the Granite Hills," respectively.[21]

Jackson was an electoral and political prototype in many ways beyond his blazing a trail for others to use military credentials to seek the White House. Some historians refer to his presidency and the decades that followed, the Antebellum era of Democratic Party political dominance over the Whigs, as the "Age of Jackson" because of his large imprint on national

---

18. Ward 1955, 55.
19. The Seminoles and other Indian tribes Jackson battled did not call him Old Hickory. For them, given his commitment to pressing the fight into Florida and winning, he was "Sharp Knife." O'Brien 2003, 201.
20. Jackson's victory in New Orleans loomed largest when considering what created his great prestige, but his less important role in the Revolutionary War was not entirely ignored. He was also called the "Hero of Two Wars," a reference to his youthful "service" in the first war with Great Britain. See Jamieson 1984, 6. During the Revolutionary War, a British officer ordered the then-teenage Jackson to polish his boots, but the lad refused. The officer took out his weapon and slashed Jackson, which left a scar on his forehead.
21. Greenberg 2012, 32; Nichols 1958, 208.

politics.[22] Jackson is in many ways more typical than Washington in showing how military service shapes who enters presidential politics and why. As the first man to ascend to the presidency, and the only conceivable man enjoying universal acclamation, Washington was unique in his path to election victory. Jackson, a mere mortal, made a path to the presidency that more closely resembles those who ran on military records after him. He also did not move simply from the battlefield to the White House. He continued in uniform in more controversial campaigns than his victory against the British.

Jackson's political antagonists were either actually concerned about the rise of a military chieftain or used the concern to raise issues to diminish his popularity.[23] Historians remind us of the context, that "Napoleon Bonaparte's subversion of the French republic had given fresh warning of what could happen if a military chieftain rose."[24] And, as the epigraph from Alexis de Tocqueville, the famous French observer of American politics, that begins the chapter makes clear, he disparaged American voters' attraction to the winner of the Battle of New Orleans.

Jackson's first presidential attempt in 1824 was an intraparty contest. Each candidate ran under the fading remains of Jefferson's Democratic-Republican banner. Jackson would compete with John Quincy Adams, son of the second president and secretary of state; John Calhoun, secretary of war; Henry Clay, former Speaker of the House; and William Crawford, secretary of the treasury. Of these men seeking the White House at the end of the ostensible "Era of Good Feelings," only Jackson relied on military exploits to attain political viability. Jackson was known only for his military adventures as late as 1818. Most people outside Tennessee knew "The General" by his famous victory at New Orleans but not beyond. He was "a military silhouette," without political details to fill in the heroic outline.[25]

The outcome of the 1824 election depended on the famous "corrupt bargain," from the Jackson viewpoint, struck between John Quincy Adams and Henry Clay concerning the outcome of the presidential race. The wide field of candidates, each with geographic bastions of support, made obtaining a majority of Electoral College votes in 1824 difficult. The apparent quid pro quo involved Henry Clay's selection as secretary of state, a likely stepping-stone to the presidency, in exchange for him tilting support toward Adams in the House of Representatives. Despite having

---

22. Remini and Miles 1979.
23. Ekirch 1956.
24. Ratcliffe 2015, 114.
25. Dangerfield 1952, 123.

won a plurality of popular votes, more than Adams by a wide margin, Andrew Jackson watched as the mechanisms of the Twelfth Amendment moved the contest into the legislature's lower chamber. There among the elected representatives, America's political elite, Jackson's military victory in New Orleans may have done his candidacy more harm than good. His appeal among the people, especially in the West, was his source of strength, not allies in Washington. Even Thomas Jefferson doubted Jackson's qualifications for president, reportedly claiming, "One might as well make a sailor of a cock, or a soldier of a goose, as a president of Andrew Jackson."[26] The final decision depended on congressmen, including those with their own political ambitions. Had the convention system existed in 1824, perhaps Jackson's support would have helped narrow the field of candidates and leverage his supporters in the electorate to have more influence prior to the election.

There is no doubt that Jackson's military experience served explicitly as a theme to engender support for his candidacy within the electorate. The connection between Jackson's western origins and the Battle of New Orleans was intentionally and concertedly cemented into the electioneering of 1824 and 1828. The song "The Hunters of Kentucky" served as the "unofficial campaign song" of those two campaigns and had been standard fare at festivities held on January 8, the anniversary of the battle.[27] "But Jackson he was wide awake, and wasn't scared at trifles, / For well he knew what aim we take with our Kentucky rifles" are only some of the lyrics that extol Jackson's martial virtues. The song was an explicit commemoration of the constructed history of the frontiersmen's military superiority over the British regulars in the battle that made Jackson famous.[28] The legends of Appalachian sharpshooter militias outgunning British regulars grew and served Jackson's political needs well in the 1820s, but they did not conform to the reality of the events on the actual battlefield of 1815. Mythic retelling of the battle described farmer frontiersmen temporarily engaged in a noble cause, men with crack marksmanship exceeding that of the Redcoats. These frontier skills were responsible for the victory, according to the reciting, but more rigorous examination found Jackson's artillery responsible for the victory.[29]

Key events in the election calendar transpired strategically to fortify the connection between candidate Andrew Jackson of the 1820s and General Jackson, Hero of New Orleans from 1815. January 8 had become

---

26. Quoted in Young 1855, 429.
27. Faragher 1992, 335; Ward 1955.
28. Ward 1955.
29. Ward 1955.

something tantamount to a national holiday and is still on the books as a "day of public rest and legal holiday" in Louisiana.[30] The practice did not continue past the Civil War outside Tennessee, but enough communities and states commemorated the anniversary of the battle that some sources saw it as a de facto national holiday. Major cities nationwide celebrated the holiday with balls, parades, and other civic displays. They did so at a time without official recognition of the holidays that would occupy later public attention, such as Thanksgiving, Memorial Day, or Labor Day.[31] Tennessee and Louisiana, however, celebrated Jackson and the battle anniversary with the most energy. A glance at the pages of any antebellum January 9 edition of the New Orleans *Times-Picayune* reveals accounts of how the "Glorious Eighth" was celebrated the day before. The day held clear symbolic potential. It was no accident that supporters scheduled political events on that auspicious date. Further, while Independence Day commemorated deeds and the spirit of many, January 8 feted one.

Active campaigning by a presidential candidate to which twentieth- and twenty-first-century voters are accustomed was considered unseemly and undignified in the early nineteenth century. Hence, despite invitations from communities everywhere to attend celebrations in his honor, Jackson declined them and remained in Tennessee prior to the election. He made one exception: Louisiana supporters sought to celebrate Jackson in New Orleans on January 8, 1828. He agreed to attend but "laid down one condition: the celebration must be completely nonpolitical."[32] After a stop in Natchez that included public celebration, he arrived to a massive parade and commemoration. It took on a wider significance than one city thanking a savior: it appeared as "an entire nation expressing homage to a brave soldier, a dutiful son, a living legend," as people had traveled to the city from across the country for the event.[33] The intention to keep the event nonpolitical was certainly impossible to maintain. President James Monroe bestowed a medal for the Battle of New Orleans in a White House ceremony on March 16, 1824, even though Congress had already done so years earlier.[34] Considering the dominance of the so-called Virginia dynasty—Jefferson, Madison, and Monroe—it is somewhat surprising that a military man from the West would succeed their ideological tradition, because that group "was not too fond of military heroes."[35]

---

30. Revised Statutes 1, §55A(1).
31. Fulcher 1999.
32. Remini 1963, 113.
33. Remini 1963, 115.
34. Mitchell 2004.
35. Dangerfield 1952, 124.

The way his supporters nominated Jackson befits his popular war-hero candidacy. Jackson's fledgling political party incorporated new mechanisms to nominate him as the death knell rang for the King Caucus system. The Federalists found the congressional caucus system increasingly difficult because of the dwindling size and diminished geographic reach of their representation in Congress by 1808 and 1812. While there were complaints about the caucus nomination system within Democratic-Republican ranks in 1816, the strong consensus behind Monroe in 1816 and 1820 obviated any serious conflict over the system. Later, Jacksonian followers made an issue out of the caucus system, painting it as secretive and elitist. During James Monroe's second term and the lead-up to the 1824 election, the candidates vying for the position were variously nominated by their home state legislatures. For the 1824 election, the dates of these nominations were arbitrary, but when Jackson's supporters made their second attempt at propelling Old Hickory into the White House in 1828, they timed the nominating conventions for January 8, the holiday that had come to rival the Fourth of July in its observance. The Tennessee legislature did not wait long after the results of 1824 to act; they nominated Jackson more than three years before the 1828 election. His appeal as a popular war hero would not have helped his candidacy in the congressional caucus system, but his broad popular appeal worked better with a less elite-driven nomination system.

In a pattern that occurs with other candidates, Jackson's military experience was a double-edged sword. When candidates employ some basis of legitimacy or credibility for their candidacy, the nature of electoral politics demands that opponents generally attempt to undermine it somehow. Some of Jackson's acts as a military commander, in his political opponents' view, were sufficiently controversial to provide an opening for criticism. In 1828, John Quincy Adams and his allies watched Jackson's ascendance from his popular vote victory four years earlier. Some of Jackson's decisions as a military leader did not serve him as well as his victory over the British at New Orleans did in attracting political support. One effort to diminish Jackson's military credentials was a broadsheet published in 1828 by supporters of John Quincy Adams, "Mournful Tragedy," a campaign advertisement in its era. It called attention to the fact that Jackson, after the Battle of New Orleans, ordered executions of six deserters, one of whom was a Baptist minister.[36]

---

36. See Jamieson 1984, 7. Further, Jackson maintained martial law in the city of New Orleans for two months after the victory, quite unnecessarily in the minds of its residents. This, along with the execution of the deserters, was used by those supporting Henry Clay, John Quincy Adams, and other anti-Jackson forces for years to come. See Tregle 1981.

Andrew Jackson's ability to become a viable presidential candidate by the departure of James Monroe hinged on his fame earned at New Orleans in 1815. It is certainly true that the political conflicts, such as tariffs and national banks, were the engine behind his popular vote victory, his election four years later, and reelection in 1832. Yet while issues and politics would drive his successes, his legitimacy and viability as a candidate would not have been possible without his military heroism in Louisiana. His battle against the British enabled him to ignore the de facto requirement of a "long service in high public office," and the changes to the nomination system helped remove potential roadblocks to his nomination.[37]

William Henry Harrison was another martial war hero with hopes for the White House, following Washington and Jackson as America's first and second veritable war heroes–turned–presidential candidates. Harrison was not a young man when he first sought the presidency in 1836, and his candidacy and political ascent resembled Jackson's elevation to the White House in several important ways germane to veteran candidacies. Harrison was the first nominee of the Whig Party when he ran against Martin Van Buren in 1840, and that short-lived party became a vehicle for several other subsequent candidates who made their military identities central to their electoral efforts. Harrison, following the Jackson tradition, became a model for partisans in uniform to run for the White House more on military honors than issues. It is impossible to imagine the 1840 Harrison candidacy without his reputation earned at the Battle of Tippecanoe.

To understand how Harrison would capitalize on his military credentials to obtain a new political party's nomination in 1840, it is necessary to begin with the formation of the Whig Party. The Federalists ceased to be viable after 1816, and Jefferson's Democratic-Republican Party was the only way to the presidency for several cycles. Jackson and Adams's contest in 1824 and rematch in 1828 demonstrated the fracture that began to divide Jefferson's heirs. Anti-Jackson elites coalesced under the National Republican banner in 1824 and then again in 1832 to nominate Henry Clay, but his unsuccessful attempt to defeat Jackson's vice president and heir apparent Martin Van Buren deferred the question for another cycle.[38]

The anti-Jackson coterie morphed and coalesced sufficiently to be active in the 1836 contest to challenge Martin Van Buren, but its members were not sufficiently organized to rally around a single candidate. They also remembered the means by which Adams beat Jackson in 1824: run multiple candidates to move the decision from the Electoral College into

---
37. Phillips 1976, 489.
38. Zinman 2016.

the House of Representatives. Their inability to agree on a consensus candidate along with the memory of 1824 provided the conditions for the Whigs' plural candidacy. The leader of these sectional choices for the new party was William Henry Harrison. They could not consolidate sufficiently to hold a convention that year, remaining an "inchoate" party until the 1840 contest.[39]

The Whigs were centrally a party against Jackson. They depicted him as a despot and used the Whig label to paint Jackson a tyrant, similar to what the English political party by the same name had done in the seventeenth century. As a party label, it invoked the spirit of the American revolutionary efforts to throw off the power of an autocrat. In this incubation period for the Whigs, they had not settled on a standard-bearer, but the one who led in votes and support was William Henry Harrison.

What were this man's military experiences that propelled him to appear more electorally viable than other leaders of this new party? Harrison's first experiences with military life occurred years before his battle at Tippecanoe, when his commission was signed by President Washington in 1791 inducting him as an ensign into the 1st United States Regiment of Infantry.[40] He served in the regulars, received promotions up to captain, and resigned in 1798. He saw combat at the Battle of Fallen Timbers in 1794, during one of the Indian Wars preceding 1812.[41] The origins of Harrison's military record and political namesake came much later, after his rise as a political force. He first was a delegate from the Northwest Territory and then governor of the Indiana Territory until 1812. He earned his martial namesake at the Battle of Tippecanoe as he straddled civilian and military roles commanding troops a year before the second war with the British began.

The Battle of Tippecanoe was not large, and looking objectively at what we know happened makes it somewhat surprising that martial glory could have been squeezed from it. While retaining his title of governor, Harrison led a group of about a thousand men to challenge Tecumseh, who had been seeking alliances with other Indian tribes to repudiate past treaties that had ceded land to the white settlers. Negotiating treaties with the Indians was one of Harrison's primary roles as territorial governor, and he had been doing so to push western expansion. With his followers, Tecumseh's brother, the Prophet, defended their enclave with a shared vision of nullifying what Indians' felt were unfair treaties through force. Harrison camped for the night, awaiting a possible parlay the next day

---

39. Holt 1999, 39.
40. Gunderson 1993.
41. Owens 2007.

that might forestall fighting. The Indians decided to launch a surprise attack and assassinate Harrison in his tent during the night.

The Americans awoke to find their camp encircled, though the sentries prevented the plan to kill their general. The Americans, mostly militia with 250 regulars, beat off the Indian attack but suffered higher casualties. One biographer notes that Harrison's forces suffered "worse than literal decimation," and initial accounts of the battle did not characterize it as a victory for the Americans.[42] Harrison was criticized for unpreparedness, allowing his camp to be encircled in a likely hostile situation. Others claimed credit for the questionable victory, accusing Harrison of incompetence, though the critics had motivations for their version of events. Irrespective of what actually happened, and even though the strategic reason behind the campaign went unfulfilled until its settlement in the War of 1812, Harrison became viewed as the hero of the battle not long afterward. Increased tensions with the Indians and the outbreak of war with the British "retroactively justified Harrison's campaign," and President Madison promoted him to major general.[43] After his experiences against the Shawnee, his leadership at the battle made his name well known, and the resulting fame enhanced his ability to attract volunteers for his troops.[44] This ability was needed after the outbreak of the war with the British. Though reluctantly, Harrison accepted his new commission as major general.[45]

One campaign issue arose in 1836 directly related to military experience regarding Tecumseh. Who actually killed Chief Tecumseh was never settled, but Van Buren's running mate, Richard Johnson, most vocally claimed credit to further his political credibility. His campaign slogan, "Rumpsey, Dumpsey, Rumpsey, Dumpsey, Colonel Johnson Killed Tecumseh," as well as the response from Whigs, "Rumpsey, Dumpsey, Who Killed Tecumseh?" were both heard on the campaign trail. Johnson received more credit for slaying the Shawnee chief, but others believed Harrison did the deed, though the former likely enjoyed more credit given his palpable battle wounds.[46]

It was not the individuals themselves who claimed credit but their advocates and campaign loyalists who made the assertions through songs,

---

42. Owens 2007, 218.
43. Owens 2007, 223.
44. Bond 1927.
45. Sources differ on the nature of the appointment; some assert that it was to brigadier general rank. See Peterson 1989, 18. Beverley Bond's claim is that the rank was major general. See Bond 1927, 501. Either way, the appointment occurred in Frankfort at Clay's side when a call for reinforcements was imminently needed.
46. For the historical record on who killed Tecumseh, see Sugden 1985.

speeches, and illustrations. The nineteenth-century equivalents to campaign advertising and online ads were broadsheets and campaign tunes, and Johnson loyalists created many. Why would there be a competition for who could claim credit for Tecumseh's death? For John Sugden, "the lure of public office sharpened the discussion" of who killed the chief. "For decades veterans of the battle claimed votes in local and national elections on account of their contributions to the defeat of the arch Indian enemy."[47]

After the loss, the Whigs chose to use a party convention to select their nominee, a decision that favored the war hero Harrison. He had not been politically passive between his loss in 1836 and his nomination in 1839 for the 1840 presidential election. Party leaders like Thurlow Weed believed that Harrison could have prevailed in 1836 if the incipient party had not been splintered among four candidates' supporters. The innovation of the party convention as a means to nominate candidates was still new. The Whig Party's delegates from the states met in December 1839 in Harrisburg, Pennsylvania, to decide who should oppose Martin Van Buren the following year. Examination of the convention's proceedings makes it clear that the delegates thought of Harrison as a general. The minutes of the speeches reveal that delegates referred to Harrison as "General Harrison" or "General William Henry Harrison," and some of the speakers, when justifying their state's preference, based Harrison's qualification for office on his military experiences on the frontier against Tecumseh.[48] The events in Harrisburg determined Clay's fate: though the senator from Kentucky enjoyed southern support in addition to that of his home state, the delegates ultimately chose Harrison for his personal charisma and reputation over the consummate legislator Clay.

Another innovation of this decade helped military veteran candidates unfurl their service to voters: the rise of the mass campaign. Electioneering in 1840 innovated a new hullabaloo in the form of parades, floats, huge rolling balls with slogans, and other public spectacles. During the parades, supporters sang songs to denigrate their rival and extol the virtues of their candidate. One song for Harrison offers a sample of how his military experience was central to his candidacy:

> Hurrah for the Log Cabin, chief of our choice!
> For the Old Indian Fighter, hurrah!
> Hurrah! And from mountain to valley the voice of the people re-echoes hurrah!
> Then come to the ballot-box, boys! Come along!

---

47. Sugden 1985, 136.
48. Burnet 1839, 34–40.

He never lost battle for you:
Let us down with oppression and tyranny's throng,
and up with Old Tippecanoe![49]

Other electioneering efforts typical of the 1840 election were pamphlets and brochures. One example, *Sketches of the Civil and Military Services of William Henry Harrison*, was a favorable biography. One of its authors, Charles Todd, helped campaign with Harrison and "sought support among other veterans of the Indian wars in which he had won fame, as well as among the numerous militia companies scattered around the country, just as Jackson had done in the 1820s."[50] *Sketches* details Harrison's military life in a flattering fashion and spends considerable pages on his time in uniform, concluding with "parallels between him and Washington."[51]

As is true for the other candidates discussed throughout this historical analysis, it is important to remember that military service is but one aspect of the campaign narrative. Even Harrison's identity as a general, which was based largely on his nickname's martial origins, sat astride other identities in his successful run in 1840. Given that he would be sixty-eight years old at inauguration, Democrats eagerly portrayed Harrison as too aged for the office and painted him as senile. Antagonist John de Ziska characterized him as "Granny" Harrison: "Give him a barrel of hard cider, and settle a pension of two thousand a year on him, and my word for it, he will sit the remainder of his days in his log cabin by the side of a 'sea coal' fire, and study moral philosophy."[52] Whigs turned this barb around successfully and used the imagery of the log cabin and hard cider to associate their candidate as a frontiersman and a man of the people rather than the son of privilege from a Virginia dynasty, though the latter was closer to the truth. The Democratic attempts to disparage Harrison in the press had four facets: "(1) that he was a Federalist; (2) that he had been an incompetent and cowardly military leader; (3) that Harrison was in favor of white slavery; and finally (4) that the Whig candidate was abolitionist."[53] Hence, the Democrats understood that the military aspect of Harrison's candidacy required a counter.

Campaigns do not choose which parts of a candidate's past to highlight in an arbitrary fashion. They select them because they believe some

---

49. Quoted in Griffin 1873, 77.
50. Holt 1999, 91.
51. Todd and Drake 1840, 219.
52. Quoted in Gunderson 1956, 443.
53. Hampton 1984, 95.

experiences attract voters and do not dwell on experiences that are unlikely to stoke interest or might detract from the image they seek to convey. Military service about which voters are unaware can hardly influence voter perceptions and attract support. Nothing changed about Harrison's past military service in the four intervening years between the two elections, so it is difficult to understand why it was salient in one but not the other race. More than just the campaign emphasis on the Battle of Tippecanoe in 1840 but not 1836 explains the different outcomes. In fact, the more memorable difference between the 1836 Harrison and the 1840 Harrison was the "hard cider" sloganeering.

Yet it is clear that Whigs backing Harrison celebrated and exulted in his battle heroism with a new style of stumping for votes. Those who study the memorabilia, songs, and other features of presidential election campaigning mark 1840 as a watershed. In parades for Harrison, large canoes were pulled by horses covered with "Old Tippecanoe Forever" banners.[54] Those sorts of efforts exemplify electioneering for a military hero in a new era of mass vote drives. This comparison is not perfect for understanding the influence of Harrison's military service, because 1836 and 1840 are not a controlled experiment in which nothing changes except the way Harrison's people presented his military record. Even before his contest against Van Buren and the others in 1836, "Tippecanoe clubs" had formed and he was referred to as "Old Tippecanoe."[55] It is difficult to specify by how much, but Harrison's campaign deployed his martial history as a campaign tool more in 1840 than in 1836. Part of the explanation is that campaign craft underwent a sea change in 1840, with more rallies, songs, trinkets, and other facets, which beg for a theme around which to rally.[56] Harrison's reputation born at Tippecanoe provided just that theme the second time around.

Lewis Cass provides another example of a battle hero nominated for president, this time by the Democrats in 1848. Unlike the others, however, Cass's critics successfully lampooned his martial exploits, as the campaign and battle were not perceived as successful. Ohio made a call for volunteers in the War of 1812 when Cass was commissioned as a colonel to lead one of the regiments from Ohio. Approximately twelve hundred men had descended on Dayton to join, and leaders split them into three regiments, with Cass commanding the third. One flattering biography recounted that his first words as an officer came after he planted an American flag in front of them: "The standard of your country is displayed. You

---

54. Cleaves 1939, 320.
55. Cleaves 1939, 297.
56. Gunderson 1957.

have rallied around it to defend her right and to avenge her injuries. May it wave protection to our friends and defiance to our enemies! And should we ever meet them in the hostile field, I doubt not but that the eagle of America will be found more than a match for the British lion!"[57]

Cass's men fought against the British in a small battle over a bridge south of Detroit, "the war's first land engagement . . . won the first victory, and received wide acclaim in the eastern press which dubbed him the 'Hero of the Tarontee.'"[58] The acclaim was exaggerated. In the scope of the War of 1812, the only benefit from this minor battle's outcome was the capture of two prisoners. Further, the battle took place in a campaign that went poorly overall. This front against the British was to become an "inglorious campaign" and ended very poorly for the Americans, though the blame for the military debacle would end up with Cass's commander, William Hull.[59] The American forces surrendered at Detroit, where Cass, consistently furious with his commander's lack of aggressiveness, reportedly snapped his sword in half when seeing the white flag. After the loss and surrender, Cass returned to Ohio after transport to Montreal but was appointed major general of the militia after his parole from British capture elapsed. He was quickly elevated to brigadier general in the regular army by March 1813 and served out the rest of the war aside General Harrison as aide-de-camp. Cass had been a minor officer, but exaggerated reports of a minor battle earned him a nickname and the potential for political ascent.

His military service would ultimately be a ticket to political office, but not through the mechanism of electoral appeal to nominating party elites. Rather, after the Battle of the Thames effectively ended the 1812 war for the Northwest Theater, President Madison appointed Cass as governor of the Michigan Territory. How important was Cass's distant military service when considering his presidential nomination in 1848 by the Democrats and its role in the general election against General Zachary Taylor? Cass was a longtime leader among Democrats and had earned support for the presidential nomination in 1844, surpassing Van Buren's support on several of the ballots taken at that year's convention. While Democrats hoped they could replicate the hero-general archetype that had worked well for Jackson and Harrison, Cass's experiences were less compelling and their power as a campaign tool correspondingly weaker.

---

57. W. Smith 1856, 35.
58. Woodford 1950, 61.
59. McLaughlin 1899, 62. Later accounts reconsider how much blame to place on Hull. Upton points out that Hull's volunteers had been unruly and insubordinate up to that point, and Hull likely perceived that failing to surrender would portend a slaughter. Upton 1912, 98–99.

One Whig congressman from Illinois took issue with the Cass campaign championing his military exploits in 1848, an effort that no doubt was done because he was running against General Zachary Taylor, commander and victor of the early phase of the war with Mexico. That congressman, Abraham Lincoln, took to the House floor to mock the more dubious portions of Cass's military record, made all the more effective by his humble descriptions of his own brief time in the Black Hawk War:

> There is one entire article of . . . the military tail you Democrats are now engaged in dovetailing on to the great Michigander. Yes, sir, all his biographers (and they are legion) have him in hand, tying him to a military tail, like so many mischievous boys tying a dog to a bladder of beans. True, the material they have is very limited; but they drive at it, might and main. He *in*vaded Canada without resistance, and he *out*vaded it without pursuit. As he did both under order, I suppose there was, to him, neither credit nor discredit in them; but they are made to constitute a large part of the tail. He was not at Hull's surrender, but he was close by. He was volunteer aid to General Harrison on the day of the battle of the Thames; and, as you said in 1840, Harrison was picking whortleberries two miles off, while the battle was fought[.] I suppose it is a just conclusion, with you, to say Cass was aiding Harrison to pick whortleberries. . . . By the way, Mr. Speaker, did you know that I was a military hero? Yes, sir, in the days of the Black Hawk War, I fought, bled, and came away. . . . I was not at Stillman's defeat, but I was about as near to it as Cass was to Hull's surrender, and like him, I saw the place very soon afterwards. . . . If General Cass went in advance of me in picking huckleberries, I guess I surpassed him in charges upon the wild onions. If he saw any live, fighting Indians, it was more than I did; but I had a good many bloody struggles with the mosquitoes. . . . Mr. Speaker, if I should ever conclude to doff whatever our Democratic friends may suppose there is of black-cockade [Continental Army] Federalism about me, and thereupon they shall take me up as their candidate for the Presidency, I protest they shall not make fun of me, as they have of General Cass, by attempting to write me into a military hero.[60]

Lincoln's sarcasm reveals that Cass was not a terribly compelling military-hero candidate, but we can infer something else, too. While it shows that

---

60. Appendix to Cong. Globe, 30th Cong., 1st Sess. (1848), 1042 (emphasis in original).

Hull's surrender was probably still in the public memory almost forty years later as the nadir in the War of 1812, more important, it reveals to at least some extent that members of the Cass campaign or its confederates had been using the candidate's distant military record to burnish his biography in the face of General Taylor's. The Democrats believed either that they needed to counter Taylor with a battle hero or that his military heroism would go some way toward that goal. Lincoln's mockery, and the fact that Taylor won, suggests it was insufficient.

General Franklin Pierce was a Mexican War veteran, one with established political credentials prior to his service in the war. He won elections to state legislative seats in the 1820s, ultimately becoming speaker of the state house. He was also a member of the state's militia, occasionally drilling and holding officer's rank. In the 1832 elections, he won a U.S. House seat and became a loyal Jacksonian Democrat on most national issues. He won a U.S. Senate seat in 1836. He was generally a doughface on abolition, but military issues were another focus for him. He favored modernization and bills that strengthened and enlarged the regular army as well as supported state militia. He resigned from the Senate in 1842 to return to practice law at home.

When war with Mexico was declared in 1846, Pierce jumped at the chance to join the war. He lobbied to join, but militia units from southern states were the first to enter service. President Polk offered him the job of attorney general in August 1846, but Pierce declined, partly because he hoped to secure a position in the war.[61] In early 1847, months after General Taylor's victories in northern Mexico, Pierce was able to secure a colonelcy with an infantry unit headed to the invasion force under General Scott at Vera Cruz. Pierce's unit was to serve as a reserve unit. As they arrived in Vera Cruz in June, two months after Scott, the Americans had already fought their way inland and won at Cerro Gordo. Now a general, Pierce commanded his brigade of twenty-five hundred men, moving slowly toward Mexico City and joining Scott in time for the Battles of Contreras and Churubusco in August near the capital.

At Contreras, Pierce led his men in a frontal attack against a part of the Mexican line while another unit was supposed to attack their flank, but the coordination failed, leaving Pierce's unit to draw all the artillery fire. Pierce's horse, a gift from friends in New Hampshire, was a "high-spirited war horse" but unaccustomed to combat and lurched wildly at the onset of the artillery blasts.[62] The horse's rearing drove the saddle pommel deeply into the general's crotch, sufficient to render him unconscious

---

61. Nichols 1958.
62. Winders 1997, 47.

when the horse fell. Another officer from an adjacent unit, unaware of exactly what happened, yelled, "Take command of the brigade, General Pierce is a damned coward,"[63] a line that would dog him later. The fall also severely twisted his knee, as he had trouble walking and riding after he regained himself.

The next day, after he had turned command over to someone else because of his condition, he appeared before Scott with one foot in the stirrups and the wounded one dangling. Scott tried to send him back to base, but Pierce insisted he stay: "For God's sake, General, don't say that. This is the last great battle, and I must lead my brigade," a sentiment that Scott apparently found persuasive.[64] Pierce's bad luck failed to leave him, however. At Churubusco, he regained his unit and led them toward battle, but he had difficulty riding and guiding the horse over the rough terrain because of his injuries. When they approached the Mexicans and drew their fire, Pierce and his horse fell again and the general fainted once more. The battle, and the war, moved on without him. One man, who was at the battle and was no political ally, felt that Pierce's loss of reputation was deeply unfair. Ulysses Grant wrote long after the war that Pierce had not fully recovered from the day before but led his men anyway, and the situation "gave rise to exceedingly unfair and unjust criticisms of him when he became a candidate for the Presidency. Whatever General Pierce's qualifications may have been for the Presidency, he was a gentleman and a man of courage."[65] Despite Grant's defense, it is difficult to see how Pierce could have converted his war stories into effective campaign themes.

Pierce's nomination at the 1852 Democratic Convention fits the "dark-horse" mold, similar to Polk's nomination in 1844. Lewis Cass, the nominee in 1848, came into the convention as a front-runner, winning pluralities of the vote over James Buchanan for many ballots. The supporters of each of those two men were dead set against the other, and some Democrats understood that before the votes and kept Pierce as a quiet candidate to introduce after the deadlock. His appeal was twofold: primarily he had been out of office for the past decade without the baggage of controversial votes, and "his more recent experience in the public eye as a minor general in the Mexican War could be exploited."[66] After more than thirty deadlocked ballots, Pierce's supporters placed him into consideration. First Buchanan's supporters defected to Pierce, and then the Cass supporters joined.

---

63. Nichols 1958, 161.
64. Kennedy 1895, 773.
65. Grant 1885, 1:114.
66. Bain and Parris 1973, 44.

The general election in 1852 saw Pierce run against the final Whig candidate who was also his commander in Mexico, General Winfield Scott. Both of their military biographies were central to the electioneering that autumn, and both were skewered in the press for their respective foibles.[67] Once Whigs had unearthed reports of Pierce's apparent cowardice on the first day at Contreras and subsequent fainting the next day at Churubusco, their partisan broadsheets wasted no time lampooning him ferociously in the press. Even in Congress, Abraham Lincoln lampooned Franklin Pierce's "claims of military glory" by self-effacingly describing the last muster of his own militia:

Among the rules and regulations, no man is to wear more than five pounds of cod-fish for epaulets, or more than thirty yards of bologna sausages for a sash; and no two men are to dress alike and if any two should dress alike the one that dresses most alike is to be fined. . . . Flags they had too, with devices and mottoes, one of which latter is "We'll fight till we run, and we'll run till we die."[68]

John Frémont was an explorer with a military commission nominated for his reputation on the frontier more than his ability to mend the splintering Union in 1856. Frémont's "military exploits" in the war with Mexico and his "colorful exploration trips" gave him a national reputation to enable his nomination.[69] His father-in-law was influential Thomas Hart Benton, Missouri senator and powerful Democrat. Being the son-in-law of a political powerhouse comes with costs and benefits. One cost is that some people perceived Frémont's rise as a product of little beyond his connection to Benton. One joke at the Republican Convention that made the rounds emphasized Frémont's sponsor: "It is proposed, if Colonel Frémont's friends succeed in procuring him the nomination for the presidency, to head their ticket thus: for president col. j. fremont, son in law of thomas h. benton."[70]

Frémont had a reputation for charisma and adventure because of his well-known expeditions in the West, but his "primadonna temperament" was also well known.[71] Frémont's first military career ended with a court-martial, not generally the exit from the armed forces leading to an easy path to the White House. In the war with Mexico, Polk promoted him to

---

67. Boller 1984.
68. Quoted in Prokopowicz 2002, 89.
69. Bain and Parris 1973.
70. Halstead, Hesseltine, and Fisher 1961, 86.
71. T. Williams 1938, 178.

lieutenant colonel to lead approximately three hundred men to California to seize Santa Barbara and Los Angeles. The Mexican forces put up only token resistance in California. The trouble began when squabbles erupted between the U.S. naval commodore and the U.S. Army general, who both also convened there. The general charged that Frémont failed to show appropriate deference, and because of delays in communication, conflicting orders, and Frémont's pride, the general charged him with disobedience and mutiny.[72] While the military trial convicted him, his political patrons pardoned him soon afterward, but the taint followed him.

The first Republican political convention did not choose Frémont because of his positions on issues, as his "political experience was limited to a brief service as senator from California, and [his] political opinions were almost unknown."[73] That fact argues that his charisma and personal reputation helped bolster his candidacy. Democrats in 1856 mainly assailed Frémont as a catalyst that would sever the Union because of his abolitionist views, but they also used the more controversial times and events of Frémont's first military career against him. Despite its rocky first attempt at winning the presidency, the Republicans nominated Abraham Lincoln in its next try in 1860. Frémont was no ally of Lincoln's, though the latter recommissioned him with a substantial promotion to the rank of general. Frémont repaid the favor by running against him, at least for a time, in 1864 from the Radical wing of the Republican Party, stating that Lincoln was "politically, militarily, and financially a failure."[74]

Partisan Generals: Taylor and Scott

General Zachary Taylor, the only other Whig to win the presidency besides Harrison, earned the nomination in 1848 on his military career and war record. Arguably, he was until now the most military candidate nominated by a major party—he served in uniform longer than Jackson and Harrison combined. He also entered presidential politics laterally, having never served in local, state, or federal government. Taylor is a classic case of a "blank slate candidate."[75] These are men whom the out-of-office party nominates to challenge the party in power with evident chinks in its armor: internal issue differences or regional conflict that can be seen in midterm losses or other symptoms. Yet the out-of-office party has its own inabilities to unite behind an issue-based candidate, so it relies on an

---

72. Rolle 1991.
73. Stanwood 1892, 270.
74. Quoted in Thomas 1987, 45.
75. Crockett 2008, 54.

"ambiguous centrist" to unite the party around a personality whose lack of issue baggage inoculates him from easy partisan criticism. Taylor perfectly embodied this role for the Whigs in the election immediately following the Mexican-American War in 1848.

Thurlow Weed, New York newspaperman and political leader in the Whig Party, identified Taylor as presidential material in 1848 and urged him to "avoid statements on political issues and ignore political letters," to prevent him from doing anything public that might harm his chances.[76] The very uncertainty about Taylor's political feelings, indeed, even uncertainty about which party he favored, was considered to be one of his key advantages. Many Whigs who had backed Henry Clay in 1844 began to feel he had earned too many political enemies to win a presidential election and cast about for an alternative who shared Clay's views.

What Taylor had achieved to make him the leading choice for Whigs in 1848 was not just a calling in the army but specifically his command leadership in Mexico. His career started in 1808, commissioned as a lieutenant, and he first saw combat in the War of 1812 when the British-allied Indians attacked his fort. He continued in the army, gaining promotions in the U.S. Army regulars, leading various garrisons on the frontier during the Black Hawk War and other Indian conflicts. His campaign against the Seminoles in Florida in 1837 elevated his stature and rank and earned him the nickname "Old Rough and Ready" from his men because he was willing to undergo the worst conditions along with them.[77] In 1844, on the eve of the war with Mexico, President Polk ordered Taylor to garrison Fort Jesup on the Texas border. Once the question of Texas annexation became more likely, Polk gave the famous order in 1846 for Taylor to lead his men "on or near the Rio Grande" without attacking Mexican troops.[78]

By spring of 1846, war had begun. General Taylor's army fought the Mexicans first at the Battle of Palo Alta and then Resaca de la Palma, which pushed Mexican forces southward past the Rio Grande. Resaca de la Palma was an important victory for Taylor's army because they displaced the Mexican army and moved the fighting out of Texas and did so against a numerically superior foe. Taylor's troops now controlled the river valley and were positioned to engage retreating enemy forces at Monterrey. His victory in the first battles of the war also increased Taylor's rank and political viability—Congress passed an official joint resolution of gratitude, and he was brevetted his second star.

---

76. Quoted in Bauer 1985, 216.
77. *General Taylor* 1848, 81.
78. Sellers 1966, 229.

In September, Taylor moved on Monterrey, where Mexican forces had stockpiled resources, and mounted a defense within the citadel city. The battle took three days, but the preparations had been difficult because of supply and transportation issues. The outcome was an American victory, with forces attacking from both sides that wore down the defenses. The Mexican generals sought a conditional surrender, and the terms of the submission became a blemish on Taylor's reputation. He and Polk quarreled over the agreed terms after the fact, the latter admonishing Taylor for allowing the Mexicans to surrender the city but leave with their army. The difference in their views was essentially the difference between military and political considerations, because from Taylor's view, his men and supplies were exhausted, while from Polk's consideration, the speediest end to the war was paramount. The battle, a "costly victory," would add to Taylor's honors.[79] While they had started on "good terms," Polk and Taylor fell out over the aftermath of Monterrey, and their "mutual respect" descended to "intense hatred," clouded by partisan motivations.[80]

After the battle, Polk faced a diminished array of options, both with respect to the war and with his hopes for creating a military hero with unambiguous Democratic credentials. Fellow Whig General Winfield Scott wrote to Taylor, wishing that Taylor would "defeat [his] enemies, both in *front* and in *rear*."[81] Polk sought an invasion closer to Mexico's center and wanted to deny Taylor further command and hence further martial glory to bolster his political viability. The campaign at Veracruz, far to the south, would need a new commander to lead a landing on Mexico's eastern shore to attack Mexico City. His explicit criteria for choosing the commander rested on whether the person was a likely presidential candidate. Eventually, Polk chose Scott, as his confidants believed Scott "politically harmless" and the alternative Democrats as worse.[82] This invasion from the east would require a substantial amount of troops from Taylor's army in the north, who peeled away to join Scott's forces on the coast over Taylor's objections. The Mexicans intercepted American orders detailing the split and decided to take advantage by attacking Taylor's numerically diminished forces, eventually clashing at Buena Vista. The battle that would give Taylor the nickname "Hero of Buena Vista" saw American forces led by Taylor hold off General Antonio Lopez de Santa Anna's army.[83] Santa Anna hoped to defeat Taylor for strategic purposes

---
79. Eisenhower 1989, 151.
80. Winders 1997, 33.
81. Letter from Scott to Taylor, September 26, 1846, quoted in Coleman 1871, 258 (emphasis in original).
82. Eisenhower 1989, 164.
83. Scriabine 1983, 167.

as well as to enhance his reputation toward his own political goals. Through timely use of artillery and reinforcements, Taylor's men, including Jefferson Davis and Braxton Bragg, parried the Mexican attack long enough to convince Santa Anna to break off and retreat. It was Taylor's last battle in the war and his career. One of his campaign's 1848 slogans echoed a command he issued to artillery officer Bragg at the battle, to "double shot your guns" or "a little more grape, Capt. Bragg."[84] News of the battle in the American press made Buena Vista into a heroic triumph. It became a "signature victory" in the war, proof that a small band of brave American volunteers could outfight a Mexican army four times its size."[85] A year later, the "Hero of Buena Vista" transitioned from military leader to presidential candidate for the 1848 election.

While Taylor enjoyed the support of many, Henry Clay also began with old allies, and General Winfield Scott and Daniel Webster were also in the race.[86] Taylor's nomination at the third Whig Party nominating convention in 1848 over these men occurred after he expressed the barest possible political convictions. In letters made public, he expressed willingness to accept nomination from either party, not thinking of himself as a "party candidate."[87] However, he eventually referred to himself as a "Whig" but not an "ultra Whig," presenting himself as a blank slate to the party.[88] He extolled the fact that he had never voted in an election as a badge of honor. Thus, Taylor is the most blank of the blank-slate candidates—and being a Mexican War hero was the prerequirement to making the lateral entry into politics without the burden of issue positions.

Having had a long military career and explicit, long-held presidential ambitions, General Winfield Scott best represents the Antebellum era with its blurred or even broken lines between civil and military spheres. He obtained votes at the first four political conventions of the Whig Party in 1840, 1844, and 1848, while finally capturing the nomination in 1852. Scott was the Whig Party's final nominee and the central character in its tragic ending. By the time of the convention, the discord within the party was already sufficiently known that party leaders considered scotching the convention.[89] Scott was also the superlative case in this book for

---

84. See the image "A Little More Grape Capt Bragg," depicting General Taylor at the Battle of Buena Vista, February 23, 1847, available at http://hdl.loc.gov/loc.pnp/cph.3b50648.
85. Greenberg 2012, 160–161.
86. When told by Weed that Taylor would be the Whig most likely to win the election, Webster exclaimed in a widely quoted line, "Taylor is an illiterate frontier Colonel who hasn't voted in forty years!" Weed 1884, 168.
87. Montgomery 1850, 52.
88. Quoted in Holt 1999, 310.
89. Gienapp 1984.

extending the overlap of his political aspirations and military career the longest amount of time.

The role that Scott's military service plays in understanding his candidacy is total. As much as any other candidate of his era or others, Scott's identity was thoroughly linked to his army career. He wore the uniform for more than fifty years and was the senior ranking military officer in America for decades. His service in the U.S. Army began in 1808 at age twenty-two, though he had served in a Virginia militia unit previously. His first years in uniform did not appear to portend the success he later enjoyed. He tendered his resignation and then rescinded it to rejoin. Later he was court-martialed for vocally criticizing a superior and spent months out of uniform as punishment. His star began to rise with the War of 1812. By the time of American forays along the Niagara River in 1814 in that war, Scott was a one-star general leading forces against the British. He saw several battles and was severely wounded at the Battle of Lundy's Lane. He was rallying his men for a charge when his horse was shot out from under him. Undeterred, he tried to wave his men forward on foot when he was shot through the shoulder. After the war, he continued in the army, eventually becoming its highest-ranking officer in 1841.

The Mexican War during the Polk presidency transpired well after Scott had earned national name recognition and had been in contention for the Whig presidential nomination, so further military valor was probably unnecessary toward his political aspirations. Despite this, he was positioned to accept Polk's reluctant offer to lead the final campaign in Mexico. As we have seen when discussing General Taylor's military reputation, President Polk's decisions about whom to put in command were based on political more than military considerations. In Senator Thomas Hart Benton's view of the Polk administration, "They were men of peace, with objects to be accomplished by means of war. . . . They wanted a small war, just large enough to require a treaty of peace, and not large enough to make military reputations, dangerous for the presidency."[90] Scott's relations with his commander in chief, President Polk, were rocky at best, though better than the relationship between Taylor and Polk. Given that Scott had previously sought the Whig presidential nomination, it was only because Polk felt that Scott was past his presidential prime that he chose Scott to command the invasion force at Veracruz to assault Mexico City. Polk's position in having to choose between two generals, Zachary Taylor and Winfield Scott, was especially problematic after Whig gains in the midterm elections of 1846 made clear that a victory in Mexico

---

90. Benton 1854.

would be needed in short order if Democrats wanted to retain the White House in 1848.

Scott's political views emerged far before the eve of his candidacies. During Jackson's presidency, while Scott was a high-ranking general, his political views were well known and chafed his commander in chief. At a White House dinner in 1836, Jackson complained that Scott opposed all of his policies. Scott protested, citing support for Jackson's antinullification views and a French foreign policy matter. "That's candid! He thinks well of two—*but two!* of my measures," was the president's reply.[91] It was clear prior to the 1840 presidential election that Scott was "bitten by the presidential bug."[92] His disappointment at watching Harrison win the nomination that year was clear, though his ability to disguise it far exceeded Henry Clay's. They played whist with others in a hotel when they received word of Harrison's nomination, and Clay, frustrated, physically struck Scott on the shoulder that bore the wound he received at Lundy's Lane. To the extent that is clear from the historical record, Scott also sought the 1844 Whig nomination for the presidency in earnest. At the advice of Pennsylvania's Thaddeus Stevens, Scott published a thirteen-page pamphlet in October 1841 that explicated his views on many national issues but was mute on the most controversial, his views on Texas annexation. Scott wrote to Stevens in August 1842, complaining that President Tyler was sidelining his military activities and keeping him in Washington rather than allowing him to travel, plainly implying that Tyler's preference for Henry Clay motivated his actions.[93]

Irrespective of why Polk chose Scott to lead the campaign to capture Mexico City in 1847, the old general in his sixties planned the invasion to attack Veracruz on the Gulf Coast of Mexico in March 1847 to take the fight directly to the Mexican capital. Polk had chosen him, but the president did so out of lack of other options, and the two men had a strained relationship. One nasty interchange led to embarrassment for Scott. In one of the letters quarreling with the administration while he planned the invasion, Scott complained of political backbiting as "fire at his rear" in contrast to fire from the front, that is, Mexico. He began another quick and quarreling response letter to beg sarcastic pardon for not responding earlier, as he had left his office "to take a hasty plate of soup."[94] The White House leaked the letter, and "Hasty Soup" (and variants of it) became a

---

91. Peskin 2003, 89 (emphasis in original).
92. Eisenhower 1997, 205. Letters revealed that Scott was disappointed when the Whig nominating convention chose General Harrison rather than him. See T. Johnson 1998, 137.
93. Eisenhower 1997.
94. Henry 1950, 70.

frequent and unflattering nickname thereafter. His unfortunate sobriquet even became the name of an opposition campaign newsletter in 1852.[95] The fact that by this time he was very overweight made this nickname even more stinging. Part of his nature made him difficult to imagine as a successful political candidate, who must be able to relate to voters. His vanity was well known, and he insisted on the formal fastidiousness of rank and military protocol. He was rarely without his full dress uniform, and prior to his "Hasty Soup" nickname, he was most often called "Old Fuss and Feathers."

Despite the political infighting between Scott and the administration, the attack plan was drawn up and the men mustered for the fight. In a series of battles across spring and summer, Scott led the army to victory after victory that took them to the gates of Mexico City. After the decisive Battle of Chapultepec, Santa Anna surrendered to Scott. The campaign achieved tremendous success, and its victories cemented Scott's reputation as an unequaled military commander. While not the right man for 1848, he would try again in 1852.

The convention motion in 1852 that finally put Scott ahead and made him the Whig nominee explicitly commended his army years and justified his nomination on that service: "Whereas, Gen. Winfield Scott, in consideration of his life having been wholly devoted and actually spent in the service of his country, and that by such service he has preeminently advanced its honor and renown at home and abroad, has shown himself justly entitled to the gratitude and affection of his countrymen."[96]

He did not resign his commission in the army while he sought the presidency. In a nation founded with explicit phobias over standing armies, this may appear at first blush to be concerning. However, three points explain why this was probably not politically problematic. First, there were many precedents for military men to ascend to the civilian presidency. Second, the size of the regular army's officer corps was very small, fewer than a thousand officers, so it could not make up a viable political bloc. Third, the officer corps was divided in their loyalties between Whigs and Democrats.[97] By the time Scott had won his party's nomination, the party had foundered. Sectional conflict over the expansion of slavery was undoing the Whig Party, and Scott's decision to hedge his bets and remain in the army to await the 1852 election's outcome turned out to be wise.

---

95. Huff 1966.
96. "Latest Intelligence" 1852.
97. Dempsey 2009.

The Common Veterans: Polk, Buchanan, and Lincoln

James K. Polk's military experiences played little role in his political career that placed him in the White House after the 1844 election. From an early perspective, he was not supposed to be the Democratic Party's nominee in 1844. Prior to the convention, sentiments among Democrats pointed largely toward former president Martin Van Buren, who had lost in the general election to Harrison in 1840, with few guessing that Speaker of the House Polk would obtain the party's nomination. The Texas annexation issue, as the question of bringing Texas into the Union as a slave state became dominant, derailed the inevitability of Van Buren's recapture of the nomination. A newly surfaced letter Van Buren had written earlier characterized his opposition to annexation, a position at odds with the preponderance of his party, so Polk won the nomination in late voting.

If the general election campaign turned at all on the biographies of the two candidates, no record of attention paid to military experience is evident. Secondary sources suggest that attacks on Polk's biography used his weakened health as a result of his having been a duelist, the assertion that Polk had Tory ancestors, and a widely circulated report that a group of slaves branded with his initials were seen heading toward southern markets.[98] Few biographical accounts mention that Polk had joined the Tennessee militia in 1821 when he was in his mid-twenties and was eventually promoted to colonel. This service probably did not occupy much of Polk's time or attention, as he had just finished his education, had begun to practice law by the early 1820s, and was elected to the state legislature by 1823 and Congress by 1825. Andrew Jackson, when referring to his protégé, usually used the title "Colonel Polk."[99]

James Buchanan's brief experience in the War of 1812 did not play a role in his later electoral life or Democratic nomination in 1856, but it was important to his very early political life. He was a staunch Federalist and critical of the Madison administration's conduct of the war in late 1814 when the conflict was going badly for the Americans. He was a young lawyer in Pennsylvania with political aspirations. In his own retelling, he gave an address in his home county not long after the British had sacked the White House in August 1814, expressing the need for voluntarism to defend the country despite party differences. As the British threatened Baltimore, Buchanan retold that he was "among the first to register [his] name as a volunteer."[100] The speech was important because Buchanan had

---

98. C. McCoy 1960.
99. Seigenthaler 2004, 25.
100. Curtis 1883, 8.

very recently been nominated to be a candidate for the Pennsylvania state legislature. It is likely that he saw the British army's advance as a personal political opportunity just as much as he saw the need to defend a potential invasion of Pennsylvania, only thirty miles from Baltimore.[101] He followed through and volunteered, mustering in a unit of dragoons, and rushed to Baltimore. While he did not see combat, it is clear that his political aspirations and brief sally were intertwined.

Buchanan's presidential successor, Abraham Lincoln, was not dissimilar. Lincoln served in impromptu military units for a short duration, he did not see combat, and the service did not shape his presidential ascent. While much scholarship has focused on his skills in managing generals and the cabinet during the trying times of the Civil War, we do not remember Lincoln as a soldier himself. Neither his election to Congress as a Whig nor his victory in the three-way presidential election of 1860 as a Republican rested on Lincoln's military credentials. He did, however, enlist in small military units three times during the short 1832 war with Indian chief Black Hawk when Lincoln was twenty-three years old. While the experience may have given Lincoln the opportunity to experience military life before his role as commander in chief during America's largest war, his personal military experience contributed little to his election in 1860 or reelection four years later.

The young Illinois frontiersman and the others in his community received word in 1832 that the governor had called for men to volunteer to counter an increasingly belligerent Black Hawk near the Mississippi River. Lincoln joined other men and then took part in the typical method for determining who would take charge of the company: election. He became the company captain, winning the initial support of the other men, and led them across the state where they were sworn in as federal forces. In his service as captain, Lincoln experienced difficulties as a military leader over reluctant men in poor conditions. While they did not see combat against Black Hawk's elusive Sauk forces, they did arrive at the scene where some soldiers had been routed by Indians. After only a month, the unit disbanded. He then reenlisted as a private in a mounted unit that did not last beyond its intended twenty-day duration. The third and last company with which young Lincoln volunteered and served a thirty-day stint was the "Spy Corps," seeking the shadowy Black Hawk.[102] They rode north into Wisconsin and discovered the remains of an ambush. Lincoln remembered each with a telltale scalped head. The future sixteenth president honorably mustered out without having seen battle, but he traveled on

---

101. S. Donovan 2005.
102. Hearn 2012, 8.

wartime footing through many miles of frontier prairie.¹⁰³ He ran for the state legislature to represent New Salem shortly after mustering out. One characterization of his stump speech made no mention of his very recent service in the Black Hawk War.¹⁰⁴

Abraham Lincoln's brief marches to find Black Hawk did not factor into his presidential candidacies. If they played any role in his political life, his experiences may have assisted in a small way in bolstering a young politician's stump skills. As a congressman, he used his past military time to diminish Democratic presidential candidates Cass and Pierce—a rhetorical move made possible and more legitimate given his own service. It would have been harder to make these comments if he had never mustered into armed duty. He humorously denigrated his own service to lampoon theirs, but one biographer has stressed that Lincoln felt deep pride in having served.¹⁰⁵

---

103. Sandburg 1926, 28–32.
104. Mansch 2005.
105. Davis 1999.

5

Civil War Generals and the Bloody Shirt

George McClellan through William McKinley

An officer fit for duty who at this crisis would abandon his post to electioneer for a seat in Congress ought to be scalped. You may feel perfectly sure I shall do no such thing.
—RUTHERFORD B. HAYES, QUOTED IN T. WILLIAMS, *HAYES OF THE TWENTY-THIRD*

I accept the banner of the bloody shirt. I am willing to take as our ensign the tattered, worn-out, old gray shirt, worn by some gallant Union hero, stained with his blood as he gave up his life for his country. . . . When they purge their party of the leprosy of secession . . . we will bury the "bloody shirt" in the grave with the honored corpse who wore it and not before.
—BENJAMIN HARRISON, QUOTED IN SIEVERS, *BENJAMIN HARRISON*

Those seeking the presidency from 1864 until the turn of the century are bookended by George McClellan and William McKinley, and that post–Civil War era featured thirteen presidential candidates. Three were West Point graduates and career officers whose military role culminated in the Civil War. Four were high-ranking officers with short but meteoric wartime experiences. Five never joined the armed forces, and of these, one paid a substitute to go to war on his behalf. The remaining one had a brief stint in the army but fell ill.

World War II and the Civil War both produced numerous veterans among the political class. And while World War II was an external and arguably existential conflict without meaningful domestic ideological implications, the Civil War was a highly partisan conflict that was resolved with bullets rather than ballots. For a World War II veteran entering electoral politics, there was no partisan or ideological implications to having fought against the Axis powers. But Union veterans had fought on one side of a domestic civil war, a culmination of differences over states' rights and slavery. These issues vexed the republic throughout the antebellum years, as territorial expansion kept reigniting the debate over expanding slavery. Periodic compromises put temporary salves on divisive conflict, but the emergence of the antislavery Republican Party in the 1850s and its nomination of Abraham Lincoln in 1860 were the justifications used by the South to secede and attack Federal forces at Fort Sumter in 1861.

The war to restore the Union was therefore a violent extension of domestic political conflict, not an external war against foreigners without partisan substance. George McClellan, Ulysses Grant, Rutherford Hayes, James Garfield, Winfield Scott Hancock, Benjamin Harrison, and William McKinley were each men who served in Lincoln's martial efforts to reunify the states. They wore uniforms to militarily achieve a domestic, political outcome. This fact, stemming from their peculiar domestic military role in a civil war between Americans over long-simmering political issues, means that their service held an undeniable partisan edge. The political legitimacy that Civil War service embedded in their electoral candidacies took a more nuanced partisan dimension than service in overseas wars.

The post–Civil War era was also distinctive from other eras because of the promotion of high-ranking officers for presidential consideration. World War II was dominated by men who served briefly as low-ranking officers and generally started political lives at the lower rungs as young war veterans, but the Civil War cohort were generals (and a major) who were able to grab higher rungs on the electoral ladder. Union generals obtained their commands as much for political considerations as for military competence. "High command was entrusted to individuals whose claims to preferment rested exclusively upon political considerations."[1]

The Civil War: Troop Strength and Means of Recruitment

While some of the men with military experience who ran for president between McClellan and McKinley did fight in the Mexican War, I consider that war as the entrée for candidates of the Antebellum era, such as Franklin Pierce, Winfield Scott, and Zachary Taylor. For the post–Civil War candidates, that was more important and certainly created more veterans. It was more recent and more political. So for men like Winfield Scott Hancock, who did fight in both wars, it was his service in the 1860s that made him presidential timber much more than his time in Mexico.

---

1. Warner 1964, xviii.

To consider the conflict from the Union side, the Civil War required more than 2 million men in the various state- and federally organized units. The VA estimates 2.2 million men served in the armies of the North.[2] The regular army as it existed after the war with Mexico was far too small for what was needed, and a wave of volunteers answered Lincoln's calls for the creation of a citizen army to restore the Union. The ability to muster new troops became more difficult as the war grew longer and bloodier, but the initial surge of enthusiasm created the army that would form the military structure that endured.

With seven or eight veterans among the thirteen major-party presidential nominees of the era, a bit more than half of the men running for president had military experience.[3] How does this compare to the male population at large? There were approximately 10 million men living in the census-classified areas of the Northeast and the North Central, and roughly half of the men of that era were between the ages of fifteen and forty-four.[4] With roughly more than 10 million men living in the non-border-state North, 4.5 million men were of the appropriate age to be eligible for serving under arms.[5] If slightly more than 2 million men made up the Union army, approximately half of the northern men who could have served did so.[6] This book considers the post–Civil War era as including those candidates from McClellan to McKinley, indicating that about half of the presidential candidates and slightly less than half of age-eligible males served in the war.

Before the war, the country maintained a small professional army, strung out across the frontier and other scattered locations. In 1860, there were about one thousand officers in the army and a total of about sixteen thousand soldiers. To summon the needed armies that would grow to more than two million strong, the Union relied on a combination of volunteers and volunteer units that would be subsumed into the U.S. Army. The old militia units in each state had ceased to be anything resembling a deployable military force.[7] Some of the militia units that were able to summon themselves to the war were "transformed into companies of volunteers; but when this happened they lost their distinctive character

---

2. Other estimates are higher. See Weigley 1967.
3. William Jennings Bryan, who ran both as a nonveteran in 1896 and a veteran of sorts in 1900, inhibits one's ability to count easily.
4. U.S. Census Bureau 1975.
5. This does not take into consideration the number of men ineligible because of infirmity or other reasons.
6. The proportion is approximately 37 percent of northern males. Juul 2009.
7. Mahon 1983.

as a force partially under state control."[8] Through "indifference," the various states fatally neglected the militia system.[9]

Congress instituted a system in the summer of 1862 whereby states would need to conscript if they did not fill quotas of volunteers, and the militia rolls provided the lists used to impress men into uniform. This provision did not generate many soldiers. However, the use of the draft impelled uncounted volunteers who sought to avoid the stigma of the draft but did not have the means to hire a substitute.

An important facet of how regiments were assembled has important implications for understanding the political viability that stemmed from Civil War service. In today's regular armed forces, members are recruited from anywhere, sent to central basic training or officer training, and deployed irrespective of their origins. In the Civil War, the creation of volunteer regiments occurred geographically. Approximately a thousand neighbors from the same community would muster together. The energy behind its creation often came from entrepreneurial political elites, using their own local social network to assemble men. For example, the Wisconsin 15th Volunteer Regiment contained a majority of recent Norwegian immigrants from the same communities, with companies in the regiment called "St. Olaf's Rifles" and "Odin's Rifles."[10] Therefore, the fundamental fighting unit in the Civil War, the regiment, was often geographically homogeneous in its membership and often duplicated existing civic and political networks. Part of the reason that military service fortified the electoral prospects for the colonels and generals of the Civil War was the regional way that military units were assembled. Whether these men already had a political identity, such as Hayes, or whether their political life was still entirely ahead of them, such as McKinley, making a name for themselves by leading men from their home state or even home community fortified their later electoral appeal in that community. For the presidential candidates of this era, the means by which regiments were mustered were a political boon for their postwar elections; the "principle of localism" for the Union army had positive electoral consequences.[11]

Casualties in the Civil War were high and framed the debate over whether to continue the war. The necessity of fighting the Civil War was a central debate between vying factions of Republicans and northern Democrats. The war started with an outpouring of voluntarism as men scrambled to get into a unit before they thought the slots would be full. This

---

8. Riker 1957, 41.
9. Riker 1957, 25; P. Smith 1919.
10. Blegen 1920, 155.
11. Goebel and Goebel 1945, 203.

early enthusiasm wore off, however, as the amount of time it would take to win became more obviously longer, to say nothing of the staggering number of casualties. Counting the dead in the Civil War is, and has always been, inexact. Poor record keeping, both before and after the battles, made counting casualties difficult, as "mass modern warfare had not brought with it the bureaucratic apparatus appropriate to its unanticipated scale."[12] The estimate for total dead on both sides is 750,000, about 360,000 on the Union side. Suffice it to say that the war toll was massive. It is common in writings on the subject to point out that the number of war dead from the Civil War outnumbered American war dead in all the other conflicts combined. This fact is approximately true, and even with the necessary asterisks attached to it, the sheer number was unfathomable.

Not only was the number great; its size as a proportion is more overwhelming. It was sixfold larger than the ratio for World War II. How much these casualties influenced public perceptions of the war is hard to quantify, but the existence of peace Democrats attests to rising unpopularity after the rosy estimations of a quick and easy war disappeared. They were replaced with the realities of costly victories such as Shiloh and Antietam, and even more disheartening losses in the Seven Days Battles and Manassas. The midterm elections were a setback for Republicans, who lost seats in both chambers. Among others things, war deaths likely shaped the public view of the war, but empirical estimates of their effects show them to be small.[13] As it would be in later wars, the North's patience with the war rested more on progress toward war aims than casualty rates. The 1864 election was in many ways a referendum on the war itself, not just a choice between two candidates. Lincoln's reelection tells us which side of this debate won.

Federalization, Partisanship, and Professionalization of the Military

The lines between military institutions and aims and domestic civilian politics have never before or since the Civil War been more blurred. The domestic political dissension over the destiny of slavery, territorial expansion, and state autonomy was a long-simmering political conflict made more problematic by the rise of cotton and territorial growth of the republic. This melding of martial and political aims created a unique type of electoral candidate, one who combined martial glory and domestic political issues. Many candidates for high elected office explained why they were a credible advocate for their political stands. For example, a candi-

---

12. Faust 2008, 252.
13. Carson et al. 2001.

date could demonstrate his view against tariffs by telling voters that he had introduced a bill to eliminate the tariff in Congress. A candidate who stood for the Union, however, and did so with voters knowing he had worn the blue uniform on bloody fields, enjoyed an obviously higher level of authority.

Those who study wars and military matters have always been challenged by how to classify civil wars. Similarly, it is tempting to somehow omit the intrastate Civil War in the 1860s from the other interstate conflicts that created a class of military veterans, who in many cases would become their parties' leaders in the following years. While the difference between intra- and interstate wars may be large from a conceptual standpoint, those differences do not make it difficult to assess this book's thesis; in fact, the central war aims of the Union were the intense expansion of both prewar aims, such as strengthening the federal government, and the newer more radical views within the Republican Party, such as abolition.

Further, the postwar domestic political schisms were reverberations of the prewar conflicts. While the war ended at Appomattox, the only way for northern Republicans to enforce what they had won on the battlefield was to continue to militarily occupy the former Confederate states. Reconstruction not only was a postwar extension of the North's war aims; it had to be carried out by the military. For the period between the war and the final collapse of the North's ability to maintain Reconstruction in 1876, the U.S. Army was deployed to carry out Congress's domestic policy agenda under arms.

Given his prerogative for choosing and sacking his generals, Lincoln might be expected to select generals who toed his political line. While Lincoln certainly had the opportunity to reshape the partisan identity of the army as an institution by use of strategic appointments and assignments of generals to particular command, he did not take it. He followed a balanced pattern in appointments and did not purge Democratic-leaning generals from the army after he had consolidated his own power.[14] This difficult postwar period for the military was perhaps the worst state of affairs in civil-military relations.[15] This era was only the beginning of a long professionalization of military institutions, given that McClellan "may well be considered the first thoroughly professional officer."[16] The civil-military tension stems principally from the use of the military not only to maintain Reconstruction but to respond to labor unrest. This

---

14. Polsky 2002.
15. Langston 2003.
16. Weigley 1993, 37.

backdrop did not diminish the Civil War veteran candidacies, however. While the popularity of the armed forces was not high, certainly not among Democrats, the political legitimacy gained on the battlefields of the 1860s was rooted in the Civil War, not in the current woes of the beleaguered U.S. Army.

Political Changes outside War and Military: Parties and the Presidency Evolve

It is also important to look at nonmilitary political dynamics to understand how and why military veteran candidates ran for president. While there were not significant changes to how parties nominated presidential candidates or the stature of the president, one of the most important political innovations in the postwar years relates to the rise of what we would call the interest group, if we merged a huge grass-roots interest group with chapters and local members across the North with a nationally oriented, deep-pocketed issue-advocacy group. The Grand Army of the Republic (GAR), a group likely unfamiliar to most twenty-first-century readers, played a central role in politics after the Civil War. It is the progenitor for all veterans' organizations in America that followed, such as the American Legion or the Veterans of Foreign Wars. The GAR was a nineteenth-century organization that played a strong role in helping Republican candidates win in exchange for support for the pensions that the group sought. Founded in Illinois, the group began with an explicitly political raison d'être. Most scholarly recognition of the GAR has centered on its "pension lobbying and staunch bloody-shirt Republicanism."[17] The organization relates to military candidacies in at least two ways. First, it was a strong electoral auxiliary of the Republican Party. It used its local organizations as electioneering arms, though not with the same force in all northern areas or in all elections. Thus, the GAR remained a force for bolstering Republican election fortunes after the Civil War. Second, it forged a common bond with other Union veterans. For its members, Grant, Hayes, Garfield, and the others were true heroes who bled with them on the battlefields and deserved their support.

Civil War Veterans: George McClellan through William McKinley

Table 5.1 depicts the thirteen individuals who belong to the post–Civil War cohort. (Lincoln is included in the table because he was a candidate

---

17. McConnell 1987, 18.

TABLE 5.1 ELECTIONS OF THE POST–CIVIL WAR ERA

Election year	Candidate	Party	Veteran type	Detail
1864	George McClellan	D	Career general	Union commander, Civil War
	Abraham Lincoln	R	Common veteran	Black Hawk War, militia
1868	Horatio Seymour	D	Nonveteran	
	Ulysses Grant	R	Career general	Union commander of all forces, Civil War
1872	Horace Greeley	D	Nonveteran	
	Ulysses Grant	R	Career general	Union commander of all forces, Civil War
1876	Samuel Tilden	D	Nonveteran	
	Rutherford Hayes	R	Battlefield general	Union commander, Civil War
1880	Winfield Scott Hancock	D	Career general	Union commander, Civil War
	James Garfield	R	Battlefield general	Union commander, Civil War
1884	*Grover Cleveland*	D	Nonveteran	Paid a substitute
	James Blaine	R	Nonveteran	
1888	Grover Cleveland	D	Nonveteran	Paid a substitute
	Benjamin Harrison	R	Battlefield general	Union commander, Civil War
1892	*Grover Cleveland*	D	Nonveteran	Paid a substitute
	Benjamin Harrison	R	Battlefield general	Union commander, Civil War
1896	William Jennings Bryan	D	Nonveteran	
	William McKinley	R	Combat veteran	Enlisted and officer with combat experience during Civil War
1900	William Jennings Bryan	D	Common veteran	Joined army between presidential attempts in 1898, fell ill
	William McKinley	R	Combat veteran	Enlisted and officer with combat experience during Civil War

Note: Winners are italicized. D = Democratic Party; R = Republican Party.

in 1864, but he substantively belongs with the Antebellum cases.) Three substantive groups delineate them. The career generals, George McClellan, Ulysses Grant, and Winfield Scott Hancock, share distinctive circumstances that led to their presidential nominations without previous office seeking. Rutherford Hayes, James Garfield, and Benjamin Harrison were the battlefield generals, who, along with William McKinley, each had brief military careers with fast promotions and used their Civil War credentials to begin political careers as Republicans, which led to presidential politics. The rest of the candidates were nonveterans. Horatio Seymour, Horace

Greeley, Samuel Tilden, Grover Cleveland, James Blaine, and William Jennings Bryan were Democrats who each contested their first presidential election without military service.

The Careerists: McClellan, Grant, and Hancock

McClellan, Grant, and Hancock were West Point graduates who joined the U.S. Army as a career. Excepting some years away from the army by Grant prior to the war, the three spent the mainstay of their adult lives in the army, earned wide acclaim during the Civil War, and entered presidential politics at the very top. The Republicans nominated Grant, and the Democrats nominated McClellan and Hancock with logic not dissimilar from that of past examples. Party elites doubtlessly thought of Washington, Jackson, and Harrison when placing these individuals on the ballot.

The first man to earn a presidential nomination with Civil War military experience was General George McClellan. He did so in 1864, before the war was over, and his military identity was an important part of the Democrats' efforts to make the case to voters that the war should end with a hope to return to the status quo ante. He began the war with an excellent reputation, but his nomination was a mixed blessing for the Democrats' hopes to unseat Lincoln for two reasons: he had been fired by Lincoln for lack of action, and it was paradoxical that the Democratic Party was the peace party that nominated a general.

McClellan was a bright, second-in-his-class cadet at West Point and notable among its graduates for having entered near his sixteenth birthday and finished at age twenty. His first combat experiences happened the same year he graduated when he went to Mexico with the army. He had sought a command role but found that the slots were already full. He used connections to try to get a leadership spot in one of the fighting regiments, but he bitterly blamed the Polk administration for allowing political appointments to fill those spots rather than choose him. He remained in the engineer company for the Battle of Vera Cruz and was exposed to fire during the city's siege. He and his men were scouting to build temporary roads, and the city's defenders took shots at them, which McClellan described as "whistling like hail around me."[18]

McClellan found himself in the middle of what would be a typical problem for this era when political alignments were palpable among officers. McClellan served under General Gideon Pillow, an ally of President Polk from Tennessee, who in turn served under General Winfield Scott, a

---

18. McClellan and Myers 1917, 56.

devout Whig who had previously sought the presidency. Historians have rated Pillow's military skills below his political ones, and he and Scott shared no affection. Scott accused Pillow of exaggerating his role in victories in his official reports and denying credit to those who deserved credit, including himself. The matter would later play out in courts-martial for all involved, but the feud was problematic during the war. McClellan saw firsthand how Scott had deployed his political rival to a less important part of the fight. Scott's "battle plan had been designed to pacify the president's friend and keep him occupied."[19]

In the Civil War, McClellan engaged in well-known clashes with President Lincoln over the speed and cautiousness with which he commanded the Army of the Potomac. McClellan's letters reveal utter disdain for the president, further showing the deep problems between them.[20] Their toxic relationship was not McClellan's first issues with those above him—his entire military career was a history of bristling against those who gave him orders. The two men had met in Illinois before the war in 1858 when McClellan supported Lincoln's opponent, Stephen Douglas, though Lincoln did not hold that against him and selected him to lead. But Lincoln's choice proved the wrong one. McClellan delegated ineffectively and suffered from large fears of failure that caused him to move overcautiously against Richmond. Despite urging from Lincoln and his own political allies, McClellan suffered from, as Lincoln put it, "the 'slows.'"[21] He overestimated enemy numbers and never moved with initiative or boldness. He thought Stanton, Lincoln, and other Republicans sought his failure when, in fact, success for the Army of the Potomac was a shared war aim for all in the North. Lincoln, having exhausted every shred of patience, and probably more, finally relieved McClellan of command in the winter of 1862.

His ascent from little-known veteran following the Mexican-American War to the first suggestions of his presidential potential did not take long, sped up by the crucible of war and other personnel changes. When his actual presidential campaign began, even informally, is more difficult to determine. He wrote an advisory letter in 1862 to Lincoln in which he acknowledged it was not his official role to give advice on the matter but nonetheless recommended that the Union forces not conduct total war. He advocated a softer strategy that avoided freeing the slaves and confiscating or destroying nonmartial property. The letter, known as the Harrison

---

19. T. Johnson 2007, 92.
20. Glatthaar 1994.
21. T. Williams 1952, 177.

Landing Letter, became public, and some believe it marked his de facto candidacy for the presidency against his commander in chief.[22]

After sacking McClellan from his position, the administration had no particular role for him, so it assigned him to an obscure position without duties away from the front and away from Washington, ostensibly for him to finish his report detailing his time commanding the Army of the Potomac. He went to New York City, a redoubt of Democratic strength, where he was celebrated and met with party elites. One biographer asserts that the evidence suggests his presidential ambitions were uncertain when he was fired: "There is nothing to indicate that during the winter ... McClellan's ambition was strongly focused on the presidency, yet there is nothing either to indicate any effort on his part to discourage those who wanted to make him president."[23]

Military necessities forced Lincoln to carry out an unpopular war measure leading up to the election in 1864. One historian asserted that "the military disasters in May and June necessitated the issuing of a proclamation calling for an additional 500,000 troops, all deficiencies on each state's quota to be made good by a draft beginning September 5. The prospect of a draft on the very eve of the state elections in Indiana, Ohio, and Pennsylvania filled many with forebodings of defeat."[24] For the Democrats, this represented an opportunity. Democrats' 1864 national committee convention was in Chicago on August 29. After adopting Clement Vallandigham's written platform, which called for immediate end of hostilities, McClellan was selected as their presidential nominee on the first ballot—virtually entirely on the basis of his experience as a Union general. The difficulty for Democrats lay in marrying two hard-to-reconcile facts: their key issue was that the war has been a failure, and their nominee was the leader of the war for a good part of it. McClellan's military service was important in his acceptance of the nomination. Despite having created and adopted a peace platform, the Democrats proceeded to nominate a Union general. Taking a week for "soul searching,"[25] McClellan accepted the nomination as he rejected the peace plank in the newly minted platform. His words show his sentiments, which would doom the Democrats: "The Union is the one condition of peace—we ask no more. . . . I could not look in the face of my gallant comrades of the army and navy, who have survived so many battles, and tell them that their labors, and

---

22. See Royster 1993; Rafuse 2012.
23. Sears 1988, 347.
24. Zornow 1954, 109.
25. Balsamo 2001, 194.

the sacrifice of so many of our slain and wounded brethren had been in vain."[26]

Another presumption that may have inspired the Democrats to put their faith in McClellan as their nominee was that the men in uniform loved him. Yet to the extent that available evidence allows, the soldier vote leaned unequivocally toward Lincoln, and wartime "Republican efforts to enfranchise military personnel were clearly in their party's interests."[27] While the Democrats doubtlessly hoped that McClellan's wartime laurels would serve as an unmitigated boon, Republicans cast his command of the Army of the Potomac negatively. One thrust aimed at his caution and inability to push on to Richmond. Another angle of attack aimed at his tendency to lead from the rear. A political cartoon titled "The Gunboat Candidate" depicts McClellan astride a saddle mounted to a boat far from the battle, looking on with spyglasses.[28]

The tenor of the presidential election of 1864 reflected the war during which it happened. A beset incumbent president sought a second term to pursue total victory in a hard war. His favorite general, Ulysses Grant, had been spoken of as a political rival, yet another general who Lincoln sacked would instead become the antagonist he would defeat. And while Grant made it very clear that his presidential ambitions were a future consideration, 1864 revealed his obvious popularity and electoral charms. Not unlike a Jackson after New Orleans or even a Washington after Yorktown, Grant basked in the warm glow of public affection based on military victory. In another way, he trail-blazed a pattern that would continue to the candidacy of William McKinley, almost to the turn of the century. The men who commanded Union troops to carry out Lincoln's wartime aims would become the Republican Party's greatest electoral asset.

Unlike Jackson, Grant represented a true lateral entry to the top of the electoral ladder. While Jackson was a soldier-planter-politician, Grant's political qualifications were entirely martial; he had made no attempts to seek lower office. At the very beginning of his farewell address in 1876, he reminded Americans that "it was my fortune, or misfortune, to be called to the office of Chief Executive without previous political training."[29] His rise to become a credible presidential candidate was remarkably fast, rivaling other meteoric political careers like that of Teddy Roosevelt. Grant was a West Point graduate, left the army in 1854, but returned when the Civil War began. He led and won important battles in

---

26. Quoted in Sears 1988, 375.
27. Inbody 2016, 44; McSeveney 1986.
28. Scriabine 1983, 168.
29. Whitney 2003, 201.

the western sphere of the conflict, and Lincoln saw him as the man who could win the war—history showed it was a correct assessment. He stayed in uniform after the war and avoided the taint of the Johnson administration to become the only credible candidate for Republicans in 1868. His war record made him—he rarely lost in battle and proved to be the tenacious and aggressive general that Lincoln had been seeking.

Grant's military career began when he earned a spot at West Point. It would not be the only time that induction into the armed services would inadvertently rename a future U.S. presidential candidate, but his name, Hiram Ulysses Grant, was mistakenly conveyed as Ulysses S. Grant when he started as a cadet (a similar error befell Wendell Willkie). Grant was a middling cadet and began as an officer serving in the west before the Mexican-American War pulled him south. As it was for several officers who would become important leaders on both sides of the Civil War, the invasion of Mexico was a formative training ground for a much bigger conflict later.

Grant played a small but reportedly clever role in the American assault on Chapultepec in General Winfield Scott's army near the end of the war, but this was after his unit was transferred from General Zachary Taylor's forces in the north, where he had fought in the earlier stages. His first taste of combat came in May 1846 at the Battle of Palo Alto. He had assumed command because his superior officer was with scouts. Grant led a charge and captured Mexicans in what was a small battle. As the army moved south, so did the need for its supplies. Grant was a lieutenant and quartermaster, though he was unhappy about supervising mules and supplies when others were given combat outfits. During one assault at the Battle of Monterrey, on hearing the cannonade, he left the rear guard without orders to join the frontline forces on horseback. Days later, he volunteered to ride to the rear with a message for more ammunition. After American forces under Taylor finally took the city, several of his units, including Grant's, were moved under General Winfield Scott to make an assault on Mexico City to the south.

Grant's role there was still as quartermaster, but he continued to find a way to get into combat. In 1847, he led a company of men to gain control of the San Cosme gate in Mexico City. He flanked a Mexican howitzer position and captured the gun. On his own initiative, he had his men transport the howitzer across "several chest-deep irrigation ditches" to a church.[30] Grant ignored the wishes of the local priest, and the men hoisted the gun up to the church's belfry and made a tactically advantageous bead on the gates and defenders behind it. The shots scattered the defenders

---

30. Brands 2012, 49.

and facilitated the swift entrée into Mexico City. Grant's actions earned him commendation from his division commander, but Grant's initiative at Chapultepec was not glory that would make him known to all Americans. As a low-ranking officer, he was not afforded any opportunity to show the strategic prowess he put to the test against Robert E. Lee in 1864 and 1865.

The years between the wars were lean times for Grant and his family. The army stationed him in several places for years. His promotion to captain was in 1853, but his military career dead-ended in 1854 after troubles with alcohol. The years from 1874 until the attack on Fort Sumter were difficult. While he swore off booze, his civilian years would see him "struggle to support his family, without capital, occasionally destitute, working with his hands to make ends meet."[31] He became a failing farmer in Missouri without a national or even regional reputation. The war, as it did for so many others, changed everything. Historians' assessments of Grant as a president rate him a poor executive, but it is undeniable that the war years earned him a national reputation on the most vital matter of the era.

He reentered the army as a colonel and then was quickly promoted to general under Frémont in the west. After commanding northern forces to victories at Fort Henry and Fort Donelson in early 1862, Grant engaged in his first large battle at Shiloh. While the two-day battle was a Union victory, turning the Confederate army in the west southward, it diminished Grant's reputation. Dubious reports that he had been drinking before the battle appeared in newspapers. These reports, whether or not they were true, meshed well with the fact that Grant had been unprepared for and surprised by the Confederate attack on the first morning of the battle. General Don Carlos Buell received more credit for the victory in the press, and high casualties spurred some to urge Lincoln to sack Grant. The president resisted these calls, telling a confidant, "I can't spare this man; he fights!"[32] In 1863 his siege of Vicksburg succeeded, and he led victories at Lookout Mountain and Chattanooga. He earned promotion to three-star general in command of all Union forces in March 1864 and began the final push against Lee in Virginia.

Attitudes toward the war depended on the fortunes of the army. Hence, views in the North toward Grant tended to rise and fall depending on the outcomes of battles. Grant's lowest point probably stemmed from the one battle he definitively lost to Lee, Cold Harbor, during which he ordered a charge that created high Union casualties without turning the

---

31. J. Smith 2001, 90.
32. McClure 1901, 166.

tide of the battle. Grant's willingness to press on despite casualties earned him nicknames such as "Grant the Butcher."[33] He finally checkmated the exhausted and dwindling Confederates by the spring of 1865, sealing his reputation for victory.

Following Lincoln's assassination, Grant politically understood that remaining out of the fray during the turbulent Johnson presidency was his best stratagem. He played his cards quietly but well as Radical Republicans fought with the president after the war. He avoided involvement with the impeachment proceedings and went on to win the Republican nomination unanimously on the first ballot at the 1868 convention and easily won renomination and reelection in 1872.

With his rapid military ascent and lateral entry to the presidency, Grant differed from the others discussed in this chapter. Grant was more a soldier than Hayes, Garfield, and the others, and his politics were less obvious. Chapter 2 differentiates the professional generals from the political ones, and the contrast between Grant and the others embodies the contrast. Grant's military and political experiences prior to his nomination in 1868 are more similar to those of Eisenhower than to those of the other Union generals who succeeded him. What Grant, Hayes, Garfield, Harrison, and McKinley share, however, are the cause and overlapping spheres of political and military that created this unique party system that refought the Civil War repeatedly with elections rather than cannons.

The third careerist, Winfield Scott Hancock, was nominated by a Democratic Party hungry for a presidential win after five straight Republican victories. The 1880 election featured two generals: the Democrats nominated Winfield Scott Hancock, and the Republicans chose James Garfield. Hancock was a professional soldier and well known as a hero from Gettysburg. Like his namesake, General Winfield Scott, his ultimate nomination came after previous failed attempts to win it. He was a serious contender for the Democratic nomination in 1868 and 1876 before earning it decisively in 1880. Unlike Hayes and Garfield, Hancock was a career army officer with much longer and more important leadership positions in the Mexican-American War and the Civil War and other military roles.

Hancock began his adult life at West Point, graduating in 1844. In 1847, after spending uneventful time on the frontier and as a recruiter in Kentucky, he joined a regiment led by General Winfield Scott in the Mexican War. His service there was important, as it was for other future Civil War officers on both sides. His first combat experiences were at the early

---

33. The label is unfair, when one applies the same casualties-to-victory ratio standard to Lee. See Bonekemper 2004, xiv.

Battles at Contreras and Churubusco in August 1847. He was wounded there, preventing his participation in the final battles of the campaign. After the Mexican War, he was a quartermaster in Florida during conflict with the Seminoles, earning the rank of captain by 1855. Transferred to California, Hancock served under soon-to-be Confederate general Albert Sidney Johnston when the Civil War began, so he headed east to be a part of the Union effort. The Civil War is the conflict in which Hancock made his national reputation.

He received quick promotion to brigadier general in September 1861 because West Point–trained leaders were a scarce commodity in the Union army. His first combat command took place during the Peninsular Campaign of 1862 under McClellan, the first northern attempt to take Richmond in the Eastern Theater. Hancock's first victory that helped him accumulate a reputation was at the Battle of Williamsburg during this campaign. He cleverly feinted a slow retreat that tempted Confederates to attack his unseen position behind a hill, waiting for them to draw close, at which time he screamed for a surprise bayonet charge. His counterattack succeeded, spurring McClellan to write of "Hancock's brilliant engagement" to Washington, adding that "Hancock was superb." The northern press, hungry for heroes, found one in Hancock, and he was frequently referred to as "Hancock the Super" from then on.[34] After the Peninsular Campaign's failure to capture Richmond after McClellan's withdrawal, the next major clash for Hancock was Antietam in September. Taking command of a division after its general had fallen in terrible fighting at the "bloody lane" during the battle, Hancock assumed control and held the center after the possibility of a Union attack had stalled. He earned his second star later that year and then saw battle again at two Union defeats, Fredericksburg at the end of the year and Chancellorsville in the spring of 1863. The battle that would elevate Hancock to true national fame was the turning point of the war in summer of 1863: Gettysburg.

The clash in Pennsylvania between Generals George Meade and Lee was the largest battle in the war, and its importance in the war is difficult to overstate. In the long view, historians generally view Gettysburg as the high-water mark of the Confederacy, and Pickett's Charge was the turning point in the battle that led to a decisive Confederate retreat from which the southern cause never recovered. Turning back Pickett's Charge was also Hancock's finest hour. General Meade trusted Hancock to command the II Corps in the center on Cemetery Ridge—exactly where Lee intended

---

34. Quoted in Jordan 1988, 44.

to force a breakthrough and shatter the Union lines with a frontal infantry assault. More than twelve thousand Confederate soldiers marched toward Hancock's well-formed lines after an artillery barrage and then charged the final two hundred yards. With grapeshot, bullets, and bayonets, the assault was repulsed with staggering Confederate casualties. Unable to sustain the attack with more than 50 percent casualties and loss of many officers, the Confederates retreated from the battlefield and ultimately from Pennsylvania, never to threaten northward in numbers again. While rallying his men, Hancock was seriously wounded in the leg with a "ten-penny nail" and some wood, likely shrapnel from a shell hitting a fence post or his saddle.[35] He refused to leave the battle line until victory was clear. The next year, after convalescing, he served under General Grant in the Virginia Campaign. He led his II Corps in the battles of that campaign, including the Battle of the Wilderness.

After the Union victory in 1865, the military shrank dramatically, but its role in securing and maintaining Reconstruction had only begun. Against Grant's counsel, Hancock assumed the military governor role in 1867 and made himself popular in the South for rolling back some of the perceived excesses of Reconstruction's implementation. President Johnson thought that the Republican generals originally selected to govern the former Confederate states were poor choices, particularly Philip Sheridan. Johnson therefore sought Democrats in uniform and wanted to switch Hancock into Sheridan's role governing Texas and Louisiana. Hancock consented reluctantly, knowing the difficulty. Northerners and former slaves in New Orleans had gathered to demonstrate, and the convulsions turned into "bloody race riots."[36] On his first day, Hancock issued "General Order No. 40," essentially blunting the spirit of Reconstruction, turning over many authorities back to civil control. His act became a national controversy; it heartened Southerners and Johnson, inflamed Radical Republicans, and worried the black population in the South. His tenure as military governor converted Hancock in the public eye. His public conflict with Grant and the Radicals in Washington over matters in Louisiana and Texas made clear that he was no longer simply a hero of Gettysburg. His time in the South signaled clearly his identification with conservatives on postwar politics and made obvious his alignment with the Democrats. He procured a unique identity, gaining credibility with Democrats as a national leader while no one forgot about his unimpeachable record on saving the Union earned at Gettysburg.

---

35. "Generals Killed" 1863, 4.
36. J. Taylor 1965, 188.

Hancock's stock as presidential timber was already nearly enough in 1876, but his nomination was assured in 1880. Introduced to the convention as "the soldier statesman with a record as stainless as his sword," he led on the first ballot and won nearly unanimously on the second. As evidence of the pervasiveness of the military candidates who entered presidential politics at the time, during the 1880 election the Greenback Party nominated James Baird Weaver and the Prohibition Party chose Neal Dow. Weaver heeded Lincoln's call for volunteers and joined an Iowa regiment and served nearby General Garfield in the western front for a time. Dow, at age fifty-seven, entered military life as a colonel of a Maine unit. He commanded and fought in Louisiana, suffered wounds, and was a prisoner of war.

In the general election, Hancock's expertise in financial matters was revealed not to be deep. He inartfully articulated a position on the national tariff policy that it was "a local issue."[37] A political cartoon by Thomas Nast on the cover of the November 13, 1880, issue of *Harper's* portrayed him wearing his epaulet stars and sword, straining to understand who this "Tariff" person was. While the military candidacy was thought of as having advantages, it could also be a way for opponents to paint candidates with the brush of political naïveté.

These three career army men—McClellan, Grant, and Hancock—who served in the highest echelons of the U.S. Army during the Civil War, ran for president in a way similar to that of other generals. Not unlike Scott or Taylor previously, or Eisenhower in the twentieth century, this trio of candidates used a lifetime of service and leadership in the army and little else to win over delegates at party nominating conventions and voters in the election. As noted earlier, Huntington makes the point that career generals enjoy less electoral success than military veterans for whom military service was a short part of their life.[38]

Battlefield Heroes–Turned–Ambitious Politicians: Hayes, Garfield, Harrison, and McKinley

The next group of post–Civil War candidates differs from the career candidates in important ways. Hayes, Garfield, Harrison, and McKinley were far from career military men. Their service generally started and stopped with the beginning and end of the Civil War. These four candidates joined regionally based, freshly created regiments that were then put under federal command. The careerists had a national outlook as members of the

---

37. Boller 1984, 143.
38. Huntington 1957.

permanent regulars, but the battlefield generals maintained association with home by serving in a state-based unit comprising men from the same town or community—a boon for aspiring politicians seeking political allies. These men differed from the career generals in terms of political experience. Hayes and the others used their brief but meteoric military careers to start public life in state or legislative roles and worked their way up to a presidential nomination.

Rutherford B. Hayes served as a general in the Union army and hailed from Ohio. These two attributes appeared to be a winning formula for presidential elections in the Gilded Age. His path to the presidency began with his service in the Ohio 23rd Regiment of Volunteers. He received battlefield wounds and a rapid elevation to general rank followed by a return to civilian life and politics. He won U.S. House and gubernatorial elections leading up to a messy Republican nominating convention in 1876, only to head into a controversial general election that saw his inauguration despite having fewer popular votes than his rival. Between Election Day 1876 and the inauguration, before he knew if he would indeed have the required Electoral College majority, he gave a speech to his fellow citizens in his home city as he departed for the nation's capital. That Ohio city, named after the ancient Roman who left his homestead to lead an army to victory and returned home a civilian, was Cincinnati. His speech recounted that sixteen years earlier, he had marched down the same street with a thousand others to muster into the Ohio Volunteers and on to war. His four years in uniform were central to his identity; he viewed them as his golden years. That experience was also near essential for political viability in the Republican Party during the later years of the nineteenth century.

He began as a major in his regiment in 1861, and he was almost forty, older than the enlisted men under his charge. He graduated from both Kenyon College and Harvard Law School. He practiced law in Cincinnati and had begun a public life. He was elected as city lawyer the year before the Civil War and had been an active Whig and more recently, Republican. When the shots at Fort Sumter spurred Lincoln to call for volunteers, Hayes joined the Burnet Rifles, a "volunteer home company" made up of his peers from a literary club.[39] The company was named after the current president of the club, who also provided money for weapons, and the thoroughly civilian Cincinnati Literary Club was quickly transformed. In short order, it changed from a local civic organization to a group of Cincinnati's civic elite eager for military service in Lincoln's army. These local ad hoc

---

39. Hoogenboom 1995, 115.

units that appeared after the administration's first calls for volunteers did not always remain intact. They were sometimes subsumed into larger units commanded by others. In Hayes's case, Ohio's governor offered him a spot as a major in a regiment to be commanded by a regular army, West Point–educated colonel.

His experience in the Ohio 23rd Regiment began and ended more or less with the war. In summary, he led troops in the eastern regions of the war and was wounded in battle several times. He fought at Carnifex Ferry, Second Bull Run, and other battles. At South Mountain in September 1862, he was shot in the arm while leading a charge. Under the command of General George McClellan, Hayes's Ohio 23rd Regiment met entrenched Confederate forces while trying to flank the larger Rebel position at Fox's Gap. His wound put him between the lines as the battle progressed, and he lost and then regained consciousness and summoned aid.[40] His charge was a help to the Union side that day; it "carried the day, or at least that part of the day."[41] His wounds, including a broken humerus, kept him convalescing for the next few weeks on the home front before he would return to his regiment as a full colonel to assume command.

The next summer, in 1863, Hayes and the Ohio 23rd fought in present-day West Virginia in a handful of minor battles. The summer of 1864 saw the regiment fight in the Shenandoah Valley, where Hayes was wounded again. Federal forces were surprised by General Jubal Early's fast-moving cavalry, which were causing both military damage by wrecking train lines and political damage. It was an election year, and Confederate forces ranging around the Shenandoah Valley close to Washington did not reflect highly on the administration.

Early surprised Union forces at Kernstown, just south of the border in Virginia. Hayes and the Ohio regiment "took the brunt of the Confederate assault," necessitating a retreat toward a wall.[42] During the retreat, Hayes's horse and his own shoulder were hit. Union forces had to limp back to Union-held ground, but Hayes's wound was not as bad as the one he sustained in 1862, and he remained with the unit and continued through the summer, fighting a handful of other small clashes as Confederate forces retreated.

Hayes had put himself on a political trajectory prior to the war, and in 1864 it was clear that his service in the Union army made him an increasingly appealing electoral candidate for Republicans in southern Ohio. While Hayes and the other Bluecoats fought in the Shenandoah Valley, his

---

40. T. Williams 1965, 139.
41. Perry 2003, 170.
42. Hoogenboom 1995, 168.

political allies back home nominated him as the Republican candidate to run for the U.S. House of Representatives. He did not avoid the nomination and felt gratification but promised to do no electioneering whatsoever, as his words quoted in the epigraph at the start of the chapter attest. Later eras would view a commissioned officer in the field appearing on a congressional ballot as a breach of the firewalls between the political and military spheres. But in the nineteenth century, as we also saw in the Antebellum era when generals with presidential aspirations attacked Mexico City, the civil-military waters were much muddier.

Not long after his election in November 1864, Hayes was promoted to general, and the war concluded in the spring of 1865. His four years were spent leading infantry troops from the front with a sword in hand. He had been shot more than once and had horses shot from under him. He led men in victories and defeats. He was in a congressional viewing stand for the Grand Review in May, and the Ohio 23rd Regiment, along with most of the rest of Union forces, disbanded. Hayes was recognized for his combat valor with a symbolic brevet promotion to major general (two star) on completion of his four years in the army as he transitioned from General Hayes to Congressman Hayes. His time as a legislator was remarkable given the tumult of the difficult postwar issues regarding stitching the country back together, but Hayes himself was not a remarkable legislator. His popularity among Republicans in Ohio, including the northeastern part of the state, where a large share of the old 23rd Regiment called home, ensured his nomination for governor in the 1867 elections. On the campaign trail, his speeches hammered at the Democratic Party's disloyalty in the war. His former soldiers were a large presence in the campaign, an important part of his coterie, and a symbolically powerful reminder of the war.

After winning, Hayes defended his gubernatorial seat in 1869 against Copperhead Democrat George Hunt Pendleton, McClellan's presidential running mate in 1864. Pendleton attempted to resurrect a story of Hayes's military malfeasance from his first year in uniform, "retailing the unsubstantiated story that his first commander . . . threatened to kick Hayes out of camp for a gross violation of military rules." Pendleton's attempt to smear him failed, however, when the commander in question, a Democrat, said that Hayes "had both my respect and esteem as an officer and a gentleman, and still retains them."[43]

The Republican Party in 1876 was not united. The favorite at the start of the campaign was not Hayes but the former Speaker of the House,

---

43. Quoted in R. Morris 2003, 64.

James Blaine of Maine. The "Plumed Knight" did not earn that moniker from Civil War service—he was a political leader in the Maine legislature at the outbreak of war and then won a U.S. House seat during the war. While Blaine led early voting, Hayes ultimately prevailed. His victory was more likely a reflection of perceptions of scandal in Blaine's past than it was Hayes's war service. His life and presidency were cut short by his assassination in 1881, less than a year after his election.

James Garfield, like Hayes, was an Ohio Republican who came of age before the war and volunteered when Lincoln called. He started as a high-ranking officer with little military knowledge, served in the field, obtained fast promotion, was nominated to run for Congress while he was still in uniform, and was put on a path to his nomination and election in 1880 through his political life as a congressman.

Garfield turned twenty-seven and married in 1858 in Hiram, Ohio, after graduating from Williams College, his first experience away from his native Ohio. He had returned home to Hiram College as a young professor pursuing a law career while the final compromises that kept the Union together strained and failed in 1860. His single prewar political experience was his successful nomination as a Republican to run for the Ohio Senate, and he won the seat in 1859.

After the outbreak of war, Garfield quickly offered his service to the governor. He had always been strident in his Unionist and antislavery views.[44] He campaigned for Frémont in 1856, and his biographers note that his political ambitions began before the war. While he was quick to join, he was more than hopeful that he deserved a commission with a rank of at least colonel. His letters to others also reveal his perception that martial experiences would help foster his already palpable political aspirations, a recognition of a widespread understanding. Once the war had begun, he wrote that he occupied his free time by reading "military science and the campaigns of Napoleon and Wellington," at the same time writing of his congressional ambitions: "If I should go to Congress we would move there for the winter. (Isn't this a fine specimen of unhatched chicken?)"[45] His hopes for being commissioned as a general were not realized. He received an offer to serve as a lieutenant colonel, but he declined it in June. By summer's end, he had joined an as-yet-unmanned regiment as a lieutenant colonel and was shortly made colonel of the Ohio 42nd Regiment. He received credit from contemporaries, his men, and later biographers in his next months of labor spent busily organizing, supplying, and training his unit.

---

44. Booraem 1988.
45. Quoted in Houdek 1970, 29.

In December 1861, Hayes led the 42nd to eastern Kentucky as part of General Don Buell's army in a minor campaign. Buell tapped Garfield to lead a brigade (a handful of combined regiments) to the Big Sandy River valley to counter Confederate forays there. The war, Bull Run aside, was still in its initial phases as Garfield marched his men south, months before the major battles of the Civil War in the summers of 1862–1864. In January 1862, Garfield's brigade met Confederates at Paintsville, Kentucky. Garfield commanded all Union forces in this rare winter battle, the Battle of Middle Creek. It was a small battle with fewer than five thousand men involved and was a Union victory, the only battle that Garfield would win as the most senior commander. Garfield showed both aggressiveness bordering on recklessness and clever trickery. He ordered his men to conduct a large marching motion to extend his lines into a longer, thinner force to give the impression of more numbers than he had. This move had the desired effect, as the Confederate commander, General Humphrey Marshall, was already under the erroneous impression that Garfield's brigade outnumbered his troops. It was also intended as a demonstration of the Union troops' fighting and marching abilities to intimidate the Rebel troops. While the battle played little role in the major turning points of the Civil War, it dramatically shaped James Garfield's political destiny.

His victory instantly increased his fame, and important actors began paying attention to him. An article in the *New York Times* headlined "Movements in the West" noted that "Col. Garfield whipped . . . Marshall on the 7th, drove in his pickets on the 9th, completely routed his 2,500 men on the 10th."[46] Garfield's political allies in Ohio worked hard to bolster his career. The Ohio Senate wrote collectively to President Lincoln to urge Garfield's promotion to general, and Treasury Secretary Salmon Chase also supported his follow Ohioan. General George McClellan also praised Garfield for his victory.[47] He was soon promoted to brigadier general in March, backdated to the day of the battle.

His interest in politics was never dormant. Replying to a letter from an Ohio ally who suggested he should throw his hat in the ring for the 1862 congressional elections, Garfield replied that he "should be pleased to take part in the legislation of the next few years. If the people should of their own motion see fit to call me to that place, of course I should be greatly pleased," and "I am free to confess that I would like to be a member of the next [Congress]." He appears to have grasped the potential of making his military career too obvious a springboard to political ascent, writing home that "I remember to have promised . . . not to use the military as

---

46. "Movements in the West" 1862, 2.
47. Houdek 1970; Dearing 1952.

a stepping stone to political preferment, and I shall make no effort. But if the people want me, they can say so even if I should not be out of the army till December."[48] In those letters and others, Garfield indicates that it was unseemly at the time for a candidate to attempt actively to run on military honors. A larger tendency of the times was that candidates carefully concealed their political ambitions while relying on allies to do the overt work. The office should appear to be seeking the man, not the man the office. Garfield's letters reveal that he understood that military valor held political potential, but he also knew that battle honors must be deftly played to demonstrate hesitant, reluctant service.

Garfield would not again see action like he had at Middle Creek. His forces rejoined Buell's army and then General Ulysses Grant's by April 1862, coming to the Battle of Shiloh in Tennessee late on the second day of the bloody affair. Garfield's men arrived a day late for the surprise Confederate attack and saw only the very end of the fighting and its terrible aftermath.[49] The mistakes made by his commanding generals fomented an already-developed antipathy toward the West Point professionals, but it was more than their military mistakes that chafed Garfield. His larger interpretation of the war was more antislavery than that of others, before and during the war. His early Unionist views made him feel that his citizen-soldier brigade pursued a just political outcome, implicitly seeing the army as a joint civilian-military political effort to restore the Union without concessions to the Confederacy.

Garfield's military career would tilt more to the political side the summer following Shiloh in 1862. The Union forces, smarting from the surprise attack, made overcautious progress toward Corinth, Mississippi. This laborious movement in poor conditions made sickness prevalent among the troops, and Garfield also fell ill. He was granted leave to convalesce and spent the time in Washington, D.C., living with Secretary Salmon Chase. During this time, his allies in the Ohio 19th congressional district worked to secure Garfield's nomination and election while he stayed in the capital. For the rest of 1862 he was assigned to administrative duties while his Republican allies carefully coaxed local party elites to abandon the incumbent in favor of Garfield. This nomination was the real hurdle to overcome, as the heavily Republican district would certainly elect whoever ran on their ticket in November. From afar, Garfield was nominated and elected to the U.S. House of Representatives a month before his thirty-first birthday. Congress would not convene for another year, so Garfield would be able to fulfill the term of his military obligation.

---

48. Quoted in Houdek 1970, 35–36.
49. Peskin 2003; Goebel and Goebel 1945.

The year 1863, Garfield's final year as an officer, not only shows his growing political instincts and connections but also demonstrates just how permeable the thin membrane was dividing political and military matters during the Civil War. The year also held a series of frustrations for Garfield, as he was without a command and seeking to return to the field. In January he met with Secretary of War Edwin Stanton to seek to be reunited with his original regiment. The general currently in command there was an Ohio Democrat who strongly objected to the use of freed slaves as soldiers, so Republican Stanton and the devoted antislavery Garfield sought but failed to replace the general with Garfield for political reasons. While Garfield got on well with Stanton, he counted Chase as his closest friend in Washington. Machinations in the cabinet and among superior generals put Garfield in a holding pattern as he tried and failed to secure a mission. He was considered for operations in South Carolina and along the Florida coast, but neither panned out. Garfield was both a party to and victim of political clashes between Democrats and factions within the GOP and the administration, as the conduct of the war was always a struggle for Lincoln in balancing disparate parts of the political and military effort. One suspects that Garfield would have worn a title "Political General" with pride. His final days in the army were as chief of staff to General William Rosecrans, commander of the Army of the Cumberland in Tennessee. The position kept him out of the saddle and away from combat, but the role likely sharpened his political skills, as rivalries between generals and between Rosecrans and Washington required delicate communications. The role was a "great deal of work and not much glamour."[50]

After Chickamauga in September 1863, Garfield went home in November and was in Washington by year's end. He still held hopes that as a two-star general, he might find another command and defer his legislative destiny, but Lincoln personally persuaded him to join Congress. With his uniform still on, Garfield met his future legislative colleagues in December and shortly assumed civilian garb to be the Ohio 19th district's representative in Congress. From his final year in the middle of the war to his simultaneous nomination as senator and president in the 1880 election, he climbed the ranks in the U.S. House. He did not seek to be governor of Ohio, though the Republicans in the state frequently entreated him to run. In 1879, having already decided to leave the U.S. House, he campaigned across Ohio for fellow Republicans to ensure their majority in the state capital, and it was Garfield the legislature chose as U.S. senator the next year.

---

50. J. Taylor 1970, 82.

While his Civil War service was crucial to his nomination in 1863, it is difficult to see how much it helped him obtain the presidential nomination in 1880. It could hardly have hinged primarily on Garfield's past military experience, as Grant and Blaine led the first round of balloting. Grant had taken two years for a world tour and returned to the United States to more parades. The initial alignment of rivals preceding the convention was Grant versus Blaine supporters, with reformers, Easterners, and Midwesterners in the Blaine camp. The convention was a long affair with more than thirty ballots. Grant's support never wavered but stayed around 40 percent of delegates through the balloting—insufficient for the nomination. When Blaine supporters, along with those who backed General William Tecumseh Sherman's brother, shifted to Garfield, the deadlock was broken. Beating Grant was not the result of his military service biography but his position as a dark horse in a contentious and divided party convention. In the general election, Garfield faced a fellow Civil War general, Winfield Scott Hancock. Military service issues did surface, with some questioning Hancock's bravery, but the most salient issues swirled around the bargain of 1876.

At age twenty-eight with two children and another one on the way, the politically well-connected practicing attorney Benjamin Harrison did not initially join the throngs who volunteered in the days following the attack on Fort Sumter. Winning elections as Indianapolis city attorney and as reporter for the state supreme court, Harrison had begun his political career and needed to provide financially for his family. In July 1862 the grandson of President and General William Henry Harrison met with Indiana's governor, a strong Lincoln ally. Oliver Morton bemoaned the lack of enthusiasm from Lincoln's recent call for volunteers, and reportedly, Harrison decided to join on the spot.[51] He declined the colonelcy because of his inexperience, so the governor made him a second lieutenant with the principal aim of recruiting a company. After he had collected eighty-five men, the governor made him a captain to head Company A within the Indiana 70th Regiment in late July; by August he was its colonel.

His regiment held ground and defended railroads in Kentucky and Tennessee, largely away from more active theaters during the war up to 1864. Harrison and his men joined Sherman's southward push toward Atlanta and were marching south by spring. The Atlanta Campaign was a long string of battles in which Confederate forces mounted an entrenched defense and Sherman's Union forces flanked and fought, pushing General Johnston's forces backward, closer to Atlanta, to try to firm up another

---

51. Sievers 1952, 179.

defensible position. The fighting took place all summer, culminating in the capture of Atlanta in September. Harrison, having been promoted to leading a brigade, commanded men in a series of battles. The Battle of Resaca became the one on which Harrison's martial reputation was solidified.

While Harrison's martial glory does not shine as brightly as some of the other Civil War stories used on the campaign trail, he did fight gallantly in a daring charge to capture Rebel artillery. Resaca was a three-day battle that ended with both sides sustaining casualties, neither obtaining conclusive advantage, and ending with the Rebels seeking better position to hold back the assault closer to Atlanta. On the morning of the last day, May 15, Harrison noticed that Confederate infantry responsible for defending an artillery position were faltering, so he led a charge through them to capture the guns. Hand-to-hand combat ensued, and Harrison's Indiana soldiers temporarily held the position. The lines shifted again, but Harrison's men were able to retrieve the artillery after nightfall. One of the men nearby wrote home, describing "Harrison standing up there right in front of the rebels, waving his sword in one hand and brandishing a revolver in the other."[52] Harrison and his men won praise from both General Joseph Hooker and Sherman.[53] He earned a brevet general's star in January and returned to Indianapolis at war's end.

After his return, Harrison showed political promise: "Benjamin Harrison was well known in Indianapolis. Before the interruption of war, he had already won a moderate success in both law and political life. At the moment a war hero, his true forte was not that of a solider."[54] In 1876, the Republican nominee for governor of Indiana removed himself from the ticket in August amid a scandal, and party supporters hoped Harrison would run in his place at that late hour. His campaign for the position embodied the bloody-shirt tactics of Republicans in the postwar years. While the contemporary issues were actually centered on money policy and Reconstruction, Harrison was, in one scholar's view, the most ardent at waving the bloody shirt, as the example in this chapter's epigraph demonstrates.[55] Union veterans who saw action in the bloody conflict shared the passion he explicitly invoked a decade after peace.

With just a few weeks before Election Day, September 20, Republicans in Indianapolis organized a massive rally with martial themes. Brass bands, drum corps, parading veterans, cheering civilians, and ornate orations substantiated General Garfield's feeling that "war issues were

---

52. Long 1888, 366.
53. Long 1888, 365.
54. Sievers 1960, 5.
55. Dearing 1952, 228.

dwarfing all others."⁵⁶ With help from the GAR, the event looked like a garrison or camp of supporters more than a typical rally. With only weeks remaining, a third-party candidate backed out of the race and endorsed Harrison, and his public letter of support based his decision on the fact that Harrison's nonveteran opponent had "during the trying ordeal of the war evinced no special patriotism."⁵⁷ It was not enough to propel him to a win in the close election. His successful 1888 presidential election was won in the Electoral College despite garnering fewer popular votes than Grover Cleveland. Cleveland had not made veterans his allies with his opposition to Civil War pensions.

The last Civil War veteran to run for president was William McKinley. The war experiences of McKinley follow those of his commanding officer, Colonel Rutherford B. Hayes, as they both saw combat in what is now West Virginia, Virginia, and Maryland for the entirety of the conflict. McKinley fits the battlefield general mold almost perfectly. He was a civilian when the war broke out, enlisted in a home-state unit, served and fought, earned rapid promotions, and left the army not long after the surrender at Appomattox. The only technical hiccup in placing his candidacy in the battlefield general category along with Harrison, Garfield, and Hayes is that he did not make it to the rank of general, though he probably would have had he joined with a commission or had the war lasted longer.

Sworn into the ranks by General Frémont, seventeen-year-old McKinley began a three-year hitch in the army as an enlisted soldier in Hayes's Ohio 23rd Regiment of Volunteers. After some months of minor skirmishes, his officers promoted him to commissary sergeant in April 1862. His skill at this task, "distributing rations, checking on fodder for horses, and attending to the endless stream of paperwork necessary in the quartermaster division," made Hayes notice him, and the two were to be connected thereafter.⁵⁸ At Antietam, he earned recognition among his regimental soldiers by making a daring supply run to the front under fire. His courage and ability at the battle earned him lieutenant's bars. He stayed with the 23rd, serving as aide to his commanders, and eventually earned brevet major in March 1865 after many battles in the Shenandoah Valley. At Kernstown, he made another "daring gallop under fire" to get a signal to a cut-off unit.⁵⁹ Four years a soldier, Major McKinley returned to civilian life at age twenty-two.⁶⁰

---

56. Sievers 1960, 118.
57. Sievers 1960, 120.
58. H. Morgan 1963, 23.
59. Leech 1959, 7.
60. Armstrong 2000.

Again following Hayes, McKinley strongly supported and campaigned for his former commander in the gubernatorial contest in 1867. McKinley's electoral experiences began very early when he was only twenty-six. He became a county prosecutor but was unseated two years later in 1871. Five years later, when Hayes claimed the White House after the close election of 1876, McKinley won his first congressional election. It is difficult to imagine that McKinley did not have presidential aspirations during his years in Congress. Three Civil War comrades-in-arms from Ohio won the White House in 1876, 1880, and 1888 as McKinley gained seniority in the U.S. House and then won the governor's mansion after being gerrymandered out of Congress.

McKinley's nomination in 1896 was more solid and more calculated than those of his Buckeye predecessors. His victory appeared easy but was actually the product of a "carefully planned and superbly executed campaign" years in the making.[61] He united the party with far more consensus than Hayes, Garfield, or Harrison—each of whom obtained his nomination at more fractured, divided conventions. Astute campaigning and clever managing by Mark Hanna avoided the infighting seen at previous conventions. William McKinley, the last of the Civil War Republicans, did not rely on his military honors in 1896, or at least did so far less than his predecessors. He defeated William Jennings Bryan in the general election on the issues of 1896, denouncing free trade and free silver rather than running on the past in a fundamentally transformative election.[62] While his time in the army was essential to his political legitimacy in the early phase of his public life, by 1896 his election success and the reshaping of the American electorate and direction of the Republican Party finally buried the bloody shirt and turned the page.

This group of candidates in the years following the war shared a common, terrible experience: fighting their former countrymen in a total war to restore the Union. Because of the inherent intermingling of domestic politics and use of the armed forces, a unique marriage between serving in the army and running for political office took place that opened the door for several veteran candidacies. Both career and battlefield generals sought the nomination, running on platforms that held the 1860s Union cause central for decades after the war. The Republicans who ran invoked the bloody shirt to remind voters which party sought a compromise on union and which party seceded. The power of the bloody shirt waned by McKinley's election in 1896, and at the turn of the century the country moved on.

---

61. Glad 1964, 95.
62. Key 1955; Rove 2015.

6

Early Twentieth Century

Theodore Roosevelt through Adlai Stevenson

We made presidents out of military men for more than thirty years after the Civil War but there doesn't seem to be any sentiment for a military candidate at the present time.
—WARREN HARDING, QUOTED IN PIETRUSZA, 1920

The early twentieth century is the period when the fewest number of military veterans ran for president. Six of the eighteen Republicans and Democrats between Theodore Roosevelt in 1904 and Adlai Stevenson in the 1950s served in the army, two saw combat, and Roosevelt is the only one with a reputation of military service woven into his public persona. This hiatus of veterans in public life is a product of changes since the Civil War. The first and most obvious is that there were far fewer veterans in the United States in the decades between the Civil War and World War I. From 1866 at the end of the war, the U.S. Army had about 40,000 men on active duty year to year, with a brief surge in 1898 for the Spanish-American War, thereafter maintaining between 100,000 and 150,000 until the recruitment of the "doughboys," the soldiers of the large American Expeditionary Forces (AEF) in 1916. Assuming no connection between prior military service and elections, one should not expect as many veterans running for president if there are fewer veterans to run. However, as the earlier Harding quotation suggests, war-hero fatigue among the political class is apparent. After two eras of generals seeking the White House, the American political system avoided veterans, and the political appeal of a military general declined. With the important exception of Dwight Eisenhower, parties stopped seeking generals to be their standard-bearers. This chapter looks at the period between Roosevelt and Stevenson, when candidates were of an age when they might have served in either the Spanish-American War or World War I.

Spanish-American War and World War I: Troop Strength and Recruitment

The two wars of the era in which presidential candidates served were the short war with the Spanish in 1898 and America's late entry into World War I. In explaining its role in shaping military affairs in the twentieth century, Samuel Huntington pointed out the importance of the Spanish-American War despite its relatively small force size and duration. The Civil War was far larger in scope and magnitude but did little to change the military establishment and its policies. The Spanish-American War, however, spurred radical changes to American military institutions and recruiting.[1] It was short, of course, lasting all of ten weeks, with John Hay giving it a characterization that, from the American perspective, would stick: it was "a splendid little war."[2] American motives included a growing global ambition. While the explosion of the U.S.S. *Maine* created a catalyst for the blockade of Cuba that would trigger war, American policy elites desired a broader global role.

Veterans Affairs data claim approximately 300,000 veterans of the Spanish-American War.[3] Fewer than 30,000 were regulars already under arms when the war broke out, but the focus here is on the other path into uniform. The volunteers who crashed recruitment office doors are more important for understanding how this war might propel presidential candidacies because of one man, Theodore Roosevelt. In two waves, first calling for 125,000 and then another 75,000, President McKinley publicly asked the nation for volunteers. Many of those were National Guard units that sought entry and were subsumed into the war effort as volunteer units but kept intact.[4] But Roosevelt's path from his desk in the Naval Department to San Juan Hill was self-made. He essentially created a new cavalry regiment and lobbied for its deployment with his political skills. His entry into the war is less probative regarding typical recruiting in the Spanish-American War than it is about his irrepressible desire to fight in battle.

A war's attributes that shape its popularity toward understanding how well its veterans might fare electorally include its duration, outcome, and casualties. Casualties were light, and America's quick victory made it the almost perfect war from the perspective of public perception. Approximately three hundred to four hundred men died in combat in the short war, but more than ten times that died from disease after returning home, after attention to the war waned.

---

1. Huntington 1961.
2. Quoted in Bishop 1919, 533.
3. U.S. Department of Veterans Affairs 2011.
4. Cosmas 1971.

Despite initial isolationist tendencies, the United States joined World War I in 1917. General Leonard Wood, former president Theodore Roosevelt, and others had been pressing for the nation to be more prepared for war, especially by enlarging the size of the regular army. The sinking of the *Lusitania* in 1915 gave their movement some lift, and continued German U-boat attacks moved President Woodrow Wilson toward seeking a declaration of war, which came in the spring of 1917. The small regular army needed rapid recruiting, so Congress initiated a conscription system that drafted almost three million men, more than ten times the number deployed in the war with Spain. The 1920 census reported approximately ten million white men between the ages of twenty and forty-four in the United States,[5] making the very rough proportion of eligible men who served about 20 percent.

The reasons for creating a mass-conscripted army of regulars for World War I rather than use previous enlistment systems, such as the geographically centered volunteer units from the Civil War, are partially due to the rift between Wilson and Roosevelt. Roosevelt, America's most famous amateur soldier, was clambering to re-create a custom military unit and had "culled commanders for his units from the regular army" while seeking endorsements for his plans from Britain and France.[6] Wilson eliminated the volunteer option to spread the burden of service to all by drawing from a more arbitrary subset of the male population, denying Roosevelt his hopes to replicate his Spanish-American War glory. Conscription succeeded in raising one hundred thousand per month in the first three months and would ultimately deliver ten thousand trained soldiers to the Western Front per day. It also created the military institution in which Alf Landon and Wendell Willkie would spend very brief stints.

Federalization, Partisanship, and Professionalization of the Military

The major reforms of the American defense establishment in the early twentieth century did not have the explicit intention of taking politics out of the armed forces. As occurred in the Antebellum and Civil War eras, party politics infused military leadership, generals were openly aligned with party and faction, and recruiting and army policy were driven by interparty struggle as much as military necessity. When the American voters chose William McKinley over William Jennings Bryan in 1896, they favored the candidate who backed military enhancement and reform

---

5. U.S. Census Bureau 1975, 16.
6. Chambers 1987, 137.

and looked away from the candidate who had attempted to "rekindle an ancient American suspicion of all things military."[7]

While the Americans had indeed defeated the Spanish in Cuba and the Philippines, the war gave clear signs that the military establishment suffered from structural and organizational woes. The rapidness with which the three hundred thousand men were recruited and outfitted butted up against a system unable to contend with the size and speed needed, resulting in a "series of shortages, equipment boondoggles, transportation tie-ups, sanitation disasters, scandal, and much angry finger-pointing."[8] Inefficiency and waste detrimental to the military and its missions were too common, bringing terms such as "embalmed beef" into the popular vocabulary.[9] Major reforms to staffing, leadership structure, organization, recruiting, procurement, and other matters would mark the ensuing decades. As American military interests grew to a global scale, obvious partisan activities by its leaders diminished while professionalization grew. This postwar period saw more healthy civil-military relations, which were more successful than other peacetime reform efforts.[10]

Political Changes outside War and Military: Parties and the Presidency Evolve

During this era, political parties began to experiment with direct primaries as a way to select their presidential nominees. From 1920 to 1968, around fifteen states decided to hold primary elections to choose delegates, but only some delegates were bound to vote per the tally. Given the primaries' limited ability to actually drive the nomination, candidates rationally viewed them as a "public arena for tests of electoral strength."[11] Hence, the mechanism used by parties was undergoing reformation but with little relevance for the few veterans who won nominations. Further, this era did not see much growth in the power or stature of the presidency, especially when contrasted with the next era starting with Franklin Roosevelt. Aside from innovative use of the "rhetorical presidency" by Theodore Roosevelt and Woodrow Wilson, the institution of the presidency remained inert compared with what was to come later.[12]

---

7. Langston 2003, 45.
8. Dyal, Carpenter, and Thomas 1996, 22.
9. Keuchel 1974, 249.
10. Langston 2003.
11. Bartels 1988, 15.
12. Ceaser et al. 1981, 158.

Veteran Candidates of the Early Twentieth Century: Low in Number and Salience

For this group of candidates, there are two categories of veteran candidacies: Teddy Roosevelt and the rest. The remaining men include one combat veteran, Harry Truman, and three others who ran in the 1930s and 1940s with very brief noncombat World War I service: Alf Landon, Adlai Stevenson, and Wendell Willkie. Military service played no role in their presidential campaigns. There were simply fewer veterans in the electorate and only two years when the nation was at war. Table 6.1 lists the elections from 1896 to 1956 to convey the candidates' military experiences.

Theodore Roosevelt: A Rough Rider Rides to the White House

Theodore Roosevelt is unique among the men of this era, and perhaps of all the candidates for the presidency. His military credentials live large in our minds. Along with Kennedy, his campaign in Cuba was a very salient part of his electoral prospects among the nongenerals discussed in this book. The unprecedented speed of his rise to national fame catapulted him to the vacant vice presidential nomination in 1900. McKinley's assassination a year later made Roosevelt the youngest president to occupy the White House, at age forty-two. Also unique was that he campaigned in his first presidential election in 1904 as a sitting president. His appeal that enabled the second phase of his rapid ascent in New York politics, which opened the door to national-level politics, came from his short but well-known campaign in the Spanish-American War. He fought and led the Rough Riders, famously capturing San Juan Hill. For the political leaders of 1900 until the mid-twentieth century, military service was uncommon, and perhaps Teddy Roosevelt's tenacity at trying to get into the fight demonstrates that men in the political class of the age needed to work very hard to find themselves in uniform.

Observers of the young Roosevelt probably would not have predicted that the sickly child, born into a wealthy family, would grow up to be an exemplary physical presence who could ride, march, shoot, hunt, and fight. He became a leading voice for military preparedness and martial virtue in the latter half of his political life, while attempting to take advantage of any opportunity to serve under arms. The interplay between military experience and electoral identity was unique to Roosevelt. Unlike most of the presidential candidates with military service, Roosevelt spent his time in uniform after his initial entry into electoral politics. In this sense, the second of his two different military roles punctuated and

TABLE 6.1 ELECTIONS OF THE EARLY TWENTIETH CENTURY

Election year	Candidate	Party	Veteran type	Detail
1896	William Jennings Bryan	D	Nonveteran	
	William McKinley	R	Combat veteran	Enlisted and officer with combat experience during Civil War
1900	William Jennings Bryan	D	Common veteran	Joined army between presidential attempts in 1898, fell ill
	William McKinley	R	Combat veteran	Enlisted and officer with combat experience during Civil War
1904	Alton Parker	D	Nonveteran	
	Theodore Roosevelt	R	Combat veteran	Rough Rider officer, Spanish-American War
1908	William Jennings Bryan	D	Common veteran	Joined army between presidential attempts in 1898, fell ill
	William Taft	R	Nonveteran	
1912	*Woodrow Wilson*	D	Nonveteran	
	Theodore Roosevelt	P	Combat veteran	Rough Rider officer, Spanish-American War
	William Taft	R	Nonveteran	
1916	*Woodrow Wilson*	D	Nonveteran	
	Charles Hughes	R	Nonveteran	
1920	James Cox	D	Nonveteran	
	Warren Harding	R	Nonveteran	
1924	John Davis	D	Nonveteran	
	Calvin Coolidge	R	Nonveteran	
1928	Al Smith	D	Nonveteran	
	Herbert Hoover	R	Nonveteran	
1932	*Franklin Roosevelt*	D	Nonveteran	
	Herbert Hoover	R	Nonveteran	
1936	*Franklin Roosevelt*	D	Nonveteran	
	Alf Landon	R	Common veteran	Brief commission in army near end of World War I
1940	*Franklin Roosevelt*	D	Nonveteran	
	Wendell Willkie	R	Common veteran	Brief commission as army lawyer, World War I
1944	*Franklin Roosevelt*	D	Nonveteran	
	Thomas Dewey	R	Nonveteran	
1948	Harry Truman	D	Combat veteran	Artillery officer, World War I
	Thomas Dewey	R	Nonveteran	
1952	Adlai Stevenson	D	Common veteran	Brief World War I service
	Dwight Eisenhower	R	Career general	Commander of Allied forces, World War II
1956	Adlai Stevenson	D	Common veteran	Brief World War I service
	Dwight Eisenhower	R	Career general	Commander of Allied forces, World War II

Note: Winners are italicized. D = Democratic Party; P = Progressive Party; R = Republican Party.

accelerated his political career rather than simply existed as an earlier biographical footnote.

The senior Theodore Roosevelt's decision to remain a civilian during the Civil War shaped the son's views. In the Civil War, the wealthy could remit a fee to allow a substitute to be conscripted rather than themselves. Along with the others of his social class, Theodore Roosevelt Sr. legally circumvented the draft and did not fight. The story is more complex than social class, however, as Roosevelt's mother was a transplanted Southerner with brothers fighting on the Confederate side. How his father's lack of service influenced Roosevelt is difficult to understand perfectly. On every other subject, the son worshipped the father, but he felt this act was a stain. Roosevelt's sister believed that Roosevelt subsequently perceived his father's decision as "the glaring single flaw in the life of an idolized father and one he would feel forever compelled to compensate for."[13]

In 1880, Roosevelt graduated from Harvard and moved back to his native New York City to begin law school at Columbia at the age of twenty-two. The next year his district's residents in Manhattan elected him to represent them in the New York State Assembly, starting his life of public service. However, he also continued developing his interests in military policy. His youthful authoring of an impressive book on naval warfare demonstrated his interest and expertise in martial matters. Roosevelt was a prolific author of books and articles throughout his life, but his first forays into his identity as a scholar and writer analyzed naval policy. While a student at Harvard, he began a research project that culminated in his publication of *The Naval War of 1812* after his graduation. Contemporary and later critics hailed its detail and analysis, giving Roosevelt an identity as a military expert.

Roosevelt's military fame that launched him into rapid political ascent was not his uneventful time in the National Guard in the 1880s. It was his

---

13. McCullough 1981, 57. All four of Roosevelt's sons served in World War I, and one did not return. According to one source, Theodore's cousin, Franklin Delano Roosevelt, "had vigorously pressed for US intervention and tried in vain to resign his position and join the fighting" of World War I. See Neal 1984, 14. Franklin Roosevelt, aside from party, shared much with his cousin Theodore, whose career was a political template that Franklin followed. Both attended Harvard and Columbia, and both became assistant secretary of the navy. Franklin Roosevelt did not step down from that appointment when the war broke out. See J. L. Thompson 2013. "Unlike TR, who in 1898 resigned as assistant secretary of the navy to 'join the fun' in the Spanish-American War, Franklin stayed at his post, a course that became a subject of some bitterness between his wife Eleanor and 'Uncle Ted,' who urged her husband on several occasions to get into the fight more directly. . . . Franklin was aware that the Colonel's war record had been instrumental in his rise to the presidency but became convinced that he could make a much more important contribution by staying in Washington to keep the US naval effort on track. Many influential friends in and out of the administration let him know in no uncertain terms that he would be 'crazy or derelict' to enlist." J. L. Thompson 2013, 181.

entrepreneurial endeavoring to do anything to get to the front lines of the Spanish-American War and its brief window of glory in the summer of 1898. The future Congressional Medal of Honor winner (awarded posthumously) held a long-standing and profound fear of missing American military action. A minor controversy between Mexico and the United States regarding an American killed by Mexican authorities in the summer of 1886 impelled Roosevelt to request sounding the bugle. Writing from his ranch, Roosevelt pleaded with Secretary of War William Endicott to consider his proposal to mobilize "an entire regiment of cowboys" and begged Endicott to keep him informed of the possibility of war.[14] Long after his charge up San Juan Hill in 1916, when U.S. forces were chasing Pancho Villa in Mexico and some predicted war might break out, Roosevelt asked Secretary of War Newton Baker conditional permission to create and command a volunteer force if war did begin.[15] On the eve of America's entry into World War I in 1917, Roosevelt, almost sixty years old and less than two years before his death in January 1919, energetically sought to organize and lead another volunteer force to war. His possible death in action was on his mind, and while he wanted to avoid dying "if it could be legitimately avoided," the historian J. L. Thompson points out that in his correspondence at the time, he believed there would be utility in his death: "[Roosevelt] believed at this point the most good he could do the country would be by 'dying in a reasonably honorable fashion, at the head of my division in the European War.'"[16]

The war in which Roosevelt would be able to make the muster was the short war with Spain. After it started, during the call for volunteers McKinley created a special role for those with "special qualifications as horsemen and marksmen. Secretary Alger would not have to look for someone to be colonel of the first regiment, since the nation's most prominent frontiersman, horseman, and marksman was already pounding on his desk."[17] Roosevelt's counteroffer was to allow Leonard Wood the command, and he would be the unit's second in command. They convened in San Antonio to drill and train Roosevelt's Rough Riders for two weeks in May 1898 before racing to Florida.

What Roosevelt's experiences in the Spanish-American War do to help one understand his political destiny is a broad question, but they do demonstrate sterling evidence of the tenacity he showed to get into combat.

---

14. E. Morris 1979, 339.
15. J. L. Thompson 2013, 137.
16. J. L. Thompson 2013, 166, quoting a letter from Roosevelt to William Allen White, February 17, 1917. See also Morison 1954, 1152.
17. E. Morris 1979, 613. See also Coffman 2004.

The Rough Riders' train arrived to a traffic jam of units coming to the Florida embarkation site near Tampa. The train did not proceed, so they marched ahead in the night and awoke to a huge camp city with other units awaiting cargo ships. The Rough Riders then received disappointing news: not all of them could go, and the cavalry would have to leave their horses behind. Wood and Roosevelt tried to learn to which ship they were assigned, but chaos and disorganization made this impossible. One ship that was ready was assigned to two other units that were not yet in position, so Roosevelt "double-quicked the rest of the regiment up to the boat . . . and then [held] her against the [other units] who had arrived a little too late, being a shade less ready." From on board, Roosevelt nodded to the other units' protesting commanders yelling from shore. He "listened with polite sympathy to the protests . . . but his final argument was conclusive: 'Well, we seem to have it.'"[18] He then noticed two press photographers who could not find a vessel to board; he saw their value and welcomed them along.

Once they sailed around to the south shore of Cuba, they organized and marched to Siboney, just thirty miles west of Guantanamo Bay. They marched north into the brief Battle of Las Guasimas, Roosevelt's first true combat experience, before the Spanish retreated northward, with casualties on both sides. After a tough march toward Santiago, Roosevelt's day of martial glory arrived. July 1, 1898, found Roosevelt as acting colonel of the men because of Wood having to take someone else's place. Roosevelt and the unmounted cavalry had the task of taking Kettle Hill, and then they charged San Juan Hill. It was a bloody day; men were shot and killed around him, but he did not waver. He led his men ably and sealed his long-sought military reputation. Less than two months later, he was the Republican gubernatorial nominee in New York. On the campaign trail, he traveled with fellow Rough Riders, who referred to him as "The Colonel," putting his time in Cuba center stage. However, he had implicitly criticized other New York units when making his case that his unit would be three times the quality of any other.[19] Also, one of the units that had been "a shade less ready" at the transport ship in front of which Roosevelt jumped the queue was the New York 71st Volunteer Regiment, and they had not forgotten. Roosevelt won in a close election, and one biography points out that the counties in which he campaigned recently and hard had "paid dividends."[20] Republicans made the subsequent choice to place him on the presidential ticket with McKinley, and he strode to the stage with his Rough Rider hat on his head.

---

18. E. Morris 1979, 629.
19. Corry 2000.
20. Corry 2000, 275.

After he lost in the 1912 election, Roosevelt was a leading voice for military preparedness after the outbreak of war in 1914, but the nation remained unwilling to join the conflict in Europe. One of his allies advocating military readiness was his former commander of the Rough Riders, General Leonard Wood. If Roosevelt provided enthusiasm, Wood offered detailed plans. This effort was running directly counter to President Wilson's more pacific intentions, and both men debated with dueling speeches. Roosevelt offered endorsement for a new volunteer civilian group of veterans who could be ready to fight if the United States were attacked. Called the American Legion (not to be confused with the veterans group that would be created a few years later), it was meant to be an answer to what those opposing Wilson called the nation's unpreparedness. After the sinking of the *Lusitania*, lines continued to be drawn between neutral-minded pacifists in and outside the administration and the preparedness-minded men, exemplified by Roosevelt. By calling for a Swiss-style system of armed preparedness, he criticized pacifists as "mollycoddlers" and "neo-copperheads," but public opinion remained on the side of nonintervention even as war crept closer.[21] On the eve of the U.S. entrance into the war, Roosevelt begged again for permission to raise a Rough Rider–inspired division for quick deployment while the U.S. Army prepared for war. To justify his qualifications, he pointed out his experience in Cuba as well as his service as commander in chief. When Wilson demurred, Roosevelt made the same offer to Britain and France.

There was some will within the Republican Party to nominate Roosevelt in 1916, but support for Charles Hughes was overwhelming. The remnants of the Bull Moose Progressives did nominate Roosevelt, but their 1912 hero not only saw a certain Wilson victory in a third-party run but also had lost affection for the party. Once U.S. involvement in the war was imminent in 1917, Wilson appointed General John Pershing to command American forces, and Roosevelt wrote Pershing a congratulatory letter. He hoped that Pershing could find room for his sons as officers while regretting that his own physical condition at almost sixty years of age prevented him from serving and doing "work you would consider worthwhile on the fighting line (*my only line*)."[22]

Other Veteran Candidacies of the Early Twentieth Century

William Jennings Bryan, the Democratic nominee in 1896 and 1900, is unique for contesting one presidential election as a nonveteran and

---

21. J. L. Thompson 2013, 82, 123.
22. Quoted in J. L. Thompson 2013, 184 (emphasis added). See also Morison 1954, 1192–1193.

another after brief military service. After his loss to McKinley in 1896, the thirty-seven-year-old Bryan volunteered to serve in a Nebraska militia unit after the battleship U.S.S. *Maine* exploded in Havana. He wrote President McKinley after the war declaration seeking a military posting: "I hereby place my services at your command . . . and assure you of my willingness to perform to the best of my ability any duty to which you . . . may see fit to assign me."[23] He was left, however, to form his own regiment of Nebraska volunteers in May, was elected as its colonel, and raced to Florida by train to try to embark to Cuba. Their late arrival, and probably not intentional poor treatment by McKinley as some claimed, precluded their deployment. Bryan contracted typhoid fever in Florida rather than honors in battle.

General Leonard Wood attracted attention in 1920 as Republicans cast for a nominee to replace Woodrow Wilson. The primaries in this era were new and often featured candidates seeking to make a name for their candidacies in the only way they could outside the convention selection method that favored party elites. Wood sought the presidency and enjoyed some support in the not-quite-yet-relevant Republican electorate. Wood was a law-and-order candidate whose central political goals were Americanism, the Red Scare, and military preparedness. His army career stalled largely because of his alignment with Roosevelt during the Wilson administration. When World War I broke out, Wilson chose John Pershing to lead the AEF and assigned Wood to a much less prestigious post in Kansas to train solders, a "calculated humiliation."[24]

The Republican landscape after the war during Wilson's second term did not feature an obvious candidate for 1920, save for Theodore Roosevelt himself. Roosevelt's popularity among Republicans did not wane afterward, and as 1920 approached, he was perceived as a standard-bearer for the party. His death in the first week of 1919 left party elites searching for a new choice. There were sparks of interest in General John Pershing, who had led the AEF, but not enough to ultimately generate any interest at the nominating convention. Instead, Leonard Wood was a "formidable candidate," along with Warren Harding.[25] Indeed, Wood "seemed well on the way toward capturing the Republican nomination" as 1920 began.[26] However, Wood was not an ideal candidate. Party elites eyed him with suspicion, and he ran in the primaries without sensitivity to political machines within states, often upsetting native-son candidacies down ballot.

---

23. Kazin 2006, 86.
24. Pietrusza 2007, 170.
25. Hagedorn 1931, 2:326.
26. Lane 1978, 240.

Military preparedness and anticommunism suited his oratory and campaign well, but when domestic issues such as economic or social matters arose, he "became vague and platitudinous."[27] There was a "Wood Boom" in 1919, a sharp increase in his appeal for the office—"Wood Leagues" popped up in various states. That year in October, Wood led troops to referee a strike in Gary, Indiana. Given the incendiary nature of labor relations in the country then and the nastiness of this particular strike, the likelihood of troops having to use violence to maintain order was more than slight. Earlier that year, Wood used his soldiers to restore order after a race riot in Omaha, keeping his name in the newspapers.

Wood's second campaign manager believed that Wood needed to be presented to the electorate in a less obvious military guise. "A corps of writers sent out highly-colored romances and countless photographs of Wood intended to make the public forget that this man was a soldier, exhibiting a nonentity in civilian dress, the grim marks of struggle removed, the granite features softened to resemble some amiable small-town bank president."[28] Wood seemingly ignored his campaign manager. He stumped in uniform, much to the dislike of his handlers.[29] When Wood ran in the South Dakota primary, the governor at the time and strong ally, Peter Norbeck, found only one fault with Wood: he insisted on wearing his uniform on the campaign trail.

At the convention, Wood, as many failed candidates have, won early rounds of voting among the delegates. Perhaps Harding's perceptions of Wood were shared among Republican delegates at the 1920 convention, and perhaps to a broader mood in the United States collectively: "I think General Wood is very much of a fellow himself but I do think his military connection and his militaristic ideas are going to put an end to his candidacy."[30] It is likely Wood's failure to seize the nomination demonstrates that the country had military-general fatigue after the Civil War cohort, but his issues and campaigning were not helping his efforts either.

Alf Landon served as a lieutenant in the waning days of World War I.[31] He joined in October 1918 and shipped to Virginia for chemical-warfare training, but the armistice ended the war less than a month later. Landon was a civilian before Christmas of that year, returning home on December 9.

---

27. Bagby 1962, 29.
28. While it is an adoring biography, Hagedorn 1931 (2:339) is a helpful treatment of the man.
29. Thomas 1987, 289.
30. Quoted in Sinclair 1965, 125.
31. D. McCoy 1966.

Wendell Willkie's military service does not feature prominently in his biographies or accounts of his White House attempts. He finished law school before World War I began, but with American involvement in 1917, Willkie enlisted. During his induction into the service, an army clerk mistakenly inverted Willkie's actual first name, Lewis, with his middle name, a legacy he never remedied, and he lived the rest of his life as Wendell L. Willkie. He joined at age twenty-five on the same day that President Wilson asked Congress to formally declare war on Germany. He trained at Harvard University, Camp Zachary Taylor in Kentucky, and Fort Sill in Oklahoma before shipping to France in September 1918.[32] Arriving too late for action, he became an officer and worked as a lawyer in uniform. In one instance he "became a counsel for enlisted men involved in courts-martial," defending men who had gone AWOL.[33] He shipped overseas a month before the war's end, was not near combat, and returned a lieutenant in February 1919. He was disappointed that he never received captain bars though he was recommended for the promotion, and after discharge Willkie stated that he was "recommended for captaincy," having come close to promotion without obtaining it.[34]

Harry Truman spent more time in the armed forces than anyone else of the era, including Theodore Roosevelt. He joined the National Guard in 1905, drilling occasionally with his Missouri unit. It was a locally organized military unit, and it expanded Truman's contacts to include those who would become political allies later.[35] He left the ranks for a time but rejoined when World War I loomed, and his regiment was federalized and became the 129th Artillery. Truman led his men and practiced artillery drills in France initially and then was sent near the front. He fought artillery duels against the Germans on several occasions. Constantly shifting to reposition and gain tactical advantage, Captain Truman and his men saw much combat and danger before the end of the war. Truman expressed that his war experiences were essential for his political career. However, it is probable that his meaning was that it forged connections to a political network in Missouri that formed the basis for his ascent rather than his using his service as an electioneering theme.[36] Compared to many other cases in this book, Truman probably campaigned on his wartime combat experiences the least in proportion to the wartime danger he faced. After he had firmly established his political career as a U.S. senator in 1941, he

---

32. Neal 1984.
33. D. Johnson 1960, 51.
34. Barnard 1966, 54.
35. Hamby 1995.
36. Daniels 1950.

had not forgotten his time in the army. Immediately after Pearl Harbor, when he was approaching sixty years of age, he spoke to the army chief of staff and offered to rejoin the army to command a field artillery regiment, an offer that was declined.[37] So Truman, despite having fought in combat in World War I, did not see his military service become important in presidential election politics. His elevation to president without an election obviated most of the possibility of using biography to win a party nomination.

Because he ran in the 1950s against the man most associated with World War II, Dwight Eisenhower, it is somewhat awkward to place Adlai Stevenson with the men of the early twentieth century. Yet his age and type of service, and the lack of its role in elections, make him a better fit here. Stevenson left his studies at Choate in 1918 and joined the U.S. Navy as an enlisted man as World War I wound down, but he spent that time in training at Princeton. Less than two months after he was inducted, the armistice had been signed. His brief service in the navy was not salient in his political life, other than it may have done a minimal job to inoculate him against being a nonveteran running against Eisenhower.

These case studies demonstrate a pattern that makes the candidates in the first decades of the twentieth century different from the other postwar cohorts. Fewer of the men had military experience, and those who did made little of it. Excepting Theodore Roosevelt and a couple of doughboys, this era was a veteran hiatus, born of a diminished supply of veterans and military-candidate fatigue following the Civil War generation.

---

37. R. Donovan 1977.

7

The "Greatest Generation"

Dwight Eisenhower through Bob Dole

Smoke and fire upon the sea
Everywhere they looked was the enemy
The heathen gods of old Japan
Yeah, they thought they had the best of a mighty good man.
—JIMMY DEAN, "PT-109"

I'm very proud of that service and proud of the
opportunity to serve this country, and I hope that is the
last we will hear about a discussion of my military service.
—MICHAEL DUKAKIS, QUOTED IN LENTZ, "DUKAKIS"

If presidential candidates after Theodore Roosevelt rose to political prominence during an era in which military service was uncommon and lacked salience, the period following World War II was the opposite on both counts. That generation, or to borrow Tom Brokaw's oft-repeated honorific, the "Greatest Generation" in presidential politics, spans from Dwight D. "Ike" Eisenhower in 1952 to Bob Dole in 1996.[1] So prevalent were military veterans in presidential elections, it is far easier to mention the sole candidate who was not: Hubert Humphrey, denied entry into service on medical grounds. The remaining men with military service varied in their type of experience in uniform. Some of them, such as Jimmy Carter and Richard Nixon, joined the armed forces and served in noncombat roles. Lyndon Johnson had a tenuous claim on serving in uniform. Others lived through harrowing combat experiences during World War II. John Kennedy, George McGovern, George H. W. Bush, and Bob Dole each survived direct attacks from enemy forces and almost did not return alive to begin their political careers.

In one way, this era of presidential elections resembles the Antebellum era of partisan generals in regard to the number of veterans contesting elections. But it differs dramatically regarding the nature of the candidates'

---
1. Brokaw 1998.

service records. In the 1828–1864 period, those candidates with military service tended to have been army generals with partisan inclinations with a short span between their time in uniform and appearance on a presidential ballot. The World War II generation, however, generally consisted of low-ranking navy or army officers who served in their youth during the war.

The magnitude of World War II defies comparison to other wars. The conflict raged around the globe nearly a decade, chewing through resources, property, and lives. Some countries were rent whole; others, created from the ruins. The Soviet Union, Poland, China, France, and many other countries were hosts to the combat, and the war changed them fundamentally in enduring ways. And while American soil remained mostly untouched, the war was a seismic shock to the United States in terms of its economy, societal changes, subsequent role in world politics, and need to raise the largest army it has ever mobilized.

The country went on a total war footing until the end in 1945. A draft regime impelled a generation of young men into uniform, the country's factories made Sherman tanks instead of Buicks and DeSotos, women entered the workforce as "Rosie the Riveter," and citizens cultivated "victory gardens" on the home front because of enforced rationing of needed supplies for the front. Although the war had been going on overseas for several years, after the Japanese attacked Pearl Harbor in December 1941, the United States entered World War II mightily. Although it is frequently written that December 7, 1941, transformed a reluctant but nascent superpower from an isolationist one into the decisive ally of the war, the United States had already begun to prepare for the conflict. The war years presuppose a war footing that by the end inducted sixteen million men into uniform, created a massive war machine to engage in two theaters of strategic wars of survival, refitted industrial output from civilian to military purposes to create the "arsenal of democracy," and redefined life in many domestic spheres.[2]

The war ended in a staggered fashion: the European war ended in the spring of 1945, and Japan had surrendered by that fall. But the world did not transition from world war to global peace and harmony. The Soviet Union, devastated by the Nazi invasion it successfully repulsed, emerged from early setbacks in the war as a superpower in 1945 and a counterweight to postwar American hegemony in Europe and elsewhere. The Cold War was the struggle between the Soviet Union and the United States

---

2. Gropman 1999, 150.

from the end of World War II until the collapse of the USSR in 1991. It never involved direct hostilities. Instead, it was a contest of combat with proxy regional wars, a nuclear arms race, war planning, and burgeoning military budgets for both sides. The presidential candidates of this time period were veterans of a victorious war against fascism who ascended the political ladder during a tense Cold War against a major power, punctuated by two active wars: the United States played a dominant role within a United Nations coalition in the Korean War in the early 1950s and fought a protracted war against communist North Vietnam in the 1960s and 1970s.

World War II: Troop Strength and Means of Recruitment

While there are several ways to explain why all but one man in this group served in the armed forces, the sheer size of the army the United States fielded is the overriding one. Its ability to easily eclipse the preceding "Great War," World War I, in its magnitude, scope, stakes, and tragedies made World War II a global conflict with no equal in human history. From an American perspective, the war reshaped lives for many. The war healed the economy, grew the federal government, and brought women into factories to build a war machine. Perhaps the war's influence was felt most intimately by the approximately sixteen million who served in uniform during World War II. This number of men in the ranks was the historical peak for the size of the American military. Without engaging a realpolitik debate of America's role in the war, the cause for the U.S. entry into both spheres of the global conflict was understood then and now as a war against aggressive tyranny. The formal declaration of war against Japan came immediately after the attack on U.S. soil. Joining Great Britain and the Allies in the fight against Nazi Germany pitted the United States in a war against fascism, a war for liberation, and a war against a regime that sought global dominance. Hence, the men who served in American military uniforms in the 1940s took part in a moral crusade to liberate countries overrun by the Axis powers rather than to expand America's borders.

How large was the army the United States fielded? What share of America's young men entered the armed forces? About 16 million underwent the transition from civilian to military life and served in uniform during the war. The size of this cohort appears even larger when one considers that the 1940 census counted about 22 million males between the ages of fifteen and twenty-five, with many of them ineligible to serve for medical or other reasons. Further, there were 20.1 million white males in that same age range counted in the census, a more realistic number.³ Even though it is difficult to determine a perfectly accurate proportion of the generation who served in uniform, we can estimate a reasonably solid figure of 21.5 million—16.1 million World War II veterans and 5.7 million Korean War veterans—and subtract the approximately 150,000 Korean War vets who were also World War II vets.⁴ This leaves about 21 million men who served in uniform during these two conflicts. Using the 1940 census, we know that there were 30 million white males born between 1906 and 1935, an imperfect but usable range for "fighting age" during these two conflicts. Therefore, approximately 70 percent of the white men of this cohort were in the military. This proportion, even as a rough estimate, is staggering. No other period in American history saw so many men serving their country under arms. It is the largest number in absolute terms and even higher when one considers it as a proportion. If somewhere around three-quarters of that generation's men served in uniform, we should not be surprised to see a similar proportion of veterans as presidential candidates.

The U.S. military dramatically grew to a size sufficient to fight and win in two large theaters of operation through recruiting and conscription. Unlike soldiers in the conflicts of the nineteenth century, the fighting forces of World War II were almost entirely federal troops with inductees joining the regular U.S. Army instead of state-identified units. At the beginning of the war in Europe in 1939, the U.S. Army contained fewer than two hundred thousand men. After Germany's invasion of Poland, budgets and manpower at the Department of Defense increased. By the time of the British evacuation of mainland Europe in May 1940 and the capitulation of France a month later, President Franklin Roosevelt and his war planners had already formulated policies for federalizing and mobilizing the National Guard units and beginning a compulsory conscription program. Yet isolationists remained an obstacle to fully implementing these plans, so the mobilization prior to American entry into the war was a half measure, given the "hesitancies and doubts" about the direction of the war for

---

3. The draft rules did not initially allow induction of African Americans into the armed forces at the beginning of the war, and many southern political elites opposed black soldier suffrage. See Parker 2009. Given that the viability of a black presidential candidate was a remote prospect for much of the era, we can use a white-only figure to determine a ratio of service among the eligible.
4. U.S. involvement in the Korean War began only five years after the end of World War II, a short span that makes it difficult to disaggregate the veterans of each war from each other. It is possible that someone was age eligible for both conflicts and served only in the former conflict or the latter, or both. Given their proximity in time, one way to determine the ratio is to lump the conflicts together and use males in the population born roughly between 1910 and 1935 to encompass both conflicts. See Teigen 2006.

the United States.[5] Even so, before American entry into the war, draft registration and conscription had begun.

Once the Japanese attacked Pearl Harbor in December 1941, triggering the start of the war for the United States, the ranks swelled with volunteers and conscripts. The reasons for men to join the fight after Pearl Harbor differed from those for the previous World War. In one telling, the men who joined the campaigns against Germany and Japan in the 1940s were more resigned than the soldiers of the AEF of 1917–1918 who fought in Europe during World War I. In the cultural and literary descriptions of the AEF, the World War I doughboys, volunteers were more naïve and idealistic and more motivated by romantic notions of war than the more grim and determined 1940s soldiers. While easy contrasts obscure the fact that every war's soldiers face many inducements to join the armed forces, "in reality, a mix of enthusiasm, resignation, and resentment can be found among those serving in each of the wars."[6]

The draft of World War II was a federally directed institution, but it worked with local draft boards comprising community leaders. In this way, the 1940s Selective Service System, a euphemism for conscription to be sure, was not a complete reinvention of military recruitment but an extension of the political compromises of the 1917–1918 debates over conscription in World War I. The same issues that vexed the previous generation made policy making difficult for a draft system that was intended to be at least ostensibly fair and universal. Issues such as race, hardship, and deferments for fathers, husbands, college students, and clergy, along with selecting the appropriate age range for draft eligibility, made passing a draft bill in Congress difficult in 1940.[7] This political challenge in a presidential election year happened despite the fall of Poland, Denmark, Norway, and France to Hitler's Germany by the time of the bill's passage. The mechanism of its procedures included sixty-four hundred local draft boards and their classification of draftees into different draft categories, leading to a draft ordering. The federal government would then conduct a lottery that determined the order of induction, held on the eve of the 1940 election between Franklin D. Roosevelt and Wendell Willkie.

Why is it important to understand how recruits were inducted during wartime? The fact that a large proportion of able-bodied young men of a generation were draft eligible in what was potentially a war of national survival created a climate in which most were expected to take part in the

---

5. Weigley 1967, 435.
6. Kindsvatter 2003, 4.
7. Flynn 1993.

war effort. It seems that no rungs of the socioeconomic ladder were untouched by the need for wartime manpower. The sons from political families of privilege joined those from blue-collar families in creating the largest army the United States has ever fielded and the largest proportion of a generation ever put into war. Candidates such as George H. W. Bush, John Kennedy, and Gerald Ford were men raised in families of means and with political connections. Others, like Richard Nixon and Bob Dole, came from families of more humble origins and also served in the war.

The war ended with Allied victories over the Germans in Europe in late spring and Japan's defeat in August 1945. The war represented a total victory with unconditional surrenders of the Axis powers. The U.S. military faced the tricky problem of how to demobilize its large armed forces back into civilian life. The services quickly shrank. While not without logistical and political headaches due to a priority system that sent combat veterans and fathers home before others, more than two-thirds of the forces were returned to civilian life within a year after Victory over Japan (V-J) Day.[8] This opened the door for returning veterans to embark quickly on their next stages in civilian life, which for some was a public life.

American society's perceptions of World War II likely shaped the pattern of veterans in politics. If we suspect that a war's popularity might influence how veterans of that war would be seen by a voting electorate, World War II vets were seen as men who fought in a necessary war. To consider the popularity of World War II is different from trying to estimate the popularity of other wars in which the United States fought. When we speak of the high popularity of the Mexican-American War or the flagging support for the Vietnam War, we are discussing elective conflicts in which the United States chose to engage. The United States in World War II arguably faced a fight for survival after a surprise attack on a U.S. Navy base in 1941, and hence the conflict was certainly a popular war but in the sense that maintaining sovereignty is a popular idea. While isolationism was a potent political force constraining Roosevelt prior to the war, once the United States joined the war, the isolationist voices fell silent.

The attributes of war that fray public support are its duration, increasing casualties, loss in battle, and financial burdens.[9] American involvement in World War II was short compared to that in later American wars such as Vietnam, Operation Iraqi Freedom, and Afghanistan. Given the

---

8. D. Ross 1969.

9. There is long and vibrant scholarly debate on the ways that the American public reacts to wars, their duration, causes, financial costs, elite consensus, and battlefield outcomes. See, e.g., Berinsky 2009; Gelpi, Feaver, and Reifler 2009.

size and scope of the war and the number of forces deployed into Europe and the Pacific, there were low casualties. The VA reports that 291,557 died in combat and another 113,842 died in uniform away from combat. As a proportion of the total size of U.S. forces, the chances of a soldier returning from war were far better in World War II than for soldiers in the Civil War, the Mexican-American War, or earlier wars generally speaking.

Yet the financial burdens were very high. The U.S. Treasury wrote checks for more than 4.1 trillion dollars (in 2011 dollars). War spending represented an unprecedented and unrepeated share of the nation's gross domestic product, more than a third.[10] While defense costs have certainly skyrocketed since the end of the Cold War and the United States never got to enjoy a peace dividend thereafter because of post-9/11 military spending, these costs pale in comparison to the outlays needed to defeat Germany and Japan. A final ingredient in maintaining public support throughout the war despite the costs was durable consensus on war aims among political elites in Washington.

Service in World War II was the norm for most of the major-party candidates of this era. However, the logic emphasized early in the book not only places importance of the role of wartime experiences of presidential candidates in their youth but also stresses that conflicts that happen during this era offer a context in which candidates' past military experiences are viewed. Hence, it is important to understand how personal World War II experiences interact with the backdrop of what was happening in the Cold War: Korea and Vietnam. For the candidates running between 1952 and the 1990s, matters of foreign policy, especially regarding the rivalry with the Soviet Union, were salient to political elites as well as the electorate. As parties deliberated over candidates, they perceived that military service could signal that veterans of a past war could effectively handle present and future conflicts in Korea and Vietnam.

The conclusion of World War II in the Pacific Theater along with the rise of the Soviet Union as an international power set the stage for rival governments in northern and southern Korea. The division of the Korean peninsula at the 38th parallel was a decision codified in the final summer of the war in 1945 at the Potsdam Conference by the United Kingdom, the Soviet Union, and the United States. Tensions between North and South Korea rose after the war's end, and a new war broke out in 1950 when North Korean forces attacked Seoul and successfully occupied the capital. Through the newly created United Nations, the United States became the dominant power to bolster South Korea's defense and retook Seoul after

---

10. Daggett 2010.

some months. After a push northward in North Korea's territory, the war grew in scope as Mao Zedong ordered Chinese forces into North Korea to assist Pyongyang and directly engage American troops. After fierce battles, the sides stalemated in 1951, and by 1952 American involvement and the fate of the Korean War became a central issue in the presidential election between Dwight Eisenhower and Adlai Stevenson.

While direct American involvement did not commence until 1964, the conflict in Vietnam also stemmed from the realignment of borders, colonial legacies, and the occupations of World War II. Colonized by the French and then occupied by the Japanese, Vietnam started the postwar era divided, not unlike the Korean precedent. Unlike Korea, the situation in Vietnam would vex a string of presidents because of the length of the conflict and America's changing involvement there. Eisenhower, Kennedy, Johnson, and Nixon each made decisions about America's role in Southeast Asia and the war in Vietnam, though its role in presidential elections was trivial in 1956 and 1960 but grew in subsequent contests. U.S. support for South Vietnam became more than ideological when Eisenhower and then Kennedy authorized American military advisers to deploy and support the South Vietnamese regime in the 1950s and 1960s, but perceptions and awareness of Vietnam as an issue heightened sharply in August 1964. In early August, as the presidential campaign season began, the media reported on the Tonkin Gulf incident, writing that North Vietnamese naval vessels attacked the U.S.S. *Maddox* in international waters. This war became the backdrop of the 1968 and 1972 elections and would also have important ramifications for the baby boomer candidates.

Federalization, Partisanship, and Professionalization of the Military

Another factor that shapes the pattern of military veterans becoming presidential candidates regards the degree and way military institutions take on partisan tendencies in a given era. In the nineteenth century, party politics were entangled with the nation's military institutions. High-ranking officers, including top-tier generals such as Taylor and Scott, held and publicly maintained partisan associations. Staffing and appointment for military positions sometimes used partisan criteria, either to reward loyalty or provide a partisan balance to various units and deployments. Further, the largest conflict of the 1800s was a partisan war, a civil war between the states on constitutional matters of central political identity. After U.S. involvement in the Spanish-American War, military institutions underwent uneven but palpable progress in modernizing. After its first large-scale conscription regime toward mobilization for World War I, the armed forces had left its partisan entanglements largely behind as an artifact of the nineteenth century.

Three large changes to military institutions and how they plugged into civilian society were brought about by the 1903 Militia Act, World War I, and the National Defense Act of 1920.[11] With the World War I draft as a rough template that inducted men nationwide rather than relied on volunteer or local units, the draft of the 1940s inducted men into a massive war fighting machine, serving in an unequivocally federal force. World War II was therefore the culmination of many of the military reforms of the Militia Act and World War I period.[12] Thus, by the mid-twentieth century, the legacies of regionally based recruitment for war and overt partisan generals were largely left in the past.[13]

Political Changes outside War and Military: Parties and the Presidency Evolve

Another potential source for distinctive patterns of military veteran candidate nominations is the propensity of veterans to be civically active. Many observers have celebrated the civic health of the body politic once the World War II generation returned from the war. Brokaw's 1998 book, *The Greatest Generation*, gave them a name long after their contributions were obvious. The cohort that came of age in the Depression and World War II have been credited as civic-minded joiners. The veterans of the war especially have been lauded for returning, taking the G.I. Bill and going to college, and shaping society for the better.[14] One metric of this positive treatment is that World War II did not spawn a new, large veterans organization. One study of returning veterans in the 1940s compares them first to the embittered World War I veterans who had created the American Legion to help organize for fair treatment after their return, second to the Union troops who formed the GAR to win pensions, and third to the more elitist Society of the Cincinnati formed by the officer corps of the Revolutionary War. Davis Ross interprets World War II's lack of such a

---

11. Ekirch 1953.
12. Todd 1941.
13. There was still some shading of the lines between military and civilian duties among government agencies under the Roosevelt administration. Roosevelt directed military personnel to assist the alphabet soup of federal governmental agencies in accomplishing their goals. Army engineers helped Works Progress Administration (WPA) facilities and flew the civilian airmail routes.
14. Brokaw 1998; Putnam 1995; Bennett 1996; Mettler 2005.

new, aggrieved group of veterans as a policy success story.[15] While certainly not without bumps and missteps, plans for the huge and rapid return of millions of young men stateside anticipated their needs.

The rise of binding presidential primary elections is another source of change for military veteran presidential nominations. America's political parties had wrestled with how to choose their candidates in the beginning after Washington's reelection. Aside from Election Day itself, party nominating conventions became the most important events in American democracy because they choose the candidates who would compete for the presidency; there was no other path to the White House outside the major-party structure. As they did in the nineteenth century, the national conventions convened in large part to select their presidential and vice presidential candidates. Some states in the early twentieth century began adding a small wrinkle to the process of choosing candidates, a development that would become the most important step toward the decision by the 1970s: primary elections. For the parties during this period of 1952–1996, states held primaries, and how much they shaped the nomination increased dramatically.

Unlike the parties' nomination decisions of the Antebellum era that chose famous generals to enter politics at the top, parties after World War II tended to reward men who worked their way up the political totem pole. Most of the party nominees had started their political ascent by winning U.S. House seats, moving to statewide office, and then entering the White House chase. The only candidate to skirt the partisan ladder was Eisenhower, who entered presidential politics the way that his nineteenth-century antecedents did: prominent generals entered national standing through war and made a lateral entry without a legacy of partisan identity. The earliest electoral efforts of the others tended to feature their military service record, and for many of them, the experience was very recent.

Post–World War II Major-Party Nominees

The individual case studies detail the candidates' military records as the electorate generally would have known them, characterize how that service played a role in the candidates' pre-presidential electoral experiences, and then describe how military service emerged as a theme or story in candidates' presidential campaigns.

---

15. D. Ross 1969. He does not explain, however, what the continued existence and reinvigoration of the American Legion meant.

The candidates, listed in Table 7.1, are organized into three categories that exhibit distinctive ways that military service factored into presidential candidacies. Dwight Eisenhower represents the only general of the era. Next is the mainstay of this era: brief wartime officers who used military experience to characterize their service in initial, pre-presidential electoral efforts. This group includes John Kennedy, Richard Nixon, Lyndon Johnson, Gerald Ford, George H. W. Bush, and Bob Dole. The third group includes candidates who also served, but for various reasons their

TABLE 7.1 ELECTIONS OF THE POST–WORLD WAR II ERA

Election year	Candidate	Party	Veteran type	Military service
1952	*Dwight Eisenhower*	R	Career general	Commander of Allied forces, World War II
	Adlai Stevenson	D	Common vet	Brief World War I service
1956	*Dwight Eisenhower*	R	Career general	Commander of Allied forces, World War II
	Adlai Stevenson	D	Common vet	Brief service, World War I
1960	Richard Nixon	R	Common vet	Navy supply officer, World War II
	John Kennedy	D	Combat vet	Navy, World War II, *PT-109*
1964	Barry Goldwater	R	Common vet	Army Air Forces pilot, World War II
	Lyndon Johnson	D	Common vet	Navy liaison and observer, World War II
1968	*Richard Nixon*	R	Common vet	Navy supply officer, World War II
	Humbert Humphrey	D	Nonveteran	None
1972	*Richard Nixon*	R	Common vet	Navy supply officer, World War II
	George McGovern	D	Combat vet	Army Air Forces bomber pilot, World War II
1976	Gerald Ford	R	Combat vet	Navy officer, World War II
	Jimmy Carter	D	Common vet	Navy submariner, post–World War II
1980	*Ronald Reagan*	R	Common vet	Public affairs officer, World War II army reserve
	Jimmy Carter	D	Common vet	Navy submariner, post–World War II
1984	*Ronald Reagan*	R	Common vet	Public affairs officer, World War II army reserve
	Walter Mondale	D	Common vet	Enlisted, army, Korean War
1988	*George H. W. Bush*	R	Combat vet	Navy torpedo bomber pilot, World War II
	Michael Dukakis	D	Common vet	Army, postwar South Korea
1992	George H. W. Bush	R	Combat vet	Navy torpedo bomber pilot, World War II
	Bill Clinton	D	Nonveteran	None
1996	Bob Dole	R	Combat vet	Army officer, World War II
	Bill Clinton	D	Nonveteran	None

Note: Winners are italicized. D = Democratic Party; R = Republican Party.

military service never became an important or secondary part of their electoral identity: Barry Goldwater, George McGovern, Jimmy Carter, Ronald Reagan, Walter Mondale, and Michael Dukakis. Only Hubert Humphrey, denied military entry for medical reasons, is omitted from consideration. (Adlai Stevenson and Bill Clinton are included in the table because of their candidacies in 1952, 1956, 1992, and 1996, but Stevenson substantively belongs with the early twentieth-century cases and Clinton with the Vietnam cases.)

General Dwight "Ike" Eisenhower

In contrast to the other men of this era, Eisenhower's candidacy and nomination depended entirely on his generalship of the Allied war effort. The first World War II veteran of the political era following that massive war to contest a president election differed substantially from the others who followed. In Americans' eyes, Dwight David Eisenhower won the war. An unassuming man from Kansas, Eisenhower rose in the army to command Allied forces to victory in World War II. He graduated from West Point before World War I but was disappointed that the armistice ended the war before his tank unit was to deploy. Between the wars, Eisenhower's military career was not marked by rapid promotion, but he served on the staffs of many high-ranking generals, including Douglas MacArthur. Some of his political skills likely improved in these years, as he had been a speechwriter for MacArthur. After Pearl Harbor and America's entrance into the war, Eisenhower led campaigns to push back German advances in North Africa and Italy. In 1944, he planned and led the Normandy invasions to retake mainland Europe. His name was universally known, and he enjoyed wide respect and acclaim for his leadership during the war. He would also become the first and last professional general to win a major-party nomination since the nineteenth century. Quite simply, "he was a war hero with a shiny reputation whose name was a household word throughout the country."[16]

He entered politics at the top, unlike most presidential candidates of the twentieth century. Entering politics at the presidential-election level has benefits and costs related to partisan identities and track records on the issues. Five years before the election, Gallup polled the nation about Eisenhower and asked respondents if they regarded General Eisenhower as a Republican or as a Democrat. About a fourth of the electorate believed each category, while the majority did not know Eisenhower's political pref-

---

16. DeSantis 1953, 148.

erences.[17] Even before the Normandy invasion of 1944, Eisenhower had been courted to run for president. The seriousness of this entreaty is not certain, but Eisenhower wrote that Harry Truman sought Eisenhower to run for president with Truman as vice president.[18] The ability to remain above the political fray can be an advantage to a potential presidential candidate. Eisenhower made no votes for or against legislation, distancing him from potential political baggage. His political ambiguity was an asset. Not known as a staunch Republican, Eisenhower entered politics from the middle. His appeal was not directly and solely a reflection of his time and success while in the U.S. Army; however, his command experience contributed to a hero status, casting him as a "man of integrity and sincerity," as well as a man with demonstrated success.[19]

Eisenhower was a reluctant presidential candidate. He did not fit the typical mold of a politically ambitious office seeker. After the war, he temporarily retired, was chosen to lead Columbia University, and then took leave from that role to be the supreme commander of the nascent North Atlantic Treaty Organization (NATO). Eisenhower believed that NATO was important to foster European peace and stability, and he had to excuse himself from the presidency of Columbia more than once to lead its development. These experiences did not come across as typical pre-presidential posturing or positioning, such as running for statewide office to build and demonstrate electoral viability.

Eisenhower's candidacy in 1952 placed the general in a contest with Robert Taft, the man conventional wisdom would have predicted as the Republican nominee before Eisenhower's entry. Before Eisenhower became the Republican's standard-bearer in the 1952 general election, his supporters had to convince the Republican Party that he was the better choice over "Mr. Republican" Robert Taft.[20] Taft was a well-known senator from Ohio, son of former president William Taft, and he long held presidential aspirations. He had dueled with Wendell Willkie in 1940 and Thomas Dewey in 1948, losing in both attempts. Taft earned the "Mr. Republican" name because he had been a chief antagonist to Roosevelt's New Deal policies in the 1930s and placed himself ideologically to the right of the moderate Eisenhower. While Taft's family was not one with a "longstanding family tradition of active military service," he volunteered for World War I but was turned away because of his eyesight.[21] As tensions

---

17. Saad 2016.
18. Scheele 1987.
19. Converse and Dupeux 1966, 344.
20. Patterson 1972.
21. Wunderlin 2005, 16.

heightened in Europe and the Pacific in the 1930s, Taft had also been a leading isolationist voice prior to Pearl Harbor.

Internal letters and documents among those in the campaign and those underwriting the "Draft Eisenhower" movement had commissioned pilot polls showing Eisenhower leading Taft by wide margins.[22] The public's affection toward Eisenhower was not brand new in 1952. His appeal to the electorate as a potential political aspirant came well before the 1952 election.[23] He refused to identify with either major party in the 1948 contest and flatly refused to enter the race, but he was immensely popular in the years after the end of the war in 1945. Despite this early appeal, Eisenhower did not allow his organization to officially file for New Hampshire's Republican primary contest until January 17, 1952.[24]

In public communications, Eisenhower's rank is frequently mentioned, or "General" is substituted for his name. Newspaper accounts commonly used the shorthand of "Governor Stevenson" versus "General Eisenhower" in the 1952 election. Eisenhower's campaign appeared to spend much energy and messaging on portraying him as a civilian in addition to his time in uniform and reminding the electorate of his rank and martial experiences. Some television, radio, and print spots did make explicit connections between Eisenhower's wartime successes to win votes, for example, juxtaposing "V-E Day" (Victory in Europe Day) with "Election Day."[25] One Republican-commissioned magazine ad in particular used an image of soldiers serving in Korea rather than Eisenhower's military biography for parrying Stevenson and the Democrats. Stevenson's campaign slogan, "You never had it so good," was cynically reworded to "They never had it so good" in the ad. The caption fit with an image of two bedraggled G.I.s in a foxhole with helmets and rifles: "What? We've never had it so good? COME INTO MY FOXHOLE AND SAY THAT!" With the increasingly unpopular Korean War as the Democratic Party's largest weakness, the ad attempted to use the Democrats' slogan against them.[26]

Democrats raised the specter of a military man assuming power and disrupting the tradition of civilian authority. In an apparent turnaround from his earlier warm feelings about Eisenhower, Harry Truman stated on a few occasions on a whistle-stop tour that "professional generals should not be president. . . . A man who spends all his life in the army can't pos-

---

22. Letter from Robinson to Eisenhower, January 15, 1952, William E. Robinson Papers, Dwight David Eisenhower Presidential Library, Abilene, KS.
23. Hyman and Sheatsley 1953.
24. David, Moon, and Goldman 1954, 30.
25. Jamieson 1984.
26. Magazine advertisement, "1952 Campaign and Election—Republican National Committee—Printed Material" Folder, Dwight David Eisenhower Presidential Library.

sibly learn the business of political life."[27] On October 8, 1952, late in the campaign, Adlai Stevenson spoke in Wisconsin. In his Milwaukee speech, Stevenson criticized the Republicans with an embedded barb that Eisenhower was an empty military shell: "The Republican strategy becomes increasingly clear. The political hucksters of the Old Guard have now a nice, new, fancy, khaki-colored package. They have an honored name and a trick slogan."[28] Eisenhower's pick for vice president, Richard Nixon, heard Stevenson's comments and replied, "We would rather have a 'khaki-clad president' than one clothed in state department pinks."[29] Democrats ran a series of print ads hoping to blunt the electoral value of Eisenhower's military experiences. One depicted Eisenhower astride a large Trojan horse with Joseph McCarthy, Taft, and others climbing aboard, using military themes to visually assert that electing Eisenhower would also bring in less popular elements of the GOP.[30] Beyond fears of electing a military man to the top civilian job, the other Democratic thrust against Eisenhower that had some resonance was instilling "doubt that Eisenhower as President was wholly his own man," meaning he would be a puppet for right-wing elements because of his naïveté in politics.[31]

Eisenhower's campaign team prepared a document that listed sometimes-heard criticisms of the general's wartime performance and detailed responses.[32] For example, some claimed that it was Eisenhower's fault that the Allies were "mousetrapped" in Berlin after the war, necessitating the Berlin Airlift, and that he did not move fast enough to capture Berlin, which allowed the Soviet forces to seize territory.[33]

In private letters, Eisenhower also considered concerns about a general in politics. He thought deeply about the implications of a high-ranking general like himself entering partisan politics at the highest levels. In a private letter to his sponsor and friend Bill Robinson he reflected precisely on the civilian-military problem, noting that "there is no individual anywhere who has struggled longer and harder to keep the political affairs and the military affairs of our country completely separated and to make certain that the military, neither through individual or group action,

---

27. Truman 1952.
28. "Democratic Presidential Nominee" 1952, 5.
29. Nixon 1978, 110–112.
30. Jamieson 1984.
31. Campbell et al. 1960, 57.
32. Citizens for Eisenhower, "Controversy over Eisenhower's Role in the Final Phase of the Defeat of Germany," April 23, 1952, p. 1, "Eisenhower Campaign, 1952—Literature" Folder, Box 5, Maxwell M. Rabb Papers, Dwight David Eisenhower Presidential Library.
33. Another jab came from Stevenson in Indianapolis on September 26, 1952: "From what I've seen I'm not persuaded that either their education or experience or inclination is the best insurance of thrift with public funds."

could seek to dominate the civil power." Referring to a previous statement, he continued: "When I felt forced last January to make the statement that I did, with an eye both to the still somewhat fearful populations of Europe and to my prior promises not to repudiate American friends in the political world, I felt that I could thereafter remain quite aloof from political turmoil." Thus, Eisenhower became aware of the irony that underlined the fears of a general-turned-president: "It did not occur to me that I might, myself, become sort of a symbol of unjustified intermingling of politics and military activity. I seem to have miscalculated a bit somewhere along the line."[34]

The Eisenhower-Nixon campaign of 1952 piloted what it claimed internally to be the first preplanned presidential campaign. In the summer before the conventions, Eisenhower's team formulated an overarching plan comprising campaign themes and strategy. The internal name for this short plan was "Document X." The successful 1952 election of Eisenhower followed this scripted, centrally led effort, ostensibly an innovation in the history of presidential campaigns. It was a schedule of candidate visits and themes that explicitly attempted to use a "candidate-centered approach."[35] Much of what is in the plan is unsurprising. Recognizing that Democrats substantially outnumbered Republicans in the electorate, the Eisenhower campaign placed much importance on what we would today call Independents as well as those who typically abstain in elections. Just as any challenger campaign does, the Eisenhower team sought to attach the Democratic nominee Adlai Stevenson's name directly to the unpopular Truman administration.

There is a lot of attention in Document X's campaign paid to cutting-edge technology, which in 1952 were television spots. Also expected in the plan is an emphasis on keeping down-ballot Republicans, those running for governor or Congress, in at least loose harmony. Much as they always do, the campaign also plots a path to victory by recognizing critical states to win to accumulate the necessary Electoral College votes, which is stock-in-trade for presidential victory.[36] Last, the plan fixated on the lifeblood of electioneering, raising and spending money. What is surprising about the plan is that it makes only the most oblique references to the candidate himself. It occasionally makes distant characterizations of the men, such as, "Both candidates have warm and winning personalities."[37] Yet for all

---

34. Letter from Eisenhower to William E. Robinson, March 26, 1952, "Series II" Folder, William E. Robinson Papers, Dwight David Eisenhower Presidential Library.
35. Bowen 2011, 162.
36. Shaw 2006.
37. "Document X," p. 13, Box 10, Robert Thomas Humphreys Papers, Dwight David Eisenhower Presidential Library.

its attention to the tactical view of which states to visit when and the extended discussion of strategy and theme, the plan could be for any candidate. There is nothing specific to Dwight Eisenhower, his background, his experiences, or his status as a revered general. If those who mapped out the Republican plan for victory in 1952 perceived Eisenhower's military background as an asset, they did not reveal it in this plan or connect their campaign themes to it.

The Eisenhower campaign innovated television campaign advertisements. While the Stevenson campaign ads tended to be straightforward renditions of the candidate giving speeches, the Eisenhower ads adapted to the new environment of television marketing. One spot was a question-and-answer format where people representing average citizens asked questions followed by a quick criticism of the incumbent party and a short solution. These "Eisenhower Answers America" ads intended to undercut the Democrats' claims that "You never had it so good!" as well as reinforce the image of Eisenhower as a down-to-earth, reasonable, and likable individual.[38] Some ads bordered on puerile: "Ike for President" was a filmed cartoon with "animation by the Disney studios" coupled with the iconic "I Like Ike" jingle in multiple layers of vocal harmonies.[39] Eisenhower himself likely believed the ads beneath his dignity. Eisenhower stated, "To think an old soldier should come to this," in reaction to the cartoon ads that marketed the general the same way that Madison Avenue advertised soap and cigarettes.[40]

Because television was not as ubiquitous as it would soon become, campaigns still relied heavily on print advertising. One prominent example was a biographically oriented ad to paint Eisenhower in a flattering light, giving a page to Eisenhower's various identities. There was a page for "Ike the Boy," which showed images from his upbringing in Kansas; one for "Ike the Citizen"; and another for "Ike the Administrator, Statesman, and Diplomat," which highlighted the war years and included photos of him in and out of uniform. But as an example of how the campaign worked to soften Eisenhower's military identity by portraying his public service side, the broadsheet notably lacked an "Ike the General" or "Ike the Commander" page.[41] If Eisenhower's identity as a military general and war hero was a focus for both the Eisenhower campaign and the Taft and

---

38. Jamieson 1984, 83.
39. Diamond and Bates 1992, 59.
40. Quoted in J. Smith 2012, 544.
41. "The Story of Dwight D. Eisenhower," "Campaign Literature 1952" Folder, Ione Ulrich Sutton Papers, Dwight David Eisenhower Presidential Library.

Stevenson campaigns, an important question is whether the public saw the Eisenhower candidacies through a military lens.

Unlike past elections in which generals were seeking the presidency, it is possible to find out who in the electorate felt positively and negatively about Eisenhower's time in the armed forces. The birth of quality public opinion polling in the mid-twentieth century means that we can begin to use these polls to infer public attitudes. The 1952 American National Election Study (ANES) asked respondents a series of questions unlike most polling questions. Instead of a query that forced respondents to choose among various options about why they liked or did not like a particular candidate, the 1952 ANES included open-ended questions pertaining to what potential voters thought about candidates.[42] In Eisenhower's case, potential voters in the 1952 election did report feelings about the Republican candidate's experiences in uniform.[43] A 2009 study compared the number of respondents in 1952 who saw Eisenhower's "Military service, war record" as a positive attribute of the candidate to those who saw his service as unfavorable.[44]

Many considered Eisenhower's time in the army a boon, and others considered it problematic. Among this representative sample, Eisenhower's wartime experiences and military career did not seem to give him an advantage. While many found it a positive asset for the presidential candidate, even more expressed that it was a reason to dislike him. Contemporary accounts of the same data also make clear that among the small number of negative mentions for Eisenhower, the most common objection to him was that he was a "military man."[45] Looking only at voters in the sample, 26 percent cite Eisenhower's time as a general as a reason to vote against him; while 25 percent said it was a reason to support him. This difference confounds the often-assumed conclusion that Eisenhower defeated Stevenson because he was a wartime general.

But what about the party identity breakdown of those who expressed favorable and unfavorable feelings toward Eisenhower's military experience? It is plausible and perhaps intuitive that the reason the ANES found more 1952 respondents expressing negative impressions about

---

42. Specifically, respondents were asked to say what they thought was favorable about a candidate, with any reason being acceptable. The question was repeated up to five times to allow respondents to include multiple reasons for favorable impressions. The same process was repeated for respondents to list what they did not like about candidates. In both cases, responses were later coded and grouped into similar categories. The survey data set is available at http://www.electionstudies.org/studypages/1952prepost/1952prepost.htm.
43. Campbell et al. 1960.
44. Norpoth 2009, 527.
45. Campbell, Gurin, and Miller 1954, 61; Campbell et al. 1960; Converse and Dupeux 1966.

The "Greatest Generation" 159

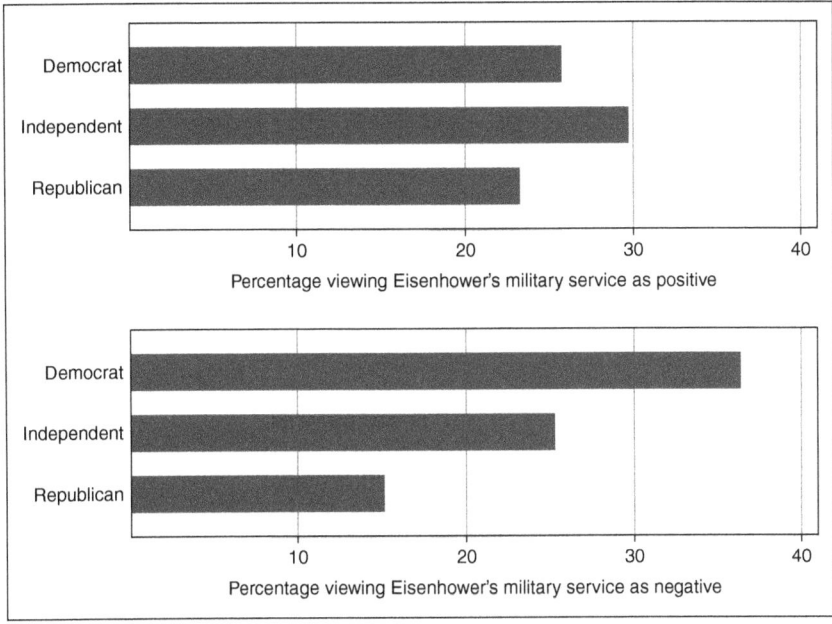

Figure 7.1 Respondents' views on Dwight Eisenhower's military service in the lead-up to the 1952 presidential election, by party identification. Data source: American National Election Study, 1952.

Eisenhower's war record and military service is that Democrats outnumbered Republicans in the 1950s. Yet closer examination of both party identification and the way respondents reported voting that year reveals a more complex pattern of party allegiance and impressions of Eisenhower's past.

This analysis uses the same questions on the 1952 ANES.[46] Figure 7.1 compares the percentage of voters who expressed favorable and unfavorable views of Eisenhower's military experience, broken down by how that person voted. From whom did these favorable and unfavorable mentions come?

Democrats who voted that year were slightly more likely (26 percent) to believe that Eisenhower's military record was a reason to support him

---

46. Respondents were asked, "Is there anything in particular about Eisenhower that might make you want to vote for him?" and "Is there anything in particular abut Eisenhower that might make you want to vote against him?" The pollster simply wrote down the response. If the respondent had an answer, the pollster noted it and then asked, "Anything else?" up to four more times for each question. In essence, each person had an opportunity to share up to five reasons to vote for or against Eisenhower. A response that Eisenhower was "a military man," had a "a successful record in Europe," or "was a successful general," was tabulated as either favorable or unfavorable, depending on which question it answered.

than Republicans (23 percent). Independents were the most likely (29 percent) to express that Eisenhower's military time was an electoral asset. While counterintuitive, the fact that Democrats rather than Republicans were willing to see Eisenhower's generalship as a boon might be that they sought reasons to express a positive aspect of him that was nonpolitical. Republicans, perhaps attempting to avoid concerns of nominating a military man, sought other reasons that Eisenhower deserved support. When considering the party breakdown for those who felt the general's time in service was a reason to vote against him, party identification acts more as one would expect: Democrats were substantially more likely than Independents to see Eisenhower's military time as a problem and much more so than Republicans.

We can break down the same comparison of favorable and unfavorable mentions of Eisenhower as a military man by vote choice. Figure 7.2 shows the proportions of favorable and unfavorable Eisenhower military mentions among those who voted for him and for Stevenson. Voters who chose Eisenhower saw his time in uniform as a plus more often than Stevenson voters, approximately 27 to 21 percent. The gap between those who cast ballots for Eisenhower and those who voted for Stevenson is much more

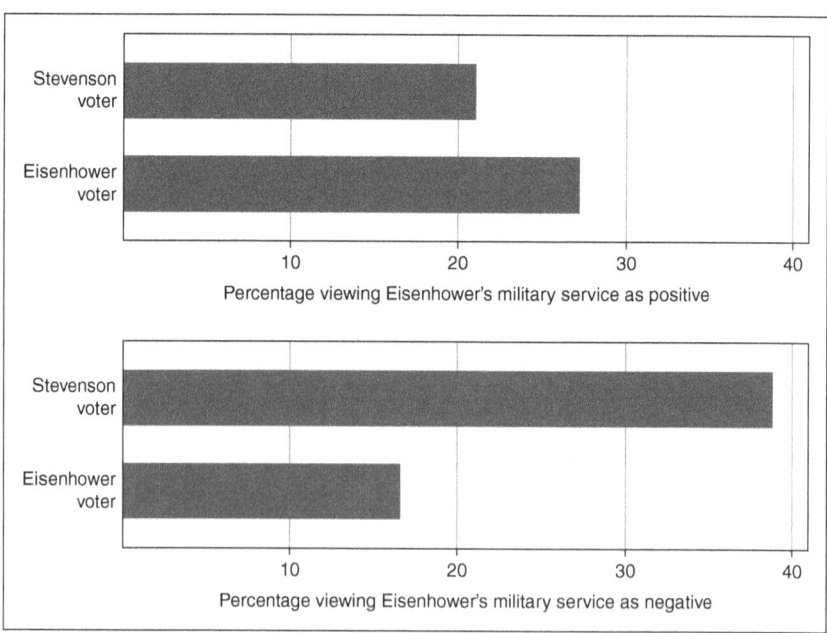

Figure 7.2 Respondents' views on Dwight Eisenhower's military service in the lead-up to the 1952 presidential election, by vote choice. Data source: American National Election Study, 1952.

stark when they were asked about reasons to vote against Eisenhower: 39 percent of Stevenson voters cited Eisenhower's time in the army as a reason to vote against him, while fewer than half that number, 17 percent, did so among Eisenhower voters. Taking both party allegiance and vote choice together, it is clear that seeing Eisenhower's military time as a negative is more polarizing than seeing it as a positive.

If military service as a central facet of a candidate's biography engenders some voters in an election year to see it positively and others negatively, why did the Republican Party nominate a general? Indeed, this question is a reexpression of the central question of this book: If voters in general elections do not seem to be moved very much by a candidate's war record, why are there so many veterans in our presidential elections? An important essay compared two military heroes vying for their nation's highest political office, Eisenhower in 1952 and Charles de Gaulle in 1958, expressing through comparison the importance of the "acclaim which a populace reserves for its conquering generals."[47]

Even though the electorate comprised more Democrats than Republicans in the era of the New Deal and more potential voters viewed a "military man" as a negative rather than a positive, Eisenhower won the 1952 election handily and the 1956 rematch by an even greater margin. The first reason for the negative mentions involves party identity. Democrats who knew they would vote for Stevenson, when pressed to list why one might vote hypothetically for Eisenhower, relied on a nonpolitical, biographical attribute of the man to avoid any issue or ideological dissonance. But when offered to come up with a reason to vote against him, Democrats and Stevenson voters were very likely to mention Eisenhower's military role. The views of Eisenhower as a military man changed between his two elections in 1952 and 1956. The salience wore off, but the negative dropped off much more precipitously than the positive.

Eisenhower enjoyed another advantage over Stevenson in 1952 precisely because of his time as a general. His military service offered more credibility on the most important foreign policy question of the election. Close to Election Day, Eisenhower delivered his most memorable campaign speech in Detroit. Eisenhower's declaration that he would seek to end the Korean War was denounced by Stevenson as a "slick plan." "I shall go to Korea," Eisenhower succinctly stated on October 24, to bring about an "early and honorable" conclusion to the war. Korea was among the chief obstacles for the incumbent Democratic Party to keep the White House, and Eisenhower's bold intention to go to Korea himself less than a

---

47. Converse and Dupeux 1966, 293.

fortnight before Election Day elevated the issue that troubled Stevenson to the fore. Eisenhower's speech was powerful; "coming from a bona fide military hero, the pledge was political gold."[48] Yet Eisenhower's appeal in 1948 should remind us that the issues of 1952 were not essential to the Eisenhower candidacy. If we entertain the supposition that Eisenhower would have won the 1948 presidential election, we must also grant that we should not overstate the role that "Korea, Communism, and Corruption" played in Eisenhower's 1952 victory.[49]

Eisenhower's role as the commander of Allied forces in World War II made him the Republican nominee. In some ways reminiscent of the nineteenth-century generals, Eisenhower was a well-known wartime general who returned to a thankful country that elevated him to the White House, not unlike Washington, Jackson, or Taylor. Yet we can see that his military experience forced his campaign to walk a fine line between extolling his service and sacrifice while calming fears of a military-minded takeover of civilian politics. Given the parity between positive and negative mentions in survey data from 1952, those cares were probably well founded.

Brief Wartime Officers Who Used Military Service to Climb the Political Ladder

Eisenhower's stature as a senior general who won the war indelibly linked him to the World War II victory. The other men who served in the war and used it as a springboard for their political careers were much younger. Eisenhower graduated from West Point before some of the following men were born. John Kennedy, Richard Nixon, George McGovern, Lyndon Johnson, Gerald Ford, George H. W. Bush, Robert Dole, and the others served in different capacities, but they all spent a short time in uniform during the war and returned home to start public life.

Of the presidential candidates who have sought the country's highest office, John Kennedy, along with Jackson, Harrison, Eisenhower, and Theodore Roosevelt, had political candidacies steeped in a compelling war story. The *PT-109* story is well known: the small torpedo boat Kennedy piloted was destroyed by a Japanese ship, yet he was a hero and survivor, helping his men to safety and rescue in the South Pacific. Kennedy explicitly played on his military service for various purposes in his rapid political ascent. It is important to briefly characterize Kennedy's military service in World War II and describe whether and how that service was

---

48. Jamieson 1984, 49.
49. Hyman and Sheatsley 1953.

salient in his political fortunes when running for the House, Senate, and White House.

John Kennedy was the second son of Joseph Kennedy Sr., an isolationist voice before the war began. Joseph Kennedy, a friend of Franklin Roosevelt, was the ambassador to Great Britain from 1938 until his resignation in 1940. He was politically incompatible with the administration, having supported Neville Chamberlain's appeasement policies and expressed pessimism about Roosevelt's policies in public. Two of Kennedy's sons were born in the 1910s and were of fighting age during World War II, Joseph Jr. and John. Both served in the U.S. Navy during the war in multiple capacities, both finding dangerous roles. Only John returned from the war. Many historical accounts have Joseph Sr. showing explicit and widely known intentions to use his financial and political assets to help propel Joseph Jr. to high political office, including the presidency. Joe Jr. became an aviator in the navy after American involvement in the war began, flying long-range bombers over the Atlantic to combat the German submarine threat. After two successful tours of duty on anti-U-boat patrols, Kennedy was eligible for safer stateside callings, but he declined them for a highly dangerous, experimental mission. To deal with heavily fortified German strategic targets, the U.S. military launched Operation Aphrodite. The United States was experimenting with remote-piloted unmanned bombers that were stripped of everything but explosives and only half-full gas tanks, to be flown over the channel and crashed directly into heavily defended targets. While these bombers could theoretically be directed remotely by radio signals once in the air, they still needed real pilots to get the bombers airborne. These pilots were to get the flying bombs aloft, get over the channel, point them at their targets, arm the explosives, switch control to the remote pilots, and bail out. However, Kennedy and his copilot were killed when the explosives detonated prematurely over England in 1944.

John was two years younger than his brother and also joined the U.S. Navy, but rather than fly over the Atlantic, he eventually became a skipper of Patrol Torpedo (PT) boats in the Pacific Theater.[50] Before he started his most known role in the war at the helm of *PT-109*, however, he had become an ensign in the Naval Reserve before the attack on Pearl Harbor in December 1941. Questions about John Kennedy's health are peppered throughout biographies of the man, with concerns about his spine, his stomach, Addison's disease, and other ailments. The back injuries from his youth may have presented challenges for Kennedy to be eligible for

---

50. He may have attempted to enlist in the army prior to his time in the navy in early 1941. See Blair and Blair 1976, 105.

military duty, but he joined all the same. U.S. Navy captain Alan Goodrich Kirk possibly pulled strings for both Joseph Jr. and John to join the navy. Kirk had been the naval attaché for Ambassador Kennedy at the U.S. embassy in London. In August 1941, John Kennedy applied to be an officer in the navy at age twenty-four. He was accepted as an ensign in the U.S. Naval Reserve.

He first worked in the office of naval intelligence, where Kirk brought him in; then he was transferred to a naval intelligence field office in South Carolina, and after a leave, reported to officer training at Northwestern University near Chicago. At this point, it appears that he volunteered for combat duty at sea and sought a role on small torpedo boats. After the officer training, he went to a navy installation in Rhode Island in October 1942 to start PT boat training. After completion, Kennedy's first post was as an instructor there, a situation about which he was not happy because many of his friends were heading to combat areas. It is possible that his medical issues kept him initially from combat duty. After about a month, Kennedy and others from the school were sent to Panama for patrol duties, but one secondary source reports that Kennedy reached out to Senator David Walsh from Massachusetts in an attempt to find a way into a PT squadron in the Pacific. He officially requested assignment to a "Motor ?Torpedo [sic] Boat Squadron now operating in the South Pacific" in February 1943.[51] Whether or not Senator Walsh had pulled strings or was even asked to do so, Kennedy was transferred to a PT boat squadron operating in the Solomon Islands by early 1943.

PT boats were small, around eighty feet long, and were intended to be flexible craft that could launch torpedoes at larger enemy ships or submarines and speed away. Another typical use of this type of vessel was to harass Japanese shipping operations. The normal crew on board was around a dozen sailors. Kennedy was the ranking officer in command of the *PT-109* after his February 1943 arrival at Tulagi Island in the Solomons, east of Papua New Guinea. Three months later, as part of an operation in the nearby Russell Islands, *PT-109* operated out of a forward, makeshift base. It was from here in August that the collision and dramatic rescue that was the basis for the Kennedy war story occurred. In the Blackett Strait in the middle of the night on August 2, 1943, near the volcano island of Kolombangara, Lieutenant JG John F. Kennedy was at the helm of *PT-109* with a crew of twelve others. The ship patrolled that area with two other torpedo boats that night because a day earlier the Japanese had bombed nearby American positions. The moonless night

---

51. Letter from Kennedy to naval chief of Bureau of Personnel, February 20, 1943, JFKPP-011-007, John Kennedy Presidential Library, Boston.

was dark, and Kennedy was running only one of the vessel's three engines, probably to reduce noise so the crew could hear enemy aircraft. Nonetheless, a fast-moving Japanese destroyer, *Amagiri*, suddenly loomed out of the darkness, bearing directly at the American boat. Without all three engines engaged, Kennedy did not have enough maneuverability to get *PT-109* out of the way. The small torpedo boat was about a fifty-ton vessel, while the destroyer weighed in at about two thousand tons, so the much larger *Amagiri* essentially plowed over *PT-109*. The encounter, while certainly destructive, was brief. Japanese vessels at that time and place were quite vulnerable to Allied air attacks during the day, so *Amagiri* was in a race. It had to get to safety before dawn, so it steamed on and did not follow up on the ramming attack.

The collision fatally crippled the torpedo boat, destroying its engines and weapons, and sent some of Kennedy's crew overboard. The fuel tanks spilled onto the wreckage and in the water, and the gasoline ignited, burning some of the sailors aboard and some in the water. Enough of the wreck stayed afloat, however, to provide a lifeline for the survivors. For the next few hours in the dark, Kennedy and other able crew members found those who had been thrown overboard by the collision and brought them back to the floating wreck. Two of the crew were killed in the collision, leaving eleven. Two had been badly hurt or burned, but life vests had kept them from drowning. By dawn, the survivors could see that they were far from land, and the possibility that the distant islands were held by the enemy was real. The wreck was unstable, so they devised a plan to lash life vests to a timber for some of the men. The most seriously injured crew member, Patrick "Pappy" McMahon, suffered from burns on his face, torso, arms, and legs and could not swim.

In what would probably become the core element of the Kennedy heroism story in August 1943, Kennedy alone carried McMahon ashore more than three miles across open ocean for at least the next four hours. Kennedy swam with McMahon on his back, towing him with a belt or strap from the burned man's life jacket in his teeth. He did the breast stroke, pulling his crewmate across the ocean, "occasionally swallowing water and coughing."[52] The other men were not strong swimmers or did not swim at all, so they worked together using the plank from the wreck to move slowly along. Kennedy's feat is even more impressive when considering he had been on alert for an extended period, under pressure, and survived a near-fatal ramming from an enemy destroyer. Kennedy had choked down salt water and gasoline in the initial rescue but swam

---

52. Tregaskis 1962, 117.

ahead with McMahon to beat the other men pushing the makeshift raft to shore.

After the survivors of *PT-109* made it ashore to the island, which had a diameter of one hundred yards, the next five to seven days were also a trying experience at survival from the elements, lack of provisions, the enemy, and the wounds suffered in the collision. The details of these subsequent days are many, but the short version is that Kennedy swam from their initial landfall to see if he could find a better spot that would be more likely to have food and make it easier for Allied rescue efforts to succeed. It was a difficult and dangerous week, but with important help from island natives and a secret message carved into a coconut shell, all eleven of the survivors were rescued and returned to their base of operations.[53] After the mission, collision, and rescue, Kennedy was awarded the Navy and Marine Corps Medal, a recognition of the noncombat heroism and danger that he faced.[54]

Another possible political use of the *PT-109* story, according to a more critical biography, was that partisan allies used the event to explain Kennedy's medical problems. The ramming had, according to the Kennedy version, exacerbated the back injury from college. Being in the water among the wreckage, choking on and swallowing gasoline, became the reason behind other ailments. Kennedy's health is disputed by scholars and others, but it is safe to state that he suffered from several nontrivial conditions, and it is reasonable to note that these medical pathologies were downplayed by his campaign and family. His back had been a problem for Kennedy from his youth, requiring repeated surgeries and treatments throughout his life. He reportedly suffered from a type of digestive disease, colitis, and was diagnosed with Addison's disease right after the war. The extent of Kennedy's medical issues, as well as the medications he required, were kept largely secret from the public.[55] Explaining Kennedy's back or digestive issues as being a product of the collision in the Pacific or swallowing the gasoline provided a reconnection to his war

---

53. Hersey 1944; R. Donovan 1961; Tregaskis 1962; Blair and Blair 1976. These accounts do not accord on all the facts. Joan and Clay Blair are the most skeptical of the near mythology, pointing out inconsistencies concerning some of the facts and questioning some of Kennedy's decisions. While noting that there is legitimate room to question the earlier and overflattering accounts, the point of this effort is to examine the influence of presidential candidates' biographies as the electorate generally understood them.
54. Joseph Kennedy Sr. complained to President Roosevelt personally that John had been recommended by his commanders to receive a medal two degrees higher than the Navy and Marine Corps Medal, but because Joseph Kennedy Sr. had been "persona non grata" in Washington by then, the "powers that be" punished him by giving the younger Kennedy a lesser medal. See Nasaw 2012, 574.
55. Altman and Purdum 2002.

service and heroism and gave a patriotic explanation for his conditions. Tregaskis, in a glowing account of Kennedy's navy experiences, wrote, "Probably the violent wrench of the collision had reactivated the old football injury."[56]

His narrow presidential election victory over Richard Nixon in 1960 was not the first time Kennedy relied on his *PT-109* heroics for electoral purposes. On returning stateside after his discharge from the navy, Kennedy was already being set up well for a congressional run, and his first campaign efforts used his military service early in his political career. He was not yet thirty years old in 1945 when he decided to run for the Boston-centered 11th congressional district. It was a Democratic stronghold, of course, so a vacancy within the party's ranks was needed for the young Kennedy. When James Curley made the move from the House to Boston's mayoral mansion, Kennedy charted his path into the opening. The narrative in historical treatments frequently asserts that Kennedy's war-hero credibility offsets possible liabilities: his youth and lack of political experience. He "had many assets as a candidate, but none more valuable than his record as a war hero."[57] Kennedy had organized a Veterans of Foreign Wars (VFW) post in Boston to be named in his elder brother's name in the spring before the primary, presumably attempting to marshal returning veterans' votes.[58] Not lacking financial muscle as a result of his father's substantial largesse, the Kennedy campaign could afford to mail large quantities of campaign literature. One such mailing excerpted John Hersey's article from the August 1944 issue of *Reader's Digest*, which was a condensed version of the original essay "Survival" that Hersey published in June of the same year in *New Yorker*.[59]

With the incumbent out of the way, Kennedy won the Democratic primary by a large margin on June 18, 1946, considering the wide field of ten, with 42 percent of the vote; the person in second place won 22 percent of the vote.[60] Kennedy won the general election in the substantially Democratic-leaning district easily in the fall. Kennedy's subsequent campaign efforts continued in this fashion. Kennedy decided to move to the upper chamber after winning reelection in 1948 and 1950. The Massachusetts 1952 Senate race was a contest between two war veterans. Kennedy challenged incumbent Republican senator Henry Cabot Lodge Jr., who was organizing Eisenhower's presidential race and would later be Nixon's

---

56. Tregaskis 1962, 121.
57. Nasaw 2012, 595.
58. Nasaw 2012.
59. Hersey 1944. The differences between the two versions of Hersey's essay are discussed in Hellmann 1997.
60. Our Campaigns, n.d.

running mate in 1960. Like Kennedy, Lodge had an impressive war record. He was elected to the U.S. Senate before the war and served two tours in the U.S. Army during the war in Europe, once as a senator and another after he resigned to rejoin the fight. He returned with combat decorations after the war in 1946 and resumed his political career by winning the Senate seat he had held before the war.

To contest the incumbent, Kennedy explicitly invoked his rescue of his shipmates after *PT-109*'s destruction in multiple electioneering efforts. One broadsheet-style leaflet took the form of a thin newspaper. The headline on the front page was "John F. Kennedy for United States Senator," with large print text saying, "He will do more . . . for the Nation, for Massachusetts, for New England" and "Here is your kind of man," along with a headshot. The first inside page had images and text telling the story of Kennedy and his rescue of the crew, under the banner headline "From the Proving Ground of War." Some of the quotations and explanations under the six images came from reporters, such as, "One of the great stories of heroism in this war," or were excerpts from the aforementioned John Hersey retelling in *Reader's Digest*. The images dominated the page, none larger than the central image: a realistic-looking pencil rendering of Kennedy swimming in the Pacific with the upturned PT boat in the background, a strap between his teeth attached tautly to McMahon.[61]

Another flier used by the campaign against Lodge was a small booklet titled "10 Reasons Why." This hand-sized booklet listed rationales to vote for Kennedy for U.S. Senate in 1952. In some of the explanations, Kennedy's wartime heroics are woven into the narrative. For example, the second reason is "He has moral courage," and the text opens with "His physical courage was proved in war. When his PT boat was sunk, Kennedy, although severely injured, helped save the lives of his shipmates. For this, he was decorated for bravery. . . . His moral courage was proved in his fight for housing for veterans." Another is "He has the persistence to see things through," and the descriptive text begins, "In 1947, Stan Allen wrote in the 'Army Times': 'While most of the young World War II veterans in Congress seem content to sit on their hands, look wise, act dumb and do nothing where vital veterans legislation is concerned, one among them at least is braving the slings and arrows of outrageous fortune to prove that even a freshman can fight.'"[62]

---

61. "John F. Kennedy for United States Senator," 1952, "Kennedy File—1952 Campaign" Folder, Box 10, Maxwell M. Rabb Papers, Dwight David Eisenhower Presidential Library.
62. "10 Reasons Why," 1952, "Kennedy File—1952 Campaign" Folder, Box 10, Maxwell M. Rabb Papers, Dwight David Eisenhower Presidential Library.

After unseating Lodge, Kennedy became the junior senator from Massachusetts, but his sights were already set on the big prize. A challenge for Kennedy's electoral prospects appeared when he sought the presidency eight years later that did not exist when he was trying to win over Massachusetts or its 11th district: his Catholicism. Partially but not entirely signaled by Al Smith, the "wet" urban Democrat who lost badly to Herbert Hoover in 1928, the difficulties of electing a Catholic to the presidency were well known. Kennedy's religion, according to Kennedy's younger brother Robert, was his largest challenge to overcome to win the election. His religion, or more precisely, the fear of it, impelled the Kennedy campaign to aggressively battle Hubert Humphrey for the nomination specifically in two states, Wisconsin and West Virginia, not because he required the delegates but because decisively beating the Protestant Humphrey outside his core areas of support would telegraph to party elites that Kennedy's religion would not sink him in November. The contest in Wisconsin in April was a Kennedy win, 56 to 44 percent, but doubts were raised about the victory. Kennedy ran strong in the Catholic areas of the state, while Humphrey did better in the Protestant portions. Additionally, the Kennedy camp had campaigned heavily and committed a lot of resources to winning the Badger State, while Humphrey had not, so Humphrey believed that Wisconsin breathed life into his own campaign.[63] Kennedy did much better and put the nail in the Humphrey coffin in May in the West Virginia Democratic primary (61 to 39 percent), a state almost entirely without Catholics in 1960. Anti-Catholic bias remained a concern after Kennedy's nomination. His most visible and remembered effort to take the issue on was a speech he made to the Greater Houston Ministerial Association on September 12. For the Kennedy campaign, the speech was sufficiently powerful that it was later developed into campaign advertising.[64]

The campaign intended this evening with the Houston ministers to be a direct conversation about the religion issue in the election and to calm doubts and fears about Kennedy's faith and its role should he win the White House. The speech was effective, and Kennedy brought up his service in the navy during the war, his brother's wartime death, and the fallen soldiers at what Texans consider the cradle of their liberty, the Alamo. By reflecting the political role of his religion through the lens of military service, Kennedy sought to blunt the anti-Catholic view. "This is the kind of America I believe in, and this is the kind I fought for in the

---

63. White 1961.
64. Cornog and Whelan 2000. Kathleen Jamieson details the ad and the strategy of where the campaign aired it. See Jamieson 1984.

South Pacific, and the kind my brother died for in Europe. No one suggested then that we may have a 'divided loyalty,' that we did 'not believe in liberty,' or that we belong to a disloyal group that threated the 'freedoms for which our forefathers died.'"[65] Kennedy thus questioned the consistency of the election-year barbs about his faith while implicitly borrowing the civic legitimacy garnered by serving under arms to declare that his political viability was as authentic as a Protestant candidate's. In addition to personalizing the logic by brandishing his own service and his older brother's sacrifice, Kennedy "invok[ed] the holiest of Texan holy arguments, the Alamo."[66]

Kennedy's language again, to push beyond concerns about his religion, used the surnames of those who died defending the Alamo to point out that "this is the kind of America for which our forefathers died, when they fled here to escape religious test oaths that denied office to members of less favored churches; when they fought for the Constitution, the Bill of Rights and the Virginia Statute of Religious Freedom; and when they fought at the shrine I visited today, the Alamo. For side by side with Bowie and Crockett died McCafferty and Bailey and Carey. But no one knows whether they were Catholic or not, for there was no religious test at the Alamo."[67] Lyndon Johnson campaigned for Kennedy in Texas as well, and he made a similar point that no one during the war asked about Kennedy's Catholicism when he skippered *PT-109*; Johnson called it his "little ole war hero speech."[68]

In the general election campaign in 1960, the *PT-109* story was explicitly used by the Kennedy campaign to bolster the military war-hero image with campaign paraphernalia. Booklets retelling the events, including Hersey's *Reader's Digest* story, were part of bulk mailings to potential voters ("hundreds of thousands" were sent according to the Kennedy Library website). Male campaign workers wore tie clips to remind potential voters about Kennedy's World War II adventure. The small golden clip was a profile of a PT boat with "KENNEDY" embossed on its miniature gunnel. By some accounts, the Kennedy campaign also used the *PT-109* heroics as a direct answer to Republican charges that the young Kennedy lacked sufficient foreign policy experience.[69]

Kennedy was victorious on Election Day, but only by an extremely close margin. Kennedy's narrow victory in 1960 did not end the attention

---

65. Casey 2009, 167.
66. Casey 2009, 167.
67. Casey 2009, 167.
68. Donaldson 2007, 108.
69. Roberts and Hammond 2004.

on Kennedy's heroics in the Pacific. A float in Kennedy's inaugural parade replicated the torpedo boat, and seven of Kennedy's crewmates rode aboard. Robert Donovan's book *"PT 109": John F. Kennedy in World War II* came out in 1961. It was complete with a vivid recounting of Kennedy and his crew's experiences. It detailed the Japanese ship ramming the small vessel, the dramatic rescue in shark-filled waters, the coconut, the help from the natives, and successful rescue. Donovan excerpted his book and wrote a summary article that was a November 1961 cover story for the *Saturday Evening Post*. Hollywood got into the act and made a movie about Kennedy's war experiences in the Pacific, hitting theaters in June 1963. It starred Cliff Robertson as Kennedy, and the screenplay was based on the Donovan book. This was not the full extent of the near hagiography of Kennedy's wartime service. Singer Jimmy Dean recorded "PT-109" in 1962, a snare-drum martial march of a country song that bullet-pointed the incident in verse. The tune made it to number 85 on Billboard's "Hot 100" rankings in 1962, beating out the Beach Boy's "Surfin' Safari" and Peter, Paul and Mary's "If I Had a Hammer."

Doubtless, Kennedy's time in the U.S. Navy during World War II shaped his electoral style and perhaps his fortunes. What his *PT-109* heroics did not do is give voters much reason to vote for or against him, according to survey data. Running the same sort of analysis detailed previously for Eisenhower shows different results. Using the open-ended question format, less than 5 percent of respondents in the 1960 ANES reported that Kennedy's military service was a reason to support him. While military service may have given Kennedy an edge in his earlier races when he needed to establish a biography as a young, returned war veteran, the voters in the 1960 presidential election weighed other criteria.

It is worth pondering whether his experiences in the Pacific might have changed him. One biographer stated, "His combat experience in the Pacific strongly influenced Kennedy's subsequent views on war and violence."[70] In a letter to his girlfriend Inga Arvad in 1943, Kennedy wrote:

> A number of illusions have been shattered. . . . We get so used to talking about billions of dollars and millions of soldiers . . . that thousands of casualties sound like drops in the bucket. But if those thousands want to live as much as the ten that I saw, the people deciding the whys and wherefores had better make mighty sure all this effort is headed for some definite goal, and that when we reach that goal we may say it was worth it, for if it isn't the whole thing

---

70. Chafe 2005, 111.

will turn to ashes. . . . This thing is so stupid that while it has a sickening fascination for some of us, myself included, I want to leave it far behind me when I go.[71]

The next candidate who used military service almost immediately on returning stateside as an electioneering effort was Richard Nixon. As Eisenhower's vice president in the 1950s and his three runs for the White House from 1960 to his reelection in 1972, Nixon was a man well known to the American electorate. However, like most other men of his generation, Richard Nixon used his military experience to help establish credibility for his initial electoral ambitions. Unlike the other men who ran for president after a stint in the armed forces, Nixon belonged to the Quaker faith, which stresses nonviolence and is better known for pacifism than for producing naval officers. He did not see combat, but his duties put him right up to seeing its aftermath.

Nixon served in the U.S. Navy during the war. He applied to become an officer in April 1942 as a twenty-nine-year-old. He had already finished college and law school and worked at the federal Office of Price Administration. Although his faith could have exempted him from active duty, Nixon went against the central plank of the Quaker faith and took a commission in the navy. He was actually immune from the draft additionally because he was employed by an important wartime federal administration. Historians have speculated about the reasons behind Nixon's decision. Patriotism is cited often, but Nixon might also have made a "political consideration," believing that sitting out the war in a civilian bureaucracy might be to his detriment.[72] Other biographers were even more explicit when explaining the political necessity of Nixon's decision to join the navy: "Veteran status was proof of patriotism and virtually a requirement for anyone entering national politics in the postwar era."[73]

He became a lieutenant JG by October 1942 and transferred to a stateside training facility. He sought to be posted closer to the action, though letters back home imply that he was not motivated by gallantry or adventurism but felt that it was his duty.[74] After some time, he was assigned to a logistics post in the Solomon Islands. His job was to manage operations in regard to moving personnel between forward areas near the enemy and rear supply areas. It was an important job, being in charge of air transport

---

71. Wills 2009, 52.
72. He would later invoke his military service in campaign speeches, leading with lines such as, "I learned in the foxholes of the South Pacific . . ." See Black 2007, 56.
73. I. Morgan 2002, 41.
74. Aitken 1993.

operations in a rapidly changing war zone, and most accounts concur that Nixon performed his duties well and enjoyed rapport with and the esteem of his men. He often saw casualties returning from combat areas. He wrote home about a particularly harrowing day when a bomber that was damaged in battle attempted to land at his airstrip but collided with a bulldozer, writing that the image of a dead crewman's wedding ring on his "charred hand" was burned into memory.[75] No Nixon biography fails to recount Nixon's most profitable activity while in the navy: five-card stud poker. Multiple accounts refer to Nixon's acumen at wagering, assessing odds, sizing up his opponents' cards, and taking money from others. He had not played before he joined the military, but he was a fast learner and reportedly amassed enough money to send home and invest in his future campaigning expenses.[76]

Nixon returned stateside and finished his time in the service until his discharge at the end of 1945. Like some of the other men whose military experiences and political aspirations are detailed here, Nixon did not wait long to launch his electoral ascent to Congress. The incumbent was a five-term Democrat running for reelection in California's 12th district in 1946, and local Republicans chose Nixon to contest the election that fall. His campaign used Nixon's naval experiences during the war in an effort to introduce the candidate positively. He did not exaggerate his service or overly glamorize it the way that Lyndon Johnson did, but he also did not go out of his way to correct journalists and biographers who overstated Nixon's proximity to combat. Sometimes he underplayed the situation: "He won two battle stars, yet when people asked him what it was like . . . in the Pacific, he shrugged . . . saying that all he did in the South Pacific was get a case of tropical fungus."[77]

Yet several sources indicate that Nixon's campaign brought his naval pedigree into the race symbolically or rhetorically. At first he even delivered speeches wearing his navy uniform while on the hustings. He discontinued the practice when he learned that the former G.I.s in the audiences, mostly former enlisted men, were sensitive to him putting on airs with his officer's uniform.[78] When he was discharged from the navy to return to California to run, he "came west with a satchelful of ideas and a set of electioneering pictures from which he learned a fundamental political truth. It was that the great majority of veterans had been enlisted men for

---

75. Quoted in Brodie 1981, 159.
76. Estimates of his haul range from $3,000 to $10,000, which is roughly equivalent to $40,000–$140,000 in 2010. See Ambrose 1987, 113.
77. Hughes 1972, 78.
78. G. Allen 1971.

whom a politician campaigning in the uniform of an officer held little attraction."[79] The campaign minimized the uniform imagery and switched the images with text, replacing "Lieutenant Commander Richard M. Nixon" with "Dick Nixon." The campaigning efforts made his navy service initially important to introducing a man struggling with name recognition but subdued the service and especially the rank. Even prior to his easy win in the Republican primary in June, Nixon crafted a standard speech that his campaign called "The Bougainville," named after Bougainville Island, his station in the Solomon Islands during the war. He described the men under his command and their duties and successes during the war. He then fast-forwarded rhetorically and discussed how each man was doing since returning home to highlight the negative "privations" suffered because of the bad economy, bureaucracy, red tape, and so on, stock-in-trade campaign tropes for challengers hoping to unseat an incumbent.[80] As the hard-fought campaign neared Election Day, Nixon's camp continued to point out that he served during the war to imply something was lacking in the incumbent's sitting out the war. His opponent tried to fend off the jab by referring to Nixon as "the Lieutenant Commander" to paint Nixon's early campaigning as elitist and obsessed with his rank.[81] Nixon went on to win easily, 57 to 43 percent.

Nixon's political career ascended with tremendous speed. His involvement with the Alger Hiss case put him in the national spotlight, and by 1950 he decided to run for the U.S. Senate. Only two years after winning that seat, he became Dwight Eisenhower's choice for the vice presidency in the 1952 election. While the Eisenhower-Nixon ticket would go on to win the election, the largest problem arose for the Republicans when news came out of a secret fund that had been illegally created for Nixon. Some presumed that after the convention, after Eisenhower had chosen Nixon, a late switch on the ticket would have to be made to save the party's chances. But Nixon battled to stay on Eisenhower's ticket in 1952 by delivering his memorable "Checkers speech." In it, he rebutted allegations that he had taken eighteen thousand dollars illegally from supporters as an underhanded windfall. He referred to his time in the navy in his attempts to portray himself as a man with modest means, as he accounted for his income and debts: "In 1942, I went into the service. Let me say that my service record was not a particularly unusual one. I went to the South Pacific. I guess I'm entitled to a couple of battle stars. I got a couple of let-

---

79. Mazo 1959, 44.
80. Aitken 1993, 121.
81. Mazo 1959, 48.

ters of commendation. But I was just there when the bombs were falling."[82] His military service became a small issue for Nixon between 1948 and his joining Eisenhower on the 1952 ticket. Journalists and biographers continued to write that Nixon had actually been in foxholes and "under fire frequently" in the war when writing background pieces on him, but by 1952 reporters looked more deeply and questioned the credibility of these claims.[83] It appears that the exaggeration of Nixon's record was a creation of both the candidate and the media.

As vice president, Nixon was the heir apparent to the Republican nomination in 1960. John Kennedy got past doubts about his religion and successfully dueled Lyndon Johnson for the Democratic nomination, while Nixon faced only scant opposition from Nelson Rockefeller. When one thinks of the use of military biography as a campaign tool in the 1960 race, Kennedy comes to mind before Nixon for an obvious reason: *PT-109*. Kennedy's war experiences meant that Nixon did not utilize his veteran status in the campaign, and Kennedy won by a slim margin. Campaign lore blames Nixon's loss on television debates and Kennedy's charm, but close elections can turn on a limitless number of factors. After losing to Kennedy, Nixon ran for governor of California two years later but lost to the incumbent Pat Brown. Nixon returned to national politics after Barry Goldwater's crushing defeat in 1964 to become the Republican nominee again in 1968. The Democratic Party was in disarray that year with internal divisions over civil rights and the Vietnam War and ultimately nominated Hubert Humphrey, the only nonveteran nominated by a major party during the post–World War II era. Nixon would go on to win in 1968 and run for reelection in 1972 against a bona fide war hero: George McGovern. McGovern did not play up his service in his political life, so in both the 1968 and 1972 elections military biography was a matter with low to no salience.

Among the post–World War II presidential candidates, and among this group who explicitly referenced their time in the war as an electoral asset, perhaps the intersection of Lyndon Johnson's military record and electoral ambition is the most complex. Through his words and actions we can see clear evidence that he believed the conventional wisdom of his era about military service: it was a requirement for political ascendancy or a negative if one lacked it. He went to extraordinary lengths to create a military chapter in his life, perhaps even more so considering he had already won a U.S. House seat. He was a congressman by the time he climbed aboard the B-26 Marauder in the Pacific in 1942 and had a Silver Star

---

82. Bochin 1990, 115.
83. Brodie 1981, 157.

pinned on his chest by General Douglas MacArthur before quickly returning to Washington, D.C.

Johnson is listed in Table 2.1 as a veteran, but some may see this classification as an overstatement of his service record given the peculiar circumstances surrounding his entry. He was a lieutenant commander in the Naval Reserve and spent less than a year in uniform during the war. His military service was not the typical early-life, prepolitical experience that it was for men born after him during this era. The criterion set forth in Chapter 2 sets a rather low bar. It assesses whether a candidate, at the time of his elevation to major-party nominee, had served in uniform in either the mobilized militia or the ranks of the federal armed forces. Johnson meets this criterion, though he did so by unusual means. Yet for all of his efforts to get near combat and the controversies surrounding his Silver Star, his military biography played little role in his path to the White House and reelection in 1964. There is no evidence to suggest that Johnson's military service record played any role in his nomination as the Democratic Party's candidate in 1964 after Kennedy's assassination. He did seek the nomination in 1960. Despite the low emphasis placed on Johnson's service during his runs for president, the tenacity with which he sought a military experience is worth detailing, given his inference that military service was necessary for his election wins later and his previous rhetoric on the campaign trail obliged him to serve.

When the Japanese attacked Pearl Harbor in December 1941, thirty-three-year-old Lyndon Johnson had already worked on Capitol Hill as a staffer and won both the Texas U.S. House 10th district in Texas and many important political allies in Washington, D.C., including Speaker of the House Sam Rayburn and President Franklin Roosevelt. Johnson's fast rise in politics hit a bump in 1941. In his only election loss, Johnson ran for the U.S. Senate seat vacated by the death of Sam Houston's son, Andrew Jackson Houston. The special election to fill the vacancy was held in summer, and Johnson ran against Texas governor Wilbert Lee "Pappy" O'Daniel for the Democratic Party nomination. In this period in Texas, winning the Democratic Party primary was tantamount to winning the election, as Republicans found it challenging to obtain percentages in the double digits in statewide elections. Hence, the short Democratic primary campaign would decide the winner, and Johnson campaigned statewide. Johnson's best line in his stump speeches was on the possible coming war and his role in it:

> Finding as the campaign progressed that that pledge was a surefire crowd-pleaser in patriotic, militaristic Texas, with its glorious history of wars against Mexico and the Comanches, he repeated it

day after day, in person and over the radio, on courthouse lawns in small towns and in big-city auditoriums. He played variations on the sentence. He promised that if war came, he would never ask for a desk job in Washington; that when the shooting started he "would be in the front line, in the trenches, in the mud and blood with your boys, helping to do that fighting..." and "If Hitler makes this an all-out war, I shall vote in the Senate for war.... And when I cast my vote I shall tear up my draft number and join the boys picked to defend our homes and Our God and our liberties. I shall never vote for war and then hide behind a Senate seat where bullets cannot reach me." The promise to be "in the trenches" became a theme of this campaign.[84]

This rhetoric is powerful, and he paired it with other electioneering efforts. He had text with similar language printed on postcards sent to voters under the title "We Need Courage Like This."[85] This speech may have also put him in a difficult position after war broke out because he was then pressured to act, at least by his own words. Candidates' promises are not always guarantees of later action, but it is easy to see how Johnson's stump speech made avoiding military service difficult once the war began. The question for Johnson was not whether to join the armed forces in some capacity, because he had already been appointed lieutenant commander in the U.S. Naval Reserve in June 1940. The motivation he felt was to attempt to live up to his pledge to somehow get to the proverbial "trenches" and see combat while keeping his seat in the U.S. House of Representatives and his political aspirations alive.

Johnson did not win the Democratic nomination for the special U.S. Senate election, so he remained a member of the House of Representatives. In December, the possibility of war that Johnson spoke about on his campaign tour became real when the Japanese attacked Hawaii, bringing the United States into the war against Japan and Germany. Johnson was in the House chamber when Roosevelt delivered his famous "Day of Infamy" speech, and Johnson was the first House member to afterward request a leave of absence from the leadership of the legislature to join active-duty forces. According to Robert Dallek, Johnson remembered "his promise during the 1941 campaign, [and] 'urgently' asked the President

---

84. Caro 1991, 19.
85. Campaign postcards, "Postcards" Folder, Box 34, House of Representatives Papers, Lyndon Baines Johnson Presidential Library, Austin, TX.

to assign him 'immediately to active duty with the Fleet.'"[86] However, he did not have any combat training, so the navy found noncombat duties for the congressman-sailor.

His first set of orders had him behind a desk in San Francisco, as the navy "planned to use Johnson's unique talents as a legislator to assist in the critical task of building up the organizational structure through which would flow men and matériel from the United States into the Pacific."[87] Johnson used his relationship with the president to directly request an assignment that would get him closer to the action at a time when Roosevelt needed a trusted ally to report back objective information about progress of war buildup. Because of some infighting among commanders in the Pacific Theater, as well as rivalries between the United States, Australia, New Zealand, and the Netherlands, Roosevelt was given biased reports and sought more objective accounting. So he approved Johnson's request, sending the legislator–turned–naval officer on a tour of various South Pacific ports important in the war mission by May 1942. Johnson reported to General Douglas MacArthur and then traveled to various ports and locations in Australia to examine the state of support logistics and war supply transport, as well as conditions among air crews who flew all-important bombing missions.

It was this latter job, which put Johnson in contact with local commanders, that offered the opportunity for him to ride along with a bombing mission. Though riding with a bombing crew probably did not provide Johnson with information germane to his mission, it afforded him an opportunity to see aviators in action and see that action himself. He rendezvoused with the combat fliers near Port Moresby, New Guinea, and boarded a B-26 bomber named the *Heckling Hare*, part of a squadron heading to strike a nearby Japanese air field. Exactly what happened in the skies between Port Moresby and the mission's targets near Lae, some six hundred miles away, is not entirely clear.

One account, published in 1964, the year Johnson was running for president, portrays the experience as harrowing.[88] Johnson's plane experienced a power failure prior to the bomb run that cut power to the right side of the airplane. This problem was due to a malfunctioning generator. This electrical failure constituted a serious emergency and meant the pilots needed to maintain a lower airspeed, making the plane much more vulnerable to attacks from Japanese "Zero" fighter planes quickly scram-

---

86. Dallek 1991, 231.
87. Caidin and Hymoff 1964, 14.
88. Caidin and Hymoff 1964.

bling to defend their airfield. The Zeroes attacked the *Heckling Hare*, scoring some hits on the bomber, but they failed to bring it down. As the Japanese attacked, Johnson reportedly remained calm and moved between the plane's gunners and pilots, allegedly sticking his head into the windows of the gun turrets to better observe the action. The crew were, according to Caidin and Hymoff's account, astonished that Johnson was able to remain calm in the face of a failing airplane being attacked by enemy fighters, with one crewman stating that Johnson was "as cool as ice."[89] Johnson returned to General MacArthur, who was perturbed that the congressman had chosen to go on a risky combat mission. However, the general decided to award him the prestigious Silver Star, a high decoration for gallantry in combat, but the motivations for this decision are unclear.[90] The Silver Star's citation read:

> For gallantry in action in the vicinity of Port Moresby and Salamaua, New Guinea, on June 9, 1942. While on a mission of obtaining information in the Southwest Pacific area, Lieutenant Commander Johnson, in order to obtain personal knowledge of combat conditions, volunteered as an observer on a hazardous aerial combat mission over hostile positions in New Guinea. As our planes neared the target area they were intercepted by eight hostile fighters. When, at this time, the plane in which Lieutenant Commander Johnson was an observer, developed mechanical trouble and was forced to turn back alone, presenting a favorable target to the enemy fighters, he evidenced marked coolness in spite of the hazards involved. His gallant actions enabled him to obtain and return with valuable information.[91]

It is very difficult to infer that this award went to Johnson because of gallantry. The other crew members aboard the *Heckling Hare* received no stars, silver or otherwise. Johnson's actions after returning stateside are also telling. His return to Washington, D.C., as a war veteran in mid-July 1942 put him back in civilian clothes as he resumed his role representing the 10th district of Texas in the U.S. House of Representatives. Very soon

---

89. Caidin and Hymoff 1964, 114.
90. See Perret 1996, 299–302. According to Dallek, "It is not difficult to suspect political backscratching. Lyndon went home with a 'war record,' and a medal and MacArthur had a new vocal advocate in Washington with some access to the President and more to Congress and the press." See Dallek 1991, 240.
91. Copy of Silver Star order provided by the MacArthur Memorial Archives, Norfolk, VA; in the author's possession.

after returning to Washington, he scheduled lunches and interviews with journalists from newspapers and wire services. As time passed, the retelling of his war stories began to change. Caro's treatment of this point is vivid. The amount of time he spent overseas grew, the number of enemy Zeroes increased, the number of miles flown throughout his observations tripled. Instead of a mechanical failure, the crippled generator suddenly happened as a result of Japanese fire. At first he felt that he did not deserve the Silver Star, but as time went on, the award came to take on high importance. He "arranged to accept it in public. Several times."[92] From the mid-1940s on, including his time as president, he wore a miniature Silver Star lapel pin every day.

The reality of what happened in June 1942 was not as Johnson portrayed it immediately after his return and certainly did not live up to its exaggerated retelling. News sources even at the time of his presidential election were skeptical of that characterization. A September 1964 *New York Times* article reported that "accounts of the mission vary somewhat," citing official records and eyewitness accounts.[93] CNN did an investigation into the matter much later and concluded that the Silver Star was probably undeserved.[94] In it, the authors interview Caro, who points out that even if one blindly accepts Johnson's account, the simple facts remain that he was exposed to combat for less than fifteen minutes on one day and returned quickly afterward. None of the other crew members received the award, and they underwent such hazards on a regular basis. The election-year telling of the story by Caidin and Hymoff is likely quite dramatized. The CNN report interviews men who were on the mission, and they attested that the 1960s retelling of the story was exaggerated to make Johnson's experience appear riskier. It is difficult to conclude, given these historical revisions, that Johnson received the Silver Star for anything beyond a political favor from MacArthur.

Johnson was not the only person to have added hyperbole to his wartime experiences. It is likely that many war stories retold stateside by other veterans underwent embellishment. What distinguishes Johnson's inflated recounting are the magnitude of the exaggeration and the motivations behind it. He overstated the role he played in World War II, transforming a brief encounter with enemy planes while his craft experienced substantial mechanical trouble into a ferocious dogfight. He gradually extended the amount of time he spent in the air and magnified the sacrifices he made. The reason for these stretches was to further his political

---

92. Caro 1991, 51.
93. Hailey 1964, 22.
94. McIntyre and Barnett 2001.

ambition. In Johnson's mind, combat experience was a prerequisite to furthering his political career. He went through extraordinary measures to get near combat, and as soon as he found a sufficiently qualifying experience, he returned stateside immediately after receiving a likely undeserved medal from a very politically minded general.

Lyndon Johnson also had the habit of screening his home movies from the Pacific, clips he had taken with a small movie camera. Caro's research revealed that Johnson would often invite journalists to see the clips "over and over again" at every dinner party, offering narration that enlarged his own gallantry at each screening, even to the same audience.[95] Johnson was not unique in making home movies; John Kerry also shot movies in Vietnam, which he showed later in life, though Kerry did not share the same habit of Johnson's exaggeration.

Caro describes the disappointment that Johnson felt at having to return to Washington as a mere member of the House as Johnson's darkest days. Johnson aspired to run for the Senate again while he continued his work in the lower house of the legislature. His political clout there diminished in the years immediately following the war, at least in part because of the death of his patron, Franklin Roosevelt, in 1944. The announced retirement of Senator "Pappy" O'Daniel in 1948 meant that both Johnson and popular governor Coke Stevenson sought the Democratic nomination for the seat. Johnson's win in 1948 was likely a product of several things, not least of which was his novel use of the helicopter on the campaign trail. He also frequently made explicit references to his war service. His time in uniform during World War II was "one of the major themes of his campaign."[96] He wore the Silver Star award on his lapel at every stop, and his advance team would try to find a Johnson-supporting amputee war veteran to be the one to introduce him onstage at rallies. About not running for Senate in 1942, he said, "When that election came around I was in the jungles of New Guinea."[97] His exaggerations continued, though he never claimed to have engaged in the fighting. The outcome of that process in the Democratic primary, the election that almost certainly would decide who would become the next U.S. senator from Texas, forced a runoff. It was extremely close, certainly involved ballot stuffing, required much postelection adjudication, but broke in Johnson's favor. His ascent to the Senate, not done without questions about its legitimacy, allowed him to begin his mastery of that body. He became majority leader as he looked to his higher trajectory, the presidency.

---

95. Caro 1991, 49.
96. Caro 1991, 229.
97. Caro 1991, 479.

Johnson sought the presidency in 1960, losing to John Kennedy at the Democratic convention. Parties had begun to use primary elections as part of the process to select nominees, but their role was secondary to the decisions made by delegates at the convention. Johnson decided not to participate in the 1960 contests, though Kennedy did. Kennedy's motivation related to his hopes to demonstrate to party elites that he could win over Protestants. In an attempt to slow the Kennedy momentum, Johnson challenged him to a televised debate during the Democratic convention. Kennedy accepted. In one of the few barbs during the debate, Johnson brought up, albeit politely, that the Massachusetts senator had been absent for many of the important civil rights votes earlier that year (Kennedy had been campaigning). Newspaper accounts of the debate make no mention of either candidate speaking about his biography. After Kennedy won the nomination, he invited Johnson to be his vice presidential candidate, and they took office in 1961.

Johnson became president following Kennedy's assassination in 1963, so his first presidential election was run as an incumbent against Arizona's Barry Goldwater in 1964. Johnson's military service played little role, diminished from its more central role in his postwar House and Senate contests. If anything, Johnson's 1964 presidential campaign, rather than champion his military credentials, sought to explicitly highlight his opponent as a trigger-happy hothead in the nuclear age. Airing only once, the "Daisy" ad of that year probably remains the most famous presidential television spot since the beginning of TV advertising. Johnson's uncommon and brief military service record meant a great deal to the man himself, but its role in his electoral experiences is minor.

Gerald Ford represents a unique case in terms of his electoral prospects. Before the Watergate crisis unfolded during the Nixon administration, Ford was a Republican congressman from Michigan who rose to leadership. When Spiro Agnew, Nixon's vice president, resigned in 1973 over a tax evasion scandal, the president selected House minority leader Ford to fill the position. When Nixon resigned as president less than a year later, Ford took the oath of office and became the thirty-eighth president without ever having been on a presidential or vice presidential ballot. Republicans nominated him as the incumbent to run in 1976 after fending off a challenge from the right by Ronald Reagan. Hence, Ford's path to the nomination was atypical. His military service was not. Like most of the other nominees of the post–World War II era, Ford served during the war as a low-ranking officer prior to launching his political career.

Ford finished law school in 1941 and entered the U.S. Naval Reserve in April 1942 at the age of twenty-nine, five months after the attack on

Pearl Harbor. He was an ensign who was quickly assigned as an instructor of preflight recruits, specializing in physical fitness. This role is not surprising, given that Ford was a standout football star at the University of Michigan in the early 1930s. He volunteered for sea duty, and by 1943 Lieutenant JG Gerald Ford was aboard the U.S.S. *Monterey*, a small aircraft carrier that had been hastily converted from a light cruiser. Ford served as "one of ten gunnery officers," tasking him to "stand on the fantail and direct crews" firing the defensive antiaircraft guns.[98] Ford later wrote that his role there was dangerous: "The Japanese planes came after us with a vengeance. . . . It was every bit as much action as I had hoped to see."[99] The *Monterey* was involved in several actions against the Japanese. Most of the action was seen by the bombers the ship launched, but occasionally the Japanese attacked the carrier.

The most harrowing moment of Ford's naval time did not involve the Japanese, however.[100] The *Monterey* was hit by a powerful storm in December 1944. Typhoon Cobra struck the fleet near the Philippines. The storm was furious, killing more than eight hundred sailors, with six of the lost aboard the *Monterey*. The typhoon was destructive enough to create waves exceeding one hundred feet—sinking three U.S. vessels. Aboard the *Monterey*, Ford was nearly washed overboard himself. When the Klaxon sounded, smoke was already coming from fires on board. Ford rushed to his battle station on the bridge. En route, the ship pitched violently when he stepped on the deck, sending him hurtling toward the sea. He slid across the entirety of the 109-foot-wide deck before he was able to grab the narrow catwalk on the port side of the carrier. He got back to the bridge and saw that the bombers and fighters on the flight deck had come loose from their moorings and many had washed away. The fuel from the aircraft, however, had ignited the planes that were still in the hanger bay underneath the deck. Some sources state that Ford himself pulled on a gas mask and fought the fires with others to repair the boilers needed to pressurize the water to fight the fires.[101] Ford's autobiography, however, refers to the rescue party in the third person.[102] Either way, the *Monterey* was in grave danger and minutes from having to be abandoned—and rescue of the crew by the embattled fleet was uncertain because of the storm. In either retelling, Ford unquestionably showed courage in the face of danger.[103] By all accounts, his superiors and the men in his charge thought

---

98. Ford 1979, 58.
99. Ford 1979, 58.
100. Drury and Clavin 2007.
101. Brinkley 2007.
102. Ford 1979, 60.
103. Brinkley 2007, 10, 162n16.

highly of him. He served out the rest of the war stateside and left the U.S. Navy in February 1946 after a promotion to lieutenant commander.

How did wartime experiences influence Gerald Ford? First, he wrote in his postpresidency autobiography that his war experience changed his political attitudes. While at Yale, he had spoken out that the United States should steer clear of alliances that might bring it into wars. After serving in the fight against the Japanese, he explicitly abandoned his earlier isolationism.[104] Second, they shaped one important aspect of his first try, a successful one, at winning a seat in Congress. The returned veteran did not wait long to begin his electoral efforts. Ford ran as a Republican against an incumbent Republican in Michigan's U.S. 5th congressional district with a message of domestic restraint and internationalism in foreign policy. He "ardently championed" the Marshall Plan and the new United Nations against the more isolationist incumbent, Bartel "Barney" Jonkman.[105]

Ford explicitly highlighted his military service in his congressional challenge. The incumbent Jonkman was the pick of the local Republican political power broker, Frank McKay. McKay had brushed off Ford before the war, so the young veteran decided to take his campaign fight to both Jonkman and McKay. To highlight his service and take on McKay directly, Ford's campaign used a well-known fixture of military life to be a campaign office: Ford rented a navy surplus Quonset hut. These prefabricated half cylinders were ubiquitous on military bases during the war and made an unambiguous visual reference to wartime service. Ford had the structure painted red, white, and blue with large "Jerry FORD Jr. for CONGRESS" written across its length. What made the Quonset hut even more politically important was where the campaign located it. They parked it in a small rented lot under the windows of Frank McKay's office.[106] Ford campaigned hard, won important newspaper endorsements, and beat the incumbent Jonkman in the primary and went on the win the general election easily.

Ford remained in the U.S. House of Representatives for more than twenty years, turning down opportunities to run for statewide office in Michigan. He joined the Republican leadership in the 1960s after enjoying easy reelections. After his unusual promotions to the vice presidency and then the presidency, Ford faced difficult reelection prospects in 1976. The 1974 midterms, the first national elections after the Watergate scandal,

---

104. Ford 1979, 61.
105. J. Cannon 1994, 49.
106. A photograph of the hut is available on the Gerald Ford Presidential Library website, at http://www.fordlibrarymuseum.gov/avproj/hseries/h51-1b.gif.

saw large gains for the Democrats. From the right, Ford faced and narrowly survived a Republican challenger, Ronald Reagan. Gerald Ford's thirty-second biographical television ad from 1976 does mention his Eagle Scout award, his football accolades at Michigan, and his "courageous" service in World War II.[107] In short, Ford explicitly used his military service to position his initial run for Congress, but his unusual path to the presidency made biography unimportant because his first presidential election was as an incumbent.

The final two candidates in this category of brief wartime officers were both combat veterans of World War II who survived harrowing experiences before returning home: George H. W. Bush and Bob Dole. Yet both of their political careers got a later start than those of the previous candidates, and the passage of time and other factors, including their own reluctance, made their wartime service less salient.

The first President Bush was Ronald Reagan's vice president in the 1980s after a long career of public service. Though he ran against Reagan in the 1980 Republican primaries, he endorsed Reagan after losing and became vice president in 1981 and the heir apparent to the presidential nomination for 1992 when he was nearly seventy years old. Well before he began his political life, however, he was a very young navy flier who piloted many combat missions. After the war, and after a successful twenty-year career as a Texas oilman, he began a long political career that saw him serve in many roles. He had been the director of the Central Intelligence Agency, ambassador to the People's Republic of China and the United Nations, and chairman of the Republican Party leadership. All of these notable posts came after a short legislative career. He has a mixed electoral record in his first forays into federal office. He unsuccessfully challenged sitting Democratic U.S. senator Ralph Yarborough in 1964 but won two terms as a U.S. congressman from Houston. In 1970, Bush relinquished his House seat to challenge Yarborough again, but this time the Democrat lost in the primary to Lloyd Bentsen. Bush ended up losing in the general, so both his attempts to win a Senate seat bookended his legislative career. He would then go on to several key appointed positions during the Nixon and Ford administrations that would lead to his first presidential aspirations in 1980.

Bush's wartime service was dangerous, and most would describe it as gallant. When America was pulled into World War II after the Japanese attack on Pearl Harbor, Bush was still in prep school, but on his eighteenth birthday the next summer he enlisted in the U.S. Navy. He learned to fly and specialized in torpedo bombers, practicing carrier takeoffs and

---

107. The advertisement is archived on the Living Room Candidate website, at http://www.livingroomcandidate.org/commercials/1976/biography#4374.

landings as well as combat tactics. He earned his commission the next summer, 1943, before his nineteenth birthday, so Bush held the distinction of being the youngest navy pilot. He was sent to report for duty aboard the U.S.S. *San Jacinto*. It was a "fast, light aircraft carrier" because a flight deck had been welded atop a cruiser's hull, a practice the navy had to employ to rapidly increase the number of carriers operating in the Pacific.[108] Bush piloted TBF Avengers, which were three-man planes that were primarily bombers but could also do reconnaissance. They were small enough for carrier deployment but large enough to hit ships with torpedoes or ground targets with bombs. Bush's plane was personalized: "Under the cockpit, his gunner . . . in contravention of navy practice, had long ago painted Barbara, the name of Bush's fiancée."[109]

By May 1944, as the fortunes of the Pacific War changed because the U.S. Navy drastically shrank the amount of ocean the Japanese controlled, the *San Jacinto*'s air crews were continuing to participate in aerial combat. The aviators, including twenty-year-old Bush, flew missions against enemy destroyers and supply vessels and against Japanese island bases and installations. Bush's most harrowing moment of the war occurred on September 2, 1944. He and his crew, a rear gunner and a bombardier/radioman, flew in an attack on a strategically important radio transmitter on the island of Chi Chi Jima, about halfway between Saipan and Japan proper, six hundred miles from Tokyo. As they made their bombing approach around sunset, Japanese antiaircraft shells exploded around them. One of his crewmen was killed instantly, while another shell hit the Avenger's engine, setting it ablaze. With smoke in the cockpit, Bush continued toward the installation and dropped two five hundred–pound bombs and "was able to score hits on the enemy installations . . . before he wriggled out of the smoking cockpit."[110] Bush jumped from the plane and deployed his parachute; his remaining crewman got out as well, but his parachute failed to open and he was killed.[111] When he hit the water, Bush opened his inflatable raft and paddled madly to get away from the Japanese-held island. An enemy boat launched from the island to intercept Bush, but one of the American escort planes dove to strafe it, giving the future president a long head start. After three hours,

---

108. King 1980, 27.
109. Hyams 1991, 8.
110. King 1980, 30.
111. One of the eyewitnesses to the events that day disputes Bush's (and the navy's) characterization. In August 1988, a navy veteran who was a gunner on another plane in Bush's squadron claimed that Bush's plane was not aflame and that he could have attempted a water landing, potentially increasing the likelihood of survival for all three in the plane. See "Gunner in Squadron" 1988.

because a fellow pilot who saw Bush get shot down radioed in the location, an American submarine surfaced and pulled the lucky aviator aboard. He stayed aboard the submarine, the U.S.S. *Finback*, while it finished out its patrol before he got to enjoy some free time at Pearl Harbor. Though he had the option to return stateside and accept a role to train future combat fliers, Bush instead chose to return the *San Jacinto*. He flew eight more combat missions before his unit rotated out, so Bush had flown fifty-eight missions in total.[112] He was awarded the Distinguished Flying Cross for the attack on the Chi Chi Jima radio installation as well as three Air Medals.

In his 1960s congressional runs, his campaign literature briefly listed his military experiences from World War II. His service more than merited its inclusion on a campaign handbill. Despite the experience in combat and danger that George Bush faced, his campaigns made them less prominent in his electioneering efforts than in those of some of the other World War II veterans. The campaign handbill mentioned previously refers to the candidate as a "war hero" and states that he was a carrier pilot who was "shot down" and "awarded the Distinguished Flying Cross and three Air Medals."[113] His military service is just one item on the list. With bullet points the brochure lists his business acumen, world travels, and civic leadership. Compared to another U.S. Navy vet who almost lost his life from a Japanese attack, John Kennedy, Bush made subtle and almost perfunctory appeals to his military experiences. While Kennedy had made his experiences in the Pacific central to his early political runs, Bush, only seven years younger but running for the House twenty years after the war, added his military time as a standard-looking résumé entry and did not appear to make it a dominant part of his public persona. And by the time of his presidential attempts in 1980, when he lost to Reagan in the primaries, and his 1988 successful and 1992 unsuccessful runs, his military service was not an important part of his candidacy.

Perhaps the reason for Bush's subdued use of his military service in his election campaigns was that he felt it was inappropriate to draw too much attention to it. A Bush White House insider, when brought in for speechwriting duties, felt that the Bush team had "missed the importance of placing references to the president's military service and valor." He brought that idea to the head speechwriter but was rebuffed: "Look, this president is a bona fide war hero. No one will argue the point, but you have to understand how he sees it. There was a time when I put references to his

---

112. Tanner 2004.
113. Campaign handbill, [1966?], "Congressional File, General" Folder, Box 1, George Bush Congressional Campaign Literature, George Bush Presidential Library, College Station, TX.

war record in speeches. He would call me over to the Oval to review the speech, and there I would stand as he drew a red line through every reference. George Bush apparently viewed references to his personal heroism as irrelevant, perhaps indulgent, and certainly awkward."[114] His reluctance to make use of his military service on the campaign trail predated his presidential runs. In Bush's first race, trying to unseat Senator Ralph Yarborough, the incumbent did not hesitate talking about his time in the war. Cramer's account of Bush's early run imagines a conversation: "C. Fred Chambers heard Yarborough talking about his war record, so he said to Bush, 'Why don't you mention your own service? Give people a feel for your life. . . .' 'Nah . . . I'd just feel funny doing that.'"[115]

Another reason might be the time that had elapsed since the war. Kennedy, Nixon, and Ford made explicit attempts to use their military service to electoral gain when they ran for the U.S. House of Representatives in the 1940s when V-E Day and V-J Day were very recent memories for American voters. For candidates like Bush, whose political careers began later, World War II service may have diminished in its electoral luster as America's more recent and less popular wars were in the headlines. As the share of the voting public who lived through the war declined, the use of World War II military service in campaigns diminished as well.

We can speculate that had Bush been a bit older, closer to the age of Ford, Nixon, or Kennedy, and had he began his political career earlier in life with memories of the war more vivid in voters' minds, perhaps his campaigns would have made more hay out of his experience in and out of torpedo bombers in the Pacific. However, secondary sources indicate that Bush himself was uncomfortable with overplaying his biography in such a fashion.

As a one-term president, Bush has a mixed electoral record, having beaten Michael Dukakis in 1988 but losing to Bill Clinton in 1992. Those two elections each saw military service records become an issue covered by media, but in ways that were salient for the Democrat, not George Bush. Questions about Dukakis's draft deferment during the Korean War lingered, while Clinton's disingenuous letter to an ROTC officer gave the impression of him as a draft dodger during the Vietnam War.

In neither case, however, did Bush explicitly take advantage of these issues on the campaign trail by donning a war-hero mantle. One can imagine a campaign ad or press release that could have tried to sway voters by explicitly inviting comparisons of Bush's wartime combat experience dur-

---

114. Charles 2004, 57.
115. Cramer 1992, 420. The Bush campaign possibly aired a newsreel from World War II that showed Bush being rescued by the *Finback*.

ing World War II to Dukakis's time as a clerk away from the front lines or Clinton's avoidance of service altogether during Vietnam. One of Bush's biographical ads showed a brief black-and-white image from the 1940s depicting him in uniform, but this visual came in a sequence with others, so it did not have great impact.

Much more memorable was the "Tank" ad that year. In 1988, the George H. W. Bush–Dan Quayle campaign repackaged Dukakis's own video footage of his infamous ride on an M1 Abrams tank, but it did not explicitly highlight with text on the image or by voice-over any of the brief controversy over Dukakis's draft deferments. Rather, it attacked Dukakis in terms of his opposition to 1980s defense programs. With the image of Dukakis in the ill-fitting helmet and the perception that he looked out of place riding atop a battle tank, the Bush people sought to diminish the credibility of Dukakis as commander in chief. It is possible that the ad might implicitly remind voters about the draft deferments.

Four years later in 1992, the Bush-Quayle campaign ran the "Gray Dot" ad, which paired two Bill Clintons on a split screen to illustrate apparent inconsistencies. According to the ad, one candidate "stood for military action in the Persian Gulf, while the one on the right agreed with those that opposed it," and one version of Clinton "was called up for military service while this one claims he wasn't." It is important to note that this jab was not directly at Clinton's lack of military service but underlined his evasive answers about the 1968 letter. Bush's loss to Bill Clinton in the 1992 election stung, not merely because he had been unseated in an era of two-term presidents but also because of who beat him. In interviews with his 2015 biographer, he still thought of Clinton as a "draft dodger," even after twenty years.[116]

In terms of actual combat experience and risk, George H. W. Bush and John Kennedy both volunteered for frontline combat duty, led others in combat against the Japanese in the Pacific, and lost men in risky encounters. Bush's service experience was arguably as valorous as Kennedy's time in the navy and probably equivalent in its potential as a campaign narrative. But in contrast to Kennedy's overt and frequent references to his harrowing *PT-109* event, both Bush presidential campaigns made little use of Bush in the cockpit of his TBM Avenger, unlike other veterans who had used their war records in their first electoral and presidential runs.

---

116. "'God, it was ghastly,' he told Meacham. 'Your whole life is based on trying to accomplish stuff, and losing hurts.' But what also stung was who he lost to: a man he considered a 'draft dodger' for avoiding service during the Vietnam War. . . . So much for 'duty, honor, country,' Bush wrote in his diary." Kelly 2015.

The last veteran of the World War II generation to obtain a major-party nomination was Bob Dole in 1996. After a grievous combat injury, Dole started his political life in 1950 for state legislative office in his home state of Kansas. Then he successfully won a U.S. House seat in 1960, and his long tenure in the U.S. Senate began after the 1968 elections. His use of military service for electioneering purposes was subdued, similar to George H. W. Bush's, which is not surprising given the similarity in their age and the amount of time between the war and their first election experiences. He was, however, somewhat more willing than Bush to connect his own wartime experience in the 1940s to his presidential campaign.

Dole joined the U.S. Army in June 1943 as an enlisted man. He entered Officer Candidate School and became an officer in the fall of 1944, after the Allies retook Paris following the successful D-Day invasion. He would not miss combat despite his late entry into the war, however. At the age of twenty-one, he took command of a platoon that had successfully landed in Italy the year before. His outfit deployed to the rugged terrain between Florence and Bologna, where fighting between the advancing Americans and the Germans was fierce as the front moved slowly north. Dole's platoon was a small part of the famous 10th Mountain Division. On April 14, just days after President Roosevelt died, three regiments sought to take Hill 913, just one of the many steps toward pushing the Germans out of Italy. An official army report cited German diaries captured from the area, revealing that German troops thought the "Tenth Mountain division was about to attack and . . . would not take any prisoners."[117]

On a field going up the slope of Hill 913, Lieutenant Dole and his experienced sergeant crossed a ravine when the German defenders attacked with machine guns and rockets. The radioman was hit, and Dole rushed to grab him and began to pull him to safety, but the soldier had been killed instantly. At the very moment Dole realized the radioman was dead and with less than a month before the total German surrender, a burst of German machine-gun fire hit Dole's right shoulder. His sergeant got Dole out of the line of fire to field medics, who found him a grim case. They administered morphine. Days later, after an initial diagnosis of shoulder damage, exploratory surgery found that Dole had sustained damage to his spinal cord in addition to the bone and muscle wounds. The prognosis was not good; he was not expected to ever walk again. He had a long and difficult recovery, but Dole proved his initial diagnoses wrong. While his right arm remained paralyzed, Dole recovered and began his law career and political life in Kansas.

---

117. J. H. Thompson 1994, 29.

Dole's first electoral experiences were in the 1950s when he ran for the Kansas lower house in the state legislature and for a county attorney seat. The headline following his first victory in 1950 was "Young Veteran Elected from Russell County."[118] In the 1960s, Dole won four terms in the U.S. House of Representatives before setting his sights on the U.S. Senate in 1968. His campaign materials in the House campaigns of the 1960s and the Senate campaigns of the 1970s made explicit reference to Dole's wartime service, the fact that he volunteered, and his difficult convalescence. One emblematic campaign flier from his senatorial contests in the 1970s stated, "You can sum up Senator Bob Dole with a 4-Letter Word: GUTS."[119]

Dole's presidential aspirations did not begin on the eve of the 1996 election. Rather, Dole had been a perennial competitor for the Republican nomination since his early years in the Senate. As a freshman senator, Dole was chosen as the Republican Party's National Committee chairman. Gerald Ford chose Nelson Rockefeller to be his vice president in 1974 after Nixon's resignation but selected Dole to be his running mate in 1976. Ford needed to shore up his right flank, and ideology explains choosing Dole more than his military biography does. He ran for president in 1980 but was not a factor in the race dominated by Ronald Reagan and George H. W. Bush. In 1988, Dole and others challenged Bush, the heir apparent, in the primaries, but Bush's lead was too formidable.

After those disappointments, 1996 was Dole's year. He spoke with a fellow senator about the age issue, and Warren Rudman said the military story inoculated any negatives about being too old to run for president. Rudman said, "Bob, it's hard to be the last of anything," referring to the fact that Dole was the last of the World War II generation, "but because Clinton didn't serve in the military and had clearly worked to dodge the draft during Vietnam, the contrast could all be used to Dole's advantage." Rudman concluded, "I don't think we have to be defensive about the age issue."[120] He invoked his World War II service in his announcement speech, though its inclusion was more ceremonial than strategic.[121] He outpolled Pat Buchanan and Steve Forbes in the primaries, winning most states, while retired general Colin Powell decided to stay out of the race. At the convention, some of the Republican delegates still thought highly of Dole's

---

118. Kalbfleisch 1950, A1.
119. Campaign flier, 1974, "Personal/Political Campaign Advertising, Campaign Literature, Dole for Senate 1974" File, Robert and Elizabeth Dole Archive and Special Collections, Lawrence, KS.
120. Woodward 1996, 43–44.
121. Woodward 1996, 164. The political cartoon *Doonesbury* lampooned Dole because he decided to announce his presidential run on the fiftieth anniversary of his World War II wound. See *Washington Post*, March 19, 1995.

war service. A survey of Republican attendees revealed that 8 percent of delegates felt that Dole's "war record" was still his greatest strength as a candidate.[122]

Dole formally accepted the Republican nomination at the convention in August 1996. His speech made both implicit and explicit references to his wartime service in World War II but did so in a fashion to connect that experience with other themes. There was a version of his campaign lapel pin that was in the shape of a Purple Heart medal with "DOLE '96" at the top.[123] He mentioned his 10th Mountain Division, the unit in which he served in Italy when he was wounded, and in the same sentence connected it to the African American 92nd Division fighting nearby. Dole referred to his long hospital stay by describing how his family cared for him. The speakers who were at the podium prior to Dole's acceptance speech also talked about his World War II experiences.

Dole's running mate, Jack Kemp, made it difficult to tag Clinton with the "draft dodger" label in 1996. Kemp achieved name recognition through his time as a quarterback on a professional football team. Kemp's medical exemption excused him from being called up from the U.S. Army Reserve for active service. Kennedy had called up the reserves in October 1961, and Kemp's unit was selected, the 977th Transportation Company. In essence he received a medical exemption that kept him out of active duty while he played for the San Diego Chargers, making it hard to credibly attack Clinton for dodging service during the Vietnam War.[124]

The incumbent Bill Clinton defeated Dole as he had done in 1992 against another World War II combat veteran. It is also important to see Dole in the context of the 1990s and how that decade saw the passing of the torch from the World War II generation to the baby boomers. For Dole and the others discussed here who were born around the same time or a bit earlier, World War II, with its unambiguous mission and victory, was the defining experience. For Clinton, America's tortured decade in Vietnam, with its ambiguous results and justification, was the defining conflict. But for Bush and Dole in the 1990s, World War II had occurred long ago.

Other Veterans in the Post–World War II Era

Barry Goldwater, George McGovern, Jimmy Carter, Ronald Reagan, Walter Mondale, and Michael Dukakis are the remaining presidential candi-

---

122. Lacayo 1996, 49.
123. Artifact ME02.09612, 1996, Robert and Elizabeth Dole Archive and Special Collections.
124. Frantz 1996.

dates of the post–World War II era. Each of them served in the military in various capacities. McGovern was a bomber pilot during the war who survived extremely risky missions, and Carter was a submarine officer in the postwar years. Reagan, Mondale, and Dukakis spent a relatively short time in uniform, Reagan during World War II and Mondale and Dukakis afterward, but these three did not see combat. What these men share is not just time in the armed forces but candidacies that did not rely on wartime heroics. For different reasons, personal and contextual, their campaigns either did not make their service salient or, like Dukakis's, it drew more negative attention than anything else.

The Republican nominee who would take on Johnson in 1964 was Barry Goldwater of Arizona. His path to a major-party presidential nomination went through the Phoenix City Council and the U.S. Senate. He was nominated by the Republicans to run for president in 1964, less than a year after John Kennedy's assassination. The party was not well unified behind the Goldwater nomination, and Johnson successfully painted him as an extremist. The election was a lopsided victory, with Goldwater winning only his home state and the core of the former Confederate states. During the war, Goldwater was an officer and pilot in the U.S. Army Air Forces. He flew many different kinds of planes in different areas of the war throughout the world. He had been a pilot since before the war and was a talented flier. He did not see combat, but he flew various warplanes from the home front to the front lines, ferrying the planes from the factories to the theaters of war. He also piloted supply planes that moved necessary matériel. Goldwater attempted to join combat squads but was turned down because of his poor eyesight and age, as he was already in his thirties when the Japanese attacked Pearl Harbor. He wanted to join squadrons that flew bombers, B-29s or B-17s, but he wrote, "I was always too old."[125] His contributions to the war effort were doubtless helpful, but he always regretted that he had not been able to fight in combat missions. In a 1977 letter, he expressed his feeling about lacking combat experience: "I have felt very self-conscious about the fact that I did not participate in actual combat during World War II."[126]

Goldwater's election efforts did not make his noncombat wartime experiences a large or notable part of the campaign. If anything, explicit references to his military experiences might not have played well for Goldwater in 1964 because the Democrats painted him as irresponsibly hawkish on foreign policy. Goldwater had spoken about the use of tactical

---
125. Dean and Goldwater 2008, 64.
126. Letter from Goldwater to Stephen Shadegg, June 6, 1977, quoted in Dean and Goldwater 2008, 63.

nuclear strikes in Vietnam and had joked about lobbing a nuke "into the men's room of the Kremlin."[127] These openings allowed the Democrats to characterize Goldwater as a trigger-happy hawk who, if elected, would be a danger. The 1964 election featured the single most famous campaign television advertisement since their inception. Lyndon Johnson's campaign's "Daisy" ad depicted a young girl picking and counting flower petals until a nuclear countdown takes over the audio and culminates in a mushroom cloud. Johnson's voice concludes the ad, imploring citizens to vote because "the stakes are too high."[128] The lopsided victory for Johnson in 1964 was not a product of either candidates' military service.

George McGovern was born in the early 1920s and came of age during World War II, and he volunteered for the U.S. Army Air Forces. The Democratic Party nominated George McGovern to challenge the incumbent Richard Nixon. Coming from the left of his party, McGovern was not a stranger to national-level politics when he ran in 1972. He had sought the 1968 Democratic nomination but fell far short of Hubert Humphrey's support and was also behind Eugene McCarthy. He had been a U.S. senator from South Dakota since 1963, a member of the Kennedy administration, and a U.S. congressman prior to that. He captured the 1972 nomination over Edmund Muskie, Henry "Scoop" Jackson, and others. The third brother of the Kennedy family in politics, Edward "Teddy" Kennedy, had been often spoken of as a likely nominee, but he lost viability after the Chappaquiddick incident in 1969.

If George McGovern had sought to use his military experience to his political advantage, his gallantry over the skies of Europe would not have harmed his candidacies. Compared to that of other veterans, his service was exceptionally valorous. George McGovern flew highly dangerous bomber missions during World War II. While he started his military career as an enlisted man, Lieutenant McGovern piloted a B-24 Liberator named *Dakota Queen* and survived long odds in one of the most dangerous combat duties of the war. By the time he shipped to the European Theater from his stateside training, the war against Hitler was nearing its end. McGovern's unit was stationed in a liberated part of Italy at an airstrip positioned so that Allied bombers could hit targets in Germany and across eastern Europe. During one harrowing mission, for which he was awarded the Distinguished Flying Cross, McGovern saved his crew by landing a damaged plane on a short runway.

---

127. Dallek 2004, 173.
128. The advertisement is available on the Living Room Candidate website, at http://www.livingroomcandidate.org/commercials/1964/peace-little-girl-daisy#3983.

On the way to a bombing run over an ammunition works in Czechoslovakia, one of the four engines of *Dakota Queen* quit. Undaunted, McGovern and his crew throttled up the remaining engines to stay in formation. Right before they reached their target, one of the remaining overtaxed engines gave up, so the bomber began to lose altitude. The crew dropped the bombs on target and turned toward home, but it was obvious they needed to find a landing strip closer than the one at their base six hundred miles away. The bomber limped to the Adriatic and away from enemy guns, but it was now flying below one thousand feet and still dropping. After the crew pitched nonessentials overboard to save weight, McGovern steered the plane to an island emergency runway designed for fighter planes. The bomber typically used a runway more than twice the length, but McGovern set the wheels on the first patch of pavement and stood on the brakes until the plane came to rest at the opposite end.

McGovern considered his final mission to hit a critical rail yard in Austria as his "toughest mission."[129] The antiaircraft fire was deadly, damaging the bomber's heat and oxygen supply. Further, the flak took out the heating system and destroyed the hydraulics that lower the bomber's landing gear and apply the brakes. The crew, who had suffered wounds from the shrapnel, had to hand-crank the landing gear down before McGovern landed the crippled aircraft, as it rolled without brakes to the end of the runway and finally stopped in a ditch. He performed thirty-five combat missions between 1944 and 1945 in unfriendly skies at great risk, performing excellently and earning prestigious combat medals.[130]

In 1956, McGovern ran for a U.S. House seat as a Democrat against an incumbent Republican, Harold Lovre. Feeling a strong challenge, Lovre's campaign implied that McGovern's support for allowing mainland China a United Nations seat meant he was a communist or communist sympathizer. Comparing war records helped McGovern deflect the smear.[131] Yet generally, McGovern treated his military record differently than other candidates did. He made almost no reference to his World War II heroism. In his speeches during the 1972 presidential campaign, including his announcement speech and his nomination acceptance speech, McGovern made no specific reference to his military service. Even when his biography might have helped burnish his credibility on taking controversial positions on lowering military spending and ending the war in Vietnam, he

---

129. McGovern 1977, 27.
130. Anson 1972; Ambrose 2001.
131. Sleuthing at the courthouse revealed that Lovre had not only failed to serve in World War II but earned his exemption by "crossing out 'lawyer' and writing in 'farmer' as his occupation." The embarrassing revelation did not help him maintain his seat. Knock 2016, 169.

made no biographical connection. One statement he used, "Let us create public transportation for people instead of more destruction of the dikes and rice paddies of Vietnam. Let us have smarter children instead of smarter bombs," was ready-made for an invocation of his own time in bombers thirty years earlier, yet he left it unspoken.[132] On August 24, 1972, McGovern addressed the National Convention of Veterans of Foreign Wars and made his case for ending the Vietnam War as soon as possible. Even in this setting, facing a group of fellow World War II veterans, he did not make substantial references to his own heroism in the skies of Europe when it might have helped provide credibility to his call for fewer weapons systems and decreased Pentagon spending. About the only reference he made was a quip relating his service in the air corps as predating the creation of the air force: "I belong, as many of you do, to the age when the Air Force was still in the Army, and the only difference was the amount of walking."[133]

Some historical treatments attribute McGovern's decision not to wave his war heroism during the election to his campaign managers. They saw it as clashing with the candidate's positions on issues. Working to elect an anti–Vietnam War candidate, McGovern's young staff balked at presenting McGovern in a light that might "boast of his military record."[134] If anything, the campaign's reluctance to use his war record left a void for someone else to fill, forcing McGovern to play defense with his military credentials in the summer before the campaign. In June of that election year, the archconservative Manchester, New Hampshire, *Union-Leader* reprinted a story first published by an arm of the John Birch Society that called McGovern's war record into question. In what might later be called a swift-boat-style attack on his military bona fides, the John Birch Society article claimed that McGovern had been reprimanded for cowardice and sent home from Europe after his fifteenth mission.[135] McGovern fired back immediately, and several of his crew mates also jumped to his defense.

Nixon aired an attack ad in 1972, "McGovern Defense" (ostensibly sponsored by "Democrats for Nixon"), that used toy soldiers being scooped off a table to criticize the magnitude of the defense budget cuts McGovern advocated. McGovern was campaigning on a peace platform that called for reductions in manpower and spending at the Pentagon. This ad, unanswered, held potential for McGovern to use his military experiences to

---

132. McGovern 1974, 28.
133. McGovern 1974, 104.
134. Farris 2012, 214.
135. "M'Govern Defends" 1972.

add credibility to his antiwar stance. One of McGovern's ads, "Young Vets," showed the candidate with wounded Vietnam veterans, pointing out that McGovern had spoken out against the Vietnam War when these veterans were in grade school. McGovern did briefly mention his wartime service in reference to the fact that he thought he deserved the educational benefits he received on returning stateside.

McGovern lost badly to Nixon in 1972, picking up only Massachusetts and Washington, D.C. The incumbent Nixon was reelected overwhelmingly in an election where military service was not salient. McGovern ran for president once more in 1984. He was never in a position to derail Walter Mondale's path to the nomination, but at a campaign stop in Iowa, McGovern's comments help illuminate his feelings about using his war stories to win public office. Some senior citizens who were presumably supporters, asked the sixty-two-year-old McGovern why he decided not to trumpet his heroic World War II combat stories aboard the *Dakota Queen*. Ronald Reagan, the incumbent Republican president, these supporters pointed out, did not have a real combat record from the war, only that he "starred in *Hellcats of the Navy*."[136] McGovern replied:

> Well, I don't go around boasting about my military record because there were millions of people who signed up for service. . . . I flew a string of combat missions against Nazi Germany. I would do the same thing again under similar circumstances. There isn't anybody running for President this year who has had any more first-hand experience with bloody combat than I have had, so I know what war is all about, and I am for a strong national defense. But I would prefer a more cooperative approach to the world and less of this interventionism and confrontation that we've had in the last couple of years. There is a certain amount of insecurity on the part of those who feed on some kind of a macho display—sort of a neighborhood bully mentality. It makes them feel tougher if they can push people around. I have never held to that view. I think that anyone who has a quiet confidence in the integrity and the soundness of American institutions and the American way of life is not always boiling for a fight with somebody else.[137]

Even more than George H. W. Bush, George McGovern exhibited reluctance to electioneer explicitly on wartime laurels. There were two

---

136. *Hellcats of the Navy* was a Reagan film from 1957, in which he starred as a submarine commander (his wife, Nancy Davis, was also in the movie).
137. Quoted in Marano 2003, 73.

reasons for his unwillingness to highlight his time on the *Dakota Queen*: it was a personal tendency of McGovern himself, and the politics of the times in which he ran for president provided disincentives to run explicitly as a war veteran. The unpopular Vietnam War polarized the country, and running for president against the war circumscribed the McGovern campaign's ability to use his military service in the campaign the way that others had done.

Graduating from the U.S. Naval Academy shortly after the end of World War II, Jimmy Carter served his active duty in the U.S. Navy as an officer until 1953. He was a few years younger than the other men in this cohort, so he did not serve in the war, but he did stay in uniform longer than most of the others. Being a veteran did not appear to play much role in either his first electoral efforts in Georgia in 1966 and 1970 or his run for president in 1976.

Excited about the U.S. Navy because of a relative who made a career there, a very young Jimmy Carter wrote to the U.S. Naval Academy at Annapolis as a grade-schooler to ascertain the entrance requirements. The catalog sent from the academy became a cherished icon in his life. Becoming sufficiently successful to meet the academy's entrance requirements, he said, was "the driving force in my life."[138] A setback occurred when he was at the cusp of this success because Carter's congressman had already nominated a candidate for the academy when he finished high school in 1941, so he enrolled at a local college and then Georgia Tech. He was later nominated for the academy and admitted, matriculating in June 1943. Even with an accelerated program necessitated by the country's wartime footing, the war ended before Carter graduated in 1946. After a short time on surface ships, Carter continued his career in the navy aboard submarines. Submariners are elite within the U.S. Navy, wearing "special insignia and get[ting] special pay. It is a proud service."[139] He became a "skilled officer" by the early 1950s.[140] He was selected to be on the final engineering team for a new type of diesel submarine and then entered the program for the new nuclear-powered vessels. Carter studied nuclear engineering and worked on developing the first generation of these ships, which would become the standard propulsion, leaving diesel engines behind. He was likely to be on track to command one of these new vessels himself, as his career appeared to exhibit a solid trajectory. His career was cut short by his father's death in 1953, as Carter felt the strong need to resign from the navy and care for his mother and siblings by continuing the family agri-

---

138. Bourne 1997, 45.
139. Mazlish and Diamond 1979, 111.
140. Godbold 2010, 64.

culture business back in Georgia. With some necessary political help from Georgia's U.S. senators to get the navy to agree to his release, Lieutenant James Carter left active duty in October 1953 after more than seven years in uniform. Carter had a successful navy career as an elite submariner with many accomplishments. He was an engineering officer on the U.S.S. K-1 (later named U.S.S. *Barracuda*) and worked on the development of the next generation of nuclear propulsion.

His political career began in 1962 with a run for a newly created state Senate district in Georgia, in which he served two terms. He ran for governor in 1966 and lost, but he won in 1970. Secondary sources, such as Carter biographies, do not mention any specific connections between Carter's naval service and his campaign themes. Like it did for George H. W. Bush, Ford, and McGovern, the time elapsed since Carter's military experience appears to have precluded the candidate's incentives for its use.

The political career of Ronald Reagan, a conservative voice from California, began in earnest with his endorsement and advocacy for Barry Goldwater in 1964. Yet he had already enjoyed wide name recognition in the United States because he was a well-known Hollywood actor in the 1930s and 1940s. He won his first try for elective office in 1966 when he captured the California governor's mansion. His involvement in presidential elections started in 1968 when he won a small number of delegates at the Republican Convention. He ran unsuccessfully again in 1976, taking on President Gerald Ford in the Republican primaries from the right but ultimately lost the nomination to the incumbent. He became the Republican nominee in 1980, beat Jimmy Carter in the general election, and then won reelection in a landslide in 1984. While Reagan is remembered for increasing defense spending, his own military service was not important in his elections.

The hawkish Republican, well known for his defense stands and support for increased military budgets during the closing years of the Cold War, served in the armed forces from 1937 until approximately the end of World War II in 1945. Because Reagan appeared in war films both during the conflict in propaganda films and afterward in Hollywood movies like *Hellcats*, some consider Reagan more of a pretender than veteran. While he did not raise the flag at Suribachi, he did wear a uniform during the war; hence, this book does not classify him as a nonveteran. Reagan was thirty years old when the Japanese attacked Pearl Harbor and had already developed an established career in Hollywood. By the time of the U.S. entry into the war, Reagan had earned a seven-year contract with a major studio, been nominated for an Academy Award, elected as a board member to the Screen Actors Guild, and performed in many films. He had also joined the U.S. Army Reserve in 1937. Starting as an enlisted infantryman, he quickly earned a commission and joined a cavalry unit. After the war broke out, he was called up to active duty in April 1942 but failed his eye test badly during the medical examination. The doctors apparently were surprised because he had somehow passed his previous exam and stated, "If we sent you overseas, you'd shoot a general . . . and you'd miss him."[141] He was classified as medically ineligible for overseas duty.

During his duty while in uniform, he did not stray far from home. Reagan was assigned to an arm of the U.S. Army Air Corps that leased movie studio space in Culver City, California, less than ten miles from Hollywood. The unit made training films for military men as well as patriotic films for civilians, often to buy war bonds or spur civilian recruiting. These films had wide-ranging goals. One urges women to work in factories; another pushed women to volunteer to drive buses. Some sought to have all Americans "open their homes to war workers who couldn't find housing."[142] Reagan narrated some of these propaganda films, and they were shown as newsreels in theaters across America. He also played a Catholic chaplain and sang in an Irving Berlin wartime musical.[143] While Reagan was indeed an officer in the active U.S. Army Air Corps during the war years, he was stationed at a movie studio that had been temporarily conscripted as a military studio. Those who question the legitimacy of Reagan's military service have an argument, but he was not known to exaggerate his war record.

The Democratic Party selected Walter Mondale, Jimmy Carter's vice president for four years, in 1984 to challenge Ronald Reagan. The election turned out to be a landslide for the incumbent. Reagan carried every state in the Union except Mondale's home state of Minnesota, where Reagan came within four thousand votes, and the District of Columbia. The candidates' military biographies played no role in this one-sided affair. Reagan was a known commodity as the incumbent. Mondale, as a less well-known challenger, conceivably could have attempted to employ a military biography toward capturing the nomination and contesting the general election. He did not have a substantial military record, however. Looking at the trend for the salience of candidate military biography, the 1980s elections were a nadir. Mondale's path to the nomination was complicated by Gary Hart, U.S. senator from Colorado and Jesse Jackson Jr. The Mondale-Hart contest was divisive, and the candidates were running closely in the polls. While Mondale had been an early favorite, Hart won

---

141. Edwards 1980, 44.
142. Boyarsky 1981, 56.
143. L. Cannon 1982.

in Iowa and New Hampshire. The men traded victories in the primaries, but Mondale eventually rounded up sufficient pledged delegates.[144] Military biographies did not play a role in any of the contests within the Democratic Party that year.

Mondale had indeed served in the military, completing a two-year enlistment. His record was not substantial compared to that of some of the other men of his generation running for president. It is reasonable to conclude that both Mondale and Reagan possessed roughly equivalent laurels from their time in uniform. Mondale volunteered to serve in the U.S. Army in September 1951. He stayed stateside, serving at Fort Knox as an assistant to the company clerk while the Korean War expanded. His views of his military time were sometimes doleful. In letters home, he related, "You might say my Army career has been colorless, in the sense that I am a mediocre GI who learns nothing except that class time provides a good opportunity to sleep."[145] His army time mattered little for Mondale, but for the next Democratic nominee four years later, it did.

During his presidential run against George Bush in 1988, Michael Dukakis faced some questions about the nature of his service during the Korean War. He was born in 1933, too young for service during World War II, but he was eligible for the draft during the Korean War, when American involvement centered on the years 1950–1953. He joined the U.S. Army in 1955 and served two years as an enlisted man in Korea after the war as a clerk, and in his pre-presidential campaigns, he "invariably cited his military service in his campaign literature."[146] He is reported to have said, "I have to have that [the army] on my record."[147]

Dukakis faced several other Democrats seeking the nomination in 1988. Al Gore and Jesse Jackson both carried states beyond their home state in the primaries. Gary Hart, George McGovern's campaign manager from 1972, had been polling ahead of all the other Democrats in early 1987, but scandal took him out of the race. Time at sea certainly played a role in Gary Hart's candidacy, but it was not related to the peculiar U.S. Naval Reserve commission he obtained at age forty-three. Rather, Hart's momentum went aground after revelations surfaced of him sailing aboard the pleasure yacht *Monkey Business* with a woman who was not his wife. After successfully dueling with Gore and Jackson, Dukakis clinched the nomination in the summer of 1988 and was able to sit back and watch the

---

144. Gary Hart, as a U.S. senator at age forty-three, requested the White House appoint him to a position in the U.S. Naval Reserve. Carter, who had lost his reelection, allowed it.
145. Quoted in Gillon 1992, 44.
146. Kenney and Turner 1988, 40.
147. Quoted in Southwick 1998, 748.

Dan Quayle National Guard controversy unfold in August.[148] But the scrutiny of Quayle's service would turn toward Dukakis. Ranking Republican House Veterans Affairs Committee member Gerald Solomon attempted to move the criticism from Quayle and shift attention back to Dukakis. He accused the candidate of avoiding military service by using his college deferment to attend Swarthmore College until 1955. Dukakis reacted defensively, retorting that he hoped the issue of his service had exhausted itself.[149]

It is hard to assess any damage to the Dukakis campaign as the Republicans sought to shift the criticism away from their vice presidential candidate. Dukakis's image problem regarding the military did not stem from his actual service record but an ill-managed campaign event in September. In the end, the most salient connection between Michael Dukakis's 1988 candidacy and the armed forces was a campaign stop that backfired terribly. The Dukakis campaign sought to dull the Bush campaign's attempts to paint their candidate as soft on defense. In what would thereafter become a lesson in how not to conduct a campaign photo op, the candidate held a press event at the General Dynamics plant in Michigan where the U.S. Army's main battle tank, the M-1 Abrams, was assembled. With reporters watching and cameras rolling, Dukakis donned a combat helmet embossed with his name and rode atop the tank with his hand on a machine gun as the tank performed maneuvers. The stop concluded with the tank's driver pulling up to the reporters, aiming the main gun at the press, and Dukakis mouthing "rat-a-tat," and the event concluded with the band playing the theme song from the film *Patton*.[150] Dukakis, who had suffered minor questions about his draft deferment a month earlier, sought to inoculate himself against charges of being soft on defense and to bolster his military authority with the event. The "attendant press corps . . . could not contain its laughter" at the sight of Dukakis in the helmet as he pulled up.[151]

The Bush campaign followed suit and hoisted Dukakis on his own video petard by using the undoctored camera footage of the tank event in an attack ad. This ad was made by a team under Republican strategist Roger Ailes that included an individual who would also be involved in creating the famous "Swift-Boat" ads of 2004.[152] The 1988 Bush ad featured the backdrop of Dukakis in his ill-fitting helmet riding on top of a

---

148. Quayle and the controversy are discussed further in Chapter 8.
149. Lentz 1988.
150. Weinraub 1988, A28.
151. Greene 2000, 47.
152. Bernsteim 2007.

tank while text scrolled down the screen along with a voice-over of all the defense systems and military programs that Dukakis had opposed over the years. George H. W. Bush won the general election by an easy margin. The actual military service records of the candidates were not salient, but Bush's campaign successfully embarrassed Dukakis in his attempt to appear hawkish. Because of Dukakis's position against Reagan's Strategic Defense Initiative, his campaign felt a need to add some hawkish luster. At the campaign event that became infamous, Dukakis's speech attacked Bush by saying that the Republican's "love affair with Star Wars" would force cuts for conventional weapons like the M-1 tank in which he rode.[153] It is important to see what the Republican ad sought to do with the visual of Dukakis in the tank. It was a policy-related attack ad that hit Dukakis for opposing many of the Reagan-era defense initiatives, such as new aircraft carriers and stealth bombers, as well as for involvement in Grenada and the strike on Libya.

From Eisenhower in 1952 to Bob Dole in 1996, the presidential candidates in the post–World War II years used military service to begin their political careers. All but one served in the army or navy, some during the war, some afterward, some in combat, and others away from the fighting. Some, such as Kennedy, Nixon, and Ford, returned from the war and immediately used their experience in World War II to win over voters. Eisenhower, the case quite apart from the others in this era, embodied the reluctant centrist role and made a lateral entry to the White House as nineteenth-century generals did. Despite the high numbers of veterans running for office, for most of the presidential elections of this period, military service was not salient in the election and far from a central element of the campaigns. As we see in the next chapter, the Vietnam War, with its very different legacy from that of World War II, elevates the role that candidates' military service plays in campaigns.

---

153. Weinraub 1988, 28.

8

Mixed Legacy of Vietnam

Bill Clinton through Donald Trump

I'm John Kerry and I'm reporting for duty.
—**John Kerry**, quoted in Hollihan, *Uncivil Wars*

I wish I could have had the luxury, like you, of growing up and living and spending my entire life in a nice place like the First District of Arizona, but I was doing other things. As a matter of fact, when I think about it now, the place I lived longest in my life was Hanoi.
—**John McCain**, quoted in Povich, *John McCain*

I don't like losers. . . . [John McCain is] a war hero because he was captured? I like people that weren't captured, okay? I hate to tell you.
—**Donald Trump**, quoted in J. Johnson, "Donald Trump Has No Interest in Apologizing to John McCain"

For those of the Vietnam War generation who entered presidential politics in the 1990s and later, the legacy of that war differed substantially from the aftermaths of previous wars. Vietnam stands alone from other American conflicts in the level of substantial domestic opposition. It was a long war with debatable origins in the Eisenhower and Kennedy administrations, but the unequivocal rise in American involvement took place under Lyndon Johnson's presidency in 1964 and lasted a decade. It was a proxy war during the Cold War where U.S. forces were deployed to prevent communist North Vietnam from unifying with South Vietnam. The American forces left Vietnam not as victors but withdrew under Nixon, who weighed the domestic opposition to the war over difficulties in fighting the Soviet-backed communists. For the eight male candidates of this cohort, four served in the military, but questions about how and if candidates served became salient for five: the Vietnam War cohort of presidential candidates saw an increase in the significance of military experience in elections.

George H. W. Bush, after the United States successfully ousted Iraqi forces from Kuwait and returned home victorious, proclaimed in 1991, "By God, we've kicked the Vietnam Syndrome once and for all," meaning that the malaise plaguing the American military after failure in Vietnam was finally over.[1] In a strict wins-and-losses sense, perhaps he was correct. However, if he believed that the echoes of Vietnam would stop recurring in American politics, he was wrong. For the presidential candidates between Bill Clinton and Donald Trump, the echoes of the Vietnam War reverberated in foreign policy debates that defined the elections. For especially Clinton, Kerry, McCain, George W. Bush, and Trump, the candidates' experiences and decisions in the 1960s about the Vietnam War framed discussion and debate over contemporary wars.

While the proportion of candidates in the post–Vietnam era with time in uniform is less than that among the post–World War II group of candidates, Vietnam War service remained more striking in presidential elections. The World War II veterans' glory from a hard-won and popular war had developed the patina of age. For the men of the Vietnam generation, military service would become an issue once more, but more complex. Far more so than occurred in other postwar eras, issues about who did not serve were as fraught a question as who did. Negative campaigning focused on attacking, for example, Bill Clinton, Mitt Romney, and Donald Trump for avoiding the armed forces despite being age eligible during the draft. During George W. Bush's run (and Dan Quayle and Jack Kemp if we include vice presidential candidates), attention zeroed in on how those with political connections received safe National Guard roles that would not rotate to combat duty.

This chapter proceeds as the previous ones do, with one addition. Given the increased salience of military service in this era, the chapter also empirically assesses the salience of previous military service among the post–Vietnam War presidential candidates. It is possible to quantify how the electorate perceives candidates' military experiences by using survey data from 1992 to 2008.

Vietnam: Troop Strength and Means of Recruitment

As a formative experience for the young adults who vied for the White House from 1990s to the 2016 election, the Vietnam War shares some characteristics with other era-defining wars but also differs in important

---

1. Dowd 1991, A1.

ways. The means by which individuals were recruited was large-scale conscription, and millions of soldiers were inducted into the armed forces as volunteers or draftees. Certainly conscription had been used to create the large forces required to wage both world wars, and the draft continued as an induction tool for Korea and Vietnam, but it drew a smaller share of the male population than World War II did. Most men who served in Vietnam were volunteers, but the motivation for their voluntarism varied, with many volunteering for noncombat roles to avoid being conscripted into infantry units.[2] The draft also became an important point of criticism for antiwar protesters as public opinion turned against the war in the late 1960s.

The major-party nominees of the post-Vietnam generation were all born strikingly close together around the end of World War II, making them early baby boomers. The oldest, John McCain, was born in 1936, but others were born between 1946 and 1948. This places them all, except Barack Obama, within the age range of being between seventeen and thirty-five in 1965 and thus among those who might serve in Vietnam.[3] Almost nine million men served during the Vietnam War, mainly in the U.S. Army, in the decade between 1964 and the disgraced conclusion of Nixon's presidency in 1974. Of these, more than three million served in Southeast Asia. The Census Bureau's estimate of the male population between ages seventeen and thirty-five in 1965 is approximately twenty-five million, comprising men born between 1936 and 1948.[4] Hence, very roughly less than a fifth of age-eligible men in the United States served in Vietnam.

Of the eight male major-party nominees in this cohort of presidential candidates, four served in some capacity and four did not. That half of them were in uniform reveals that while the proportion of nominees with service is far less than among the World War II cohort, it is still larger than the approximate proportion of age-eligible males who served. In other words, parties nominated veterans to be their standard-bearer more than one would expect if they were simply drawn randomly from the population.

The path that led to the military, or avoided it, differed for the candidates in this chapter. For John McCain, it is difficult to imagine a path outside the U.S. Navy. The son and grandson of admirals, McCain began

---

2. Angrist 1991; Shields 1981.
3. Hillary Clinton does not receive consideration here given the gender restrictions and social norms of the Vietnam era, though she did claim to consider joining the Marines. See Kessler 2015.
4. U.S. Census Bureau 1995.

his studies at the U.S. Naval Academy in 1954, and his retrospective view was that the decision was inevitable, "an immutable fact of life."[5] John Kerry decided to serve in some capacity while an undergraduate at Yale before 1966, and his decision to join the navy was in part a reaction to his likely conscription into the army. Al Gore volunteered to enlist and serve in Vietnam when he probably could have avoided it. One biographer of failed presidential candidates saw a bond between these three men, sons of privilege who could have avoided Vietnam but instead sought to serve there because of a mix of idealism and a "misapprehension that a military record would be necessary to pursue a career in public office."[6]

Even though the Cold War had ended, America's military role in the world continued, and Americans would debate how and where American force should and should not be projected. These debates occurred with Vietnam as a backdrop. This era saw the transition of American conflicts from large, conscripted land armies fighting conventional wars into smaller but difficult asymmetric wars against a range of enemies that vary in their ease of definition. The first conflict of the era was Operation Desert Storm, America's first war on live television, for which the combat action lasted less than two months. America's role in the Middle East underwent a fundamental change after terrorists attacked New York City and the Pentagon on September 11, 2001. Under George W. Bush's administration, the United States attacked Taliban forces in Afghanistan later that year for harboring Al-Qaeda and Osama Bin Laden, the mastermind of the terrorist attacks. Two years later, Bush pushed for a war with Saddam Hussein in Iraq, using various justifications to win over public opinion and Congress, which opened the door to the invasion of Iraq in 2003. While the successful invasion of Iraq and toppling of Hussein took only six weeks, American involvement in occupying Iraq during a protracted and difficult stabilization of the country and region continues. American boots on the ground outlasted Bush's two terms in office, leaving President Obama to declare troops out of the country by the end of 2011, but the U.S. commitment to both broken countries remains as of this writing. The declining popularity of these wars, along with few options to proceed, has made them difficult foreign policy challenges and keep military and defense issues important in campaigns and governing.

Vietnam, partially responsible for dividing the Democratic Party in 1968, continued to create schisms in society and the political realm. Some of these echoes of Vietnam that continued to reverberate centered on who

---

5. McCain and Salter 1999, 110.
6. Farris 2012, 260–261.

served and what service meant.⁷ There are several examples of events long after the war demonstrating that the United States had still not fully recovered from Vietnam. Hollywood films about Vietnam were dark, remarkably different from films about World War II in the decades that followed that conflict.⁸ The unveiling of the controversial Vietnam War Memorial in Washington, D.C., in the 1980s reopened the only partially healed wounds.

That memorial's central feature is a list of all the names of American casualties in Vietnam, all 58,307 of them. Casualties increased in the Vietnam War as the war escalated in 1966. As a proportion of all the servicemen deployed in Southeast Asia, around three million, the casualty rate at less than 2 percent appears very low when compared to the rate in nineteenth-century wars when medical care was poor. Yet the American electorate did not observe casualties in comparison to those in the Mexican-American War more than one hundred years in the past; they saw this human cost of war in the face of cloudy military goals and a sense that the United States was not winning. The growing toll of American war dead shaped Americans' attitudes toward the war, in concert with perceptions that the war was not going well.⁹ As Christopher Gelpi, Peter Feaver, and Jason Reifler point out, the Tet Offensive in January 1968 was a turning point concerning public attitude toward the war. War dead, negative views toward returned Vietnam veterans, and the lack of achieving war aims all contributed to how citizens in subsequent times would continue to think about the war.

This mixed legacy of Vietnam, still real, also had implications for those seeking political office. The Vietnam generation began entering politics in the 1980s and 1990s. The selection of Indiana's Dan Quayle as George H. W. Bush's running mate made him the first Vietnam-era name on a presidential ballot. After that, from Bill Clinton on, baby-boomer presidential candidates would see Vietnam issues reemerge again and again. Another way that Vietnam manifested in this era with regard to military service is the coining of the term "chickenhawk," an epithet to disparage political elites seeking wars who had not been to war themselves.¹⁰

Military service during this time declined as a proportion of Washington insiders, as well as in the population at large. The share of congressmen with military experience peaked in the 1970s and declined afterward. However, parties began to recruit military veterans explicitly

---

7. Ricks 1997; Webb 1978.
8. Dittmar and Michaud 1990.
9. Gelpi, Feaver, and Reifler 2009.
10. Ryan 2009.

in congressional elections in the 2000s.[11] Perhaps this occurred because of a lingering sense that military service is a necessary ingredient or a boon for attracting votes inherited from the World War II era of political leaders. With the supply of veterans diminishing across the 1990s and 2000s, parties began to increase their demand for candidates with military experience.

Federalization, Partisanship, and Professionalization of the Military

As we have seen in the past eras, changes to the political hue of the military institutions were related to how candidates' military experiences were perceived in elections. For those earlier eras, the debates about federalization were important. Fights over the role of militia forces versus that of federal regulars were important before, but for this era, the federalization of the armed forces had long been a settled issue. The key question relates to a fissure forming between the military and civilian worlds, which diverged after the Cold War, with important implications for both.

Richard Kohn wrote a stunning indictment of the growing divide between civilian society and its civilian leaders in government and the armed forces and a rise in the political maneuvering of top military personnel. He and others recognized a growing gulf in values and political identities that had been occurring quietly in the postconscription years but had reached a more critical and demonstrable point when Bill Clinton became president. Due in part to the president's avoidance of military service, the relationship between him and the Pentagon became strained. Clinton came to the table with "less experience, interest, understanding, and credibility in military affairs" than previous presidents.[12]

On the military side, Chairman of the Joint Chiefs of Staff General Colin Powell was a household name because of his leadership during the 1991 war with Iraq. If Clinton entered office lacking clear military credibility, Powell had become a highly persuasive actor in shaping military policy since before Operation Desert Storm, even though he was a soldier at the time. By consolidating many of the avenues with which the president as commander in chief influences the military, Powell had created a more influential chairmanship, and he used it.[13] One of the two most public breaches of the deferential military role that Powell committed was a *New York Times* op-ed he wrote about President George Bush's decision to

---
11. See Rothenberg 2007; Dao and Nagourney 2006.
12. Kohn 1994, 3.
13. Avant 1998. Others see Powell's political actions in a less problematic light. See Hooker 2003.

use limited air power over Bosnia in October 1992 during the presidential election. Powell's op-ed was not a full-throated criticism of Bush's decision to conduct war on a limited scale, but it did not "signal a clear endorsement," making it publicly distinct from the White House's position.[14] The second political dispute into which Powell publicly waded was the debate surrounding gays serving openly in the armed forces. His opposition, in uniform, to President-elect Clinton's proposed policy showed lack of deference that spilled into public view.[15]

As the armed forces became smaller and relied on volunteers, those in the ranks began to look less and less like a representative cross section of the public at large. Data began to reveal increasing identification with the Republican Party among members of the active military.[16] The gap was not the same for subgroups, but among whites and officers a demonstrable Republican tilt was evident. The public's perception about which party enjoyed more credibility on national security and defense issues rewarded the Republicans as well. From before the 1990s until approximately George W. Bush's second term, respondents told pollsters by wide margins that they trusted Republican more than Democratic political leaders to handle defense issues.[17]

As a backdrop to the individuals who ran for president as this gap between the civilian and military worlds grew, veterans became a focal point and a potential bridge. Yet rather than help ameliorate the gap, the presidential elections with salient military service issues only highlighted the differences between the military institutions' culture and that of the civilian world. Clinton's reputation as a draft dodger made it difficult to be commander in chief. As military elites became more Republican, the gulf between them and civilian Democrats in politics made the relationship less easy. While the Clinton years put this problem in sharp focus, the schism continued after his administration.

Political Changes outside War and Military: Parties and the Presidency Evolve

In the 1992–2016 period, the parties continued to make small changes to their nominating systems, but what had begun in the 1970s after the McGovern-Fraser reforms remained largely in effect. The typical path to

---

14. Feaver 2003, 261.
15. Drew 1994.
16. Holsti 2001; Inbody 2008.
17. Goble and Holm 2009.

successfully clinch a party presidential nomination meant garnering momentum from early victories in Iowa and New Hampshire to tackle subsequent contests in larger states. Some elections were close-run contests, while others were lopsided; some years featured many candidates, while other years saw only a pair of viable candidates.

The stature of the presidency did not diminish in this era. If Cold War presidents were seen as commanders in chief in a nuclear standoff with the Soviet Union after World War II, the Vietnam-era presidents also faced military threats, albeit of a very different nature. While nineteenth-century transformational changes to political parties and the presidency itself held implications for understanding the role that candidates' military service played, there was little change in either factor from the post–World War II to post-Vietnam generations with important implications for veterans running for the White House.

Vietnam Era Veterans: Echoes from an Unwon War Reverberate

Table 8.1 lists the nine candidates of this post-Vietnam cohort between 1992 and 2016. (George H. W. Bush and Bob Dole are included in the table because of their candidacies in 1992 and 1996, but they substantively belong with the World War II cases.) They are arranged into substantively similar categories. Five ran for the White House and found that Vietnam remained relevant to their political lives. Four, John McCain, John Kerry, George W. Bush, and Al Gore, served in the armed forces, all but Bush going to Vietnam. Bill Clinton's maneuvering to avoid the draft made the politics of military service important to understanding his candidacy. The appropriate way to group them in terms of the role that Vietnam played is to study McCain and Kerry together as combat veterans and then consider the Gore candidacy. While his short time in the army and Vietnam was not as salient as it was for others, it was an important political matter for both him and his father, a U.S. senator. Then the analysis moves to Bill Clinton, Bush, and Trump, because of criticism about avoiding Vietnam. Even though they did not obtain major-party nominations, former generals Wesley Clark and Colin Powell each feature importantly for different reasons. Clark actively contested the 2004 Democratic nomination, while Powell served in George W. Bush's cabinet after retiring from the army and frequently was spoken of as a potential Republican candidate. Hillary Clinton, the first female major-party nominee for president, did not serve in the military, as very few women of her generation enlisted.

TABLE 8.1 ELECTIONS OF THE POST–VIETNAM WAR ERA

Election year	Candidate	Party	Veteran type	Military service
1992	George H. W. Bush	R	Combat vet	Navy torpedo bomber pilot, World War II
	Bill Clinton	D	Nonveteran	None
1996	Bob Dole	R	Combat vet	Army officer, World War II
	Bill Clinton	D	Nonveteran	None
2000	*George W. Bush*	R	Common vet	Texas Air National Guard pilot, Vietnam War
	Al Gore	D	Common vet	Brief enlistment as military journalist in Vietnam
2004	*George W. Bush*	R	Common vet	Texas Air National Guard pilot, Vietnam War
	John Kerry	D	Combat vet	Navy swift-boat officer, Vietnam War
2008	John McCain	R	Combat vet	Navy pilot, POW, Vietnam War
	Barack Obama	D	Nonveteran	None
2012	Mitt Romney	R	Nonveteran	None
	Barack Obama	D	Nonveteran	None
2016	*Donald Trump*	R	Nonveteran	None
	Hillary Clinton	D	Nonveteran	None

Note: Winners are italicized. D = Democratic Party; R = Republican Party.

Vietnam Combat Veterans: Kerry and McCain

John Kerry and John McCain did not share similar paths in their prewar years that would lead them to Vietnam. Kerry attended Yale and thought heavily about the U.S. role in Southeast Asia, while McCain's military career and life were almost foreordained by his family's long military legacy. Vietnam and their role in it created a frame for understanding both of their political candidacies. McCain's service was seen almost entirely positively, but Kerry's Vietnam service and antiwar activities afterward colored his presidential bid in two contrasting ways.

John Kerry was a Vietnam combat veteran who returned after the war to begin a successful political career and later run for president with a keen focus on his military experiences in a wartime election. His service record would become the topic of the most memorable attack on him in 2004. Karl Rove, top campaign strategist for George W. Bush, in summing up his side's estimation of the Democratic nominee in 2004, saw John Kerry's "record as a veteran [as] a big asset—though not as big of an asset as he thought it was."[18] Perhaps Rove was right on both points. Based on

---

18. Rove 2010, 370.

the way the Kerry-Edwards campaign behaved, it seems clear that those running the campaign agreed with Rove. Few presidential candidates have made their military service so central to their candidacy as John Kerry did in 2004—certainly among the nongenerals. And no other candidate's military service would be the center of such contrast: the Kerry campaign and the Democrats hoped to put forward a bona fide war hero with Purple Hearts to dispel the inherent advantage that Republicans enjoyed on national defense and war, while Republicans and affiliated groups worked overtime to show that Kerry exaggerated his combat experience and then dishonored himself by protesting the war after his return. My point here is not to establish which depiction more closely hews to the truth but to convey how both versions of John Kerry were central to understanding the 2004 contest, a wartime election with important consequences.

John Kerry was born during World War II and graduated from Yale in 1966—after Kennedy's assassination in 1963 and the Tonkin Gulf Resolution in 1964. Two biographies that rely primarily on interviews with Kerry's college friends show that he thought a great deal about America's involvement in Vietnam while in school. Prior to more widespread opposition, Kerry's skepticism about the possibilities of American military policy increased when he was at Yale, but he was also firm in his belief that he should serve his country. One of Kerry's close friends was the nephew of William Bundy, assistant secretary of state on East Asian affairs under President Johnson. Bundy visited Yale to speak and had a late-night conversation with Kerry and others. Bundy spoke earnestly about the importance of their military service. The conversation made a deep impression on the young men, including Kerry.[19]

Kerry was probably also influenced by the templates of public service laid forth by his idol, John Kennedy. Kerry was very conscious of the role that the *PT-109* story played in Kennedy's rapid political ascent. While it is clear that Kerry felt the pull toward joining the military as Vietnam escalated, it is less clear what role he wanted to serve in the war. The draft weighed heavily in his life, as it did for other able-bodied students heading toward graduation and the end of draft deferment. Prior to graduating and facing a draft that inducted more and more men each month, Kerry volunteered. Rather than join the army, marines, or air force, which might have appealed to him given his training as a pilot, he joined the navy—the branch with a low likelihood of combat. He enlisted with a deferral until graduation and would be sent to Officer Candidate School (OCS). He was

---

19. Kranish, Mooney, and Easton 2004, 49; Brinkley 2004, 42.

certainly aware of the increasing role that the U.S. military had begun to assert in Southeast Asia—all while recognizing his political ambitions.

His first months in uniform were in training; he spent the fall of 1966 at OCS and earned his commission by December. He spent time in further training in 1967 and 1968 and was assigned to the U.S.S. *Gridley* by June 1967, which sailed on the Pacific to various locations, including the Tonkin Gulf, the Philippines, and New Zealand. He commanded sailors on the guided-missile frigate, a combat vessel that typically sailed with a carrier group in a support and antiaircraft role. Kerry's task as a junior officer was generally to keep the sailors busy with cleaning and maintaining the seaworthiness of the ship. He decided in 1968 to request a change of station and volunteered for duty on smaller, shallow-water craft that operated in and around the shores and rivers of Vietnam. He sought more action and less monotony, and he was keen to be in charge of a boat and its crew. By the summer's end in 1968, he was in training to serve on swift boats in Vietnam. Swift boats and other shallow-water navy craft in the region typically patrolled rivers and inlets, making sure fishing vessels and other boats were not transporting enemy weapons and supplies.

Kerry's first taste of combat was a brief firefight in December 1968, though decades later, he characterized it as "half-assed action that hardly qualified as combat."[20] While patrolling in a small skimmer, Kerry and his men surprised a group of Viet Cong in the night. A brief firefight resulted in a small shrapnel wound for Kerry, one that did not prevent him from normal duty the next day but did qualify him for a Purple Heart. He was later assigned his own swift boat, *PCF-44* and then *PCF-94*, and tasked to more dangerous areas.

Headquarters gave a diverse array of missions to swift-boat crews. Sometimes the boats would simply patrol, while other missions involved extraction of American or allied forces. They might also be sent to inspect targets after air strikes, provide fire support for others, ferry navy SEAL teams, or sometimes wait to ambush Viet Cong forces at night. The locations of the missions also ranged widely. Sometimes orders kept them in coastal waters, while other missions took them upstream into rivers, far beyond friendly territory. The risk on these missions also varied but was never zero. Mines, ambushes, Viet Cong posing as fishermen, and other threats faced the patrols. A rocket-propelled grenade fired from a riverbank sent shrapnel into Kerry's leg on February 20, 1969, earning him a second Purple Heart, though the injury was minor.

---

20. Brinkley 2004, 146.

One week after the shrapnel wound, Kerry led a group of swift boats upriver on the Dong Cung River with a mission to deploy a group of South Vietnamese forces. Anticipating ambuscades, Kerry and the other officers decided to alter their response to the inevitable ambushes. Rather than return fire and continue sailing, they chose to turn their craft directly toward the enemy fire to beach the craft and disembark to engage the attackers directly. When the swift boats took fire, they turned toward the source and beached quickly, eliminating a lookout and fanned out to look for more enemy soldiers. Kerry ordered his boat to continue upriver, and two hundred yards later, Viet Cong forces fired a rocket at *PCF-94*. Beaching again, they discovered a surprised soldier as he ran off. Kerry dashed after him and came back with his weapon after he and the other Viet Cong were dead. Kerry received the Silver Star for this action not long after the events.

Accounts of the action on that day, February 28, 1969, differ. The men who appeared in the Swift Boat Veterans for Truth campaign advertisements in 2004 claim that credit for Kerry's actions and tactical successes belong to others. John O'Neill and Jerome Corsi's book, *Unfit for Command*, also raises doubts. "Kerry . . . took off, perhaps with others, following the young Viet Cong as he fled, and shot him in the back, behind a lean-to. . . . Whether Kerry's dispatching of a fleeing, wounded, armed, or unarmed teenage enemy was in accordance with the customs of war, it is very clear that many Vietnam veterans and most Swiftees do not consider this action to be the stuff of which medals of any kind are awarded."[21] Even before his presidential campaign, some doubts appeared. A *Boston Globe* reporter wrote an article on the eve of Kerry's 1996 Senate reelection, questioning whether Kerry's actions that day had been a war crime: the piece implied he shot a wounded and potentially unarmed man in the back.[22]

Kerry's service in Vietnam presents a complex case. Ascertaining the degree to which John Kerry deserved his war medals is not my intention. Official reports favor Kerry's rendition of events. Kerry's superiors had incentives to award him and other officers medals. The admiral in charge "had dozens of Swift boats getting shot at and he wanted to make sure his junior officers were given proper honor. . . . The Silver Star . . . was an 'impact' award, given shortly after an action to lift morale."[23] It is very clear that Kerry's political candidacy brought both supporters and detractors to the surface, each using his Vietnam experiences for different purposes decades later. Irrespective of how different partisan messaging played out,

---

21. O'Neill and Corsi 2004, 83.
22. Warsh 1996.
23. Brinkley 2004, 293.

it is certain that John Kerry, unlike others of his privileged background, volunteered for combat leadership in Vietnam and served under dangerous conditions. As we have seen for other presidential candidates, that type of service is more than sufficient for trying to win over voters. Kerry would see political value in his time in Vietnam almost immediately upon returning stateside.

There were many young Vietnam veterans in the late 1960s. What gave John Kerry name recognition was not precisely his use of Vietnam experiences to run for office. Rather, his time in the navy as a combat veteran with medals gave him a unique platform to engage in politics as an antiwar activist. There was no shortage of antiwar protesters in 1971, but there were few Yale-educated, Boston Brahmins in fatigues with war medals and top-notch debating skills. His Senate testimony on the nature of the war in April 1971 was powerful and established his political future. He called the war an error in vivid terms with compelling oratory; few in the congressional chamber were not "shaken" when Kerry asked the committee and country, "How do you ask a man to be the last man to die in Vietnam? How do you ask a man to be the last man to die for a mistake?"[24] Kerry's appearance on the *Dick Cavett Show* two months later further signaled his growing importance and political potential. He was a leader and spokesman for Vietnam Veterans against the War (VVAW), an antiwar group of returned vets that held events and protests. He, with VVAW, wrote a book the same year, *The New Soldier*, which detailed their movement and protests.

The mixed legacy of his Vietnam service emerged as a political attack on Kerry in his first run for political office in 1972. He had beaten a large field of Democrats to face Republican Paul Cronin in the 5th congressional district of Massachusetts, but he fell short in the general election. His loss was explained by critical editorials in the local paper and attacks from an independent candidate who ran Kerry's *New Soldier* book cover as a visual, which featured antiwar veterans mocking the famous Iwo Jima flag-raising photo and statue while flying the U.S. flag upside down as a protest. While hostile editorials and his opponents did not help Kerry's chances, he also suffered criticism for being a latecomer, having changed residences three times in the previous year in search of a congressional district in which he had a chance. His identity as an antiwar protester and carpetbagger, not the composition of the district, shaped the outcome of the race.

Later, he would use his service as a foil against nonveteran opponents. During a race in 1996 when he defended his U.S. Senate seat, he often

---

24. Nicosia 2001, 138.

reminded voters of his challenger's lack of experience in the armed forces by highlighting his own, using subtle and unsubtle means. In debates, he frequently touched on his own service experience when answering questions. When asked about a recent terrorist attack in Saudi Arabia that killed nineteen U.S. airmen, he answered that Americans are united in their anger and followed with, "I have a particularly strong sense of what it's like to stand watch in a lonely place and never know when the danger is going to hit."[25] In an earlier debate, the candidates clashed over the death penalty. Bill Weld challenged Kerry, an opponent of the death penalty, to explain why a convicted cop killer's life was worth more than the slain officer's. Kerry responded by connecting a hot-button domestic issue to his war record. He said, "It's not worth more. It's not worth anything. . . . It's scum that ought to be thrown in jail for the rest of its life. . . . I know something about killing. I don't like killing. And I don't think a state honors life by turning around and sanctioning killing."[26]

Among the Democrats seeking the presidential nomination in 2004, Kerry was not the only one with military experience. The 2000 presidential election addressed education policy more than foreign policy, but the terrorist attacks of September 11, 2001, and wars in Afghanistan and Iraq made the 2004 election hinge on America's wars and military direction. In response to 9/11, the Bush administration had launched two wars—one immediately after the attacks against Al-Qaeda and Taliban forces in Afghanistan and another against Iraq in 2003. If the United States had enjoyed a period of post–Cold War attention to domestic issues, the 2004 election thrust defense and security matters to the fore. The Democratic Party faced a decision between four main rivals for the presidential nomination to try to unseat President Bush in the 2004 election. Howard Dean, a nonveteran medical doctor from Vermont, appeared to be the front-runner in 2003. He was the most critical of the Iraq invasion among the Democratic candidates and had not been in the Senate to cast the vote authorizing action. John Edwards's candidacy centered more on domestic issues than the other candidates' campaigns. General Wesley Clark, commander of the Allied campaign to liberate Kosovo and valedictorian of his West Point class, came to the race late.

Wesley Clark, whose military credentials were obviously sterling, never edged beyond single digits in polls. While there had been a "Draft Clark" movement afoot for some time in 2003, he did not officially begin the campaign until September of that year, long after a presidential primary effort should begin to be competitive in the early states. His identity

---

25. "Massachusetts Senatorial Debate" 1996.
26. Dewar 1996, A4.

as a Democrat was another issue, with some stalwarts in the party questioning him based on positive comments about notable Republicans. His public-speaking style, prone to offer complicated and nuanced answers to predictable political questions, was also a matter that attracted the wrong kind of media attention. In short, while the party sought someone with military credentials who could challenge Bush, Clark's negatives outweighed his service record. He later retracted the words as a joke, but he told the *New Yorker* that he was a Democrat only because Karl Rove failed to return his calls.[27]

With the primaries in the rearview mirror, the American voter considered two candidates of approximately the same age, both of whom had spent time in uniform during the Vietnam War, though the nature of their service substantially differed. John Kerry, a combat veteran in Vietnam who came home to found an antiwar organization, ran against the incumbent George W. Bush, a man with a thinner, controversial military service record. People wondered how he had remained out of combat and speculated about his absences from duty. Hoping to make the contrast clear, the Democrats organized the 2004 convention to highlight Kerry's military past. It took place in Boston, Kerry's hometown. He arrived at the convention center by boat, crossing Boston Harbor with fellow swift-boat veterans who served with him under arms. Retired generals and admirals spoke in person and appeared in videos during the convention to continue to bolster Kerry and the Democrats' defense chops. The candidate's acceptance was introduced by Max Cleland, a former U.S. senator and triple amputee wounded in Vietnam. Kerry took the stage and began with a military salute to the crowd, stating that he was ready for duty. He reminded listeners, "I know what kids go through when they're carrying an M-16 in a dangerous place, and they can't tell friend from foe." The Democrats obviously hoped to convey throughout the convention an "unspoken message: Kerry served in combat, while George W. Bush served stateside in the National Guard."[28]

The response did not come from the Bush-Cheney campaign directly but from an election advocacy group attacking Kerry right at that point of credibility that the Democrats worked hard to convey at the convention. A week after the convention, Swift Boat Veterans for Truth put their ad in three small media markets, but it would become the most memorable part of the 2004 election.[29] Titled "Any Questions?" it begins with John Edwards's claim, "If you have any question about what John Kerry's made

---

27. Boyer 2003.
28. VandeHei 2004, A28.
29. Teigen 2007; Ball 2005.

of, just spend three minutes with the men who served with him." The music then swells as Edwards fades out, shifting to a low, ominous tone, and segues into a minute-long series of critical statements by military veterans. They either directly contradict Kerry's valor and actions that led to his medals or attack him for his antiwar advocacy after his return stateside. The lines were powerful broadsides that directly undermined the image established by the convention in Boston. Comments from swift-boat veterans sought to cast doubt on the heroism that others had lauded, such as "I know John Kerry is lying about his first Purple Heart because I treated him for that injury," and "John Kerry lied to get his Bronze Star. I know, I was there, I saw what happened."[30]

The Swift Boat Veterans for Truth "527" organization, the type so named because of its status within the tax code, would make and air more ads, but the first was its most well known. The group received criticism from Democrats and Republicans alike, with John McCain and even George W. Bush singling out the ad as an unfair smear.[31] Important campaign decision makers in the Kerry campaign retrospectively regret not reacting to the ad sooner. Key Kerry campaign consultant Bob Shrum revealed after the election that waiting two weeks to respond to the swift-boat attacks was one of the campaign's tactical errors.[32] So important was the organization in 2004 that the term "swift-boating" lived on as a political verb in our electioneering jargon, meaning to level an unfair or false ad hominem attack on the campaign trail.[33]

Vietnam cast contrasting light on Kerry's political life. His time as a combat veteran lent credibility and allowed him to speak to defense issues more than other Democrats. Yet his antiwar activities after the war would allow detractors to diminish any boon from his time in the navy. In a time with American troops in two active wars, the candidates' past military service was a central concern of the 2004 presidential campaign. A video game company even produced a first-person combat simulation so players at home could relive Kerry's experiences in Vietnam.[34] Kerry's dual identity, combat veteran and war protester, along with attacks on his service from an outside group proved that while military service was salient, it was also complex.

---

30. A video of the ad is available at http://www.livingroomcandidate.org/commercials/2004/any-questions. Later investigations revealed that some of the same veterans had spoken highly of Kerry previously. See Coile 2004.
31. Journalists would later find links between the Bush-Cheney campaign and the leadership of the Swift Boat Veterans for Truth organization. See Zernike and Rutenberg 2004.
32. Shrum 2007.
33. Major and Andersen 2016, 891.
34. Snider 2004.

The other Vietnam combat veteran nominated in this era was John McCain. His military service was, like John Kerry's, also central and salient in his presidential bids. Unlike Kerry, it was seen mostly positively. With deep military history and roots among his family, a career as a combat naval aviator during the Vietnam War, long and harrowing experiences as a prisoner of war from 1967 to 1973, and substantial wounds from the crash and torture, McCain was, and is, simply inseparable from his military biography. He ran for president twice, once losing in the primaries in 2000 and once in the general election in 2008. Among the men who have won a major-party nomination since the World War II generation left the stage, McCain had the longest military career and probably experienced the most arduous and painful time in service than any presidential candidate of any era.

After his education at the U.S. Naval Academy, McCain became an aviator and piloted carrier-based A-4 Skyhawks. These single-seat small planes were used during the Vietnam War as fast, light bombers. For his twenty-third bombing mission, McCain flew with his squadron to attack a power station in North Vietnam's capital, Hanoi, in October 1967. McCain watched the radar tracking alarm light up, signaling a likely incoming surface-to-air missile (SAM); engaged countermeasures; and then dove and dropped his payload. After dropping his bombs, his plane's wing was destroyed by the SAM, forcing McCain to eject over hostile territory.[35] Ejecting from a small combat aircraft even when not in hostile conditions is dangerous. The process to push the pilot from the aircraft uses controlled explosives to quickly launch the seat from the cockpit—the intention being to save the life without excessive concern for the limbs. McCain's arms and legs were severely injured by the ejection. While he survived and landed in a lake, he sustained many injuries and broken bones that were made worse by the crowd that pulled him from the water and beat him, as well as neglect and abuse by his captors.[36]

During McCain's five-and-a-half-year stay at Hoa Lo Prison in Hanoi, his captors routinely tortured and interrogated him despite his serious wounds from the ejection. His identity as a POW was made more complicated by the fact that his father was an admiral. On the one hand, it probably moved the Vietnamese to give him medical aid once they found out his identity, but, on the other hand, he had great value as a propaganda tool. McCain's ordeal in Hanoi was terrible. He spent the five years suffering from dysentery, eventually weighing around one hundred pounds. Sometimes he was kept with other American POWs; at other times he was

---

35. Timberg 1999.
36. P. Alexander 2008.

confined in solitary. For some stretches, he was ignored, but at other times he was shackled or bound during interrogations. Beyond the concerted efforts to punish and extract information from him, McCain was also routinely subjected to demeaning and painful abuse from low-level prison guards. At one point he was offered early release, but he refused it—he wanted no special treatment, feeling that prisoners should be released in the order of capture, not by who happened to be an admiral's son. After the Paris Accords, McCain was finally released in March 1973.

McCain had been in the U.S. Navy since his graduation from Annapolis in 1958 until his retirement as a captain in 1981. In the years following Vietnam, McCain had tried to regain his flying status and continue his navy career, but his wartime injuries precluded him from flight and the promotions he sought, so he filed his retirement papers. His final role while in uniform perhaps portended his next career. He was assigned to the navy's liaison office with the U.S. Senate, which, in his words, would "mark my real entry into the world of politics and the beginning of my second career as a public servant."[37] His political activity began immediately after retirement, as McCain ran for the open U.S. House seat in the Arizona 1st district in 1982.

McCain enjoyed some name recognition at the time of his first House race, as his capture and return were national news and he had given speeches widely. The district leaned heavily Republican, so winning the primary was tantamount to obtaining the seat. He deflected carpetbagger accusations memorably by saying that Hanoi was where he had spent the most time in one place.[38] In Congress as a House member for two terms and U.S. senator since the 1986 elections, McCain became a leading voice, well known for defense and veterans' issues. He was at least twice on vice presidential short lists, for George Bush in 1988 and Bob Dole in 1996, but being passed over both times, he opted to run for the top slot himself.

McCain first ran in 2000, when he lost the Republican nomination to George W. Bush, and then again in 2008, when he secured the Republican Party nomination but lost to Barack Obama in the general election. The role of McCain's military biography in his 2000 run gave him credibility as a commander in chief, but it also inspired underhanded questions about his mental stability. In his contest against Texas governor George W. Bush in 2000, McCain won an early victory in the New Hampshire primary, a state that allows both Republicans and Independents to participate in the Republican primaries and a place where McCain had placed most of his electioneering resources to challenge the better-funded Bush.

---

37. McCain and Salter 2002, 14.
38. Povich 2009.

After his tour of New Hampshire in his famous campaign bus, the "Straight Talk Express," he beat Bush by a large margin, gaining momentum toward the South Carolina primary three weeks later. That southern state, however, held fundamental advantages for Bush, and the lead-up to its February 19 contest is frequently noted as among the nastiest intraparty fights in recent memory. The Bush side inadvertently allowed comments by a notable military veteran at a Bush rally, J. Thomas Burch, chair of a veterans' organization. He forcefully attacked McCain's record as a legislator on veterans' issues, claiming that McCain "forgot" veterans and their issues when he got to Washington.[39] Bush was on the stage during these comments, which were contrary to the way Bush and his campaign had treated McCain's military and veteran credentials up to that point. Bush had generally complimented McCain on his stance on veterans' issues. These comments gave McCain an opening and put Bush on the defensive. Republican and Democratic senators wrote a public letter admonishing Bush, and even an assistant secretary of veterans affairs from George H. W. Bush's administration conceded that the attack on McCain's record was "over the line."[40]

A central voice from within the Bush campaign saw the event as a "blow" from which it took days to recover because McCain kept the comments alive by bringing the "insult" up in media events, town hall meetings, and debates.[41] Burch's criticism of John McCain on veterans' issues was tantamount to criticizing his identity as a war hero and respected military veteran. The magnitude of this moment on the 2000 campaign trail and the way Bush had to scramble to get past it represent a stark contrast to the aftermath of comments that Donald Trump would make fifteen years later. Donald Trump himself offered a far more withering and disrespectful attack on John McCain's service yet suffered little for it.

It is difficult to know how much traction McCain gained or Bush lost because of the event. The polls were volatile, but it is important to note that South Carolina was and is a closed-primary state, allowing only registered Republicans to vote in the GOP contest. McCain's more politically centrist identity made it harder to win over voters in South Carolina than in New Hampshire, which allowed Republicans and political Independents to participate. Bush won by a smaller margin than McCain's win in New Hampshire, but it was sufficient to put Bush back in the driver's seat; McCain's hopes for the White House in 2000 were largely dashed.

---

39. Gamerman 2000, A1.
40. Lacey 2000, A10.
41. Rove 2010, 146.

Even before his run for president, McCain had felt the barbs of political attacks from critics who believed he had not done enough to press Vietnam on releasing soldiers who were missing in action—there had been innuendos and accusations that his time as a prisoner of war "left him prone to violent fits of temper, perhaps even rendered him mentally unstable."[42] Whispers of mental instability borne from his POW experiences also came out in the 2000 cycle, or even worse was an accusation that McCain was a brainwashed Manchurian Candidate.[43] These ideas were reportedly spread by push polling and other under-the-radar methods.[44] As it did for Kerry, military service offers both opportunities and vulnerabilities for presidential candidates.

In the years between his presidential attempts while George W. Bush was in the White House, McCain remained a U.S. senator who enjoyed wide name recognition nationally. McCain and Bush had buried the hatchet in some ways since 2000, and McCain was traveling with the president during the election and stumping on his behalf. Perhaps Bush gained additional support by having his former rival endorse him. The American people generally felt positively toward McCain while he was not a presidential candidate. In a national poll during the 2004 presidential election that measured Americans' general feelings toward various political leaders, John McCain earned more than a 60 on the 0–100 "feeling thermometer" used by the ANES. Further, military veterans in the electorate felt even more positively than nonveteran civilians. Of the two presidential candidates, Kerry came in at 53 and Bush at 55.[45]

Perhaps it was this number that kept McCain's presidential aspirations alive, and he decided to run after the Bush years. The race in 2008 was "open seat" in the sense that a second-term president could not run and Bush's vice president, Dick Cheney, was not going to run. The three main rivals for the Republican nomination were John McCain, former Massachusetts governor Mitt Romney, and former Arkansas governor Mike Huckabee.

In summer 2008, long after McCain had won enough delegates to become the presumptive Republican nominee, an episode occurred involving his veteran status. Wesley Clark proved the rule that for most people it is very difficult to criticize a candidate's military service, even if the critic has well-known military experiences himself. Wesley Clark was

---

42. M. Allen 2009, 292.
43. Gooding 2004.
44. Push polls are telephone-bank electioneering efforts that resemble survey research but ask leading questions meant to shape opinions rather than measure them. See Streb and Pinkus 2004.
45. Teigen 2007.

a valedictorian from West Point and combat officer in Vietnam and rose to four-star general and Allied commander of NATO forces during the Kosovo War. Yet even a man with such military credentials is not immune to the apparent prohibition making it tough to criticize a candidate's military service. Clark went on television to make the case for Obama's candidacy on a Sunday-morning news program, *Face the Nation*. Clark started by honoring McCain's sacrifices as a POW but then asserted that McCain's time as a naval aviator did not give him any executive experience. He stated further, "I don't think riding in a fighter plane and getting shot down is a qualification to be president."[46] It was a flap that generated outrage from Republicans. Obama was forced to give a speech the day after Clark's comments about patriotism and tried to rise above the spat by asserting that no party has a monopoly on patriotism. Clark's comments, which Obama had to characterize as inartful, forced both Clark and Obama to try to recontextualize Clark's words and spend time expressing admiration for McCain's service for days afterward. Again, Donald Trump's negative language about John McCain as a prisoner of war in 2015 makes clear this formerly taboo treatment of veterans is subject to change.

Aside from how campaign proxies and events on the campaign trail play out, it is also important to understand how the public viewed McCain and his military service. Survey evidence shows that his military service helped McCain in some ways. The American people, at least before the realities of the financial meltdown led all headlines by autumn, found in June 2008 that John McCain was far more able to handle the responsibilities of the commander in chief role than nonveteran Barack Obama. While more than half (55 percent) believed Obama could handle the duties, 80 percent thought that McCain had what it takes to bear the military responsibilities of a post–Cold War president. This sample was not otherwise disposed to favor McCain, as a majority of the same people in the survey intended to vote for Obama. What this means is that McCain, likely because of his own well-known experiences during his military service, earned more credibility as commander in chief from Democrats than nonveteran Obama did from Republicans.[47] This credibility was expressed more in abstract than specific terms. McCain's military service was more salient to the American public than that of most of the candidates for whom we have polling data. In the ANES of that year, respondents were asked for reasons to support McCain, and their open-ended responses were recorded. Of those who could think of any reason to like him, more than a fifth specifically mentioned his military service or time as a

---

46. Zeleny 2008.
47. Saad 2008.

prisoner of war.⁴⁸ This number puts McCain's service below Eisenhower's in terms of salience but above Kerry's and Dole's.

Kerry and McCain ran for president while the country was at war, and each campaign highlighted their combat experience. For both, military service framed their first candidacies for congressional races that would be a stepping-stone to the U.S. Senate. And while supporters found each candidate's military service a compelling attribute to value, detractors attempted to cast each man's wartime involvement in a negative light. While this is recognition that campaigns perceive military service as an electoral advantage that requires a response, it is clear that the mixed legacy of Vietnam and the politics of the 1960s can extend for decades thereafter.

A Senator's Son Goes to Vietnam: Al Gore

Al Gore stands apart from the combat veterans as well as the candidates who avoided Vietnam. He neither garnered any great advantage or narrative frame of military experience to shape his candidacy nor attracted attacks on his military service. For having enlisted and gone to Vietnam, he fulfilled an obligation as he saw it, for country, himself, and his family. Al Gore faced the same difficult decision that the other men seeking the White House did during the Vietnam War years. For the senator's son, deciding to volunteer and enlist was a difficult family matter. In June 1969, immediately after graduating from Harvard, his student deferment ended and his draft eligibility became real. The war was near its height, and while Al Gore Jr. had his concerns about his short- and long-term life plans and political viability, his father was facing political challenges of his own.

Al Gore Sr. was a Democrat representing Tennessee, a three-term incumbent first elected in 1952 after having already been a House member before World War II. The one-party hold that the Democratic Party had on the South generally, including Tennessee, was waning, and Gore Sr. faced a challenge both in the Democratic primary in 1970 and then a serious challenge in the general. One of his electoral weaknesses was his opposition to the Vietnam War, being out of step with public opinion among his constituents. Vice President Spiro Agnew declared that unseating Gore was the "Nixon Administration's number-one target" in the midterms.⁴⁹

---

48. That year, 189 of 707 (21.1 percent) who said something positive about McCain referenced his military service. Among all respondents (2,322), 8 percent mentioned it. Both proportions are unweighted.
49. Barone, Ujifusa, and Matthews 1972, 757.

One biography cites Gore Jr.'s Harvard friends to show that he had mixed feelings about serving in the war.[50] The younger Gore had misgivings about the war but also knew that his father's electoral prospects would not be helped by having a draft-dodging son. Overt pressure does not appear to have been applied by the father, but rather the son accepted the political reality. Had he different parents, his decision to voluntarily enlist would likely have gone the other way.[51] But different parents would have given him a different surname, denying him his greatest asset when beginning his political life. Gore's own description of his joining the military places fairness at the center of his decision: if he pulled strings to get out of the draft, some other young man from Carthage, Tennessee, would have to go to Vietnam in his place. Once in uniform, there is no evidence that Gore ever asked for special treatment, even though the army was acutely aware of whose son he was. Four-Star General Westmoreland singled him out during a drill to have a chat about why young people opposed the war.[52]

Rather than wait for the draft, Gore enlisted in the U.S. Army in August 1969. Given his journalistic experiences and Ivy League education, the army saw value in placing Gore into service as a public affairs staffer. His recruiters were cognizant that he was a senator's son, but it was not unusual for anyone of his qualifications to be given a job outside the infantry (one of the recruiting sergeants said Gore had "just about maxed everything" on the entrance exams).[53] After basic training and then less than a year at Fort Rucker, Alabama, Gore shipped to Vietnam. He had requested the move, hoping to be assigned to a public affairs unit in South Vietnam. Some sources speculate that his orders to Vietnam were delayed from the White House—to deny Gore Sr. any positive press from his son shipping to the war zone. One of his campaign ads showed Gore Sr. sitting in army uniform with his son, the father teaching the son patriotic life lessons.

In Vietnam, Gore worked as a newspaper reporter in a public information role from January to May 1971. He flew and traveled around South Vietnam, covering stories for the army paper and writing press releases for consumption back home. He was not in a combat role and did not see action, but he saw and interviewed many G.I.s recently returned from fighting. It was a short, five-month tour for Gore during his relatively brief time in the army, having served about two years. He applied for graduate school and requested an early separation in May 1971, and the future senator and presidential candidate was a civilian in Tennessee by that summer.

---

50. Turque 2000.
51. Turque 2000.
52. Henneberger 2000.
53. Maraniss and Nakashima 2000, 114.

Al Gore Jr. ran for the U.S. Congress in 1976, after working in journalism, but made no notable use of his army time in his successful attempt to win the Democratic nomination for the 4th district. He ran a bit to the right, befitting his district, but won on his name, dogged campaigning, and issue positions. It was a crowded field, but Gore narrowly won with about a third of the votes. His subsequent general elections for his House seat were never in doubt. He ran for U.S. Senate in 1984 when the seat opened from a retirement, and he won that handily, paving the way for his premature bid for the Democratic nomination for president in 1988.

Al Gore did not place his time in the army front and center for any of his campaigns but did include it as a biographical entry. Gore's presidential runs in 1988 and 2000 both used images from his time in the army. It is likely that the imagery was meant to convey that despite growing up with all the advantages of coming from an elite family, he volunteered to do his duty like anyone else.

Avoiding Vietnam: Clinton, Bush, Romney, and Trump

Bill Clinton, George W. Bush, Mitt Romney, and Donald Trump each received scrutiny for the means by which they sidestepped the draft to avoid going to Vietnam. The circumstances and political fallout for their actions differed dramatically, but the common thread is central to this book's question: How do candidates' military biographies shape presidential elections? In their cases, military biography is important because they were draft-eligible young men at a time when the United States fought in Vietnam. Bush stands apart because he did join the military, but questions of how he obtained a post in a National Guard unit arose in 2000 and 2004, making his case similar to those of the other three. It is important to stress that many men did what they could to avoid the draft during the Vietnam War, especially men in high socioeconomic positions. Only about a dozen of the approximately eleven hundred graduating from Harvard in 1969 went to Vietnam.[54] But for those seeking the highest office in the land, skipping Vietnam in the 1960s would resurface in each candidate's political lives later.

The first presidential candidate in this era was Bill Clinton, and his avoidance of the draft during the Vietnam War illustrates how fraught the matter of past military service became after the World War II cohort passed the torch. If candidates' military service in World War II played a minor but positive role, questions of who served and who did not and why became more salient and divisive for the Vietnam generation. Clinton,

---

54. Henneberger 2000.

from before the primaries in 1992, put the politics of past military service back on the front page of the papers. Clinton's lack of service might have been noteworthy in itself, as he was the first nonveteran to win a nomination since Hubert Humphrey. Before he officially entered the race, Clinton himself expressed that his lack of service might constitute an electoral liability in the wake of the popular liberation of Kuwait in 1991. When brainstorming the decision to run, he thought it would be very challenging to upset an incumbent who presided over a successful war because he "never served in Vietnam."[55]

But simply lacking service was not the whole of the issue. It was how he had avoided the draft in 1969 that dogged him, as early as 1978 in the Arkansas gubernatorial race, but it also arose in 1992 when he ran for the Democratic presidential nomination. Clinton had graduated from Georgetown University in 1968, ending his draft exemption as a college student. He was against American involvement in Vietnam and wanted no part of it. He planned to attend law school, which in the past would have extended his exemption from conscription, but the Pentagon ended postgraduate deferments in 1968. What he actually did is still difficult to understand completely because of conflicting accounts. Even biographers contend it is a "difficult episode to sort out, muddled by Clinton's various accounts . . . and by a scarcity of documentary evidence."[56] While he was a Rhodes Scholar after college, Clinton explored options to avoid the draft legally. He spoke to an ROTC recruiter, perhaps exaggerating his interest in the program at the University of Arkansas, which led the program to offer an exemption contingent on his attending law school there. He ultimately decided not to accept that offer, but the draft lottery gave men with his birthday a number that made his induction extremely unlikely. When he made the decision to decline the offer, Clinton wrote the recruiter to notify him, and the letter reveals his thinking:

> The decision not to be a resister and related . . . decisions were the most difficult of my life. I decided to accept the draft in spite of my beliefs for one reason: to maintain my political viability within the system. . . . When the draft came, despite political convictions, I was having a hard time facing the prospect of fighting a war I had been fighting against, and that is why I contacted you. ROTC was the one way left in which I could possibly, but not positively, avoid both Vietnam and resistance.[57]

---

55. Goldman et al. 1994, 39.
56. Maraniss 1995, 190.
57. Ifill 1992, A1.

Claims that he had avoided Vietnam by gaming the ROTC deferment came out in 1978 when he ran for governor, but his explanations were at the time apparently sufficient. When Clinton sought the presidency in 1992, the letter became national front-page news. The New Hampshire primaries were important as a contest to ascertain how much support there was for Clinton. With less than a week before the New Hampshire primary, the letter came out and cemented Clinton's reputation as a draft dodger, though he did not technically evade conscription. Clinton's campaign staff worried deeply that it would harm Clinton's chances, especially given that a war hero, Bob Kerrey of Nebraska, was also running: "You didn't have to be a war hero, but you couldn't be seen as a draft dodger."[58] That reputation was not a fatal blow to his electoral viability. Clinton beat expectations, coming in second place in New Hampshire, despite the draft letter not even being the largest crisis for the Clinton campaign that week. Around the same time a woman with an audiotape of a phone conversation claimed she had been Clinton's mistress for years while Clinton was governor. Yet it was exactly Clinton's ability to win votes in the primaries despite these setbacks that propelled him to the nomination.

In the general election, the way Clinton avoided Vietnam continued as an issue, made even more problematic when his role in antiwar demonstrations overseas became known. President Bush repeatedly criticized Clinton's organization of peaceful antiwar protests in front of the U.S. embassy in London while he was a student in England: "I cannot . . . understand mobilizing demonstrations against your own country . . . when you are in a foreign land. Maybe I'm old fashioned, but to go to a foreign country and demonstrate against your own country when your sons and daughters are dying halfway around the world, I am sorry but I think that is wrong."[59] The Bush campaign ran its most negative advertisements against Clinton on the radio, drawing listeners' attention to Clinton's actions during the Vietnam War. One spot referred to Clinton as a waffler, using evidence that "Clinton said he respected the military but then never joined" and "Clinton at first said he never received a draft notice but later reversed his story."[60] Polls at the time revealed that more than 20 percent of voters believed the issue to be "very important" to their vote.[61]

---

58. Stephanopoulos 1999, 70. Kerrey earned the Congressional Medal of Honor in Vietnam as a navy SEAL.
59. Kelly and Johnston 1992, A20.
60. Newman 1994, 112.
61. Frankovic 1993, 123.

Clinton unseated Bush in 1992 and became president, yet his actions in 1969 continued to color perceptions of his administration. He earned the enmity of some skeptics within the military establishment when he pledged to overturn the ban on gays serving openly in the military. Clinton's difficulty selecting an effective secretary of defense in his first term contributed to the impression that he had trouble with security issues, reinforcing the draft-dodger image. The matters that continued to connect the administration's problems with Clinton's actions in 1969 showed that "the perception . . . that he was a 'draft dodger' during the Vietnam War shadowed him and seemed to compromise his status as commander in chief."[62] His lack of service engendered unprecedented open criticism from high-ranking officers.[63] His not being a veteran, the letter to the ROTC recruiter, his emphasis on repealing the ban on gays serving in the armed forces, and his trouble finding a secretary of defense added up to an "impaired legitimacy" that constrained his ability to preside over military matters.[64] Clinton entered 1990s politics with a 1960s history that "invited confrontation with the military,"[65] which made his presidency more challenged than it would have been otherwise.

George W. Bush's service also engendered controversy in his presidential campaigns, though quite different from Clinton's because of his decision to join a Texas-based Air National Guard unit. In both his presidential election in 2000 and reelection in 2004, Bush faced criticism about his military record during the Vietnam War. Bush came from a political family. His grandfather had been a U.S. senator from Connecticut for more than a decade, and his father had an even longer Washington résumé, culminating in his presidency. At the time that George W. Bush was graduating from college and losing his student deferment status in 1968, he moved to Texas to join the Texas Air National Guard.

The *how* he joined is important, but explaining *why* points to a common strand among all the men in the post-Vietnam cohort. Like Gore, Bush was sensitive to his father's electoral concerns. Bush the elder had lost a U.S. Senate race in 1964 but won his House race two years later, and everyone knew that he had his sights on higher office. According to a close college friend, George W. Bush understood that "in order not to derail his father's political career he had to be in military service of some kind."[66] He told reporters that he was not willing to hide in Canada or "shoot my ear-

---

62. Adler 2003, 480.
63. Feaver 2003.
64. Betts 2005, 10.
65. Hooker 2003, 10.
66. Minutaglio 1999, 116.

drum out" to obtain a deferment—and he wanted to be a pilot like his father.[67] So right before he graduated from Yale, he signed up in the Texas Air National Guard to begin after graduation in 1968. How much Bush believed that military service would be a necessary stepping-stone to his own political career is not clear. However, as the son and grandson of politically powerful men, Bush had to have at least entertained thoughts of a public future and likely shared the conventional wisdom about the perceived necessity of military experience.

How Bush obtained a spot in the Texas unit, which was unlikely to deploy to Vietnam, had been a matter of speculation and controversy since the early 1990s.[68] Two questions dogged Bush: whether he had been offered a coveted spot in the Texas Air Guard because of his name and political connections and whether he had completed his military duties in the Alabama Air Guard when he was temporarily assigned there.

For those who sought military service without risk of going to Vietnam, or sought legal means to fend off the draft, state National Guard units held appeal. Very few of the men serving in Air National Guard units rotated to Vietnam for combat duty. Other well-connected political families, such as those of Senator Lloyd Bentsen and Governor John Connally, had acquired spots for their sons in what some called a "champagne unit."[69] How Bush earned a role in a full-rostered unit with a waiting list that kept him from Vietnam became an important question on the campaign trail. Bush repeatedly maintained that no one from his family made a call on his behalf to obtain preferential treatment. However, in 2004, Democrat Ben Barnes, lieutenant governor of Texas in 1969, went public with how Bush got into the National Guard. Barnes reported that he was approached by a close ally of the Bush family in 1969 about finding a spot for the younger Bush. The favor may have worked both ways. From the perspective of the National Guard unit, there were incentives to doing a favor to a congressman's family.[70]

George W. Bush joined the 147th Fighter Group, a unit with a mission not terribly dazzling: defend American airspace over Texas and the Gulf of Mexico. Threats to this space were not many. Bush trained to fly F-102 Interceptors, fighter jets that were becoming obsolete. By the time Bush was a pilot in the 147th, the roles that the plane played were dwindling, having been replaced by newer craft. Bush finished basic training and shipped to Moody Air Force Base in Georgia to train on the jets. He was

---

67. Minutaglio 1999, 116.
68. Perhaps the most critical account can be found in I. Williams 2004.
69. J. Smith 2016, 18.
70. Mann 2015.

awarded his wings in December 1969 and rotated to a Houston, Texas, air base. Bush spent the time there before he started his MBA at Harvard in 1974 by flying part-time. There is little doubt that he enjoyed his time training and flying fighter jets—one of his biographers assessed Bush's autobiography, concluding that the "excitement at being a pilot is the only part that literally leaps off the pages."[71]

Another controversy during Bush's presidential campaigns related to a temporary reassignment he was granted. He helped a Republican candidate run a U.S. Senate election in Alabama in 1972, a time when he had apparently received an official approval for his requested transfer to an Alabama Guard unit. Journalists in 2000 and 2004 and subsequent historians have been unable to find compelling evidence that he appeared for duty at his temporary unit, though some first-person accounts recall his time there. Establishing the veracity of Bush's claims and those made by Democrats is not important for our purposes. What is important is that Bush's National Guard duty emerged in his presidential runs, and in two elections against men who served in Vietnam, some voters saw the appearance of preferential treatment that kept Bush from Vietnam.

The template for this perception was created by Bush's father's vice president in the 1988 election, Dan Quayle. He joined the Indiana Army National Guard in 1969 as an enlisted man near the height of American involvement in Vietnam. The heart of the controversy over his military service was the appearance or reality that his politically powerful family had used its influence to guide Quayle's service into the Indiana National Guard rather than in the active force likely to deploy to combat in the Vietnam War. Reports at the time were that he replied to questions from Tom Brokaw and Dan Rather that "phone calls were made," but he was "almost certain that the Governor or Lieutenant Governor were not involved in that."[72] A snubbed Bob Dole, who had actively sought the vice presidency, retorted, "And I must tell you, in my generation, you knew who was in the Guard and who was in uniform and fighting for their country."[73]

George Bush's military service became an issue in his presidential elections because of the appearance that he received preferential treatment to avoid Vietnam as a result of his father's connections and because of the irregular reassignment to Alabama and doubts about him actually reporting for duty. Yet he did wear a uniform and fly fighter jets. Romney and Trump, however, never joined, though the importance of this gap on their résumés seems to have receded with time.

---

71. Renshon 2004, 38.
72. Oreskes 1988.
73. Dowd 1988, A1.

Mitt Romney used religious and academic exceptions to avoid the draft during the Vietnam War. His lack of service was never an above-the-fold story during the 2012 presidential election. After college, he followed the Mormon tradition of missionary work, traveling to France in 1966, justifying the ministerial deferment. The year before his first presidential bid in 2008, Romney discussed his deferments and told an interviewer, "I was supportive of my country. . . . I longed in many respects to actually be in Vietnam and be representing our country there, and in some ways it was frustrating not to feel like I was there as part of the troops that were fighting in Vietnam."[74]

Religious exemptions for the draft are granted at the state level, and because Romney lived outside Utah, his chances of getting a missionary exemption were good. As a Mormon seeking a Michigan missionary-based exception, Romney had an easier path than Mormons in Utah seeking exceptions because the demand exceeded the supply. The relatively small numbers of Mormons in Michigan made it all but certain that his deferment would be granted. After his educational and religious deferments expired, Romney became draft eligible in 1970, but his favorable draft number and the diminishing force size in Vietnam meant that he had a very small chance of selection. Except for an awkward news cycle in which he defended his sons for not serving in the armed forces by insinuating that their work on getting him elected was comparable to military service, there was little overlap between veteran politics and the election in 2012.[75] Considering the field, it was likely that the GOP would nominate a nonveteran in 2012. Of the front-runners among the candidates, only Rick Perry, governor of Texas, and Ron Paul, congressman from Texas, had served. Neither former Speaker of the House Newt Gingrich nor former senator Rick Santorum had served.

Donald Trump appeared to break so many rules in his ascent to the presidency in 2016 that it was largely overlooked that he suffered little to no criticism for avoiding military service during the Vietnam War. Bush, Clinton, and Quayle each faced harsh and repeated criticism for missing the war, though in different ways. Trump repeatedly demonstrated how his candidacy conformed to a different set of rules concerning what statements, actions, and gaffes might doom a White House run. Some are directly related to military-service issues.

His lack of service and varying explanations of how he avoided Vietnam received comparatively little attention compared to similar scenarios facing past presidential candidates. Trump graduated from a

---

74. Wines 2012.
75. Ryan 2009.

military-themed prep school in 1964, and as American involvement in Vietnam ramped up, he applied for four educational deferments as he attended college. After receiving his degree in 1968, he applied for a medical deferment based on a physical exam disqualifying him from service related to bone spurs in both heels. He later told a biographer, "I had a doctor that gave me a letter—a very strong letter on the heels."[76] He then received a draft number that made his subsequent draft vulnerability very low.

Beyond what he did and did not do as a young man, the sacred cows relating to veterans and military service that Trump attacked as a presidential candidate are important to note. Very early in his candidacy he mocked Senator John McCain on camera, attacking him for having been shot down and captured—openly defying the spirit of black POW-MIA flags hanging in veteran organizations' posts nationwide. In January 2016 on the eve of the Iowa caucuses, he held a fund-raiser, ostensibly for veterans, as an alternative event to boycott a Fox News debate and later claimed to generate six million dollars in donations. Reporters followed up and found no evidence of such donations, forcing Trump four months later to give some money quickly to a veterans group and reveal that he raised much less.[77] Perhaps most shocking was Trump's repeated disparagement of Khizr and Ghazala Khan, parents of a U.S. army captain who was killed in combat in Iraq. He "breached multiple norms of American politics" by criticizing the Gold Star parents for saying that Trump had "sacrificed nothing" at the Democratic convention.[78] Perhaps one reason for the lack of sustained censure for his avoidance of Vietnam comes from the fact that the especially wide field of other candidates featured so few veterans. Only a couple of the other Republican candidates vying for the nomination had served, both of whom dropped out of the race early, so no obvious contrast could be used to highlight Trump's educational and medical draft deferments.

Related to his draft avoidance and comments about the military experience of others, what made Trump immune from damage that might have sunk other candidates? It is possible that some explanations are unique to 2016, and the amount of time that had passed since the Vietnam War had weakened mores related to the war. One reason that Trump's medical exemption made few headlines is that the number of times and speed with which Trump made news were high and unprecedented, so no single issue was likely to endure or invite steady contemplation. Against the backdrop

---

76. Eder and Phillips 2016, A1.
77. Fahrenthold 2016.
78. Burns, Haberman, and Parker 2016, A1.

of other scandals, such as the audio recording of his disparaging remarks about women or his tax returns being leaked, Trump's avoiding Vietnam fifty years earlier generated comparatively little interest. He was covered by the media to an unprecedented degree. Trump received four hundred million dollars' worth of free media attention in February 2016 alone. In contrast, John McCain spent about four hundred million dollars on his entire 2008 campaign.[79] It is also possible that because Vietnam was fifty years in the past, the debates over who served and who did not were simply becoming less relevant to an electorate that has fewer voters who were alive during the war. Prior to 2016, even glancing criticism of McCain by proxies such as Burch and Clark put other candidates facing McCain on the defensive. Trump showed immunity for his remarks about McCain, which would have damaged candidacies in the past. And there was no expectation that Hillary Clinton's lack of military service hampered her candidacy because women of her cohort did not generally serve. Hence, the usual contrast of military service records with two men running was absent in the general election.

Quantifying the Salience of Post-Vietnam Candidate Military Service in Presidential Elections

I include an empirical analysis of presidential candidates' military experiences for this era because of the substantive variation and partisan differences in how the public perceives the post-Vietnam presidential candidates. While the data were available for the post–World War II generation of candidates, the level of salience after Eisenhower was low and varied little. The post-Vietnam era, however, shows that representative samples of the electorate exhibited positive and negative perceptions of candidates' service, with different patterns across the candidates.

One quadrennial survey specifically measures respondents' reasons for and against supporting candidates near Election Day. It is a quality measure to see what potential voters think about presidential candidates and their service. The centrality of candidates' military service records increased in this era compared to that for the large pool of World War II veterans. Figure 8.1 visualizes the positive and negative references that survey respondents made in open-ended questions. It shows the proportion of respondents who used a candidate's military service as a reason to vote for and against the candidate. The survey questions on this set of

---

79. Confessore and Yourish 2016.

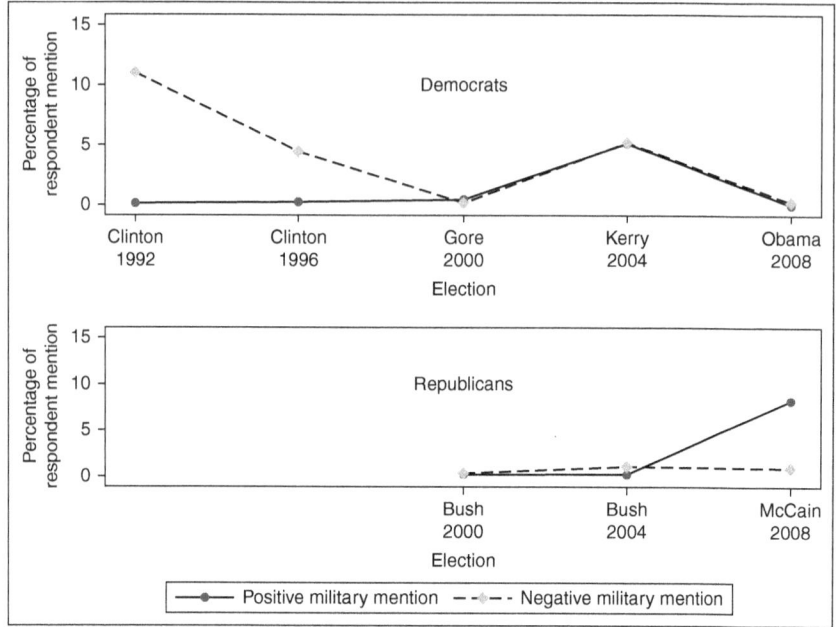

Figure 8.1 Percentage of respondents who use the candidates' military experience (or lack thereof) as a reason to support or not to support them. Data source: American National Election Study, 1992–2008.

surveys are virtually identical to the same set of questions asked about Eisenhower detailed in Chapter 7.

The survey asks, "Is there anything in particular about [candidate] that might make you want to vote for him/her? What is it?" and then asks for reasons why the respondent might vote against the candidate.[80] The survey design allowed respondents to say anything and did not predispose them to a certain view or offer choices, and up to five responses were recorded. This question was entirely apart from partisanship or vote-choice questions, so even if respondents planned to vote for one candidate, they were offered the opportunity to propose reasons to vote for and against both candidates.

As the data indicate, the presidential nominees' military service was important in all but one election, 2000. For Bill Clinton's elections in 1992 and 1996, his lack of military service and, perhaps, the means by which he avoided service, inspired respondents to express that issue was a reason

---

80. Data, question wording, and other specifics are available on the American National Election Studies website, at http://www.electionstudies.org/studypages/download/datacenter_all_NoData.php.

to oppose him (data are not currently available after 2008). In 2004, John Kerry's time in Vietnam, as well as his antiwar protest efforts, were central to the campaign, for both his supporters and detractors, during a wartime election. Different respondents, therefore, found John Kerry's Vietnam experiences as a reason to vote both for and against him. A small share of respondents also found George W. Bush's Texas Air National Guard service, and presumably the controversies surrounding it, as rationale for voting against him. In 2008, some felt that John McCain's service in the U.S. Navy as a pilot and his time as a prisoner of war in Hanoi provided reasons to support him. Taken together, this shows considerable salience for this group of candidates. Among the post–World War II veterans, only Eisenhower attracted more than a scattering of positive and negative attention about his military service.

The politics of military service was clearly more important among the post–Vietnam War candidates. Even given the fewer candidates with military service, the mixed legacy of Vietnam and a growing gap between the military and society made the politics of who served, who did not, and how they served more central to our presidential elections. This book has sought to understand the relationship between the early-life military experiences of presidential candidates, how those experiences shape the parties' decision to nominate veterans, and how veteran politics plays a role in the election itself. These data show that for post–Vietnam War candidates, whether and how one served influenced how potential voters assessed them. Respondents saw Bill Clinton's draft avoidance negatively in both 1992 and 1996, and almost equal numbers of people saw Kerry's combat experiences in Vietnam positively and negatively. While small numbers of people regarded John McCain and George W. Bush's military service negatively, many more saw McCain's military experiences positively. Both parties of this era had reasons to consider whether or not to nominate a candidate with military service. What is clear for this era is that military service is not a simple "box-checking" affair as it may have been for some of the World War II veterans in the past. The divisions and complexities of the Vietnam War reemerged in an increasingly polarized political environment beginning in the 1990s to play a role in presidential elections.

Conclusion

Contemplating a Future with Fewer Veterans in Politics

One of the reasons I ran for Congress was to make sure we didn't repeat the mistakes of the past, of going into war without a clear strategy.
—**Representative Tulsi Gabbard**, quoted in Parker and Peters, "Veterans in Congress Bring Rare Perspective to Authorizing War"

No one should ever take lightly the prospect of military action, I certainly do not. Only those who have not tasted war's bitter cup would wish another sip.
—**Senator Tom Cotton**, remarks at the Heritage Foundation, January 13, 2015

The 2012 presidential election was the first since 1944 that lacked a military veteran running under a major-party banner. That happened again in the 2016 presidential election; the Republicans nominated Donald Trump, who had sought and received draft deferments during the Vietnam War, and the Democrats nominated the first woman to be a major-party choice. The number of veterans in Congress has steadily declined as well, with the number of veterans running and winning decreasing since the 1970s. The comparative lack of military service among candidates in our national elections and among incumbents is likely to continue given the end of conscription, the small size of the U.S. military, and a reliance on careerists to fight the continuing conflicts in the Middle East.

During the 2012 and 2016 elections, it was but a footnote to contentious elections that the nominees and running mates pursued other avenues than military service in their formative years. Mitt Romney was age eligible for conscription during the Vietnam War and used religious and academic deferments as a Mormon missionary in France during the hottest period of American involvement. Romney was the first Republican candidate without military service since Thomas Dewey in 1948. Obama, like most of his peers, had decided on a civilian path in his young-adult years. The pattern repeated itself in 2016. Neither the presidential candidates nor their running mates had served, and the unusually large pool of people seeking the nominations almost entirely lacked military experience. The only 2016 aspirant with notable military service was Democratic senator Jim Webb.

The 2012 and 2016 elections, without veterans on the ballot, seem to mark a turning point to a long-standing pattern in American elections. This book argues that the number and kinds of veterans who emerged as candidates stem from a set of factors that follow wars and conflicts. It is true that more than half of those nominees spent some of their early adulthood in the armed forces, but these veterans were concentrated in postwar periods with circumstances that engendered veterans in politics. Whether it was Washington's leadership during the Revolutionary War, Kennedy's *PT-109* heroism in World War II, Theodore Roosevelt's charge at San Juan Hill, or Zachary Taylor's command at the Battle of Monterrey, military service helped define who ran for the highest office in the land.

Without trying to predict the future, it is safe to say that political parties are probably not finished nominating military veterans for high public office, including the presidency. However, the supply of veterans has declined, and we should not expect to see as many running for president or Congress as we did after World War II and Vietnam. The reasons future elections are likely to feature veterans, but fewer of them, reside in the pages of this book.

I offer a systematic explanation for the why, how, and when veterans have become presidential candidates. Political parties have perceived something attractive about running veterans since the beginning of American elections. By serving in the military, the institution most closely connected to the state itself, the institution that made separation from Great Britain real and has defended the nation since, veterans embody the glow of that patriotism. That baseline advantage applies to veterans of all eras, so while this is part of the reason behind the surfeit of veterans, it cannot explain changes over time.

By comparing the prevalence and types of military veterans running in presidential elections in some eras and the paucity in others, this book uses extant factors in military and political spheres to explain the changes. The pattern of veterans' emergence, number and types, into presidential elections is a function of differences and changes to the wars, military professionalism, and civilian politics across time. The many conflicts in which American soldiers have served have varied considerably in size, intensity, personnel needs, and duration. The conditions surrounding America's wars, as well as the domestic factors, contribute to the number and kinds of military veterans within the political class of the next generation. Not only did the number of military veteran candidacies vary, but so did the kinds of veterans. Some eras saw many generals in elections; other saw junior officers, because the voters of different eras favored different kinds of military service.

Two eras in U.S. history stand out in terms of veteran emergence in presidential elections because of the very high numbers. During the Antebellum (1820s–1860s) and post–World War II (1950s–1990s) eras nonveterans were rare in presidential elections. Between Andrew Jackson's election and General George McClellan's unsuccessful bid to oust his former commander in chief in 1864, most candidates were veterans of America's early conflicts. Only a handful lacked military experience. The rest, such as Jackson, Harrison, and Scott, were men with prominent and well-known military honors from the War of 1812, Indian Wars, or the Mexican-American War. In the wake of World War II, between Dwight Eisenhower's election in 1952 and Bob Dole's loss in 1996, there was another period full of military veterans running for president. Kennedy, McGovern, H. W. Bush, and Dole were young officers on the front lines of World War II, each with harrowing stories of heroism and valor. Others, such as Nixon, held commissions away from combat but served honorably.

The remaining eras in American electoral history did not see such high numbers of military veterans contest presidential elections. Within the early republic, Antebellum era, post–Civil War generation, early twentieth-century veteran hiatus, post–World War II generation, and post-Vietnam cohort, presidential elections exhibited substantial variation in the number and types of veterans. In the post–Cold War period and in the early republic, around half of the presidential candidates running possessed military experience.

The war's size and means of recruiting soldiers are important in explaining the patterns of veteran emergence, as large wars create large populations of veterans, making the chances of military veterans running for office greater. However, this is not to say that size alone contributes to the frequency of veterans in presidential elections. We must look beyond the size of the wars and veteran population to explain veterans in politics. While World War II was a huge conflict that enlisted a massive share of young men, resulting in a forty-year period when World War II vets were ubiquitous in presidential elections, other eras generated nearly as many military veteran candidacies without a large war. Some 80 percent of the candidates in the Antebellum era had military experience even though the wars that preceded the era produced a comparatively tiny proportion of men with wartime experience in the population.

Another factor that helps explain how many and what kinds of veterans appeared in American presidential elections is the separation between the civilian and military spheres. The degree to which military and political elites are intertwined affects whether generals are likely to be presidential candidates. The entirely federalized, well-funded, apolitical, hyperprofessional U.S. military of today has little resemblance to the militia-reliant, impoverished, hyperpartisan, and poorly trained armed forces of the early American republic. It would be difficult to expect similar patterns of later-life political results between the former and the latter.

Finally, political forces from the civilian side have implications for veteran emergence in politics, albeit smaller ones. Political parties have gone through several mechanisms for choosing presidential nominees, some relying more heavily on political elites' preferences and others using partisans in the electorate to make the decision. Military-hero candidates exemplified by Andrew Jackson, with broad popular appeal but less support from political elites in Washington, benefit from moving to a selection mechanism that taps into party networks in the states. Further, voters after World War II began to see their president more and more through the commander in chief lens, leading to discussion of whether or not the candidate had been in the ranks. Unpopular wars with conscription, such as Vietnam, make military service, or the lack thereof, an important issue on the campaign trail for years after war's end. Speculation about what the future holds, given the dwindling number of veterans, should rely on these factors.

Generations of Vets Serve and Ebb

A looming reality is that veterans in politics will be rarer going forward. When Frank Lautenberg, the last World War II veteran in the Senate, died in 2013, his departure from the legislature signaled the end of a long era when men of the "Greatest Generation" dominated national politics. As discussed previously in more detail, World War II was an epic global conflict, and the United States played a large role by fielding massive armies across the globe. Approximately three-quarters of a generation wore the uniform. And that cohort swept into Washington, D.C., not long after the war and dominated political elite circles until the entrance of the baby boomers. Presidential elections are not the only way to see the entrance and exit of war cohorts in politics.

We can use a legislature, with more cases elected more frequently across a long time span, to show that wars create veterans with political aspirations. One arbitrarily chosen state's legislative elections better

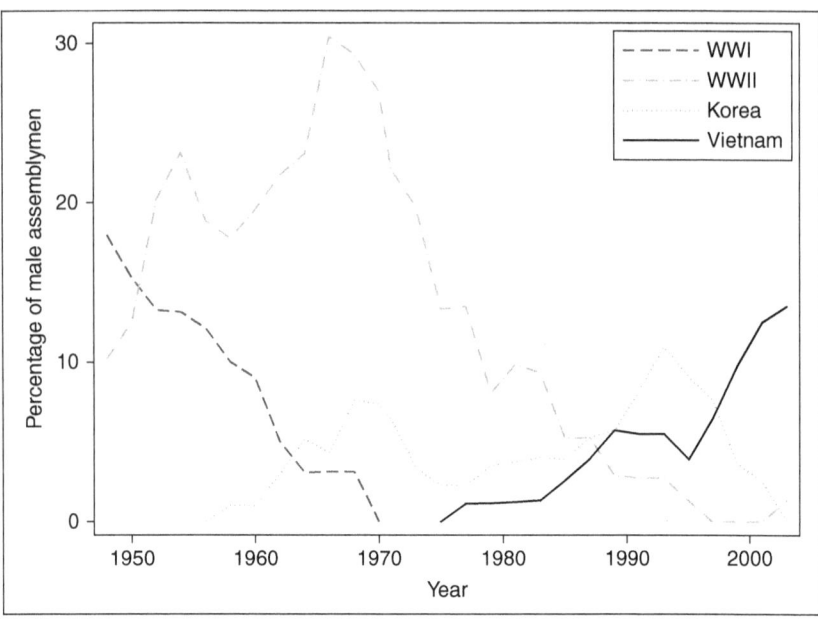

Figure C.1 Male members of the Wisconsin State Assembly who were military veterans, by war. Data source: The Wisconsin Blue Book, 1948–2003, available at https://uwdc.library.wisc.edu/collections/WI/WIBlueBks.

conveys how veterans from different conflicts emerge in political institutions. Wisconsin's lower legislative chamber has ninety-nine seats, and Figure C.1 shows the proportion of veterans from each conflict who won elections.[1] Considering only males for 1950–2000, cohorts of veterans are easy to recognize. About a fifth of male representatives were World War I veterans at the end of World War II. Veterans from World War II surged into the ranks of the legislature and hit their peak around 1970. Veterans from the Korean and Vietnam conflicts entered politics in similar patterns after those wars though in fewer numbers than the World War II vets. Veterans return from large wars, enter politics, and retire. To see what the future holds requires us to recognize that our current wars require far fewer individuals than did World War II or Vietnam.

It is possible that John McCain was the final presidential nominee who fought in the Vietnam War. It is risky to speculate, but it is worth

---

1. Wisconsin is not unique, and other states' legislatures likely show very similar patterns. Wisconsin's data are simply easier to acquire than those from other states because it has digital biographies from as early as 1950. The assembly holds biennial elections, and there were one hundred seats until 1973, when the number of districts dropped to ninety-nine. See the website of the Wisconsin Legislative Reference Bureau, at https://legis.wisconsin.gov/lrb/publications/wisconsin-blue-book.

considering the possibility that McCain shares something important with the president he most identifies with and admires, Theodore Roosevelt. To speak in probabilistic terms and not in certainties, consider a commonality between McCain and Roosevelt in terms of military service and presidential elections. Roosevelt, a candidate who catapulted from New York City politics to the national stage, was a man whose military service infused and catalyzed his political potential. His short but famous time in the Spanish-American War in 1898 was widely covered in the media, giving him the visibility and credibility for his political ambitions. For McCain as well, his time in uniform as a pilot and as a prisoner of war during the Vietnam War was an important facet of his political ascent to become a congressman, senator, and presidential candidate. It is possible that each candidate marked the end of a veteran era. Roosevelt was the last veteran after a large class of Civil War veterans, and McCain, perhaps, is the final Vietnam veteran to earn a nomination. In short, the end of conscription with smaller armies is likely to engender another veteran hiatus with few veterans running for public office.

Is candidate veteran status becoming increasingly irrelevant because of the decline in their numbers? One fact suggests that politicians remain convinced that being a veteran helps candidates win office: they still exaggerate their service records. As Lyndon Johnson's evolving tale of his time in World War II demonstrates, exaggerating military experiences is nothing new. However, today's information age and improved record keeping probably mean that embellished war stories are more likely to be revealed. Mark Kirk, a Republican running for the U.S. Senate from Illinois, won a narrow victory in 2010 despite admitting that his claims of being the navy's "Intelligence Officer of the Year" and other accolades lacked veracity.[2] He was unseated six years later by Tammy Duckworth, a combat veteran from Iraq who lost parts of her legs when her helicopter was shot down. Democrat Richard Blumenthal, who ran for U.S. Senate in 2010 from Connecticut, claimed that he served in Vietnam, but journalists discovered that he was in the marine reserves and never deployed.

It is clear that the supply of veterans has diminished as the Vietnam generation recedes. Further, while we still fight wars, we are doing so with fewer troops. The United States has clearly not stopped fighting wars since Vietnam. Two wars in Iraq and a long war in Afghanistan are the three largest recent commitments for the U.S. military. However, the men and women in the armed forces today stay in uniform longer and fight in more tours of duty than past generations of war veterans.[3] With the same

---

2. R. Smith, 2010, A3.
3. Baiocchi 2013.

individuals doing more of the fighting, our current military structure is simply making far fewer veterans than the past eras, despite continuing to fight wars.

This is not to say our elections will necessarily be bereft of veterans. With a smaller supply, it is possible that parties will see increased value in veteran candidates. As the Appendix makes clear, military service did not provide political candidates with a clear advantage at the ballot box in the past. However, those analyses largely use post–World War II and post-Vietnam candidates as data. It is possible that a paucity of candidates with military experience will enhance their electoral appeal, and the salience and value of military service will rise. Veterans from Iraq and Afghanistan are already contesting elections in state legislatures and Congress, and it seems probable that veterans will continue to engage in politics after returning to civilian life, just in smaller numbers than before.

An indirect barometer indicating whether we as a country still think of our presidents and elected leaders as military veterans is to look at popular fictional presidents. Writers who create dramatized presidents and presidential candidates for films and television often graft a military biography or connection to war on their characters. Blockbuster 1996 action film *Independence Day* explicitly filled a fighter pilot veteran background into its fictional president. More recently, television put veteran backstories on the small screen. One of *Homeland*'s fictional presidents was a mother who had lost a son in Iraq, and the imagined president in *House of Cards* faced a Republican challenger who joined the air force right after 9/11. *Madame Secretary*'s fictional president served in Vietnam. One of the several fictional presidents in *24* was a former marine. President Jed Bartlet's successor on *The West Wing* graduated atop his class at Annapolis and then flew as a navy fighter pilot.

Political Implications of Fewer Veterans in Politics

The decline in the number of military veterans in the American polity generally, and in political institutions specifically, portends change. If veterans act or think differently on important government policies, then a future with fewer veterans will potentially reshape policy in those areas. Some researchers have empirically studied this decline, finding mixed evidence that the decreasing number of veterans in Congress has shaped legislative outcomes related to foreign policy and defense matters.[4] Some evidence shows that fewer veterans in Washington, D.C., predicts higher

---

4. Bianco 2005; Kriner 2010; Howell and Pevehouse 2007; Gelpi and Feaver 2002; Horowitz and Stam 2014.

likelihood of belligerent foreign policy, while other studies question that conclusion. Gelpi and Feaver's study in particular should raise concerns about a decline in the number of veterans, as they conclude that the United States is more likely to initiate militarized disputes if fewer veterans occupy leadership positions.

However, all of these studies rely on past data when the number of veterans was relatively high—hence these studies have probed for the implications of the change from many veterans to a moderate number of veterans. They are less able to speak to what will happen when positions of power are filled by even fewer veterans. They also understand military service only through the lens of World War II and Vietnam veterans, large cohorts of veterans from a conscription regime. How well the evidence holds up is to be determined when fewer veterans—volunteers who compose less than 1 percent of our nation—from very different kinds of conflicts in the Middle East return to begin their political careers.

There are other values that military service may impart to its veterans that prepare them for political leadership. Those who served in the military since Vietnam are likely to have served in an institution that has made more progress on race relations than the civilian world. "A visitor to an Army dining facility . . . is likely to see a sight rarely encountered elsewhere in American life: blacks and whites commingling and socializing by choice."[5] Further, today's youth from the strata of society that tend to create our political leaders would be humbled by the forced equality in an institution that is largely a meritocracy and does not care about individuals' origins. To join the armed forces is to join an institution that pools its members into common experiences, forcing everyone to rub shoulders with men and women of diverse backgrounds. A young Richard Nixon, while in the U.S. Navy during World War II, wrote letters home about all the people from all walks of life he met. "He was thrown in overseas with men he never would have met otherwise or mingle with by choice. . . . It was here, in the Navy, that Nixon discovered he had a real rapport with working class Americans."[6] It would not hurt our national political institutions if more of its members had spent a few years in uniform, working in close quarters with people from all classes and races.

While those with experience in the armed forces can bring what they have learned from their time in uniform to be a better civic leader, we should be cautious about believing the military can do no wrong and candidates who wrap themselves with excessive military trappings. Andrew Bacevich reminds us that the military generals who did become president,

---

5. Moskos and Butler 1996, 2.
6. Ambrose 1987, 114.

such as Washington, Grant, and Eisenhower, worked hard to set aside their military identities, and we should eschew "militarizing the presidency itself."[7] When candidates or presidents have gone too far, such as Dukakis and the 1988 tank incident or George W. Bush's "mission accomplished" carrier landing in 2003, there was negative reaction to blurring the lines between the civilian and military spheres.

Future considerations about the politics of military service need to reflect on gender. Given that the vast preponderance of military service was done by men until recently, the military path to elected office shapes candidate emergence into a male-dominated pattern. Thus, the comparisons in the preceding chapters generally exclude women. During World War II, approximately four hundred thousand women served in uniform as cryptologists, noncombat pilots, postal clerks, nurses, and many other roles, but after the pressing needs of that war ended, women occupied a very small fraction of the armed forces. After the World War II era, the number of women in the ranks grew only after the Vietnam War, with most of the growth of women in the ranks occurring between 1973 and the end of the Cold War in the early 1990s.[8] Though not without debate, prohibitions on women serving in combat roles declined and the number of women in combat grew during the wars in Iraq and Afghanistan. When we look forward to the next era, the emergence of a small but notable group of female veterans gives us reason to pay attention to the possibility of more. We know that being a veteran makes it easier to push national security and defense legislation, so it is difficult for nonveteran females in Congress to take leadership on those issues.[9] Thus, female veterans have an advantage in gaining media attention and taking the lead on defense issues in Washington. Recent females in Congress with military service, such Tulsi Gabbard (Democrat, Hawaii) in the House and Tammy Duckworth (Democrat, Illinois) in the Senate, have found that their wartime experiences give them effective platforms to raise concerns about America's wars and military policies in Washington.[10]

I conclude with a note about the horrible phenomenon that creates large numbers of veterans in politics: war. Many have lamented the numerical decline of war veterans in public life and believe that America is losing something important with their passing. The logical deduction is that more veterans would be a boon to civic life. There is value to having people with military experience in civilian political roles. Others also be-

---

7. Bacevich 2005, 30.
8. U.S. Department of Veterans Affairs 2011.
9. Swers 2007.
10. Parker and Peters 2015.

lieve that recent military veterans in America are an untapped resource in civic life. For example, Veterans Campaign, a nonpartisan, nonprofit organization in Washington, D.C., provides assistance to interested veterans about organizing and running electoral campaigns.[11] Perhaps readers may infer a regretful tone in this book about the decline in the number of veterans in the White House, Congress, or in civic life generally. However, we should never forget that, while we may recognize the worth and advantages of military veterans in positions of power, large wars created those large legions of veterans. Wars destroy. Veterans are simply a silver lining to their carnage. The periods of American civic life replete with veterans followed terrible wars that exacted heavy tolls from all involved—measured by casualties, dollars, and lost opportunities. Hence, I stress that despite recognizing the civic value of veterans, it is with a pacific outlook that I close.

---

11. Veterans Campaign was pioneered by Seth Lynn and can be found online at http://www.veteranscampaign.org.

Appendix

This Appendix uses presidential and congressional electoral data, along with a host of other factors, to test the claim that veterans do better at the ballot box than nonveterans. I analyze presidential elections, by running statistical models used by others, to estimate the effect of military experience in terms of popular votes for candidates. Then, noting the difficulties and shortcomings in using presidential elections as data, I use congressional elections to provide another test of the same contention.

PRESIDENTIAL ELECTION MODELS

In Chapter 2, we see that past military service does not systematically enhance presidential votes. In a more extended form, Table A.1 includes two presidential election models based on different scholarly attempts to predict and explain how various factors influence the popular-vote share of the incumbent party: the Hibbs model ("Bread and Peace") and the Abramowitz model ("Time for Change").[1] Hibbs uses measures of economic growth and American war casualties to predict the incumbent party's support, while Abramowitz's model includes a different economic measure, the duration of the incumbent party's White House incumbency, and the incumbent president's approval rating. The decision to use these models was not based on any predictive accuracy criteria but on their simplicity. The point of using their models is not to replicate their prognostic insight but to add a candidate military-service variable to both models to evaluate how much, if at all, being a veteran helps a presidential candidate. I favor neither and include them both to demonstrate that the lack of a powerful veteran effect does not depend on any given model.

---

1. See Hibbs 2012; Abramowitz 2008.

TABLE A.1 PRESIDENTIAL ELECTION MODELS, 1948–2012

	Bread and Peace	Bread and Peace + individual vet	Bread and Peace + relative vet	Time for Change	Time for Change + individual vet	Time for Change + relative vet
Incumbent-party vet		−1.34			1.09	
		(1.01)			(1.25)	
Challenger-party vet		−0.26			0.32	
		(0.85)			(1.11)	
Incumbent-vet advantage			−1.13			0.053
			(0.65)			(0.66)
Per capita income change	3.53**	3.53**	3.27**			
	(0.41)	(0.43)	(0.41)			
Casualties	−0.052**	−0.061**	−0.058**			
	(0.010)	(0.012)	(0.010)			
Q2 annual GDP change				0.56**	0.59**	0.56**
				(0.14)	(0.16)	(0.15)
Time for Change				−4.35**	−4.53**	−4.37**
				(1.30)	(1.40)	(1.39)
June presidential approval				0.19**	0.17*	0.19**
				(0.05)	(0.06)	(0.05)
Constant	46.39**	48.19**	46.96**	47.62**	46.97**	47.64**
	(0.97)	(1.88)	(0.96)	(3.84)	(4.40)	(4.01)
Observations	16	16	16	16	16	16
Adjusted R-squared	0.871	0.889	0.897	0.873	0.884	0.873
Years of data	1952–2012	1952–2012	1952–2012	1948–2008	1948–2008	1948–2008

Note: Ordinary least square regression with standard errors in parentheses; *$p \le 0.05$; **$p \le 0.01$.

To graft candidate biography onto these models, I add different specifications of a veteran variable. Empirical social scientists are frequently confronted with how to measure inherently qualitative variables. While average quarterly growth and battle deaths are easily quantified for the purposes of Hibbs's model, putting a value on the nature of the candidates' military service is not as straightforward. To assess the role of military service, I offer two different measures. The first looks at the objective military experience of the candidates and gives a score of 0, 1, or 2 based on the nature of the experience (per Chapter 2, a 0 means nonveteran, 1 is common veteran, and 2 is anything higher).

The second way to model military service compares the two candidates. In most of the presidential elections from 1952 to 2012, one man had unequivocally more esteemed or prestigious military service. Perhaps voters do not weigh candidates' military service candidate by candidate but compare them directly. The second measure of presidential candidate service also has three possible scores, but it is a comparison between the candidates' service rather than a per-candidate measure. A 0 implies rough parity in the candidates' military experience, at least an equivalence for the purposes of election analysis. A positive 1 marks races where the incumbent party's candidate has a "better" military record than that of the challenger, and a negative 1 denotes that the incumbent party's candidate has a "worse" record. By calling them "better" and "worse," I hasten to add, I intend no normative values; rather, I strive to mark higher or lower notability. In 1960, for example, Kennedy's *PT-109* biography of heroism on the high seas trumps Nixon's honorable yet less exciting life as a supply officer. In only three elections (1976, 1984, and 2012) was the candidates' service roughly equivalent. The remaining races featured one candidate with a military biography advantage. It might be a dramatically large advantage, such as Eisenhower's military credentials over Stevenson's minor service or McGovern's risky piloting of B-24s trumping Nixon's routine supply role service. In other cases the gap might be real but substantively smaller, such as Gore's enlisted service in the army as a journalist in Vietnam holding higher status than George W. Bush's complicated Texas Air Guard service during the same years.

The first column in Table A.1 is a replication of Hibbs's model, showing how economic growth (specifically, weighted-average growth of per capita real disposable personal income) helps the incumbent party while American battle casualties do not. The second column lists the results of adding the individually measured military-service variables, one for the incumbent-party candidate and one for the challenger-party candidate. The third column adds the single, relative measure of military service, the one that is measured as either incumbent-party advantage, equivalent military service, or challenger-party advantage. Neither measure demonstrates a systematic "veteran effect." Candidates' experiences in the armed forces do not shape the outcome of presidential elections. The coefficients that denote the slope of the effect of military service, construed by either measurement, are not statistically significant; in other words, they are not statistically distinguishable from 0. In short, grafting candidate military biography onto Hibbs's model shows no perceptible role for a veteran effect in determining presidential election outcomes. Even with minor changes to the measurement, nothing substantially different results. For instance, if one disputed that Gore's noncombat time in Vietnam was politically more advantageous than the younger Bush's time in the Texas Air National Guard, and measured them equivalently, the quantitative results do not change more than trivially.

Figure A.1 presents the relationship of Hibbs's economic factor and presidential elections graphically, indicating years when the incumbent party enjoyed a military biography advantage (marked by an X) and years when it did not (marked by a dot). If military veterans systematically enhanced their vote share, we should see those years being higher than the other years, relative to the baseline expectation. The baseline expectation is the line, depicting the linear relationship between real income growth per capita and vote share. The years with and without a veteran advantage show no particular pattern. For every year, such as 1952, when it looks like Adlai Stevenson underperformed the economic conditions, one can find a counterexample, such as 1996, when Bill Clinton overperformed against a candidate with a clear veteran edge. Hibbs stresses in his description of 1952 and 1968 that mounting American casualties explain the incumbent party's underperformance.

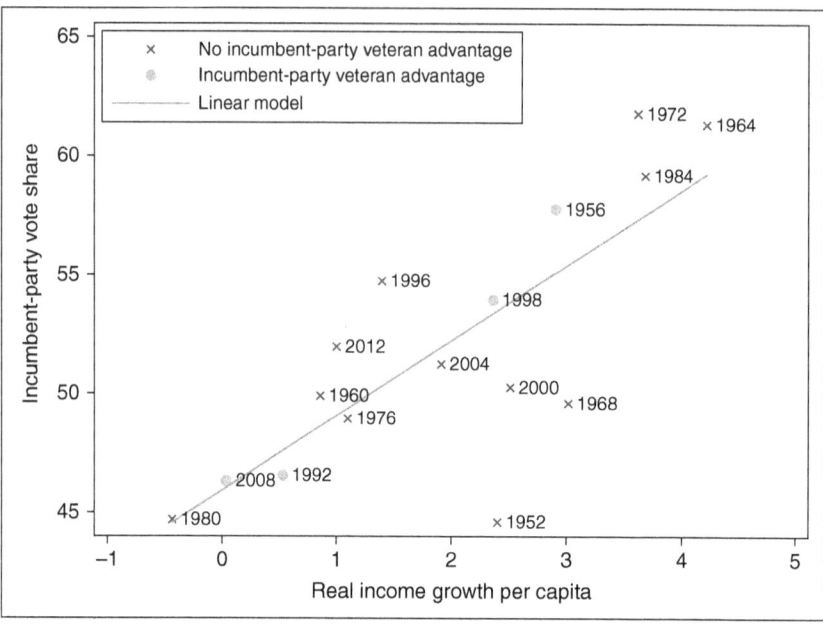

Figure A.1 Relationship between macroeconomic growth and the incumbent party's share of the two-party presidential popular vote.

While similarly reliant on economic conditions, the specifics of Abramowitz's model differ from Hibbs's. The model includes three factors: the second-quarter annual gross domestic product growth rate within the election year, the incumbent-party president's June approval rating, and a dummy variable ("yes" or "no" variable) marking each year concerning whether the administration has been in power for one term or two or more terms. Table A.1 includes a replication of Abramowitz's findings to show that positive growth in the economy helps the incumbent party, public approval of the incumbent president also helps, while the time-for-change variable demonstrates that parties who have been controlling the White House are punished for having been in office two terms or more. I augment Abramowitz's data in the same fashion as for the Hibbs data. In the separated measure that includes a variable measuring military service for each the incumbent-party candidate and the challenger-party candidate, using the 0–2 scale, we see that neither incumbent nor challenger's military service influences the vote share outcome on Election Day. The other relative veteran measure yields the same result: candidates' military service does not make a good predictor of presidential election outcomes.[2]

CONGRESSIONAL ELECTIONS

Adding congressional elections to the analysis hedges against the possibility that presidential elections are too few in number or too context dependent to be a good test

---

2. This finding corroborates bivariate research in Karsten 2012.

of past military service. With far more iterations, elections to the U.S. House of Representatives provide another means to evaluate if and how much candidates' military biography might help on Election Day. This analysis models congressional election outcomes with typical factors as well as a measure of candidates' military service. This effort uses six cycles of U.S. House of Representatives general election data, from 2000 to 2014. U.S. House races are held every two years, and there are obviously a higher number of them than presidential elections, given that there are 435 seats in the modern era.

Some of these districts are inappropriate to use for our purposes, so many cases are omitted to avoid problems in the analysis. District boundaries are almost never arbitrarily drawn, and some districts so heavily favor one party or the other that the incumbent runs unopposed. These unopposed races are omitted, along with a handful of others for comparability purposes (data availability; mid-decade redistricting; Louisiana-style "top-two" elections found in Louisiana, Washington, and California; or other irregularities). The elections of 2002 and 2012 are also left out because of redistricting. The number of cases per year is still sufficiently high to contain a healthy variance in partisan makeup of the districts and candidates.

The dependent variable is the two-party vote share obtained by the (arbitrarily chosen) Democratic candidate.[3] Using only the proportion of the major-party votes ignores the usually trivial influence of minor-party candidates. Using ordinary least squares regression, I model the Democratic candidates' two-party vote share as a function of military biography, the election result in the prior cycle, incumbency, the partisan nature of the district, the district's racial composition, the gender of both candidates, and dummy variables for each election year (except 2000). To measure the prior performance in the district, the model includes the Democratic percentage of the two-party vote in that district in the election held two years earlier. Including this measure controls for the performance of the incumbent in the district in the cases in which an incumbent is running again, as well as measures the performance of a retired incumbent whose legacy might help his successor. Incumbency is a powerful force in American politics, and perhaps nowhere more so than in U.S. House elections, where a 95 percent success rate for incumbents trying to hold on to office is routine. Given its role in explaining election outcomes, this model measures incumbency by coding each race as Republican incumbent (1), open seat (2), or Democratic incumbent (3). House district lines are not arbitrary—they are often the products of a partisan process that has incentives to defend incumbents or maintain stability. To measure the partisan disposition of district, I use the presidential election vote share as the most reasonable proxy. Even aside from who is running as a Democrat for the seat, it is important to control for how well a past Democratic presidential candidate did in that district. For example, in the 2006 and 2008 House races, the model measures partisan composition by the percentage that John Kerry won in that district in 2004. Race and politics are intertwined in American elections, so the percentage of the district that is white is used as a simple measure of each district's racial composition. Because the independent variables of interest, whether the Democratic candidate and the Republican candidate had military service, are steeply correlated with candidate gender, the model includes dummy variables for both parties' candidate's gender.

---

3. One could use the Republican candidate vote share with no difference to the results but the sign of the estimates.

Veterans are mostly male, so to run a veteran model without a gender control might mistake a true gender effect for a veteran effect.

The key variables of interest in the model are military service for the two candidates. The task of measuring candidate military service is easy for the winning candidates. Members of the House enjoy substantial biographical coverage on their own official websites, official biographies in the House records, and prolific media coverage. To obtain the military service records of the men and women who did not win is more difficult. Most losers of congressional campaigns enjoy little media attention, maintain small-budget campaign operations, and attract little attention from official biographers. Hence, the military experience of these losing candidates was obtained through local media reports, campaign websites (very much in vogue by the 2004 cycle), and Associated Press and other media candidate profiles.

If military service by the candidates themselves was explicitly listed on any of these sources, the candidate was coded as a veteran. The nature of military service varies tremendously. However, the inherent ambiguity in many candidate records made it difficult to distinguish between types of service. While it would have been ideal to distinguish those who had been in combat, those who were in the reserves or the National Guard after a stint in active duty, those who were officers, and so on, the sheer volume of names coupled with the difficulty in finding electoral losers' biographies necessitated a simple dichotomous measure of military service.

It is important to note that I did not corroborate assertions of military service with some official record, such as from the Pentagon. Nor did I attempt to prove nonservice regarding candidates who did not explicitly list military service in their biographies with official records. The question here is how voters react to their perceptions of candidates' military service. If a candidate is actually a veteran but did not publicize that fact by including it in the biographical information presented to voters, then the candidate is not a veteran for the purposes at hand.

Table A.2 lists the four different pooled models that test for the electoral influence of congressional candidates' military biography. None of the four models shows a systematic, measurable effect from military backgrounds (while the other factors perform as expected). On the contrary, Democratic veterans actually do a little worse than comparable nonveteran Democrats (more detailed analysis shows that this effect centers on 2008). Whether one examines all contests, contests between two men, the small number of open-seat races caused by retirements or deaths, or only close races (between 45 percent and 55 percent for the winner), neither party enjoys an advantage when nominating a military veteran. The dependent variable is two-party Democratic vote share, so negative and significant coefficients denote a boon for Republicans, while positive and significant coefficients would show a help for Democrats.[4]

Figure A.2 contrasts veterans and nonveterans with regard to the relationship between the partisanship of the district and the results of congressional elections, using the cases from the regression analysis. The partisanship of congressional districts is measured by the Democratic presidential candidate's vote share in that district in the previous election—a very good predictor of congressional election vote share, illustrated by the linear prediction line. (Cases include contested races only, and the figure omits third-party candidates, states with top-two primary systems, and contests with two veterans running against each other.) If veterans enjoyed a system-

---

4. Several other model permutations were tried as well, including one that assessed whether challenger veterans differed from incumbent veterans, but no effect appeared there either.

TABLE A.2 CONGRESSIONAL ELECTION MODELS AND CANDIDATE MILITARY SERVICE, 2000–2014

	All contested	Two male candidates	Open seats only	Close races (45%–55%)
Democrat a vet	−0.78*	−0.52	−2.62	−0.16
	(0.38)	(0.41)	(2.14)	(0.45)
Republican a vet	−0.31	0.06	1.85	−0.28
	(0.34)	(0.40)	(2.07)	(0.38)
Democratic candidate vote share in previous race	0.44**	0.44**	0.05	0.07**
	(0.01)	(0.02)	(0.07)	(0.02)
Incumbency status	2.52**	2.84**		0.84**
	(0.18)	(0.22)		(0.23)
Previous Democratic presidential vote share in district	0.50**	0.49**	0.60**	0.13**
	(0.02)	(0.02)	(0.10)	(0.03)
Percentage white in district	−0.04**	−0.03**	−0.17**	−0.00
	(0.01)	(0.01)	(0.05)	(0.01)
Democrat a male	0.46		2.83	0.75
	(0.36)		(1.79)	(0.39)
Republican a male	0.40		−4.13*	0.40
	(0.46)		(1.97)	(0.46)
2004 election	3.33**	2.84**	1.53	1.42
	(0.56)	(0.69)	(2.51)	(0.78)
2006 election	8.18**	8.55**	11.16**	2.92**
	(0.58)	(0.71)	(2.32)	(0.67)
2008 election	6.95**	6.81**		1.92**
	(0.58)	(0.71)		(0.68)
2010 election	−4.83**	−4.71**		−1.04
	(0.54)	(0.66)		(0.60)
2014 election	0.40	0.24		0.41
	(0.57)	(0.71)		(0.66)
Constant	−2.45	−2.93	27.01**	36.75**
	(1.52)	(1.75)	(8.12)	(2.04)
Observations	1,979	1,334	86	279
Adjusted R-squared	0.859	0.853	0.693	0.185

Note: Ordinary least square regression with standard errors in parentheses; *$p \leq 0.05$; **$p \leq 0.01$. Data include U.S. House of Representatives elections but omit unopposed races, those in post-redistricting years (2002 and 2012), and races with two candidates of the same party in the general election.

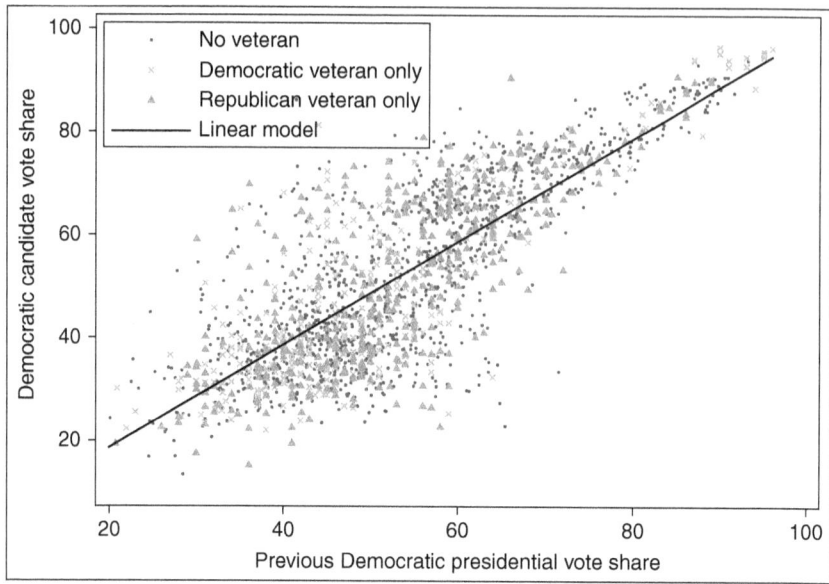

Figure A.2 Relationship between the U.S. House of Representatives district partisanship and the vote share of the Democratic House candidate.

atic advantage on Election Day, we should see veterans do generally better than the linear prediction. If true, that would show us two tendencies: races where the Democratic candidate was a veteran (marked with an X) should trend above the linear prediction, while races with Republican veteran candidates (triangles) should trend below the line. The data do not show a veteran advantage. The Republican veterans cluster roughly evenly above and below the linear prediction, as do the Democratic veterans.

Any expectations of a reliable and consistent positive veteran influence on elections are unrealistic. If there were, hypothetically speaking, a three to five percentage-point advantage for military service in the general elections, no rational party would ever nominate nonveterans. Races can be, and often are, won or lost within a five-point margin. The reason behind the negative result for Democratic veterans in the "All Contested" model stems from a trend of Democrats nominating veterans in more longshot races in 2010 and 2014. In 2014, for example, the district average Democratic presidential election votes for nonveteran Democrats challengers was 41.2 percent. For Democrats with military service experience challenging a Republican incumbent, the district's Democratic presidential election average was 38.4 percent.

This Appendix uses election data to find out whether the reason American elections have featured so many veterans was that military experience wins more votes. The results are mixed, with an ambiguous answer: sometimes veterans appear to do better than nonveterans, but the advantage depends on many other factors. If there is one statement we can rule out with these presidential and congressional election results, it is the contention that military service is a tide that floats all veterans' boats equally. Serving in the military may be a help for some candidates in some contexts, but that benefit is clearly context dependent.

References

Abramowitz, Alan I. 2008. "Forecasting the 2008 Presidential Election with the Time-for-Change Model." *PS: Political Science and Politics* 41 (4): 691–695.
Adler, David Gray. 2003. "Presidential Greatness as an Attribute of Warmaking." *Presidential Studies Quarterly* 33 (3): 466–483.
Adler, William D., and Jonathan Keller. 2014. "A Federal Army, Not a Federalist One: Regime Building in the Jeffersonian Era." *Journal of Policy History* 26 (2): 167–187.
Adler, William D., and Andrew J. Polsky. 2010. "Economic Development, Public Goods, and the Early U.S. Army." *Political Science Quarterly* 125 (1): 87–110.
Ainsworth, Scott. 1995. "Electoral Strength and the Emergence of Group Influence in the Late 1800s: The Grand Army of the Republic." *American Politics Quarterly* 23 (3): 319–338.
Aitken, Jonathan. 1993. *Nixon: A Life*. Washington, DC: Regnery.
Alexander, Arthur J. 1946. "Desertion and Its Punishment in Revolutionary Virginia." *William and Mary Quarterly* 3 (3): 383–397.
Alexander, Paul. 2008. *Man of the People: The Maverick Life and Career of John McCain*. Hoboken, NJ: John Wiley.
Allen, Gary. 1971. *Richard Nixon: The Man behind the Mask*. Boston: Western Islands.
Allen, Michael J. 2009. *Until the Last Man Comes Home: POWs, MIAs, and the Unending Vietnam War*. Chapel Hill: University of North Carolina Press.
Altman, Lawrence K., and Todd S. Purdum. 2002. "In J. F. K. File, Hidden Illness, Pain and Pills." *New York Times*, November 17. Available at http://www.nytimes.com/2002/11/17/us/in-jfk-file-hidden-illness-pain-and-pills.html.
Ambrose, Stephen E. 1987. *Nixon: The Education of a Politician, 1913–1962*. Vol. 1. New York: Simon and Schuster.
———. 2001. *The Wild Blue: The Men and Boys Who Flew the B-24s over Germany*. New York: Simon and Schuster.
Anderson, Benedict R. 1983. *Imagined Communities: Reflections on the Origin and Spread of Nationalism*. London: Verso.

Angrist, Joshua D. 1991. "The Draft Lottery and Voluntary Enlistment in the Vietnam Era." *Journal of the American Statistical Association* 86 (415): 584–595.

Ansell, S. T. 1917. "Legal and Historical Aspects of the Militia." *Yale Law Journal* 26 (6): 471–480.

Anson, Robert Sam. 1972. *McGovern: A Biography*. New York: Holt.

Armstrong, William H. 2000. *Major McKinley: William McKinley and the Civil War*. Kent, OH: Kent State University Press.

Avant, Deborah D. 1998. "Conflicting Indicators of 'Crisis' in American Civil-Military Relations." *Armed Forces and Society* 24 (3): 375–387.

Bacevich, Andrew J. 2005. *The New American Militarism: How Americans Are Seduced by War*. New York: Oxford University Press.

Bachman, Jerald G., John D. Blair, and David R. Segal. 1977. *The All-Volunteer Force: A Study of Ideology in the Military*. Ann Arbor: University of Michigan Press.

Bagby, Wesley Marvin. 1962. *The Road to Normalcy: The Presidential Campaign and Election of 1920*. Baltimore: Johns Hopkins University Press.

Bain, Richard C., and Judith H. Parris. 1973. *Convention Decisions and Voting Records*. Washington, DC: Brookings Institution.

Baiocchi, Dave. 2013. "Measuring Army Deployments to Iraq and Afghanistan." Available at http://www.rand.org/content/dam/rand/pubs/research_reports/RR100/RR145/RAND_RR145.pdf.

Ball, Moya Ann. 2005. "The Role of Vietnam in the 2004 Presidential Election." *Rhetoric and Public Affairs* 8 (4): 689–693.

Balsamo, Larry T. 2001. "'We Cannot Have Free Government without Elections': Abraham Lincoln and the Election of 1864." *Journal of the Illinois State Historical Society* 94 (2): 181–199.

Barnard, Ellsworth. 1966. *Wendell Willkie: Fighter for Freedom*. Marquette: Northern Michigan University Press.

Barone, Michael, Grant Ujifusa, and Douglas Matthews. 1972. *The Almanac of American Politics*. Boston: Gambit.

Bartels, Larry M. 1988. *Presidential Primaries and the Dynamics of Public Choice*. Princeton, NJ: Princeton University Press.

Bass, Jack, and Marilyn W. Thompson. 2005. *Strom: The Complicated Personal and Political Life of Strom Thurmond*. New York: PublicAffairs.

Bauer, K. Jack. 1985. *Zachary Taylor: Soldier, Planter, Statesman of the Old Southwest*. Baton Rouge: Louisiana State University Press.

Bennett, Michael J. 1996. *When Dreams Came True: The GI Bill and the Making of Modern America*. Washington, DC: Brassey's.

Benton, Thomas Hart. 1854. *Thirty Years' View*. New York: D. Appleton.

Berger, Thomas U. 1993. "From Sword to Chrysanthemum: Japan's Culture of Anti-militarism." *International Security* 17 (4): 119–150.

Berinsky, Adam J. 2009. *In Time of War: Understanding American Public Opinion from World War II to Iraq*. Chicago: University of Chicago Press.

Bernsteim, Adam. 2007. "Greg Stevens, 58: Operative Was behind Dukakis Tank Ad in '88." *Boston Globe*, April 20, p. 17.

Betts, Richard K. 2005. "The Political Support System for American Primacy." *International Affairs* 81 (1): 1–14.

Bianco, William T. 2005. "Last Post for 'the Greatest Generation': The Policy Implications of the Decline of Military Experience in the U.S. Congress." *Legislative Studies Quarterly* 30 (1): 85–102.

Bishop, Joseph B. 1919. "Theodore Roosevelt and His Time." *Scribner's Magazine*, November, pp. 515–533.
Black, Conrad. 2007. *Richard M. Nixon: A Life in Full*. New York: PublicAffairs.
Blair, Joan, and Clay Blair Jr. 1976. *The Search for JFK*. New York: Putnam.
Blegen, Theodore C. 1920. "Colonel Hans Christian Heg." *Wisconsin Magazine of History* 4 (2): 140–165.
Bochin, Hal. 1990. *Richard Nixon: Rhetorical Strategist*. New York: Greenwood Press.
Boller, Paul F. 1984. *Presidential Campaigns*. New York: Oxford University Press.
Bond, Beverley W., Jr. 1927. "William Henry Harrison in the War of 1812." *Mississippi Valley Historical Review* 13 (4): 499–516.
Bonekemper, Edward H. 2004. *A Victor, Not a Butcher: Ulysses S. Grant's Overlooked Military Genius*. Washington, DC: Regnery.
Booraem, Hendrik. 1988. *The Road to Respectability: James A. Garfield and His World, 1844–1852*. Lewisburg, PA: Bucknell University Press.
Boucher, Ronald L. 1973. "The Colonial Militia as a Social Instiution: Salem, Massachusetts 1764–1775." *Military Affairs* 37 (4): 125–130.
Bourne, Peter G.1997. *Jimmy Carter: A Comprehensive Biography from Plains to Post-presidency*. New York: Scribner.
Bowen, Michael. 2011. *The Roots of Modern Conservatism: Dewey, Taft, and the Battle for the Soul of the Republican Party*. Chapel Hill: University of North Carolina Press.
Boyarsky, Bill. 1981. *Ronald Reagan: His Life and Rise to the Presidency*. New York: Random House.
Boyer, Peter J. 2003. "General Clark's Battles: The Candidate's Celebrated—and Controversial—Military Career." *New Yorker*, November 17, p. 70.
Brands, H. W. 2012. *The Man Who Saved the Union: Ulysses Grant in War and Peace*. New York: Doubleday.
Brinkley, Douglas. 2004. *Tour of Duty: John Kerry and the Vietnam War*. New York: William Morrow.
———. 2007. *Gerald R. Ford*. New York: Times Books.
Brodie, Fawn McKay. 1981. *Richard Nixon: The Shaping of His Character*. New York: Norton.
Brokaw, Tom. 1998. *The Greatest Generation*. New York: Random House.
Buley, R. C. 1919. "Indiana in the Mexican War." *Indiana Magazine of History* 15 (3): 260–292.
Burk, James. 1995. "Citizenship Status and Military Service: The Quest for Inclusion by Minorities and Conscientious Objectors." *Armed Forces and Society* 21 (4): 503–530.
Burnet, Jacob. 1839. *Proceedings of the Democratic Whig National Convention*. Harrisburg, PA: R. S. Eliot.
Burns, Alexander, Maggie Haberman, and Ashley Parker. 2016. "Donald Trump's Confrontation with Muslim Soldier's Parents Emerges as Unexpected Flash Point." *New York Times*, July 31, p. A1.
Burrows, Edwin G. 1974. "Military Experience and the Origins of Federalism and Antifederalism." In *Aspects of Early New York Society and Politics*, edited by J. Judd and I. H. Polishook, 83–92. Tarrytown, NY: Sleepy Hollow Restorations.
Caidin, Martin, and Edward Hymoff. 1964. *The Mission*. Philadelphia: Lippincott, 1964.
Campbell, Angus, Philip E. Converse, Warren E. Miller, and Donald E. Stokes. 1960. *The American Voter*. New York: Wiley.

Campbell, Angus, Gerald Gurin, and Warren E. Miller. 1954. *The Voter Decides*. Evanston, IL: Row, Peterson.

Cannon, James M. 1994. *Time and Chance: Gerald Ford's Appointment with History*. New York: HarperCollins.

Cannon, Lou. 1982. *Reagan*. New York: Putnam.

Caro, Robert A. 1991. *Means of Ascent*. New York: Vintage Books.

Carp, E. Wayne. 1986. "Early American Military History: A Review of Recent Work." *Virginia Magazine of History and Biography* 94 (3): 259–284.

Carr, Robert Kenneth, Marver H. Bernstein, Donald H. Morrison, Richard C. Snyder, and Joseph E. McLean. 1955. *American Democracy in Theory and Practice*. New York: Holt, Rinehart and Winston.

Carson, Jamie L., Jeffery A. Jenkins, David W. Rohde, and Mark A. Souva. 2001. "The Impact of National Tides and District-Level Effects on Electoral Outcomes: The U.S. Congressional Elections of 1862–63." *American Journal of Political Science* 45 (4): 887–898.

Casey, Shaun. 2009. *The Making of a Catholic President: Kennedy vs. Nixon 1960*. New York: Oxford University Press.

Catton, Bruce. 1985. *The Civil War*. New York: American Heritage by Houghton Mifflin.

Ceaser, James W., Glen E. Thuerow, Jeffrey Tulis, and Joseph M. Bessette. 1981. "The Rise of the Rhetorical Presidency." *Presidential Studies Quarterly* 11 (2): 158–171.

Chafe, William Henry. 2005. *Private Lives/Public Consequences: Personality and Politics in Modern America*. Cambridge, MA: Harvard University Press.

Chamberlain, Samuel E. 1987. *My Confession: The Recollections of a Rogue*. Lincoln: University of Nebraska Press.

Chambers, John Whiteclay. 1987. *To Raise an Army: The Draft Comes to Modern America*. New York: Free Press.

Charles, Robert B. 2004. "The Moral Leadership of President George Bush." In *A Noble Calling: Character and the George H. W. Bush Presidency*, edited by W. Levantrosser and R. Perotti, 53–76. Westport, CT: Praeger.

Cleaves, Freeman. 1939. *Old Tippecanoe: William Henry Harrison and His Time*. New York: C. Scribner's Sons.

Coffman, Edward M. 1986. *The Old Army: A Portrait of the American Army in Peacetime, 1784–1898*. New York: Oxford University Press.

———. 2004. *The Regulars: The American Army, 1898–1941*. Cambridge, MA: Belknap Press of Harvard University Press.

Coile, Zachary. 2004. "Bush Lawyer Who Aided Boat-Ad Group Resigns." *San Francisco Chronicle*, August 26, p. A1.

Coleman, Chapman. 1871. *The Life of John J. Crittenden, with Selections from His Correspondence and Speeches*. Vol. 1. Philadelphia: J. B. Lippincott.

Confessore, Nicholas, and Karen Yourish. 2016. "$2 Billion Worth of Free Media for Donald Trump." *New York Times*, March 15. Available at https://www.nytimes.com/2016/03/16/upshot/measuring-donald-trumps-mammoth-advantage-in-free-media.html.

Converse, Philip E., and Georges Dupeux. 1966. "De Gaulle and Eisenhower: The Public Image of the Victorious General." In *Elections and the Political Order*, edited by A. Campbell, Philip E. Converse, Warren E. Miller, and Donald E. Stokes, 292–345. New York: John Wiley and Sons.

Cornog, Evan, and Richard Whelan. 2000. *Hats in the Ring: An Illustrated History of American Presidential Campaigns*. New York: Random House.

Corry, John A. 2000. *A Rough Ride to Albany: Teddy Runs for Governor.* New York: J. A. Corry.
Cosmas, Graham A. 1971. *An Army for Empire: The United States Army in the Spanish-American War.* Columbia: University of Missouri Press.
Cramer, Ben. 1992. *What It Takes: The Way to the White House.* New York: Random House.
Crapol, Edward P. 2006. *John Tyler: The Accidental President.* Chapel Hill: University of North Carolina Press.
Cress, Lawrence Delbert. 1982. *Citizens in Arms: The Army and the Militia in American Society to the War of 1812.* Chapel Hill: University of North Carolina Press.
Crockett, David A. 2008. *Running against the Grain: How Opposition Presidents Win the White House.* College Station: Texas A&M University Press.
Cunliffe, Marcus. 1968. *Soldiers and Civilians: The Martial Spirit in America, 1775–1865.* Boston: Little, Brown.
Curtis, George Ticknor. 1883. *Life of James Buchanan, Fifteenth President of the United States.* Vol. 1. New York: Harper and Brothers.
Daggett, Stephen. 2010. "Costs of Major U.S. Wars." *Congressional Research Service*, June 29. Available at https://fas.org/sgp/crs/natsec/RS22926.pdf.
Dallek, Robert. 1991. *Lone Star Rising: Lyndon Johnson and His Times, 1908–1960.* New York: Oxford University Press.
———. 2004. *Lyndon B. Johnson: Portrait of a President.* New York: Oxford University Press.
Dangerfield, George. 1952. *The Era of Good Feelings.* New York: Harcourt, Brace and World.
Daniels, Jonathan. 1950. *The Man of Independence.* Philadelphia: Lippincott.
Dao, James, and Adam Nagourney. 2006. "They Served, and Now They're Running." *New York Times*, February 19, p. A1.
David, Paul T., Malcolm Moos, and Ralph M. Goldman. 1954. *Presidential Nominating Politics in 1952: The National Story.* Baltimore: Johns Hopkins University Press.
Davis, William C. 1999. *Lincoln's Men: How President Lincoln Became Father to an Army and a Nation.* New York: Free Press.
Dean, John W., and Barry M. Goldwater Jr. 2008. *Pure Goldwater.* New York: Palgrave Macmillan.
Dearing, Mary Rulkotter. 1952. *Veterans in Politics: The Story of the G.A.R.* Baton Rouge: Louisiana State University Press.
"Democratic Presidential Nominee Has Praise for the 'Wisconsin Idea.'" 1952. *Milwaukee Sentinel*, October 9, p. 5.
Dempsey, Jason K. 2009. *Our Army: Soldiers, Politics, and American Civil-Military Relations.* Princeton, NJ: Princeton University Press.
DeSantis, Vincent P. 1953. "The Presidential Election of 1952." *Review of Politics* 15 (2): 131–150.
Dewar, Helen. 1996. "'96 Themes on Display as Kerry, Weld Debate." *Washington Post*, April 10, p. A4.
Diamond, Edwin, and Stephen Bates. 1992. *The Spot: The Rise of Political Advertising on Television.* Cambridge, MA: MIT Press.
Dittmar, Linda, and Gene Michaud. 1990. "America's Vietnam War Films: Marching toward Denial." In *From Hanoi to Hollywood: The Vietnam War in American Film*, edited by L. Dittmar and G. Michaud, 1–18. New Brunswick, NJ: Rutgers University Press.

Donaldson, Gary. 2007. *The First Modern Campaign: Kennedy, Nixon, and the Election of 1960*. Lanham, MD: Rowman and Littlefield.

Donovan, Robert J. 1961. *PT 109: John F. Kennedy in World War II*. New York: Crest and McGraw-Hill.

———. 1977. *Conflict and Crisis: The Presidency of Harry S. Truman, 1945–1948*. New York: Norton.

Donovan, Sandra. 2005. *James Buchanan*. Minneapolis: Lerner.

Dowd, Maureen. 1988. "Dole Says Quayle Is Damaging Bush." *New York Times*, August 22, p. A1.

———. 1991. "After the War: White House Memo; War Introduces a Tougher Bush to Nation." *New York Times*, March 2, p. A1.

Drew, Elizabeth. 1994. *On the Edge: The Clinton Presidency*. New York: Simon and Schuster.

Drury, Bob, and Thomas Clavin. 2007. *Halsey's Typhoon: The True Story of a Fighting Admiral, an Epic Storm, and an Untold Rescue*. New York: Atlantic Monthly Press.

Dyal, Donald H., Brian B. Carpenter, and Mark A. Thomas. 1996. *Historical Dictionary of the Spanish American War*. Westport, CT: Greenwood Press.

Eder, Steve, and Dave Phillips. 2016. "Seemingly Fit, Trump Avoided Vietnam Draft." *New York Times*, August 1, p. A1.

Edwards, Lee. 1980. *Ronald Reagan: A Political Biography*. Houston: Nordland.

Eisenhower, John S. D. 1989. *So Far from God: The U.S. War with Mexico, 1846–1848*. New York: Random House.

———. 1997. *Agent of Destiny: The Life and Times of General Winfield Scott*. New York: Free Press.

Ekirch, Arthur A., Jr. 1953. "The Idea of a Citizen Army." *Military Affairs* 17 (1): 30–36.

———. 1956. *The Civilian and the Military*. New York: Oxford University Press.

Eysturlid, Lee W. 1994. "'An Opportunity to Show Their Epalets and Feathers': The South Carolina Militia during the First Secession Crisis, 1848–1851." *Armed Forces and Society* 20 (2): 303–316.

Fahrenthold, David A. 2016. "Four Months after Fundraiser, Trump Says He Gave $1 Million to Veterans Group." *Washington Post*, May 24, p. A1.

Faragher, John Mack. 1992. *Daniel Boone: The Life and Legend of an American Pioneer*. New York: Holt.

Farris, Scott. 2012. *Almost President: The Men Who Lost the Race but Changed the Nation*. Guilford, CT: Lyons Press.

Faust, Drew Gilpin. 2008. *This Republic of Suffering: Death and the American Civil War*. New York: Alfred A. Knopf.

Feaver, Peter D. 2003. *Armed Servants: Agency, Oversight, and Civil-Military Relations*. Cambridge, MA: Harvard University Press.

Feaver, Peter D., and Christopher Gelpi. 2005. *Choosing Your Battles: American Civil- Military Relations and the Use of Force*. Princeton, NJ: Princeton University Press.

Ferling, John E. 1984. "'Oh That I Was a Soldier': John Adams and the Anguish of War." *American Quarterly* 36 (2): 258–275.

Finer, Samuel E. 1962. *The Man on Horseback: The Role of the Military in Politics*. London: Pall Mall Press.

Flynn, George Q. 1993. *The Draft, 1940–1973*. Lawrence: University Press of Kansas.

Ford, Gerald R. 1979. *A Time to Heal: The Autobiography of Gerald R. Ford*. New York: Harper and Row.

Frankovic, Kathleen A. 1993. "Public Opinion in the 1992 Campaign." In *The Election of 1992*, edited by G. M. Pomper, 110–131. Chatham, NJ: Chatham House.
Frantz, Douglas. 1996. "Army Allowed Kemp to Skip Army Call-Up for an Injury." *New York Times*, August 18. Available at http://www.nytimes.com/1996/08/18/us/army-allowed-kemp-to-skip-army-call-up-for-an-injury.html.
Fulcher, Bob. 1999. "The Glorious (but Forgotten) Eighth of January." *Tennessee Conservationist* 65 (1): 4–10.
Gamerman, Ellen. 2000. "A Battle for Veterans' Votes: McCain Arms Himself with War Record for S. C. Campaign." *Baltimore Sun*, February 18, p. A1.
Gelpi, Christopher, and Peter D. Feaver. 2002. "Speak Softly and Carry a Big Stick? Veterans in the Political Elite and the American Use of Force." *American Political Science Review* 96 (4): 779–793.
Gelpi, Christopher, Peter D. Feaver, and Jason Aaron Reifler. 2009. *Paying the Human Costs of War: American Public Opinion and Casualties in Military Conflicts*. Princeton, NJ: Princeton University Press.
"Generals Killed and Wounded in Battle." 1863. *New York Times*, July 7, p. 4.
General Taylor and His Staff. 1848. Philadelphia: Grigg, Elliot.
Gienapp, William E. 1984. "The Whig Party, the Compromise of 1850, and the Nomination of Winfield Scott." *Presidential Studies Quarterly* 14 (3): 399–415.
Gillon, Steven M. 1992. *The Democrats' Dilemma: Walter F. Mondale and the Liberal Legacy*. New York: Columbia University Press.
Glad, Paul W. 1964. *McKinley, Bryan, and the People*. Philadelphia: Lippincott.
Glatthaar, Joseph T. 1994. *Partners in Command: The Relationships between Leaders in the Civil War*. New York: Free Press.
Goble, Hannah, and Peter M. Holm. 2009. "Breaking Bonds? The Iraq War and the Loss of Republican Dominance in National Security." *Political Research Quarterly* 62 (2): 215–229.
Godbold, E. Stanly. 2010. *Jimmy and Rosalynn Carter: The Georgia Years, 1924–1974*. New York: Oxford University Press.
Goebel, Dorothy Burne, and Julius Goebel. 1945. *Generals in the White House*. Garden City, NY: Doubleday, Doran.
Goldman, Peter, Thomas M. DeFrank, Mark Miller, Andrew Murr, and Tom Mathews. 1994. *Quest for the Presidency 1992*. College Station: Texas A&M University Press.
Gooding, Richard. 2004. "The Trashing of John McCain." *Vanity Fair*, November, p. 193.
Grant, Ulysses S. 1885. *Personal Memoirs of U. S. Grant*. 2 vols. New York: C. L. Webster.
Greenberg, Amy S. 2012. *A Wicked War: Polk, Clay, Lincoln, and the 1846 U.S. Invasion of Mexico*. New York: Alfred A. Knopf.
Greene, John Robert. 2000. *The Presidency of George Bush*. Lawrence: University Press of Kansas.
Griffin, Gilderoy Wells. 1873. *Memoir of Col. Chas. S. Todd*. Philadelphia: Claxton, Remsen and Haffelfinger.
Gropman, Alan L. 1999. "Planning War, Pursuing Peace: The Political Economy of American Warfare, 1920–1939." *Armed Forces and Society* 26 (1): 147–150.
Gunderson, Robert Gray. 1956. "Ogle's Omnibus of Lies." *Pennsylvania Magazine of History and Biography* 80 (4): 443–451.
———. 1957. *The Log-Cabin Campaign*. Lexington: University Press of Kentucky.
———. 1993. "William Henry Harrison: Apprentice in Arms." *Northwest Ohio Quarterly* 65:3–29.

"Gunner in Squadron Disputes Bush on Downing of Bomber." 1988. *New York Times*, August 13, p. A8.
Hadley, Arthur T. 1976. *The Invisible Primary*. Englewood Cliffs, NJ: Prentice-Hall.
Hagedorn, Hermann. 1931. *Leonard Wood: A Biography*. 2 vols. New York: Harper and Brothers.
Hailey, Foster. 1964. "Johnson Was Awarded the Silver Star for Flight with Bomber Group in the Pacific." *New York Times*, September 21. Available at http://www.nytimes.com/1964/09/21/johnson-was-awarded-the-silver-star-for-flight-with-bomber-group-in-pacific.html.
Halstead, Murat, William Best Hesseltine, and Rex G. Fisher. 1961. *Trimmers, Trucklers and Temporizers*. Madison: State Historical Society of Wisconsin.
Hamby, Alonzo L. 1995. *Man of the People: A Life of Harry S. Truman*. New York: Oxford University Press.
Hamilton, Alexander, James Madison, and John Jay. 2009. *The Federalist Papers: Alexander Hamilton, James Madison, John Jay*. Edited by Ian Shapiro. New Haven, CT: Yale University Press.
Hampton, Charles F. 1984. *Michigan Log Cabins and Hard Cider*. Brighton, MI: Green Oak Press.
Hanser, Richard. 1976. *The Glorious Hour of Lt. Monroe*. New York: Atheneum.
Hayes, Danny. 2005. "Candidate Qualities through a Partisan Lens: A Theory of Trait Ownership." *American Journal of Political Science* 49 (4): 908–923.
Hearn, Chester G. 2012. *Lincoln and McClellan at War*. Baton Rouge: Louisiana State University Press.
Hellmann, John. 1997. *The Kennedy Obsession: The American Myth of JFK*. New York: Columbia University Press.
Henneberger, Melinda. 2000. "The 2000 Campaign: Off to War, for Gore, Army Years Mixed Vietnam and Family Politics." *New York Times*, July 11, p. A1.
Henry, Robert Selph. 1950. *The Story of the Mexican War*. Indianapolis, IN: Bobbs-Merrill.
Herring, Pendleton. 1941. *The Impact of War: Our American Democracy under Arms*. New York: Farrar and Rinehart.
Hersey, John. 1944. "Survival." *New Yorker*, June 17, pp. 31–43.
Hibbs, Douglas A. 2012. "Obama's Reelection Prospects under 'Bread and Peace' Voting in the 2012 US Presidential Election." *PS: Political Science and Politics* 45 (4): 635–639.
Holian, David B. 2004. "He's Stealing My Issues! Clinton's Crime Rhetoric and the Dynamics of Issue Ownership." *Political Behavior* 26 (2): 95–124.
Hollihan, Thomas A. 2009. *Uncivil Wars: Political Campaigns in a Media Age*. Boston: St. Martin's.
Holsti, Ole R. 2001. "Of Chasms and Convergences: Attitudes and Beliefs of Civilians and Military Elites at the Start of a New Millennium." In *Soldiers and Civilians: The Civil-Military Gap and American National Security*, edited by P. D. Feaver and R. H. Kohn, 15–100. Cambridge, MA: MIT Press.
Holt, Michael F. 1999. *The Rise and Fall of the American Whig Party: Jacksonian Politics and the Onset of the Civil War*. New York: Oxford University Press.
Hoogenboom, Ari Arthur. 1995. *Rutherford B. Hayes: Warrior and President*. Lawrence: University Press of Kansas.
Hooker, Richard D. 2003. "Soldiers of the State: Reconsidering American Civil-Military Relations." *Parameters* 33 (4): 4–18.

Horowitz, Michael C., and Allan C. Stam. 2014. "How Prior Military Experience Influences the Future Militarized Behavior of Leaders." *International Organization* 68 (3): 527–559.

Horowitz, Michael, Allan C. Stam, and Cali M. Ellis. 2015. *Why Leaders Fight*. New York: Cambridge University Press.

Houdek, John Thomas. 1970. "James A. Garfield and Rutherford B. Hayes: A Study in State and National Politics." Ph.D. diss., Michigan State University.

"How Many Americans Have There Been?" 2010. *A Niche in the Library of Babel* (blog), January 19. Available at https://babelniche.wordpress.com/2010/01/19/how-many-americans-have-there-been.

Howell, William G., and Jon C. Pevehouse. 2007. *While Dangers Gather: Congressional Checks on Presidential War Powers*. Princeton, NJ: Princeton University Press.

Hsieh, Wayne Wei-siang. 2009. *West Pointers and the Civil War: The Old Army in War and Peace*. Chapel Hill: University of North Carolina Press.

Huddy, Leonie, and Nayda Terkildsen. 1993. "The Consequences of Gender Stereotypes for Women Candidates at Different Levels and Types of Office." *Political Research Quarterly* 46 (3): 503–525.

Huff, Lawrence. 1966. "Joseph Addison Turner's Role in Georgia Politics, 1851–1860." *Georgia Historical Quarterly* 50 (1): 1–13.

Hughes, Arthur J. 1972. *Richard M. Nixon*. New York: Dodd.

Hünemörder, Markus. 2006. *The Society of the Cincinnati: Conspiracy and Distrust in Early America*. New York: Berghahn Books.

Huntington, Samuel P. 1957. *The Soldier and the State: The Theory and Politics of Civil-Military Relations*. Cambridge, MA: Belknap Press of Harvard University Press.

———. 1961. *The Common Defense: Strategic Programs in National Politics*. New York: Columbia University Press.

Hyams, Joe. 1991. *Flight of the Avenger: George Bush at War*. San Diego, CA: Harcourt Brace Jovanovich.

Hyman, Herbert H., and Paul B. Sheatsley. 1953. "The Political Appeal of President Eisenhower." *Public Opinion Quarterly* 17 (4): 443–460.

Ifill, Gwen. 1992. "Clinton Thanked Colonel in '69 for 'Saving Me from the Draft.'" *New York Times*, February 13, p. A1.

Inbody, Donald S. 2008. "Partisanship and the Military: Voting Patterns of the American Military." In *Inside Defense: Understanding the US Military in the 21st Century*, edited by D. Reveron and J. H. Stiehm, 139–150. New York: Palgrave.

———. 2016. *The Soldier Vote: War, Politics, and the Ballot in America*. New York: Palgrave Macmillan.

Ingrao, Charles. 1982. "'Barbarous Strangers': Hessian State and Society during the American Revolution." *American Historical Review* 87 (4): 954–976.

Jacobs, James Ripley. 1947. *The Beginning of the U.S. Army, 1783–1812*. Princeton, NJ: Princeton University Press.

Jamieson, Kathleen Hall. 1984. *Packaging the Presidency: A History and Criticism of Presidential Campaign Advertising*. New York: Oxford University Press.

Janowitz, Morris. 1960. *The Professional Soldier: A Social and Political Portrait*. New York: Free Press.

Jensen, Laura Smietanka. 2003. *Patriots, Settlers, and the Origins of American Social Policy*. New York: Cambridge University Press.

Johnson, Donald Bruce. 1960. *The Republican Party and Wendell Willkie*. Urbana: University of Illinois Press.

Johnson, Jenna. 2016. "Donald Trump Has No Interest in Apologizing to John McCain." *Washington Post*, July 12, p. A5.
Johnson, Timothy D. 1998. *Winfield Scott: The Quest for Military Glory*. Lawrence: University Press of Kansas.
———. 2007. *A Gallant Little Army: The Mexico City Campaign*. Lawrence: University Press of Kansas.
Jordan, David M. 1988. *Winfield Scott Hancock: A Soldier's Life*. Bloomington: Indiana University Press.
Juul, Peter M. 2009. "The History of Veterans Affairs." In *Serving America's Veterans: A Reference Handbook*, edited by L. J. Korb, 15–49. Santa Barbara, CA: ABC-CLIO Praeger Security International.
Kalbfleisch, Gay. 1950. "Young Veteran Elected from Russell County." *Topeka State Journal*, November 10, 1950, p. A1.
Karsten, Peter. 2012. "Veteran Electability to the Presidency: A Critique of the Somit Thesis." *Armed Forces and Society* 38 (3): 486–499.
Katznelson, Ira. 2002. "Flexible Capacity: The Military and Early American Statebuilding." In *Shaped by War and Trade: International Influences on American Political Development*, edited by I. Katznelson and M. Shefter, 82–110. Princeton, NJ: Princeton University Press.
Kazin, Michael. 2006. *A Godly Hero: The Life of William Jennings Bryan*. New York: Knopf.
Kelly, Jim. 2015. "Jon Meacham's 'Destiny and Power: The American Odyssey of George Herbert Walker Bush.'" *New York Times*, November 9. Available at https://www.nytimes.com/2015/11/15/books/review/jon-meachams-destiny-and-power-the-american-odyssey-of-george-herbert-walker-bush.html.
Kelly, Michael, and David Johnston. 1992. "The 1992 Campaign: The Vietnam War; Campaign Focus on Vietnam Reviving Debates of the 60's." *New York Times*, October 9. Available at http://www.nytimes.com/1992/10/09/us/1992-campaign-vietnam-war-campaign-focus-vietnam-reviving-debates-60-s.html.
Kennedy, James Harrison. 1895. *The American Nation*. Cleveland, OH: N. G. Hamilton.
Kenney, Charles, and Robert L. Turner. 1988. *Dukakis: An American Odyssey*. Boston: Houghton Mifflin.
Kessler, Glenn. 2015. "Hillary Clinton's Claim That She Tried to Join the Marines." *Washington Post*, November 12. Available at https://www.washingtonpost.com/news/fact-checker/wp/2015/11/12/hillary-clintons-claim-that-she-tried-to-join-the-marines.
Kestnbaum, Meyer. 2000. "Citizenship and Compulsory Military Service: The Revolutionary Origins of Conscription in the United States." *Armed Forces and Society* 27 (1): 7–36.
Ketcham, Ralph Louis. 1971. *James Madison: A Biography*. New York: Macmillan.
Keuchel, Edward F. 1974. "Chemicals and Meat: The Embalmed Beef Scandal of the Spanish-American War." *Bulletin of the History of Medicine* 48 (2): 249–264.
Key, Valdimer Orlando, Jr. 1955. "A Theory of Critical Elections." *Journal of Politics* 17 (1): 3–18.
Kindsvatter, Peter S. 2003. *American Soldiers: Ground Combat in the World Wars, Korea, and Vietnam*. Lawrence: University Press of Kansas.
King, Nicholas. 1980. *George Bush: A Biography*. New York: Dodd, Mead.
King, Rufus, and Charles R. King. 1894. *The Life and Correspondence of Rufus King*. Vol. 5. New York: G. P. Putnam's Sons.

Knock, Thomas J. 2016. *The Rise of a Prairie Statesman: The Life and Times of George McGovern*. Princeton, NJ: Princeton University Press.
Kohn, Richard H. 1970. "The Inside History of the Newburgh Conspiracy: America and the Coup d'Etat." *William and Mary Quarterly* 27 (2): 188–220.
———. 1979. *Anglo-American Antimilitary Tracts, 1697–1830*. New York: Arno Press.
———. 1994. "Out of Control: The Crisis in Civil-Military Relations." *National Interest* 35 (Spring): 3–15.
Kranish, Michael, Brian C. Mooney, and Nina J. Easton. 2004. *John F. Kerry: The Complete Biography by the Boston Globe Reporters Who Know Him Best*. New York: PublicAffairs.
Krebs, Ronald R. 2006. *Fighting for Rights: Military Service and the Politics of Citizenship*. Ithaca, NY: Cornell University Press.
Kriner, Douglas L. 2010. *After the Rubicon: Congress, Presidents, and the Politics of Waging War*. Chicago: University of Chicago Press.
Lacayo, Richard. 1996. "Where's the Party?" *Time*, August 19, pp. 44–49.
Lacey, Marc. 2000. "The 2000 Campaign: The Veterans Issue; Five Senators Rebuke Bush for Criticism of McCain." *New York Times*, February 5. Available at http://www.nytimes.com/2000/02/05/us/2000-campaign-veterans-issue-five-senators-rebuke-bush-for-criticism-mccain.html.
Lane, Jack C. 1978. *Armed Progressive: General Leonard Wood*. San Rafael, CA: Presidio.
Langston, Thomas S. 2003. *Uneasy Balance: Civil-Military Relations in Peacetime America since 1783*. Baltimore: Johns Hopkins University Press.
Larson, Edward J. 2014. *The Return of George Washington: 1783–1789*. New York: William Morrow.
"Latest Intelligence." 1852. *New York Daily Times*, April 8, p. A1.
Laver, Harry S. 2002. "Rethinking the Social Role of the Militia: Community-Building in Antebellum Kentucky." *Journal of Southern History* 68 (4): 777–816.
Leech, Margaret. 1959. *In the Days of McKinley*. New York: Harper.
Lentz, Philip. 1988. "Dukakis: 'I Volunteered' Dukakis." *Chicago Tribune*, August 23. Available at http://articles.chicagotribune.com/1988-08-23/news/8801240911_1_lloyd-bentsen-iii-korean-war-michael-dukakis.
Long, John Davis. 1888. *The Republican Party: Its History, Principles, and Policies*. New York: M. W. Hazen.
Mahon, John K. 1983. *History of the Militia and the National Guard*. New York: Macmillan.
Maier, Pauline. 1976. "Coming to Terms with Samuel Adams." *American Historical Review* 81 (1): 12–37.
Major, Mark, and David J. Andersen. 2016. "Swift Boating Reconsidered: News Coverage of Negative Presidential Ads." *Presidential Studies Quarterly* 46 (4): 891–910.
Mann, Jim. 2015. *George W. Bush*. New York: Times Books.
Mansch, Larry D. 2005. *Abraham Lincoln, President-Elect: The Four Critical Months from Election to Inauguration*. Jefferson, NC: McFarland.
Maraniss, David. 1995. *First in His Class: A Biography of Bill Clinton*. New York: Simon and Schuster.
Maraniss, David, and Ellen Nakashima. 2000. *The Prince of Tennessee: The Rise of Al Gore*. New York: Simon and Schuster.
Marano, Richard Michael. 2003. *Vote Your Conscience: The Last Campaign of George McGovern*. Westport, CT: Praeger.

"Massachusetts Senatorial Debate." 1996. *C-SPAN*, July 2. Available at https://www.c-span.org/video/?73359-1.
Mayhew, David R. 2005. "Wars and American Politics." *Perspectives on Politics* 3 (3): 473–493.
Mazlish, Bruce, and Edwin Diamond. 1979. *Jimmy Carter: A Character Portrait*. New York: Simon and Schuster.
Mazo, Earl. 1959. *Richard Nixon: A Political and Personal Portrait*. New York: Harper.
McCaffrey, James M. 1992. *Army of Manifest Destiny: The American Soldier in the Mexican War, 1846–1848*. New York: New York University Press.
McCain, John, and Mark Salter. 1999. *Faith of My Fathers*. New York: Random House.
———. 2002. *Worth the Fighting For: A Memoir*. New York: Random House.
McClellan, George B., and William Starr Myers. 1917. *The Mexican War Diary of George B. McClellan*. Princeton, NJ: Princeton University Press.
McClure, Alexander K. 1901. *"Abe" Lincoln's Yarns and Stories: A Complete Collection of the Funny and Witty Anecdotes That Made Lincoln Famous as America's Greatest Story Teller*. Philadelphia: H. Neil.
McConnell, Stuart Charles. 1987. "A Social History of the Grand Army of the Republic, 1867–1900." Ph.D. diss., Johns Hopkins University.
McCoy, Charles Allan. 1960. *Polk and the Presidency*. Austin: University of Texas Press.
McCoy, Donald R. 1966. *Landon of Kansas*. Lincoln: University of Nebraska Press.
McCullough, David G. 1981. *Mornings on Horseback*. New York: Simon and Schuster.
McDermott, Monika L., and Costas Panagopoulos. 2015. "The Electoral Impact of Military Service as an Information Cue." *Political Research Quarterly* 68 (2): 293–305.
McEuen, Kathryn Anderson. 1955. "Military Phraseology in Presidential Campaigns." *American Speech* 30 (1): 38–43.
McGovern, George. 1974. *An American Journey: The Presidential Campaign Speeches of George McGovern*. New York: Random House.
———. 1977. *Grassroots: The Autobiography of George McGovern*. New York: Random House.
McIntyre, Jamie, and Jim Barnett. 2001. "The Story behind LBJ's Silver Star." *CNN*, July 6. Available at http://medicinthegreentime.com/wp-content/uploads/2014/05/LBJ-SSM-CNN.pdf.
McLaughlin, Andrew Cunningham. 1899. *Lewis Cass*. New York: Houghton Mifflin.
McSeveney, Samuel T. 1986. "Re-electing Lincoln: The Union Party Campaign and the Military Vote in Connecticut." *Civil War History* 32 (2): 139–158.
Mettler, Suzanne. 2002. "Bringing the State Back in to Civic Engagement: Policy Feedback Effects of the G.I. Bill for World War II Veterans." *American Political Science Review* 96 (2): 351–365.
———. 2005. *Soldiers to Citizens: The G.I. Bill and the Making of the Greatest Generation*. New York: Oxford University Press.
"M'Govern Defends His Service Record." 1972. *New York Times*, June 17, p. 12.
Miller, Arthur H., Martin P. Wattenberg, and Oksana Malanchuk. 1986. "Schematic Assessments of Presidential Candidates." *American Political Science Review* 80 (2): 521–540.
Miller, John Chester. 1960. *Sam Adams: Pioneer in Propaganda*. Stanford, CA: Stanford University Press.
Minutaglio, Bill. 1999. *First Son: George W. Bush and the Bush Family Dynasty*. New York: Times Books.

Mitchell, Thomas. 2004. "The Native-Fighter Politician." *Journal of Political and Military Sociology* 32 (2): 219–235.

Moltke, Helmuth von, and Daniel J. Hughes. 1993. *Moltke on the Art of War: Selected Writings*. Novato, CA: Presidio Press.

Montgomery, Henry. 1850. *The Life of Major General Zachary Taylor*. Auburn, NY: Derby, Miller.

Morales, Lymari. 2008. "Nearly All Americans Consider Military Service 'Patriotic.'" Gallup, July 3. Available at http://www.gallup.com/poll/108646/nearly-all-americans-consider-military-service-patriotic.aspx.

Morgan, H. Wayne. 1963. *William McKinley and His America*. Syracuse, NY: Syracuse University Press.

Morgan, Iwan W. 2002. *Nixon*. New York: Oxford University Press.

Morison, Elting. 1954. *The Letters of Theodore Roosevelt*. Vol. 8. Cambridge, MA: Harvard University Press.

Morris, Edmund. 1979. *The Rise of Theodore Roosevelt*. New York: Coward, McCann and Geoghegan.

Morris, Roy. 2003. *Fraud of the Century: Rutherford B. Hayes, Samuel Tilden, and the Stolen Election of 1876*. New York: Simon and Schuster.

Morton, Louis. 1958. "The Origins of American Military Policy." *Military Affairs* 22 (2): 75–82.

Moskos, Charles C., and John S. Butler. 1996. *All That We Can Be: Black Leadership and Racial Integration the Army Way*. New York: Basic Books.

"Movements in the West." 1862. *New York Times*, January 19, p. 2.

Nasaw, David. 2012. *The Patriarch: The Remarkable Life and Turbulent Times of Joseph P. Kennedy*. New York: Penguin Press.

Neal, Steve. 1984. *Dark Horse: A Biography of Wendell Willkie*. Garden City, NY: Doubleday.

Newman, Bruce I. 1994. *The Marketing of the President: Political Marketing as Campaign Strategy*. Thousand Oaks, CA: Sage.

Nichols, Roy F. 1958. *Franklin Pierce*. Philadelphia: University of Pennsylvania Press.

Nicosia, Gerald. 2001. *Home to War: A History of the Vietnam Veterans' Movement*. New York: Crown.

Nixon, Richard M. 1978. *RN: The Memoirs of Richard Nixon*. New York: Grosset and Dunlap.

Norpoth, Helmut. 2009. "From Eisenhower to Bush: Perceptions of Candidates and Parties." *Electoral Studies* 28:523–532.

Norpoth, Helmut, and Bruce Buchanan. 1992. "Wanted: The Education President Issue Trespassing by Political Candidates." *Public Opinion Quarterly* 56 (1): 87–99.

O'Brien, Sean Michael. 2003. *In Bitterness and in Tears: Andrew Jackson's Destruction of the Creeks and Seminoles*. Westport, CT: Praeger.

O'Neill, John E., and Jerome R. Corsi. 2004. *Unfit for Command*. Washington, DC: Regnery.

Oreskes, Michael. 1988. "The Republicans in New Orleans: Convention Message Is Garbled by Quayle Static." *New York Times*, August 19. Available at http://www.nytimes.com/1988/08/19/us/the-republicans-in-new-orleans-convention-message-is-garbled-by-quayle-static.html.

Our Campaigns. n.d. "MA District 11—D Primary." Available at http://www.ourcampaigns.com/RaceDetail.html?RaceID=505122 (accessed June 21, 2017).

Owens, Robert M. 2007. *Mr. Jefferson's Hammer: William Henry Harrison and the Origins of American Indian Policy*. Norman: University of Oklahoma Press.

Pace, Eric. 2005. "General Westmoreland Dies; Led U.S. in Vietnam." *New York Times*, July 19. Available at http://www.nytimes.com/2005/07/19/nyregion/general-westmoreland-dies-led-us-in-vietnam.html.

Parker, Ashley, and Jeremy W. Peters. 2015. "Veterans in Congress Bring Rare Perspective to Authorizing War." *New York Times*, February 17. Available at https://www.nytimes.com/2015/02/18/us/bringing-a-rare-perspective-to-authorizing-war.html.

Parker, Christopher. 2009. *Fighting for Democracy: Black Veterans and the Struggle against White Supremacy in the Postwar South*. Princeton, NJ: Princeton University Press.

Patterson, James T. 1972. *Mr. Republican: A Biography of Robert A. Taft*. Boston: Houghton Mifflin.

Peckham, Howard H. 1958. *The War for Independence: A Military History*. Chicago: University of Chicago Press.

Perret, Geoffrey. 1996. *Old Soldiers Never Die: The Life of Douglas MacArthur*. New York: Random House.

Perry, James M. 2003. *Touched with Fire: Five Presidents and the Civil War Battles That Made Them*. New York: PublicAffairs.

Peskin, Allan. 2003. *Winfield Scott and the Profession of Arms*. Kent, OH: Kent State University Press.

Peterson, Norma Lois. 1989. *The Presidencies of William Henry Harrison and John Tyler*. Lawrence: University Press of Kansas.

Petrocik, John R. 1996. "Issue Ownership in Presidential Elections, with a 1980 Case Study." *American Journal of Political Science* 40 (3): 825–850.

Phillips, Kim T. 1971. "Democrats of the Old School in the Era of Good Feelings." *Pennsylvania Magazine of History and Biography* 95 (3): 363–382.

———. 1976. "The Pennsylvania Origins of the Jackson Movement." *Political Science Quarterly* 91 (3): 489–508.

Piehler, G. Kurt. 1995. *Remembering War the American Way*. Washington, DC: Smithsonian Institution Press.

Pietrusza, David. 2007. *1920: The Year of the Six Presidents*. New York: Carroll and Graf.

Polsky, Andrew J. 2002. "'Mr. Lincoln's Army' Revisited: Partisanship, Institutional Position, and Union Army Command, 1861–1865." *Studies in American Political Development* 16 (2): 176–207.

Polsky, Andrew J., and William D. Adler. 2008. "The State in a Blue Uniform." *Polity* 40 (3): 348–354.

Popkin, Samuel L. 1991. *The Reasoning Voter*. Chicago: University of Chicago Press.

Povich, Elaine S. 2009. *John McCain: A Biography*. Westport, CT: Greenwood Press.

Prokopowicz, Gerald J. 2002. "'If I Had Gone Up There, I Could Have Whipped Them Myself': Lincoln's Military Fantasies." In *The Lincoln Forum: Rediscovering Abraham Lincoln*, edited by J. Y. Simon and H. Holzer, 77–92. New York: Fordham University Press.

Putnam, Robert. 1995. "Bowling Alone." *Journal of Democracy* 9:65–78.

Rafuse, Ethan S. 2012. "General McClellan and the Politicians Revisited." *Parameters* 43 (Summer): 71–85.

Ratcliffe, Donald J. 2015. *The One-Party Presidential Contest: Adams, Jackson, and 1824's Five-Horse Race*. Lawrence: University Press of Kansas.

Remini, Robert V. 1963. *The Election of Andrew Jackson*. Philadelphia: Lippincott.
———. 1991. *Henry Clay: Statesman for the Union*. New York: W. W. Norton.
Remini, Robert V., and Edwin A. Miles. 1979. *The Era of Good Feelings and the Age of Jackson, 1816–1841*. Arlington Heights, IL: AHM.
Renshon, Stanley Allen. 2004. *In His Father's Shadow: The Transformations of George W. Bush*. New York: Palgrave Macmillan.
Resch, John Phillips. 1999. *Suffering Soldiers: Revolutionary War Veterans, Moral Sentiment, and Political Culture in the Early Republic*. Amherst: University of Massachusetts Press.
Ricks, Thomas E. 1997. *Making the Corps*. New York: Scribner.
Riker, William H. 1957. *Soldiers of the States: The Role of the National Guard in American Democracy*. Washington, DC: PublicAffairs.
Roberts, Robert North, and Scott J. Hammond. 2004. *Encyclopedia of Presidential Campaigns, Slogans, Issues, and Platforms*. Westport, CT: Greenwood Press.
Rolle, Andrew F. 1991. *John Charles Frémont: Character as Destiny*. Norman: University of Oklahoma Press.
Ross, Davis R. B. 1969. *Preparing for Ulysses: Politics and Veterans during World War II*. New York: Columbia University Press.
Ross, Sam. 1964. *The Empty Sleeve: A Biography of Lucius Fairchild*. Madison: State Historical Society of Wisconsin.
Rothenberg, Stuart. 2007. "Republican Recruiting." *Inside Elections*, October 23. Available at http://www.insideelections.com/news/article/republican-recruiting.
Rove, Karl. 2010. *Courage and Consequence: My Life as a Conservative in the Fight*. New York: Threshold Editions.
———. 2015. *The Triumph of William McKinley: Why the Election of 1896 Still Matters*. New York: Simon and Schuster.
Royster, Charles. 1979. *A Revolutionary People at War: The Continental Army and American Character, 1775–1783*. Chapel Hill: University of North Carolina Press.
———. 1993. "Comment on John Shy, 'the Cultural Approach to the History of War' and on Russell Weigley, 'the American Military and the Principle of Civilian Control from McClellan to Powell.'" *Journal of Military History* 57 (5): 59–62.
Ryan, Cheyney. 2009. *The Chickenhawk Syndrome: War, Sacrifice, and Personal Responsibility*. Lanham, MD: Rowman and Littlefield.
Saad, Lydia. 2008. "McCain vs. Obama as Commander in Chief." Gallup, June 25. Available at http://www.gallup.com/poll/108373/mccain-vs-obama-commander-chief.aspx.
———. 2016. "Gallup Vault: Americans Saw What They Liked in Ike." Gallup, June 7. Available at http://www.gallup.com/vault/192377/gallup-vault-americans-saw-liked-ike.aspx.
Sandburg, Carl. 1926. *Abraham Lincoln: The Prairie Years*. Vol. 1. New York: Harcourt and Brace.
Scheele, Henry Z. 1987. "The 1956 Nomination of Dwight D. Eisenhower: Maintaining the Hero Image." *Presidential Studies Quarterly* 17 (3): 459–471.
Schlesinger, Arthur Meier. 1955. "Political Mobs and the American Revolution, 1765–1776." *Proceedings of the American Philosophical Society* 99 (4): 244–250.
Schwartz, Barry. 1990. *George Washington: The Making of an American Symbol*. Ithaca, NY: Cornell University Press.
Scriabine, Christine. 1983. "American Attitudes towards a Martial Presidency: Some Insights from Material Culture." *Military Affairs* 47 (4): 165–172.

Sears, Stephen W. 1988. *George B. McClellan: The Young Napoleon*. New York: Ticknor and Fields.
Seigenthaler, John. 2004. *James K. Polk*. New York: Henry Holt.
Sellers, Charles. 1966. *James K. Polk*. Vol. 2, *Continentalist, 1843–1846*. Princeton, NJ: Princeton University Press.
Severo, Richard, and Lewis Milford. 1989. *The Wages of War: When America's Soldiers Came Home, from Valley Forge to Vietnam*. New York: Simon and Schuster.
Shaw, Daron R. 2006. *The Race to 270: The Electoral College and the Campaign Strategies of 2000 and 2004*. Chicago: University of Chicago Press.
Shields, Patricia M. 1981. "The Burden of the Draft: The Vietnam Years." *Journal of Political and Military Sociology* 9 (2): 215–228.
Shrum, Robert. 2007. *No Excuses: Concessions of a Serial Campaigner*. New York: Simon and Schuster.
Sievers, Harry Joseph. 1952. *Benjamin Harrison: Hoosier Warrior*. New York: University Publishers.
———. 1960. *Benjamin Harrison: Hoosier Statesman*. 3 vols. New York: University Publishers.
Sinclair, Andrew. 1965. *The Available Man: The Life behind the Masks of Warren Gamaliel Harding*. New York: Macmillan.
Skeen, Carl Edward. 1999. *Citizen Soldiers in the War of 1812*. Lexington: University Press of Kentucky.
Skocpol, Theda. 1992. *Protecting Soldiers and Mothers: The Political Origins of Social Policy in the United States*. Cambridge, MA: Belknap Press of Harvard University Press.
———. 1993. "America's First Social Security System: The Expansion of Benefits for Civil War Veterans." *Political Science Quarterly* 108 (1): 85–116.
Skowronek, Stephen. 1982. *Building a New American State: The Expansion of National Administrative Capacities, 1877–1920*. New York: Cambridge University Press.
Skrentny, John David. 1996. *The Ironies of Affirmative Action: Politics, Culture, and Justice in America*. Chicago: University of Chicago Press, 1996.
Smith, Jean Edward. 2001. *Grant*. New York: Simon and Schuster.
———. 2012. *Eisenhower: In War and Peace*. New York: Random House.
———. 2016. *Bush*. Simon and Schuster.
Smith, Louis. 1951. *American Democracy and Military Power*. Chicago: University of Chicago Press.
Smith, Paul T. 1919. "Militia of the United States from 1846 to 1860." *Indiana Magazine of History* 15 (1): 20–47.
Smith, R. Jeffrey. 2010. "Illinois Republican Senate Candidate Admits to Error on Navy Award." *Washington Post*, May 30, p. A3.
Smith, William L. G. 1856. *Fifty Years of Public Life: The Life and Times of Lewis Cass*. New York: Derby and Jackson.
Snider, Mike. 2004. "Online Game Provides Gritty Glimpse of Kerry's Vietnam." *USA Today*, September 16. Available at https://usatoday30.usatoday.com/news/politicselections/nation/president/2004-09-16-swiftboat_x.htm.
Southwick, Leslie H. 1998. *Presidential Also-Rans and Running Mates, 1788–1996*. Jefferson, NC: McFarland.
Sparks, Jared. 1855. *The Writings of George Washington: Being His Correspondence, Addresses, Messages, and Other Papers, Official and Private*. Boston: Little, Brown.
Sparrow, Bartholomew H. 1996. *From the Outside In: World War II and the American State*. Princeton, NJ: Princeton University Press.

Stanwood, Edward. 1892. *A History of Presidential Elections.* Boston: Houghton.
Stephanopoulos, George. 1999. *All Too Human: A Political Education.* Boston: Little, Brown.
Stone, Richard G. 1977. *A Brittle Sword: The Kentucky Militia, 1776–1912.* Lexington: University Press of Kentucky.
Streb, Matthew J., and Susan H. Pinkus. 2004. "When Push Comes to Shove: Push Polling and the Manipulation of Public Opinion." In *Polls and Politics: The Dilemmas of Democracy,* edited by M. A. Genovese and M. J. Streb, 95–115. Albany: State University of New York Press.
Sugden, John. 1985. *Tecumseh's Last Stand.* Norman: University of Oklahoma Press.
Swers, Michele. 2007. "Building a Reputation on National Security: The Impact of Stereotypes Related to Gender and Military Experience." *Legislative Studies Quarterly* 32 (4): 559–595.
Tanner, Stephen. 2004. *The Wars of the Bushes: A Father and Son as Military Leaders.* Philadelphia: Casemate.
Taylor, John M. 1965. "General Hancock: Soldier of the Gilded Age." *Pennsylvania History: A Journal of Mid-Atlantic Studies* 32 (2): 187–196.
———. 1970. *Garfield of Ohio: The Available Man.* New York: Norton.
Taylor, Shelley E. 1981. "The Interface of Cognitive and Social Psychology." In *Cognition, Social Behavior, and the Environment,* edited by J. Harvey, 189–211. Hillsdale, NJ: Erlbaum.
Teigen, Jeremy M. 2006. "Enduring Effects of the Uniform: Previous Military Service and Voting Turnout." *Political Research Quarterly* 59 (4): 601–607.
———. 2007. "Veterans' Party Identification, Candidate Affect, and Vote Choice in the 2004 U.S. Presidential Election." *Armed Forces and Society* 33 (3): 414–437.
———. 2012. "Conventional and Distinctive Policy Preferences of Early 21st Century Veterans." In *The Politics of Veterans' Policy,* edited by S. R. Ortiz, 263–280. Gainesville: University Press of Florida.
Thomas, G. Scott. 1987. *The Pursuit of the White House: A Handbook of Presidential Election Statistics and History.* New York: Greenwood Press.
Thompson, J. Lee. 2013. *Never Call Retreat: Theodore Roosevelt and the Great War.* New York: Palgrave Macmillan.
Thompson, Jake H. 1994. *Bob Dole: The Republicans' Man for All Seasons.* New York: D. I. Fine.
Tilly, Charles. 1990. *Coercion, Capital, and European States, AD 990–1990.* Cambridge, MA: Blackwell.
Timberg, Robert. 1999. *John McCain: An American Odyssey.* New York: Simon and Schuster.
Tocqueville, Alexis de. 1945. *Democracy in America.* Edited by Phillips Bradley, Henry Reeve, and Francis Bowen. New York: A. A. Knopf.
Todd, Charles Stewart, and Benjamin Drake. 1840. *Sketches of the Civil and Military Services of William Henry Harrison.* Cincinnati, OH: U. P. James.
Todd, Frederick P. 1941. "Our National Guard: An Introduction to Its History." *Military Affairs* 5 (3): 152–170.
Tregaskis, Richard. 1962. *John F. Kennedy and "PT-109."* New York: Random House.
Tregle, Joseph G., Jr. 1981. "Andrew Jackson and the Continuing Battle of New Orleans." *Journal of the Early Republic* 1 (4): 373–393.
Truman, Harry S. 1952. "Rear Platform and Other Informal Remarks in New York." October 10. Available at http://trumanlibrary.org/publicpapers/index.php?pid=2279&st=&st1=.

Turque, Bill. 2000. *Inventing Al Gore: A Biography*. Boston: Houghton Mifflin.
Unger, Harlow G. 2009. *The Last Founding Father: James Monroe and a Nation's Call to Greatness*. Cambridge, MA: Da Capo Press.
Upton, Emory. 1912. *The Military Policy of the United States*. Washington, DC: Government Printing Office.
U.S. Census Bureau. 1864. *Population of the United States in 1860*. Washington, DC: Government Printing Office. Available at https://www.census.gov/prod/www/decennial.html.
———. 1942. *Sixteenth Census of the United States, 1940: Population*. Washington, DC: Government Printing Office. Available at https://www.census.gov/prod/www/decennial.html.
———. 1975. *Historical Statistics of the United States: Colonial Times to 1970*. Washington, DC: Government Printing Office.
———. 1995. *Population Estimates by Age, Sex, Race: 1900–1979*. Washington, DC: U.S. Census Bureau.
U.S. Department of Veterans Affairs. 2011. "America's Women Veterans: Military Service History and VA Benefit Utilization Statistics." Available at https://www.va.gov/VETDATA/docs/SpecialReports/Final_Womens_Report_3_2_12_v_7.pdf.
———. 2017. "America's Wars." Available at http://www1.va.gov/opa/publications/factsheets/fs_americas_wars.pdf.
Uscinski, Joseph E., and Arthur Simon. 2012. "Prior Experience Predicts Presidential Performance." *Presidential Studies Quarterly* 42 (3): 514–548.
VandeHei, Jim. 2004. "Kerry Returns to Boston with 'Band of Brothers': Former Crewmates Continue to Help in His Campaign." *Washington Post*, July 29, p. A28.
Viola, Herman J. 1969. "Zachary Taylor and the Indiana Volunteers." *Southwestern Historical Review* 72 (3): 335–346.
Waller, Willard. 1944. *The Veteran Comes Back*. New York: Dryden Press.
Ward, John William. 1955. *Andrew Jackson: Symbol for an Age*. New York: Oxford University Press.
Warner, Ezra J. 1964. *Generals in Blue: Lives of the Union Commanders*. Baton Rouge: Louisiana State University Press.
Warsh, David. 1996. "Behind the Hootch." *Boston Globe*, October 27, p. E1.
Washington, George. 1987. *The Papers of George Washington*, vol. 1, edited by W. W. Abbot, Dorothy Twohig, Philander D. Chase, and Beverly H. Runge. Charlottesville: University Press of Virginia.
Webb, James H. 1978. *Fields of Fire: A Novel*. Englewood Cliffs, NJ: Prentice Hall.
Weed, Thurlow. 1884. *Life of Thurlow Weed including His Autobiography and a Memoir*. Vol. 2. New York: Houghton Mifflin, 1884.
Weigley, Russell F. 1962. *Towards an American Army: Military Thought from Washington to Marshall*. New York: Columbia University Press.
———. 1967. *History of the United States Army*. New York: Macmillan.
———. 1993. "The American Military and the Principle of Civilian Control from McClellan to Powell." *Journal of Military History* 57 (5): 27–58.
Weinraub, Bernard. 1988. "Campaign Trail: Loaded for Bear and Then Some." *New York Times*, September 14, p. A28.
White, Theodore H. 1961. *The Making of the President, 1960*. New York: Atheneum.
Whitney, Gleaves. 2003. *American Presidents: Farewell Messages to the Nation, 1796–2001*. Lanham, MD: Lexington Books.

Williams, Ian. 2004. *Deserter: Bush's War on Military Families, Veterans, and His Past.* New York: Nation Books.

Williams, T. Harry. 1938. "Frémont and the Politicians." *Journal of the American Military History Foundation* 2 (4): 178–191.

———. 1952. *Lincoln and His Generals.* New York: Knopf.

———. 1965. *Hayes of the Twenty-Third: The Civil War Volunteer Officer.* New York: Knopf.

Wills, Chuck. 2009. *Jack Kennedy: The Illustrated Life of a President.* San Francisco: Chronicle Books.

Winders, Richard Bruce. 1997. *Mr. Polk's Army: The American Military Experience in the Mexican War.* College Station: Texas A&M University Press.

Wines, Michael. 2012. "Dissecting Romney's Vietnam Stance at Stanford." *New York Times*, September 11. Available at http://www.nytimes.com/2012/09/12/us/politics/at-stanford-romney-stood-ground-on-vietnam.html.

Wood, Gordon S. 2009. *Empire of Liberty: A History of the Early Republic, 1789–1815.* New York: Oxford University Press.

Woodford, Frank B. 1950. *Lewis Cass, the Last Jeffersonian.* New Brunswick, NJ: Rutgers University Press.

Woodward, Bob. 1996. *The Choice.* New York: Simon and Schuster.

Wunderlin, Clarence E. 2005. *Robert A. Taft: Ideas, Tradition, and Party in U.S. Foreign Policy.* Lanham, MD: SR Books.

Young, Andrew W. 1855. *The American Statesman: A Political History.* New York: J. C. Derby.

Zahniser, Marvin R. 1967. *Charles Cotesworth Pinckney, Founding Father.* Chapel Hill: University of North Carolina Press.

Zeleny, Jeff. 2008. "Campaign Flashpoint: Patriotism and Service." *New York Times*, July 1. Available at http://www.nytimes.com/2008/07/01/us/politics/01campaign.html.

Zernike, Kate, and Jim Rutenberg. 2004. "Friendly Fire: The Birth of an Attack on Kerry." *New York Times*, August 20, p. A1.

Zillman, Donald N. 2006. "Where Have All the Soldiers Gone II: Military Veterans in Congress and the State of Civil-Military Relations." *Maine Law Review* 58 (3): 135–156.

Zinman, Donald A. 2016. *The Heir Apparent Presidency.* Lawrence: University Press of Kansas.

Zornow, William Frank. 1954. *Lincoln and the Party Divided.* Norman: University of Oklahoma Press.

Index

Abramowitz, Alan, 249–252
Adams, John, 50, 53, 60
Adams, John Quincy, 50, 70, 73, 76
Adams, Samuel, 35, 37
Agent Orange, 28n21
Agnew, Spiro, 182, 225
Al-Qaeda, 207, 217
Amagiri, 165
American Expeditionary Forces (AEF), 32, 127, 137, 145. *See also* World War I
American Legion (proposed ready reserve military organization), 136
American Legion (veterans organization), 104, 149, 150n15
American National Election Study (ANES), 158–159, 171, 224
American political development, 25–26
Annapolis, U.S. Naval Academy at, 198, 207, 220–221, 244
Antifederalists, 40, 61
Anti-Masonic Party, 43
Army of the Potomac, 107–109
Articles of Confederation, 35–36
Atlanta Campaign, 123–124

Bacevich, Andrew, 245
Baker, Newton, 134
Barnes, Ben, 231
Barracuda, U.S.S., 199
Battle of Antietam, 102, 113, 125

Battle of Brandywine, 51, 58
Battle of Buena Vista, 90–91
Battle of Bull Run, Second, 117
Battle of Carnifax Ferry, 117
Battle of Cerro Gordo, 85
Battle of Chancellorsville, 113
Battle of Chapultepec, 94, 110–111
Battle of Chattanooga, 111
Battle of Chickamauga, 122
Battle of Churubusco, 85–87, 113
Battle of Cold Harbor, 111
Battle of Contreras, 85, 87, 113
Battle of Fallen Timbers, 78
Battle of Fort Donelson, 111
Battle of Fort Henry, 111
Battle of Fort Sumter, 40, 99, 111, 116
Battle of Fredericksburg, 113
Battle of Gettysburg, 113–114
Battle of Kernstown, Second, 117, 125
Battle of Las Guasimas, 135
Battle of Lookout Mountain, 111
Battle of Lundy's Lane, 92–93
Battle of Middle Creek, 120–121
Battle of Monterrey, 89–90, 110, 239
Battle of New Orleans, 22, 39, 61, 63–65, 71–72, 73–77, 109; and January 8 commemoration, 74–75, 76; and martial law, 76n36
Battle of Palo Alto, 110
Battle of Resaca, 124

Battle of Resaca de la Palma, 89
Battle of Richmond, 107, 109, 113
Battle of Shiloh, 102, 111, 121
Battle of South Mountain, 117
Battle of Thames, 64
Battle of the Wilderness, 114
Battle of Tippecanoe, 22, 77–79, 82
Battle of Trenton, 56–58
Battle of Vera Cruz, 85, 90, 92–93, 106
Battle of Vicksburg, 111
Battle of White Plains, 56
Battle of Williamsburg, 113
Battle of Yorktown, 6, 51, 109
Beef, embalmed, 130
Benton, Thomas Hart, 87, 92
Bentsen, Lloyd, 185, 231
Berlin Airlift, 155
Bin Laden, Osama, 207
Black Hawk War, 84, 89, 96–97
Blaine, James, 106, 119, 123
Bloody-shirt politics, 98, 104, 124, 126
Blumenthal, Richard, 243
Bonus March, 28n21
Boston Massacre, 35
Bougainville Island, 174
Bragg, Braxton, 91
Breckinridge, John, 10n1
British army, 24, 34–35, 37, 39, 50, 55–60, 63–65, 72, 74, 83, 92, 95–96
Brokaw, Tom, 141, 149, 232
Brown, Pat, 175
Bryan, William Jennings, 100n3, 106, 126, 136–137
Buchanan, James, 70, 86, 95–96
Buchanan, Pat, 191
Buell, Don Carlos, 111, 120–121
Bundy, William, 213
Burch, J. Thomas, 222, 235
Bush, George H. W.: and Bill Clinton, 229; and Colin Powell, 209–210; and George W. Bush, 230; and Michael Dukakis, 202–203; military service of, 20, 141, 146, 185–189, 197; on Vietnam War, 205
Bush, George W.: and Iraq War, 7n11, 29, 207, 217; and John McCain, 221–223; military service of, 46, 205, 211, 218, 230–232, 237, 251; and "mission accomplished" banner, 246; presidency of, 207, 210, 217; in presidential election of 2000, 221–222; in presidential election of 2004, 21, 217–219
Byron, Lord George Gordon, 5–6

Calhoun, John, 73
Carter, Jimmy: military service of, 192–193, 198–199; presidency of, 200; in presidential election of 1976, 21–22, 198
Cass, Lewis: and Abraham Lincoln, 84–85, 97; military service of, 82–84; in presidential election of 1848, 83–85; in presidential election of 1852, 86
Casualties: of Civil War, 101–102, 111–112, 114, 124; and election models, 249, 250, 251; of Indian Wars, 79; influence of, on public opinion, 102, 128, 146; of Mexican-American War, 68; of Spanish-American War, 128, 135; of Vietnam War, 208; of War of 1812, 65; of World War II, 146–147, 171, 173
Cemetery Ridge, 113
Central Intelligence Agency, 185
Chalmette Field, 71
Chamberlain, Neville, 163
Chamberlain, Samuel, 67
Chase, Salmon, 120, 121–122
Checkers speech, 174–175
Cheney, Dick, 223
Chickenhawk, 208
Choate, 140
Cincinnati Literary Club, 116
Cincinnatus, 5–6, 55, 116
Citizen-soldiers, 6, 17n7, 19, 51
Civil-military relations, 8, 24
Civil War, 40–41, 98, 127; casualties of, 101–102, 111–112, 114, 124; compared with interstate wars, 103; conscription for, 101–102; recruitment for, 33, 101; troop size in, 32, 100–101. See also specific battles
Clark, Wesley, 19, 211, 217–218; on John McCain, 223–224, 235
Clay, Henry, 61, 70, 73, 76n36, 77, 89, 91, 93
Cleland, Max, 28, 218
Cleveland, Grover, 106, 125
Clinton, Bill: and Bob Dole, 192; on gays in the military, 210, 230; and George H. W. Bush, 189; and Vietnam War draft, 2–3, 22, 46–47, 188–189, 190–191, 209, 227–230
Clinton, DeWitt, 50
Clinton, Hillary Rodham, 43, 46, 206n3, 211, 235
Cold War, 42, 142–143, 147, 204, 207, 211

Index   279

Columbia University, 133, 153
Congressional Medal of Honor, 134, 229n58
Connally, John, 231
Conscription: for Civil War, 33, 101–102; effect of, on number of veterans, 241, 243, 245; for Vietnam War, 206, 207; for World War I, 46, 129, 149; for World War II, 18, 33, 144–145
Conservative realism, 16
Constitutional Convention, 53
Continental Army, 51
Coriolanus, 5–6
"Corrupt bargain," 73
Cotton, Tom, 238
Coups d'état, 24
Crawford, William, 73
Creek War, 62
Cress, Lawrence, 37
Cromwell, Oliver, 5, 38, 55
Cronin, Paul, 216

"Daisy" ad, 194
Dakota Queen, 194–198
Davis, Jefferson, 91
D-Day invasion of Normandy, 1, 152, 190
Dean, Howard, 217
Dean, Jimmy, 141, 171
Declaration of Independence, 5, 35–36
Democratic Party, 6, 10n1, 43, 49, 72, 106, 118, 175
Democratic-Republican Party, 10, 43, 70, 73, 77
Dempsey, Jason, 61
Department of Veterans Affairs, 12, 28
De Ziska, John, 81
Dick Act (Militia Act of 1903), 41
Dick Cavett Show, 216
Distinguished Flying Cross, 187, 194
Document X, 156–157
Dole, Robert: and Dan Quayle, 232; military service of, 20, 141, 146, 162, 185, 190–191, 203; in presidential election of 1996, 190–192
Doonesbury, 191n121
Douglas, Stephen, 10n1, 107
Dow, Neal, 115
Duckworth, Tammy, 243, 246
Dukakis, Michael: military service of, 141, 151–152, 189, 193, 201; in presidential election of 1988, 188, 201–203; in tank ad, 189, 202–203, 246

Early, Jubal, 117
Edwards, John, 217–219
Eisenhower, Dwight D.: compared to other World War II vets, 150–151, 153, 162, 203; military service of, 16, 19–22, 112, 115, 127, 150–153, 225, 235, 237, 246, 251; political naïveté of, 154–156; in presidential election of 1952, 140, 148; and Richard Nixon, 174–175; television ads of, 157; and Vietnam War, 148, 204
Electoral College, 5, 26, 37, 70, 73, 77, 116, 125, 156
Endicott, William, 134
Executive power, 35–36, 42

Fairchild, Lucius, 28–29
Feaver, Peter, 8, 245
Federalist Papers, 5, 36–37
Federalist Party, 40, 43, 52–53, 58–59, 64
Federalization of military forces: in Antebellum era, 68–69; in Civil War era, 102–104; in early republic era, 51–52; in early twentieth century, 129–130; in Vietnam War era, 209–210; in World War II era, 148–149
Finback, U.S.S., 187
Finer, Samuel, 24
Forbes, Steve, 191
Ford, Gerald, 188; military service of, 146, 162, 182–184, 203; in pre-presidential elections, 184; presidency of, 191; as unelected president, 182
Frémont, John: and Abraham Lincoln, 88; and James Garfield, 119; military service of, 65, 87–88; and William McKinley, 125

Gabbard, Tulsi, 238, 246
GAR (Grand Army of the Republic), 104, 125, 149
Garfield, James: military service of, 115, 119–122; in presidential election of 1880, 112, 122–123
Gates, Horatio, 55
Gays in the military, 210, 230
Gelpi, Christopher, 8, 245
George III, King, 35
Gerry, Elbridge, 37, 38
G.I. Bill, 26, 28
Gingrich, Newt, 233
Goebel, Dorothy, 34
Goebel, Julius, 34

Goff, Peter, 66–67
Goldwater, Barry: military service of, 21–22, 151–152, 193; in presidential election of 1964, 21–22, 175, 182, 193–194, 199
Gore, Al, Jr.: and Al Gore Sr., 230; military service of, 46, 207, 211, 226–227, 251; in pre-presidential election campaigns, 201, 227
Gore, Al, Sr., 225–226, 230
Grand Army of the Republic (GAR), 104, 125, 149
Grand Review of the Armies, 19, 118
Grant, Ulysses: in Civil War, 109, 111–112; and Johnson administration, 112; in Mexican-American War, 110–111; in presidential election of 1868, 112; in presidential election of 1880, 123; at West Point, 109–110
Greeley, Horace, 105–106
Gridley, U.S.S., 214
Griswold, Roger, 50
Guantanamo Bay, 135

Hamilton, Alexander: advice of, to George Washington, 49, 54–55; military service of, 35, 58; views of, on military, 5, 37
Hancock, Winfield Scott: at Gettysburg, 113–114; military service of, 21, 46, 99, 105–106, 112–115; in presidential election of 1880, 112–115, 123; and Reconstruction, 114; at West Point, 46, 112
Hanna, Mark, 126
Harding, Warren, 127, 137–138
Harper's Magazine, 115
Harrison, Benjamin: and bloody-shirt politics, 98, 124; military service of, 19–20, 123–124
Harrison, William Henry: as grandfather, 123; military service of, 3, 17, 22, 31, 63, 77, 78–82, 162
Harrison Landing Letter, 107–108
Hart, Gary, 200–201
Harvard University, 59, 116, 133, 139, 225–227, 232
"Hasty Soup," 93–94
Hay, John, 128
Hayes, Rutherford: assassination of, 119; military service of, 46, 98, 101, 104–105, 115–119; in presidential election of 1876, 118–119

Hellcats of the Navy (film), 197
Hessians, 34
Hibbs, Douglas, 249–252
Hiram College, 119
Hiss, Alger, 174
Hoa Lo Prison, 220–221
Homeland (TV series), 244
House of Cards (TV series), 244
Huckabee, Mike, 223
Hughes, Charles, 136
Hull, William, 83, 84–85
Humphrey, Hubert, 46, 141, 152, 169, 175, 194, 228
Huntington, Samuel, 16–18, 69, 115, 128
Hussein, Saddam, 207

Incumbency, 253
Independence Day, 23, 75–76
Independence Day (film), 244
Indiana 70th Volunteer Regiment, 123
Indian Wars. *See* War of 1812
Iowa caucuses, 197, 201, 211, 234
Iraq wars, 7n11, 29, 47, 146, 205, 207, 209, 217, 228, 234, 243–244, 246
Israel, 26–27
Israeli Defense Forces (IDF), 26
Issue ownership, 6–7

Jackson, Andrew: in Battle of New Orleans, 22, 39, 72; and George Washington, 73; and militias, 39, 52; nicknames of, 72; presidency of, 42; in Revolutionary War, 72n20; as template, 39, 72–73, 77, 162
Jackson, Jesse, 200–201
Janowitz, Morris, 17n7
Japan, 26–27
Jefferson, Thomas: and Andrew Jackson, 74–75; and Democratic Party, 61; lack of military service by, 24, 50; opposition of, to Society of the Cincinnati, 6n7; in presidential election of 1796, 43, 53; and regular armies, 35, 38, 68–69
John Birch Society, 196
Johnson, Andrew, 110, 112, 114
Johnson, Lyndon: and Barry Goldwater, 193–194; and Douglas MacArthur, 179–180; exaggerated war service of, 173, 179–181, 243; and John Kennedy, 170, 175, 182; military service of, 178–181; promise by, to serve, 176–178; and Vietnam War, 204, 213

Johnson, Richard, 79–80
Johnston, Albert Sidney, 113
Johnston, Joseph, 123
Jonkman, Barney, 184

K-1, U.S.S., 199
Kemp, Jack, 192, 205
Kennedy, John F.: Catholicism of, 169–170; health of, 163, 166–167; military service of, 16, 20, 32, 131, 141, 146, 151, 162, 164–166, 251; in pre-presidential election campaigns, 167–169; and PT-109, 22, 162–171, 175, 189, 213, 239, 251; and Vietnam War, 148
Kennedy, Joseph, Jr., 163–164
Kennedy, Joseph, Sr., 163, 166n54
Kenyon College, 116
Kerrey, Bob, 229
Kerry, John: antiwar sentiments of, 213, 216, 218; military service of, 46, 204, 181, 212–216, 223, 225, 237; pre-presidential election campaigns of, 216–217; in presidential election of 2004, 217–219, 237, 253; swift boat ad by, 21–22, 215, 218–219
Khan, Khizr and Ghazala, 234
King, Rufus, 50, 54, 59
King Caucus, 43, 69, 76. *See also* Presidential nomination process
Kirk, Alan Goodrich, 164
Kirk, Mark, 243
Kohn, Richard, 37, 209
Kolombangara, 164
Korean War: and presidential election of 1952, 161; relation of, to World War II, 147–148; troop size in, 32

Landon, Alf, 129, 131, 138
Lautenberg, Frank, 241
Lee, Charles, 55
Lee, Henry, 55
Lee, Robert E., 111, 112n33, 113
Lincoln, Abraham: appointment of generals by, 103; and Civil War, 99–100; and executive office, 42; and George McClellan, 106–107; and John Frémont, 88; on Lewis Cass, 84–85; military service of, 70, 84, 87, 96–97; in presidential election of 1860, 10n1; in presidential election of 1864, 102, 106
Lodge, Henry Cabot, Jr., 167–169
Lovre, Harold, 195

Lusitania, 129, 136
Lyons, Matthew, 50

MacArthur, Douglas, 19, 152, 176, 178–180
Madame Secretary (TV series), 244
Maddox, U.S.S., 148
Madison, James: and *Federalist Papers*, 36–37; and Lewis Cass, 83; military service of, 50, 54, 60; and War of 1812, 64; and William Henry Harrison, 79
Maine, U.S.S., 128, 137
Manchurian Candidate, 223
Marshall, Humphrey, 120
Marshall, John, 23–24, 58
Marshall Plan, 184
McCain, John: on ad against Kerry, 219; and Donald Trump, 234; military service of, 16, 20, 46, 206–207, 220–221, 237, 242; in presidential election of 2000, 221–222; in presidential election of 2008, 223–225, 235, 237; as prisoner of war, 204, 220–221; and Theodore Roosevelt, 242–243
McCarthy, Eugene, 194
McCarthy, Joseph, 155
McClellan, George: in Civil War, 103; and Democratic Party, 106, 108–109; and James Garfield, 120; in Mexican-American War, 106–107; relationship of, with Lincoln, 107–108
McGovern, George, 141, 152, 162, 175, 192–193, 194–198, 201, 240, 251
McGovern-Fraser reforms, 43, 210
McKay, Frank, 184
McKinley, William: military service of, 125; in presidential election of 1896, 126, 129–130; in presidential election of 1900, 135; and Rutherford Hayes, 125; in Spanish-American War, 128, 134, 137
McMahon, Pappy, 165–166, 168
Meade, George, 113
Mexican-American War, 85–94: casualties of, 68; popularity of, 67–68; troop strength and recruitment for, 33. *See also specific battles*
Military recruitment: in Civil War, 18, 31–32; in Revolutionary era, 51; in Spanish-American War and World War I, 32, 128; in Vietnam War, 32, 205–206; in War of 1812, Indian Wars, and

Military recruitment (*continued*)
  Mexican-American War, 33, 62–68; in World War II, 18, 31–32, 145
Military service experience: in film and television, 244; as homogenizing experience, 31, 245; and partisan spirit, 40, 69, 106, 122, 129; and patriotism, 24; as providing political legitimacy, 29; types of, 20–21; as voting heuristic, 30–31
Military-state legitimacy, 26–27
Militias: British origins of, 37–38; compared to regular army, 18; and framers' fears of standing armies, 34, 36–39; military capability of, 38–39, 52, 66; Militia Act of 1903, 149; political alignment of, 40, 52; in Revolutionary War, 51–52
Mondale, Walter, 152, 193, 197, 200–201
Monkey Business (yacht), 201
Monroe, James, 50, 54, 56–57, 58
Monterey, U.S.S., 183
Morton, Oliver, 123

Napoleon Buonaparte, 5, 63–64, 73, 119
Nast, Thomas, 115
National Defense Act of 1920, 149
National Guard, 20, 41, 128, 133, 139, 144, 218; controversial induction into, 202, 205, 227, 230–232, 237, 251
National Republican Party, 62n1, 77
Naval Reserve, 163–164, 176–177, 182, 201
Newburgh Conspiracy, 35, 56
New Hampshire primaries, 154, 201, 211, 221–222, 229
New York 71st Volunteer Regiment, 135
Nixon, Richard: Checkers speech by, 174–175; and Dwight Eisenhower, 155, 175; military service of, 12, 141, 146, 151, 162, 172–173, 251; pre-presidential election campaigns of, 173–174; in presidential election of 1960, 167; and Vietnam War, 148
Nonveteran candidates, 19
Norbeck, Peter, 138

Obama, Barack, 46, 206–207, 224, 238–239
O'Daniel, Pappy, 176, 181
Ohio 23rd Regiment of Volunteers, 116–118, 125

Ohio 42nd Regiment of Volunteers, 119–120
Operation Aphrodite, 163
Operations Desert Shield and Desert Storm, 32, 189. *See also* Iraq wars

Partisanship in military, 40–41, 69, 88–94, 99, 103–104, 142, 148–149, 155–156, 209–210
Paul, Ron, 233
Pearl Harbor, 40, 140, 142, 145, 152, 163, 176, 187, 193
Pendleton, George Hunt, 118
Peninsular Campaign, 113
Perry, Rick, 233
Pershing, John, 136–137
Persian Gulf War, 32, 189. *See also* Iraq wars
Pickett's Charge, 113–114
Pickney, Charles, 50, 54, 58–59
Pierce, Franklin, 65, 72, 85–87, 97
Pillow, Gideon, 106–107
Polk, James, 66–68, 72, 85, 87–90, 91–93, 95, 106
Powell, Colin, 191, 209–211
Presidential candidate military experience: number of veteran candidates, 10–15; types of service, 16–21. *See also specific candidates; military service*
Presidential elections: of 1789, 3, 52; of 1796, 53; of 1800, 53; of 1804, 53; of 1816, 76; of 1820, 53, 76; of 1824, 69–70, 73–78; of 1828, 70, 74–76; of 1832, 43, 76–77; of 1836, 3, 77–80, 82; of 1840, 3, 77–78, 80–82, 84, 91, 93, 95; of 1844, 83, 86, 91, 95; of 1848, 82–84, 86, 88–89, 91; of 1852, 86–87, 91, 94; of 1856, 88; of 1860, 10n1, 88, 96; of 1864, 88, 102, 108–109, 240; of 1868, 110, 112; of 1872, 112; of 1876, 112, 115, 116, 118–119, 126; of 1880, 112, 115, 119, 122–123; of 1888, 125–126; of 1896, 100n3, 126, 136; of 1900, 100n3, 131, 136; of 1904, 131; of 1920, 137–138; of 1928, 169; of 1940, 145, 153; of 1948, 153, 162; of 1952, 153–162, 174, 251; of 1956, 161; of 1960, 169–171, 175, 182, 251; of 1964, 182, 193–194; of 1968, 4, 43, 175, 194; of 1972, 194–197, 201; of 1976, 182, 185, 191, 198–199; of 1980,

185, 187, 191, 199; of 1984, 197, 199, 200–201; of 1988, 186n111, 187–189, 199, 201–203; of 1992, 22, 46, 185, 187, 189, 209–210, 228–230, 236–237; of 1996, 191–192, 236–237; of 2000, 217, 220–223, 227, 236; of 2004, 21, 202, 211–213, 217–219, 223, 227, 230–231, 236–237; of 2008, 220–221, 223–225, 235, 236–237; of 2012, 238–239; of 2016, 233–235, 238–239

Presidential nomination process, 43; in Antebellum era, 69–70; in Civil War era, 104; in early republic era, 52–53; in early twentieth century, 130; in Vietnam War era, 210–211; in World War II era, 150. *See also* King Caucus

Primaries. *See* Presidential nomination process

Professionalization of the military, 4, 23, 33–41, 45; in Antebellum era, 67, 68–69; in Civil War era, 100–103; during Civil War versus World War II, 18; in early twentieth century, 129–130; after World War II, 148–149

The Prophet (Tenskwatawa), 78

PT-109, 22, 162–171, 175, 189, 213, 239, 251

Puritans, 51

Purple Heart, 192, 213–214, 219

Quayle, Dan, 189, 202, 205, 208, 232–233

Rayburn, Sam, 176

Reagan, Ronald: defense initiatives of, 203; military service of, 152, 193, 197, 199–201; in presidential election of 1980, 187, 191; in primaries of 1976, 182, 185

Reconstruction, 26, 40–41, 103, 114, 124

Redcoats. *See* British army

Red Scare, 137

Republican Party, 6, 41, 99, 103–104, 118, 126, 210

Reserve Officer Training Corps (ROTC), 2, 188, 228–230

Revolutionary War. *See* War of Independence

Rhetorical presidency, 130

Rockefeller, Nelson, 175–191

Romney, Mitt, 205, 223, 227, 232, 233, 238

Roosevelt, Franklin: death of, 190; and Joseph Kennedy, 166n54; lack of military service by, 12, 133n13; presidency of, 42, 130, 144, 146, 149n13, 153, 163, 176–178, 181; in presidential election of 1940, 145

Roosevelt, Theodore: family of, 131–133; on military readiness, 136; military service of, 20, 46, 109, 127–128, 134–135, 243; presidency of, 42, 130–131; and Woodrow Wilson, 129

Rosecrans, William, 122

ROTC (Reserve Officer Training Corps), 2, 188, 228–230

Rough Riders, 131, 134–136

Rove, Karl, 212–213

Rudman, Warren, 191

San Jacinto, U.S.S., 186–187

San Juan Hill, 128, 131, 134–135, 239

Santa Anna, Antonio Lopez de, 90–91, 94

Santorum, Rick, 233

Scott, Winfield: and Andrew Jackson, 93; and James Polk, 90; in Mexican-American War, 65, 85–87, 107, 110, 112; as military careerist, 19, 21, 46; in War of 1812, 92; and Whig partisanship, 40, 69, 70, 90–94

Second Party System, 62

Seminole Wars, 62, 72n19, 89, 113

Seymour, Horatio, 105

Sheehan, Cindy, 29

Sheridan, Philip, 114

Sherman, William, 123–124

Shrum, Bob, 219

Silver Star, 175–176, 179–181, 215

Slavery, 36, 61, 81, 94–95, 99, 102

Society of the Cincinnati, 6n7

Solomon, Gerald, 202

Solomon Islands, 164, 172, 174

Songs, 22, 39, 74, 79–82, 141, 171

Spanish-American War, 32–33, 127, 128–130. *See also specific battles*

Stanton, Edwin, 107, 122

Stevens, Thaddeus, 93

Stevenson, Adlai, 131, 140, 148, 151–162

Swift boat ad, 21–22, 215, 218–219

Taft, Robert, 153–154, 155, 157

Taft, William, 153

Taliban, 207, 217

Tank ad, 189, 202–203, 246
Taylor, Zachary: as blank-slate candidate, 88–91; military service of, 45, 65–66, 69–70, 89–91; in presidential election of 1848, 83–85
Tecumseh, 62, 78–80
Terrorist attacks of September 11, 2001, 207, 217
Tet Offensive, 208
Texas Air National Guard, 230, 231, 237, 251
Thurmond, Strom, 1–4
Tilden, Samuel, 106
Tilly, Charles, 25
Times-Picayune (New Orleans), 75
Tocqueville, Alexis de, 61
Todd, Charles, 81
Tonkin Gulf incident, 148
Tonkin Gulf Resolution, 213
Treaty of Ghent, 65
Troop strength, 31–33; in Civil War, 99–101; in Revolutionary War, 50–51; in Spanish-American War and World War I, 128; in Vietnam War, 205–206; in War of 1812, Indian Wars, and Mexican-American War, 62–64; in World War II, 143–145
Truman, Harry: and Dwight Eisenhower, 153, 154, 156; military service of, 46, 131, 139–140
Trump, Donald, 47, 204–205, 222, 224, 233–235, 238
Twelfth Amendment, 49
Tyler, John, 65, 93

Uniform Code of Military Justice, 41
Union army, 18, 100–104
University of Arkansas, 2, 228
Upton, Emory, 63–64, 66n9, 83n59
U.S. Constitution, military provisions of, 36
U.S. Military Academy: compared to other military training, 19, 67, 113, 117, 121; graduates of, 46, 98, 106, 109–110, 117, 152, 162, 217, 224
U.S. Naval Academy, 198, 207, 220–221, 244

Vallandigham, Clement, 108
Valley Forge, 24
Van Buren, Martin, 3, 77, 80, 83, 95
Veterans: distinctive attitudes of, 7–8; female veterans, 7, 246; government benefits for, 27–28; patriotism of, 24; population size of, 11; race and ethnicity of, 29. *See also specific wars*
Veterans Affairs, Department of (VA), 28, 100, 128
Veterans Campaign, 247
Veterans Day, 23
Veterans of Foreign Wars (VFW), 167
Vietnam War: candidate veterans of, 3–4, 21–22, 28, 46–47, 192, 204; and Democratic Party, 175, 205; films about, 208; popularity of, 146, 198; presidential handling of, 147–148, 194–198; troop strength and means of recruitment for, 2, 32, 205–209; Vietnam Syndrome, 205; Vietnam Veterans against the War (VVAW), 216; Vietnam War Memorial, 208; and World War II, 148. *See also specific battles*
Villa, Pancho, 134
Volunteers, 128

Wainwright, Stuyvesant, II, 1
Walsh, David, 164
War in Afghanistan, 47, 146, 207, 217, 243–244, 246
War of 1812: casualties of, 65; Lewis Cass in, 82–83; and Mexican-American War, 67, 69; popularity of, 64–65; troop strength and recruitment for, 33, 62–65; William Henry Harrison in, 79; Winfield Scott in, 92; Zachary Taylor in, 89. *See also specific battles*
War of Independence, 3, 35–36, 50–51, 55. *See also specific battles*
War wounds, 28–29, 190
Washington, George: appeal of, to electorate, 54; military service of, 3, 35, 55–57; on militia, 52; and Newburgh Conspiracy, 56; presidency of, 53; retirement of, 56; as template, 5–6, 49–50, 54, 62, 70–71, 73, 77, 81, 106, 109, 162, 245–246
Weaver, James Baird, 115
Webb, James, 239
Webster, Daniel, 91n86
Weed, Thurlow, 80, 89, 91n86
Weld, Bill, 217
Wellington, Arthur Wellesley, 119
Western Front (World War I), 129
Westmoreland, William, 3–4, 226
West Point. *See U.S. Military Academy*

The West Wing (TV series), 244
Whig Party: collapse of, 94; consolidation of, 10n1, 69, 77–78
Williams College, 119
Willkie, Wendell, 131, 139, 145, 153
Wilson, Woodrow: presidency of, 42, 129–130, 136–137, 139; and Theodore Roosevelt, 129
Wisconsin 15th Volunteer Regiment, 101
Women in the military, 246
Wood, Leonard, 19, 129, 134–138

World War I: troop size and recruitment for, 32, 129; veterans of, 127
World War II: economic impact of, 147; recruitment for, 33, 143–146; troop size for, 32, 142–143. *See also specific battles*

Yale University, 2, 184, 207, 212–213, 231
Yarborough, Ralph, 185, 188

Zedong, Mao, 148

Jeremy M. Teigen is Professor of Political Science at Ramapo College in New Jersey.